Picturing Worlds

Picturing Worlds

**Visuality and Visual Sovereignty
in Contemporary Anishinaabe Literature**

David Stirrup

MICHIGAN STATE UNIVERSITY PRESS | *East Lansing*

♾ The paper used in this publication meets the minimum requirements of
ANSI/NISO Z39.48-1992 (R 1997) (Permanence of Paper).

Michigan State University Press
East Lansing, Michigan 48823-5245

Library of Congress Cataloging-in-Publication Data is available
ISBN 978-1-61186-352-9 (paper)
ISBN 978-1-60917-626-6 (PDF)
ISBN 978-1-62895-3-886 (ePub)
ISBN 978-1-62896-389-2 (Kindle)

Book design by Charlie Sharp, Sharp Designs, East Lansing, Michigan
Cover design by Erin Kirk New
Cover art is *Thunderbird Poses for Morrisseau* (2017), by Travis Shilling,
oil on canvas, 30″ × 30″. Image courtesy of Ingram Gallery, Toronto.

Michigan State University Press is a member of the Green Press Initiative and is
committed to developing and encouraging ecologically responsible publishing
practices. For more information about the Green Press Initiative and the use of
recycled paper in book publishing, please visit www.greenpressinitiative.org.

───────────────────────

Visit Michigan State University Press at *www.msupress.org*

CONTENTS

ACKNOWLEDGMENTS

This book has taken a long time. That may or may not be a good thing. Over the course of that time, a great many people have influenced, supported, and directed me, whether knowingly or otherwise. None of them are to blame. They all deserve my warmest thanks and recognition for the parts they have played, but I have a terrible memory. Please know, then, that if you're not included in the list below, it is not because your friendship, guidance, or encouragement was not appreciated.

In no particular order: Colleagues at the University of Kent and elsewhere in the UK, you keep me going. In particular, Jennie Batchelor, Scarlett Thomas, Patricia Debney, Sarah James, Sarah Dustagheer, John Wills, David Herd, Catherine Richardson, Danne Jobin, Padraig Kirwan, Gillian Roberts, Zalfa Feghali, Jennifer Andrews, Jeff Orr, Tasha Hubbard, Chris Andersen, Coll Thrush, Paul Whitehouse, Sharon Holm, Robin White, and Jacqueline Fear-Segal, just thank you. The wider Native American Literature Symposium (NALS) family, who have tolerated my presence with so much humor and warmth for so many years now—especially Smokii Sumac, Billy Stratton, Jesse Peters, Steve Sexton, Jill Doerfler, Niigaan Sinclair, John Gamber, Scott Andrews, Mesheki Giizhig, Meg Noodin, Kim Blaeser, Shannon Toll, Gordon Henry Jr., Heid Erdrich, LeAnne Howe, Karen Poremski, Martha Viehmann, Joseph

Bauerkemper, Connie Jacobs, Nancy Peterson, Brian Twenter, Fantasia Painter, and others I know I am forgetting—you are all inspirations, and yes, I know I should have asked you all many more questions in the course of writing this. Thank you and everyone else who showed up and sat through versions of parts of this book, generally completely unwittingly. You can point out my errors next time I see you. Our *Transmotion* team—David Carlson, Theodore Van Alst, James Mackay (*especially* James Mackay, who keeps us all writing), Miriam Brown Spiers—it's such a delight and privilege working with you all, bouncing ideas around.

I have taught several iterations of Anishinaabeg literature classes, both combined with and independent of broader Native literature classes. It wouldn't be right to not acknowledge the energy, enthusiasm, deep curiosity, and above all ethical urgency of the students who have taken those classes.

Of course, I thank my anonymous readers and all who contributed to the publication process, with profuse and particular gratitude to Julie Loehr, who keeps the cogs in motion, and Gordon Henry (again), who stuck with me every step of the way. And to all other friends and colleagues in the wider academic world who may not have suffered much of the process of this book, but who offer stimulating conversation, exacting advice, and who demand rigor while offering warmth and unstinting friendship in return. The artists featured in this book, their managers, agents, estates, and so on, have all been so generous with their artwork, too; I tip my hat and remain, as ever, in awe.

Last, but by no means least, family. Mum and dad, it's so sweet that you still tell everyone I'm a professor; your support is cherished. My siblings Matthew and Emma, who selflessly moved to the United States and Canada respectively to accommodate my need for low-cost research visits. And then Jo, Florence, Ottilie, the loves of my life. This book—the labor that produced it at least—is for you.

INTRODUCTION

This book represents an attempt to read Ojibwe-authored texts by paying attention to the uses their authors make of visual images and marks made on surfaces such as rock, bark, paper, and canvas. In doing so, I highlight the ubiquity in Anishinaabe literature of an engagement with the visual arts. Indeed, this book was conceived in the generalized observation that contemporary Ojibwe authors seem particularly drawn to characters who are artists. I argue, too, that addressing these visual aspects means recognizing a relationship between literature, both oral and textual, and the visual traditions of the Anishinaabeg. It is a simple connection, but one that has been largely overlooked in the bulk of criticism pertaining to these texts. It admits a close link between literary aesthetics and cultural resurgence that does not depend on often-reductive discourses of the oral in the written, or text as culture. In fact, it resists the false binaries of oral/ written, Indigenous/modern, that in turn permit equally reductive questions of authenticity and hybridity to continue worrying away at empowered forms of Indigenous activism that coalesce around concepts of sovereignty, decolonization, revitalization, and resurgence. In what follows, my aim is to illuminate the connections and convergences between story/text, image/vision, and resistance/resurgence in the inherently political and politicized sphere of Anishinaabe literature broadly.[1]

In describing the revivifying, healing, and decolonizing power of language and story, scholar-activist Leanne Betasamosake Simpson observes:

> Storytelling . . . becomes a lens through which we can envision our way out of cognitive imperialism, where we can create models and mirrors where none existed, and where we can experience the spaces of freedom and justice. Storytelling becomes a space where we can escape the gaze and the cage of the Empire. (2011a, 33–34)

What is most striking about Simpson's statement is the prevalence of the optical metaphor for articulating her sense of the importance of story. In a statement about the oral tradition, a form associated in literary criticism almost exclusively with the ear (heard), the centrality of such a *descriptive* role for vision is significant.[2] Simpson goes on to elucidate this triad of oral (spoken), ocular (seen), and oracular (envisioned), noting that "dreams and visions provide glimpses of decolonized spaces and transformed realities that we have collectively yet to imagine" (2011a, 35). To recount those dreams and visions, traditionally the task of specific community members, is also to lay the foundation of a system of inscription: pictographic marks and symbols on rocks, hide, and birch bark; mnemonic forms that, through an ideographic system of signs, underpin the oral tradition.

Drawing on poetry, prose, and drama by a range of Ojibwe-Anishinaabe writers—from Gerald Vizenor, Louise Erdrich, and Gordon Henry Jr., to Jane Johnston Schoolcraft, Heid Erdrich, and Marcie Rendon, among others[3]—I explore the prevalence and significance of visual artists and visual artistic motifs employed by these writers, whether it be a simple act of mark making or a fully realized multimedia stage play. In doing so, I examine the rich visuality of Anishinaabe writing in its responses to the oral, graphic, and material cultures that underpin its practice. More than this, I suggest that these works blur the category distinctions between oral, visual, and written traditions, actively unsettling the binary within Native literature scholarship into which the oral and written have commonly been inserted, illuminating the interdependence of these intellectual, aesthetic, and spiritual practices, and refusing the temporal and ideological impositions of Western taxonomies.

This theoretical approach is underpinned by the work of a number of Indigenous scholars, but one in particular demands early mention. Christopher Teuton, in *Deep Waters: The Textual Continuum in American Indian Literature*, takes to task a number of prominent critics for inadvertently perpetuating the binary limitations of "oral-literate theory" (2010, 25–26), including "essentialist claims regarding Indian identity and belief [that] are inevitably rooted in a logocentric interpretation of oral tradition as a body of unquestionable tradition and moral authority" (26). Addressing the reification of the oral tradition and the essentially logocentrist positions of some of its best-known celebrants, Teuton implies an undermining of the validity of Native writing itself, as if, to paraphrase his assessment of Louis Owens's "double bind," to write about, through, or in the spirit of the oral tradition is to necessarily take a step away from that world (2010, 18). The further implications of this double bind have long been used by proponents of the very notion of the "primitive" that these critics refute, to demonstrate the inauthenticity and assimilated quality of all Native production that utilizes postcolonization technologies. In a further ironic twist, Teuton proposes that defense of the purity of the oral tradition and its inestimable value to Native cultures—a defense that he designates both "reification and nostalgia"—leaves itself open to interpretation as a "fulfillment of the West's logocentric desires" (23). Teuton's intervention is significant—and vital in relation to the claims I make throughout this book. "Cornered into taking two untenable positions in relation to logocentrism and graphocentrism," he writes, "Native American literary criticism has been unaware of a third, crucial discourse that works to disrupt the dominance of either the oral or written discourse" (28). Inserting what he calls the "critical impulse," Teuton "spins" the binary that Abenaki scholar Lisa Brooks subverts in *The Common Pot* in a way that usefully reemphasizes the role of the graphic, the visual, in the "fluid exchange of discursive power" (Teuton 2010, 33).[4]

Although increasing attention is being paid to the "mutually constitutive language of literary and visual arts" (Bernardin 2011, 162), the majority of scholarship on the interplay between text and image to date lays greater emphasis on the visual arts. The developing critical discourse around the visual-verbal is dominated by considerations of the uses to which Native visual artists put text. Yet, as Susan Bernardin notes, an increasing number of scholars have begun to "locate indigenous literatures as part of a broader aesthetic system of related practices such as beadwork, basketmaking, and dance," alluding to "the unsung importance of visual arts in indigenous literary practice and interpretation" (162–63). The connections I point out in this book involve long-standing aspects of Native literary aesthetics, present in the mixed-genre practices of authors such as N. Scott Momaday, Gerald Vizenor, Leslie Marmon Silko, and Louise Erdrich, as well as innumerable less-well-known or less-studied Native artists and authors whose works are finally coming to prominence in critical and readership circles. Elsewhere, scholars such as Gordon Brotherston (1992), Elizabeth Hill Boone and Gary Urton (2011), and Birgit Brander Rasmussen (2012) have addressed the prevalence of writing systems in pre-Columbian America, the literal and discursive suppression of those systems, and the visual-verbal continuum in Indigenous literacies. Gathering around what Hill Boone and Walter Mignolo call the "alternative literacies" of Native North America (1994; see also Sinclair 2013a; Kelsey 2010; Low-Weso 2006; Wieser 2017), such conversations have been slowly adding depth and texture to the heart of Native literary criticism.

In *Gerald Vizenor: Writing in the Oral Tradition* (1996), the first full-length monograph of any Ojibwe author's oeuvre, Kimberly Blaeser addresses the imagic quality of Vizenor's "vision," paying close heed to the imagistic nature of his poetry and to the play with pictomyths by some of his best-known characters. Blaeser's book is exceptional for its careful and incisive analysis of Vizenor's output, yet her focus remains closely on questions of literary style, seeing the generation of his "word cinemas," through V. N. Vološinov's notion of "pictorial" style, as a function of the translation of orality to textuality.[5] This pictoriality describes the rhetoric of reproducing reported speech rather than the image or its function per se. To date, however, there has been little rigorous and sustained analysis of the specifically visual in Vizenor's work. And yet, beyond his discussion of Edward Curtis's photographs and his interest in the photographic work of Bruce White, for instance, Vizenor has collaborated with and written about artist David Bradley and about modernist painter George Morrison, has made specific use of the pictograph (in *Summer in the Spring* and *Touchwood*), and has made substantive affiliative reference to ledger art as well as to European art of the early twentieth century. Similarly, despite much scholarship on the treaty in Vizenor's work, little attention has been paid to the documentary record as it pertains to nonalphabetic textuality, either in Vizenor's work or more generally in Anishinaabe writing.

I seek to address such gaps, examining the turn to the visual in general terms and offering a direct interrogation of the development of an Indigenous aesthetic that ties the visual to the textual. Drawing on pan-Indigenous and Anishinaabe-specific forms of image making, as well as contemporary Native and European/Euro-American art, I will analyze both the nature and function of the visual arts and visual artists in these works and discuss the ways they contribute to the development of an ethics and poetics of circulation and relation. This poetics simultaneously resists colonial impositions of textualized identities (legal, political, sociological, and so on) and reinscribes the graphic, artistic, and documentary as an intrinsic element of Anishinaabe cultural and political expression through gestures of survivance, sovereignty, and decolonization. According to Alexander and Mohanty, "Decolonization involves thinking oneself out of the spaces of domination, but always *within* the context of a collective or communal process" (1997, xxviii). The visual, circulatory poetics I describe here precisely constructs that process by which Anishinaabe writers and artists think themselves out of the spaces of domination and into an Indigenous-centered framework, generating a practice of storied life that simultaneously enacts literary activism. As such, the visual and its relationship with the written in the works under scrutiny in the following chapters discursively produce an ethical reading praxis—one that takes account of Indigenous literacies and acknowledges the aesthetic sophistication of the literary forms that carry them—that has implications in the world beyond the text.

Spinning the Binary

Since the turn of the millennium, a number of literary scholars have begun to turn to what Teuton calls the graphic tradition to explore that "space" between the oral and the written in Native American literature—a space that, Rex Weeks insists, has been understood in related fields like art history and anthropology for roughly 150 years and suppressed by Eurocentric bias for a good half of that time: "A number of recent studies clearly show awareness of Native North American terms for ancestral writing, and then disingenuously embark on the study of rock art or some form of 'proto-writing'" (2004, 13). Resisting the oppositional schematic that emanates from and reinforces a colonial logic, Teuton develops an argument that demonstrates resistance to said logic alongside an even greater degree of connection and continuity between literary and traditional forms than earlier scholarship has suggested, having tended, through to the mid-1990s, to prioritize themes of cultural loss, textual hybridity, and so on. Approaching the site of the critical impulse as a focus for "engaged resistance" (Rader 2003; 2011), my project responds to Teuton's "hope that the oral, graphic, and critical impulses will encourage further study of the relationships between oral and other nonalphabetic graphic traditions" (2010, 217) by examining the centrality of the visual arts, image and mark making, and the ideographic in a range of English-language Anishinaabe texts. Taking this relationship as fundamental to what I will suggest is a complex and mutually informing visual textuality, I will go on to examine more broadly the role the mark, or image, and the visual arts have to play in contemporary Anishinaabe literature.[6] Taking Teuton's arguments as a theoretical starting point, and de-emphasizing the oppositional tendency in the oral-literate conversation, I will analyze the ways in which Anishinaabe authors develop a relationship between text and image, story and picture that governs a visual aesthetic within the literary form. This aesthetic, in turn, determines and feeds that politics and ethics of circulation and produces a literature of survivance.

In his study of the political aesthetics of Native American visual, cinematic, and literary arts, Dean Rader notes the peculiar absence "in the already-meager discourse about Native public art" of its "first forms" such as "petroglyphs, pictographs, and geoglyphs" (2011, 204). Acknowledging debates over the "meaning" of such forms and illuminating, as he does elsewhere, the strikingly diverse generic (and cross-genre) range of visual-verbal art forms in North America, which would also include such "textual" objects and structures as baskets, beaded moccasins and tunics, medallions, hide coverings, mounds, and more (see also Rader 2014), Rader nevertheless avows "that one of the functions of this early symbolic action was to express something specific about a culture and a place" (2011, 204). Rader's observation is intriguing, not least because it belies decades of debate in archaeology, anthropology, (art) history, and, more recently, literary studies as to exactly what form such expression represents. These debates are centered on distinctions between "rock art" and "picture-writing"—between, in other words, the aesthetic practices ("designs and figures") that both feed and derive from secular and spiritual traditions, and the graphic representation of speech acts—and can perhaps best be represented in their polarization by two fairly insistent claims.

On the one hand, Birgit Brander Rasmussen has asserted, "contrary to common belief, that confrontation between European and indigenous people in the Americas was often a clash between literate cultures" (2012, 2–3). In opposition to the received wisdom, which attests that European explorers encountered cultures in arrested states of linguistic and cultural development, the real story of the "discovery" of the Americas is a fantasy of denial: denial of the apprehension of sophistication evident in many early accounts of attempts to translate Indigenous languages, and denial of the validity of Indigenous practices and perspectives. On the other hand, in pursuit of a universal framework in which to situate the Chinese logogram, John DeFrancis condemns too open a definition of what constitutes writing, reiterating the truism that "isolated Indian pictographs communicate only as much as such limited symbolizations as heraldic insignia placed on coats of arms, the male-female figures seen on restroom doors, and 'No Left Turn' or 'Steep Incline' warnings pictured on highway signs" (1989, 35).

Yet DeFrancis evaluates only the early nineteenth-century documentation of pictography by Henry Rowe Schoolcraft and Garrick Mallery. Extensive though that documentation is, there is no suggestion of consultation with Indigenous intellectuals or rigorous examination of the pictograph's mnemonic, social, spiritual, or relational function in DeFrancis's critique. Drawing conclusions about the limitations of the form in this fashion, DeFrancis arguably employs the colonizing logics against which Daniel Heath Justice warns: "In discussing diverse Indigenous textualities and writing systems, there is danger in inadvertently locating non- or extra-alphabetic texts in an evolutionary trajectory by which the 'alternative' textualities are those that are illegible to a mainstream audience" (2015, 302). DeFrancis's insistence that pictographic writing is not writing (1989, 35) and that it neither does nor could constitute a full system of writing (47) does not preclude its status as alternative (or parallel) literacy. Nor does it negate the self-evident fact that the existence of the considerable wealth of texts inscribed on bone, stone, bark, hide, metal, and cloth exposes a fundamental flaw in conventional histories of the "book" in North America (see Warkentin 1999, for an excellent discussion of this question in a Canadian context).

"In general," writes Gila River Pima scholar David Martínez, "tribal languages did not possess a word for 'writing' per se, though many did adapt older terms—typically ones signifying drawing or picture making—to describe the peculiar markings on paper that settler populations brought with them, and which was a prominent part of their idea of 'civilization'" (2014, 31). A relatively common stance, Martínez's negation is nuanced somewhat if we turn to Abenaki scholar Lisa Brooks's groundbreaking examination of the function of awikhigan in the U.S. Northeast, in *The Common Pot*. She attests that "for Abenakis, as well as for Mayans, Mixtecs, and Ojibwes, writing and drawing are both forms of image making," and "*awigha-*" denotes "to draw," "to write," "to map" (2008, xxi). Acknowledging the contextual specificity of such forms, Teuton also suggests that "the privileging of writing as recorded speech has led to the perception that context-dependent forms of signification, such as Native American oral and graphic traditions, are less culturally advanced" (2010, xv). The scholarship in this area is extensive and growing rapidly. It includes treatment of Quechuan quipus, Dine sand paintings, Mayan codices, wampum belts, waniyepu wowati, or Plains winter counts, and more (see, among others, Brotherston 1992; Low-Weso 2006; Kelsey 2010 and 2014; Hill

Boone and Urton 2011). Like the discussion of writing systems prior to Columbian "discovery," the focus on pictographic and other systems as being analogous to writing could be considered determinative of a colonized pattern of thought—such as with a term like "intellectual" that, Martínez argues, is both strategic and indicative of a particular moment of response to contact[7]—as long as such studies fail to disrupt the notion that the "peculiar markings on paper" that the colonizer brought with them remain indexed to "civilization," which requires the liberation of these various texts from Eurocentric taxonomies. Several decades of study under such rubrics as Indigenous studies (in all of its institutional and geographical formulations), postcolonial studies, and, more recently, settler colonial studies, along with centuries of lived experience, have done much to demonstrate the instability of such categories and their markers. As with David Martínez's scrutiny of the term "intellectual," notions of "civilization," and the primacy of writing as a determinant of the latter's achievement, have been challenged lately by Indigenous intellectual traditions. The irony of this table-turning venture is explicit in Martínez's own language: the peculiar markings on paper might once have been peculiar markings on rock or birch bark. Where once their "peculiarity" signposted the Otherness that corroborated Euro-Western self-narratives of superiority, such phrasing begins to connote an epistemological leveling. Necessary Indigenous-language-centered practices and discourses are being produced to counter precisely the concerns Martínez raises; to entirely negate the powerful rhetorics of recuperation in the meantime seems potentially counterproductive.

The final ambiguity in Martínez's phrasing is also worth briefly dwelling on. When he writes of "their idea of 'civilization,'" he intends, presumably, to suggest the "they" who settled, the invaders and colonizers whose self-asserted superiority depended in no small part on their documents and maps and, more significantly, on their ability to comprehensively document and map the terrains and peoples they encountered. It infers a willful blindness to alternative systems of designation and representation, of course, and to the particular systems of documentation and mapping their apparently nonliterate counterparts employed. But Martínez's "their" might also apply to the Indigenous peoples themselves, to the assimilative processes of colonization that led to the gradual—though rarely total—abandonment of Indigenous systems of knowing and recollection in favor of the "gift" of alphabetic script. Brooks's project, like those of the scholars she draws on—Craig Womack, Daniel Heath Justice, and others—seeks to "spin the binary between word and image into a relational framework" (2008, xxi) as well as to show how "Native people in the northeast used writing as an instrument to reclaim lands and reconstruct communities" (xxii). Brooks's object is to show how, for Native people facing the violent rupture of colonial intervention through the imposition of alphabetic writing and other forms of discursive power, "violent rupture" is itself as much a form of rhetorical colonialism, a narrative of suppression, as it is a reality on the ground. Otherwise positive reviews of Brooks's book have suggested an inherent reductionism in the celebration of "literacy . . . as a vehicle for political engagement and cultural resistance" when, in fact, "literacy in colonial contexts has proven a much darker, more pernicious, even fatal agent in Native life" (Benson 2010, 146). I suggest, however, that the celebration of literacy through the recovery of "alternative literacies" systematically suppressed, ignored, and devalued is not to disavow the violence of colonial processes—instead, it is to confront it head on.

Those colonial processes are coercive, and often physically and spiritually violent. While it will not be the purpose of this book to recount or account for colonial displacement, we will encounter such narratives frequently. Among them, integral to the processes first referred to as "decolonizing" the mind (Thiong'o 1986) or as the "colonizing of consciousness" (Comaroff and Comaroff 1992), is recognition of the absorption of "their" ideas, of the settling for "their idea of civilization" such that to become "civilized" or to prove one's value involves subsumption into the educational and intellectual models of the colonizer. Ngũgĩ's description in *Decolonizing the Mind* of the struggle to seize back "creative initiative in history through a real control of all the means of communal self-definition in time and space" (1986, 3) has application here.[8] His rejection of English and preference for African languages—Gikuyu and Kiswahili specifically—is germane to the reclamation of epistemic frameworks that challenge, inflect, unsettle, and revise the dominance of alphabetic writing as just one aspect of the "fatalistic logic" (7) exemplified by the acceptance by colonized subjects of European languages and forms. There is, naturally, a fine line that must be carefully trodden between reification of idealized Indigenous cultures on the one hand, and the demonization of Euro-Western cultures on the other. None of the writers I look at here condemn writing, or the act of writing per se, as intrinsically damaging, even where they navigate that binary landscape in which writing is presented as a colonizing instrument. Indeed, writing can be a liberatory vehicle. Discussing LeAnne Howe's methodological-theoretical concept of tribalography, Anishinaabe scholar Jill Doerfler writes: "By acknowledging the work that can [be] and is done by writing, tribalography contains a component of activism as a part of methodology. . . . As

Howe has argued, 'A Native writer remains in conversation with the past and the present to create the future' and 'Native stories are power. They create people. They author tribes'" (2014, 65–66). Nevertheless, as many Native writers demonstrate, none more so than Gerald Vizenor, writing can be, and has been, used to enslave, incarcerate, and isolate. Despite a certain affinity with Brooks's recovery of Indigenous writing forms, Teuton resists an interpretation of out-and-out continuity à la Brooks when he insists that Euro-American colonialism, and the privileging of alphabetic writing in particular, disrupted the balance between oral and graphic. "Writing," he continues, "is unrivaled as the discursive mode with which Native Americans have faced colonialism, it is through this very medium that graphic dominance is most actively disrupted. Writing has been a tool of *both* colonialism and survivance" (2010 xix; emphasis added).

The oppressive manipulations of the written word through scripture, law, and other documentary means of ownership and suppression, along with the historical belief that writing was something—*the* thing—beyond the reach of Indigenous peoples, and that oral cultures were therefore locked in a precivilized state, has had an overwhelmingly negative effect. As Vizenor notes, "The notion in the literature of dominance, that the oral advances to the written, is a colonial reduction of natural sound, heard stories" (1994b, 72; also qtd. in Weaver 1997, 21), diminishing the vitality and authority of the oral tradition by rendering it subordinate. It infers that the movement from the oral to the written is one of assimilation, acculturation, or, at best, the abrogation of the authentically (ab)original. Several key texts in the past several decades, such as Robert Warrior's *Tribal Secrets* (1994) and Maureen Konkle's *Writing Indian Nations* (2004), have made serious inroads into decentering this once-standard narrative of degradation-by-alphabet. "By treating orature as a dead relic and thus valorizing the written over the oral," Jace Weaver writes in another of those interventions, "one renders the written version normative and a representation of a pure, authentic culture and identity over against current degraded Natives" (1997, 21). The potential ambivalence of that scenario, its implicit colonial logics, invariably places emphasis on fictive tropes of resistance and reclamation. The writers here, while frequently drawing attention to the oppressive instrumentality of particular documents, or of a certain kind of writing, continue in a variety of ways to liberate Indigenous writing from the definition of being always already the product of colonial imposition: writing as not only resistance, but a resistance to writing-as-non-Indigenous. That inherent ambivalence is reflected and refracted through direct engagement with the making of marks and images, and with writing both implicitly and explicitly as a form of image making. It is not so much a matter of asking whether Indigenous nonalphabetic graphic (and often tactile[9]) forms constitute writing, as asking how such forms, in interaction with the oral and other expressive media, constitute methods of documentation and elaboration of Indigenous knowledge, craft, and aesthetics. In asking such questions, we may more readily begin to discern the wealth and significance of the visual, the imagic, in the works of a host of Native writers.

Anishinaabeakiing and Anishinaabe Mobilities

In the conclusion to this book I make a few suggestions as to how the readings herein could take in a range of other texts and writers from different Native nations. That wider potential is considerable, and I offer broader surveys elsewhere (see Stirrup 2015). For the purposes of this study, however, I have chosen to restrict my readings to Anishinaabe—indeed to Ojibwe—authors for reasons that include subjective questions of taste. More substantively, whatever one may feel about the often-heated criticism of tribal literary nationalisms, the specificity of historical, geographical, linguistic, and cultural context such frameworks offer is of immense value and allows for a depth and rigor that pan-Indigenous approaches do not always supply. Meanwhile, critics of such approaches have objected to the ways such embordering appears to artificially narrow rather than broaden the terms of influence of tribal peoples. It is a curious objection, since national framing and cultural variety are hardly mutually exclusive. As Robert Warrior points out (see Warrior 2009), tribal nations are always already transnational and, unlike many of those who criticize tribal-centered critique yet perform their own analysis both implicitly and explicitly within the boundaries of the settler-colonial nation-state, this study—like most Anishinaabe-specific work—brings together writers from a range of communities in both U.S. and Canadian nation-states, necessarily crossing borders, engaging with diverse community contexts and, of course, different experiences of colonization.

Free from the artifice of semantic binaries, the rich textures and varieties of Anishinaabe aesthetics and cultural practices cannot easily be distilled, and certainly resist any attempt at describing them in singular terms; this is especially true for outsider critics. The rationale at work here inevitably artificially reduces the permutations of Anishinaabe studies to those writers and artists formally known as Ojibwe/Ojibwa and their related groups—including Plains Bungi, Salteaux, and Mississaugas. I will say more shortly about the cultural and historical contexts both embraced and inevitably circumscribed in a project such as this, but as the editors of *Centering Anishinaabeg Studies* make clear, "complexity is the tenet most evident and unifying in Anishinaabe life, culture, and nationhood" (Doerfler, Sinclair, and Stark 2013, xvii).

That of course reflects the wider complexity of Native lives and communities across the United States and Canada—indeed, across the Americas. The circumscriptions involved, from dwelling on (largely) Anglophone North American writing to focusing on Nation-specific literary and artistic production, are necessary in order to communicate rather than dilute that complexity. Nevertheless, the findings of Nation-specific studies can be drawn on in more general terms, and while the primary contribution of this book is to the conversation around Anishinaabe literary and visual arts, it is formed in a nexus composed of Native North American literary studies more broadly, the developing discourse of visuality and visual aesthetics in Native American and First Nations literatures, and Native North American critical interventions into postcolonial, settler colonial, and postmodern studies. Also included is the interdisciplinary dialogue between literature and history, literature and the history of art, literature and law, philosophy, and religion, and direct engagement with legal and political contexts of Indigenous sovereignties. Many of these latter interventions will be minor, but they reflect a core fact of Native American studies exemplified by the "*truly* interdisciplinary work" of Jace Weaver, whom Tol Foster characterizes, along with Craig Womack and Robert Warrior, as "deploying methods from broader cultural studies and indigenous philosophies to place American Indian literary texts in dialogue with the predominant concerns of tribal communities" (2008, 566–67). Such dynamism has only grown in intensity and accomplishment in the last decade or two of development in the field. The scholarship of Weaver, alongside other established scholars such as Emma LaRocque, Warrior, Jean O'Brien, Kimberly Blaeser, Simon Ortiz, Vizenor, and the tranche of Native and non-Native scholars specifically driving forward fields like Anishinaabeg studies (Sinclair, Stark, Doerfler, Noodin, Molly McGlennen, Leanne Simpson, Adam Spry, Joseph Bauerkemper, and many others), demonstrates an exemplary interdisciplinary reach that underscores the rigor—and the activist embrace—of Native literary studies.

The Anishinaabeg are among the most studied of First Peoples on Turtle Island. This is in part a consequence of their homelands being in the Great Lakes region, which, toward the end of their great migration, enabled them to develop a close relationship with French fur traders and voyageurs and brought them into contact with French Jesuit priests, in particular, as well as explorers such as Samuel de Champlain and, of course, the later Anglo-American Indian agents. Among the latter, Henry Rowe Schoolcraft famously devoted himself to studying his wife Bamewawagezhikaquay's people during his time in Michigan. That Bamewawagezhikaquay, or Jane Johnston, became the first female Native American literary writer, and the first to publish poetry in a Native language, is largely well known now, not least thanks to the finely detailed scholarship of Robert Dale Parker (2007).[10] For the better part of 170 years, however, she was greatly overshadowed by her husband. Schoolcraft's legacy as Indian agent, promoting the assimilative agenda of the settler state,[11] is ambivalent, to say the least. Alongside Schoolcraft's own ethnological studies, it includes the recordings of significant numbers of stories and songs, customs and practices of the Ojibwe of Upper Michigan, distributed in Schoolcraft's lifetime via his newsletter, *Algic Researches*, which included a significant number of translations by Bamewawagezhikaquay. Prior to the development of more community-minded ethnographic practices, his informants were almost entirely unacknowledged. Whether that is historically forgivable or not, a parallel legacy persists today also in misperceptions of Schoolcraft's "discovery" of the source of the Mississippi, of his (re)naming of various important locations in Michigan and Minnesota, such as Lake Itasca (Omashkoozo-zaaga'igan), and of his source-provision for his friend Henry Wadsworth Longfellow's cultural mélange, *The Song of Hiawatha*. His status as both "friend of the Ojibwe" and exemplar of the perfidious scholar-ethnographer, of which Native studies has more than its fair share, means the legacy of that outsider-study remains ambivalent.

Odawazawguh i gunning educator Edward Benton-Benai suggests that the Anishinaabe migration began in roughly 900 CE and lasted for around five hundred years (1988, 102);[12] Niigaanwewidam James Sinclair, meanwhile, asserts that the story of Niizhwaaso-ishkoden Ningaanaajimowin, or the Seven Fires Prophecy, properly begins in 600–700 CE, "when ancestors of Anishinaabeg resided on the shores of what is now the Atlantic Ocean, in a political and social alliance often called the Waabinaakii ('Day Break People') Confederacy" (2013a, 176). Beginning on the eastern seaboard and following the passage of the St. Lawrence River, the people paused at six locations in present-day Canada and the United States, before finally settling at Madeline Island (Mooningwanekaaning) on Lake Superior in present-day Wisconsin. Along the way, stops, ishkode ("fires"), or "durées," as Scott

Lyons calls them (2010), dictated by the vision of a miigis (sacred cowrie shell) and seven individual prophecies, induced groups to break away. They would either stay put as the remainder moved on in accordance with the next prophecy or explore south, west, and north, dispersing the Anishinaabeg far and wide. Besides Warren, Benton-Benai, Lyons, and Sinclair, a number of Anishinaabe writers and scholars, including both Basil Johnston and Vizenor, have put versions of the story into print. It has, of course, been told, and continues to be told, by generations of oral storytellers, and as Sinclair recounts, it is recorded in various other material forms, including as petroglyphs and on birchbark scrolls (see Sinclair's excellent account, 2013a, 175–84, for more detail). As a set of stories Niizhwaaso-ishkoden Ningaanaajimowin both provides a clear sense of continuity in a specific (if very large) geographical terrain and insists on migration and mobility as being foundational to that sense of belonging-in-place.

Although the migration itself and the stories associated with it will feature only fleetingly in this book, there are principles associated with it that are central to the temporal, spatial, and formal concerns of my argument. For Jean O'Brien, for instance, "principles of mobility existed alongside notions of fixity, as in movements between central village sites," and "multi-village geography, in concert with Indian seasonally mobile economies," govern the spatial matrices of Indian identities otherwise constituted by lineage and kinship (1997, 21). As such, "a larger Indian sense of place connected many separate locations together in an intricately webbed landscape," while "creative tensions between mobility and fixity ... were deeply etched in Indian societies and their histories" (22). O'Brien here writes about the Northeast generally, but she expresses a relationship to land, and a configuring of the social order, echoed by her fellow Anishinaabe scholars writing specifically on the Ojibwe.

Cary Miller in *Ogimaag: Anishinaabeg Leadership, 1760–1845* writes, for instance, of social organization among the Ojibwe, despite their being consistently characterized by early twentieth-century anthropologists as atomistic: "Rather than being a weakness that demonstrated a lack of organization, or worse, some sort of 'primitive' condition, fluidity strengthened the Anishinaabeg, not only helping them to survive but also binding their villages more tightly together" (2010, 5). The "fluidity" she describes pertains to the Ojibweg "acephalous" political system, a "diffuse" leadership structure readily misread by European onlookers as prevarication, failure of authority, and lack of coherent control within Anishinaabe societies. Miller insists that "the flexibility they display must be understood as a strength, supporting a complex and dynamic social system that could easily respond to environmental changes or intertribal conflict" (4). The idea of mobility with a sense of stability that defies stasis strikes me as a useful metaphor for Anishinaabe literary aesthetics, a poetics of "transmotion," to use Gerald Vizenor's now familiar term. Described by Vizenor himself in evocatively elusive terms, "scenes of transmotion are not syntactical clauses or closure, not simulations, and not an outline of absence, of want or scarcity of motion and presence" (2015, 64). The result—the storied cohesion that actively defies the fixity of conventional literary form—means that "the stories of native survivance are instances of natural motion, and transmotion, a visionary resistance to cultural dominance, the practices of monotheism, policies of federal reservations, and the heavy loads of industrial conversions" (65). In chapter 2, I explore this "migratory" poetics in greater depth, examining how visual markers of the relationship between presence and travel at the levels of the personal and familial become signifiers of a form of visual sovereignty that correlates with sovereign movement and survivance more broadly. This echoes Joseph Bauerkemper's assertion that "in relation to and well outside of the federated contours of White Earth nationhood, . . . Anishinaabeg are reconstituting themselves as transnational citizens, navigating a cosmopolitan constellation of national affiliations, obligations, and liabilities" (2015, 16). Beyond White Earth, this ethic finds an aesthetic configuration in transmotion: "Native sovereignty is the right of motion, and transmotion is personal, reciprocal, the source of survivance but not territorial. . . . Native transmotion is an original natural union in the stories of emergence and migration that relate humans to an environment" (Vizenor 1998, 182–83). That Vizenor illustrates these locutions with the reproductions of pictographs will itself come under investigation here. Thus, while the physical geographies of Anishinaabeakiing are the tangible, felt ground of Anishinaabe literatures, the conceptual terrain of Anishinaabe literary sovereignty in the work included here is unconfined by "hard" territorial, temporal, or intellectual boundaries.

If this sense of mobility is key to an understanding of a migratory poetics, it must not be understood as all-encompassing, exhaustive, or monolithic, but as simply one way of approaching the particularities of the relationship between text and image in a selective range of texts. To present a more inclusive argument is arguably beyond the reach of any single study. Even those thinkers who have more assertively put forward broad-reaching theoretical suggestions have tended to prioritize particular nations or clusters of nations, individual writers or clusters of writers within the broader Anishinaabe collectivity. These comments are not intended as either qualitative or quantitative judgments of any such projects, all of which contribute richly and rigorously to that bigger conversation. They point, instead, to Anishinaabe literary studies itself as reflective of the diversified nature of the broader Anishinaabe world.[13] As Heidi Kiiwetinepinesiik Stark explains:

> Beyond recognizing a collective identity, the Anishinaabe comprise distinct, separate nations (frequently referred to as bands) that span a vast geographic region from the Plains to the Great Lakes. They are historically and today a people who cross many political and geographical borders. Anishinaabe people share many beliefs and practices, yet individual nations are influenced by their particular histories, geographic locations, political relations, and internal conflicts. (2012, 124)

Smaller-scale interventions can and do contribute to the fuller constellation, and it is to points of connection, felicitous or intended, stylistic and intellectual, that this book turns, with an understanding of its subject matter as heterogeneous and unbordered, informed but not confined by the imposed boundaries of states and other pre- and postcolonial constructions. Where Noodin insists that "all of the authors surveyed [in her monograph, *Bawaajimo*] refer to the power and influence of the region, the *Anishinaabeakiing*" (2014a, 182), it is to a vast geographical terrain that she alludes, one stretching from north-central North Dakota to Ontario's Bruce Peninsula—a distance of roughly 1,100 miles—and incorporating four separate Ojibwe bands or nations (Turtle Mountain, White Earth, Fond du Lac, and Chippewas of Nawash Unceded First Nation) as well as two U.S. states (Minnesota and North Dakota) plus one Canadian province, not to mention two nation-states and an international border. If that is the terrain covered by the authors treated in *Bawaajimo*, Anishinaabeakiing is vaster still, home to the many bands of Ojibwe, Odawa, Potawatomi, and other closely related nations. Its geographical span spreads historically as far east as Pennsylvania and as far west as Montana in the United States and Alberta in Canada. Of course, everything after the word "alludes" points to the residue of colonization rather than to the spiritual, imaginative, expressive, political, economic, and kinship determinants of Anishinaabe life and land. In that sense, Anishinaabeakiing is limitless.

Writing, Picturing, Visuality

Indigenous arts and literatures, in ways uncommon in non-Indigenous societies, have tended to be dismissed and/or fetishized for their practical functions, for their eschewal of modern principles of art-for-art's sake, or for their status as so-called primitive artifacts. Such a statement radically reduces both the complexity of such practices in Indigenous societies and the continuity, behind the headline-act of contemporary art, of embedded and often ancient traditions in western European artistic practices. It privileges the Kantian aesthetic tradition while failing to acknowledge alternative systems for gauging both beauty and function. Needless to say, storytelling has always served highly pedagogic, religious, and socializing purposes in Native families and communities. Yet to understand the oral tradition only in mechanistic and instrumental terms is to entirely fail to grasp the "life, juice, energy" that Gerald Vizenor sees in trickster tales, for instance: "Tribal words have power in the oral tradition," he writes; "the sounds express the spiritual energies" (1984b, 24). Quoting this same sentence, Kimberly Blaeser, scholar and fellow White Earth writer, affirms:

> Spiritual energies, life, vibrancy, force, vitality, power—these are the kinds of words used by indigenous people and scholars alike to characterize the Native American oral tradition. This vitality originates in the word itself, as well as in the expansive nature, the communal quality, and the generative character of the oral tradition. (1996, 17)

Vizenor's own attempts to mimic and mirror the functioning of orality in his writing, meanwhile, include "the events of oral tradition, the occurrences, the comings into being, the community of story," through their "dialogic qualities," and the relocation of the reading experience "from the passive to the active realm of experience" (Blaeser 1996, 15–16) and through the linguistic refusal of closure and stasis.

Native art forms play more multivalent roles than functionalist assumptions permit. In the postcontact world in particular, "Anishinaabe artists and the things they make have become instrumental in describing Anishinaabe relations to the land, to one another, and to those of the outside world" (Penney 2013, 15). Similarly, it is important to note, as do Berlo and Phillips, that what art historians now refer to as Native visual arts is, in historical terms, itself an effect of Western aesthetic valuations:[14]

One of the effects of Western domination over Native American cultures has been to devalue the importance of other expressive forms, such as oratory or dance, that have traditionally been equally, if not more highly, valued in Native societies. (1998, 16)

Scholars have also devalued the interconnection between different expressive and social forms. In all of the more generalized understandings of visual and storied worlds, little attention has been paid to date to the relationship between the visual and verbal, and between the performance of oratory and the different but related "performance" or act of mark making. As will be developed through the course of this book, it is that intricate relationship between a highly visible textuality and a long-standing alphabetic textual tradition among the Ojibwe, and between the highly intimate, individual reception of the visionary tradition and the individuated "genius" of the post-Romantic literary tradition, that sets the visual-verbal nexus of Anishinaabe literary heritage apart from other considerations of image-text configurations.[15]

Pictographic practice is an intriguing orbital center, caught as it is in the taxonomic anxieties of two Euro-Western traditions. Long resisted by both art-historical and philological conventions as either art or writing in their "true" senses, pictography takes up a frequent, vital place in Native artistic and, latterly, literary articulations of visual sovereignty. The renewed attention to the production of writing systems and prewriting systems that predate the introduction of the Latin alphabet, but function in similar ways, finds its most direct exposition in Brooks's *The Common Pot*:

Transformations occurred when the European system entered Native space. Birchbark messages became letters and petitions, wampum records became treaties, and journey pictographs became written "journals" that contained similar geographic and relational markers, while histories recorded on birchbark and wampum became written communal narratives. All of these forms were prolific in the northeast long before Indian people began writing poetry and fiction. These texts, which emerged from within Native space, represent an indigenous American literary tradition. (2008, 13)

Brooks's proposition of continuity of purpose between pre- and postcontact forms of communication, while not unique, at least takes a step into a Native literary historical terrain that few scholars have dared to explore, a terrain in which Native "literature" connotes far more than the spoken domain of the oral tradition itself. Others such as Rasmussen (2012) and Kelsey (2014) develop other aspects of the conversation.

As discussed earlier, standard treatments of North America in the study of the development of writing contain a common refrain that Native Americans had no need to write (Mithun 1999, 34) or no words for writing, suggesting neither need nor desire (see Martínez 2014). This book is not concerned with the validity or otherwise of the various claims to precontact writing systems in North America. On the one hand there is an ideological imperative at work in maintaining a strict binary between script-based literacy and prewriting or symbolic—and, therefore, "inferior"—systems of expressive communication. On the other, there is a political expediency to inferring equivalence where none exists, to insisting on the illegitimacy of judgments of sophistication and so on through the use of culturally relativist mechanisms. Balance is struck by scholars such as Floyd Lounsbury, who speaks of "writing in its fullest sense in those instances where we find graphic representation of complete sentences . . . but I also accept as 'writing,' though in a more attenuated sense, those instances in which compound words and phrases are the maximum attested units" (1989, 203). Nevertheless, "writing" remains a form that is directly representative of words and phrases, rather than generative of stories in a more diffuse sense.

I am not invested directly in the argument as to what does and does not constitute "writing"; I am interested in claims for writing systems in modes significantly more attenuated than Lounsbury describes. Louise Erdrich, by pursuing its linguistic trace in the root *mazina*, correlates both "book" (as in textual script) and "rock painting" to conclude, with fascinating (and compelling) results, that "the Ojibwe people were great writers from way back" (2003, 5). I am settled, for the purposes of this study, quite contentedly in a line pursuant on Brotherston's *Book of the Fourth World*, in which he examines "the scrolls of the Algonkin, the knotted strings (*quipus*) of the Inca, Navajo dry paintings, and the encyclopedic pages of Mesoamerica's screenfold books" (1992, 4): texts in any sense of the word.[16]

Brotherston follows Derrida's deconstruction of Claude Lévi-Strauss's *Mythologiques*, noting that "for Derrida, 'writing' is present everywhere, in gesture and speech itself, in the traces and paths of landscape: Orality and script do not therefore constitute a mutually exclusive binary; still less are they moral opposites" (1992, 42). My own arguments proceed in sympathy with this refusal of hard and fast binaries between oral and written, with the placing to one side of the assumptions and oversights of Lévi-Strauss's idealization of "Rousseauesque, script-free societies" (Brotherston 1992, 42). In fact, for the broader purposes of this study, my argument concerns the relationship between image and text and the unsettling of the oppositional construction of oral and written rather than any substantive effort to persuade readers that pictures constitute writing. My analysis of the ways contemporary Anishinaabe authors employ and deploy visual images is only partially related to questions of precontact literary heritage. Nevertheless, the nature of the textuality of pictography is a defining aspect of Anishinaabe literary traditions and is suggestive of forms of continuity that remain relatively underexplored in Native studies.

The continuity to which Brooks refers in the second section resides first and foremost—and in relatively simple ways—in linguistic evolutionary connections. Brotherston notes that "even alphabets can never register sound entirely, while even the most rudimentary-seeming pictography will always imply a kind of language" (42). That "kind of language," then, is of significance. Brooks, for instance, moves from a brief mention of Erdrich's commentary on the uses of *mazina* to note:

> The same is true in the Abenaki language, which is kin to Ojibwe. The root word *awigha-* denotes "to draw," "to write," "to map." The word *awikhigan*, which originally described birchbark messages, maps, and scrolls, came to encompass books and letters. An Ojibwe scroll is an *awikhigan*. The road map that Natalie and I use to navigate our trip is an *awikhigan*. Erdrich's account of her travels among the islands of Ojibwe country is an *awikhigan*. (2008, xxi)

There is a readily discernible double significance to this linguistic relationship between actions only relatively remotely related in historical terms but explicitly connected conceptually by the people.

As Brooks continues to explain, these lines of connection serve to unsettle the conventional binary between speech and writing, established in the Enlightenment philosophy of Rousseau and that, according to Derrida, traces back to Plato's *Phaedrus*,[17] just as they undermine binaries more generally:

> Just as Native writers spin the binary between word and image into a relational framework, they also challenge us to avoid the "oppositional thinking that separates orality and literacy wherein the oral constitutes authentic culture and the written

contaminated culture," as Muskogee author Craig Womack argues in *Red on Red*. He suggests that such notions may actually hinder our understanding of a "vast, and vastly understudied, written tradition" in Native America. (Brooks 2008, xxi)

Against the currents of poststructuralist literary studies, the emphasis placed in relation to Indigenous literatures on a division "wherein the oral constitutes authentic culture and the written contaminated culture" (Womack 2009, 15) cements Indigenous cultures in an antimodern, always already passed (and therefore past) life. It is a form of stasis that renders Native intellectual traditions outside and beyond the reaches of modernity, and any written, filmed, or otherwise "nontraditional" art form as essentially hybrid at best, non-Native at worst. As such, it is an untenable burden that continues to deny self-determination, intellectual and cultural sovereignty, and enacts an ideologically motivated distinction between the modern and the Indigenous. Womack and Brooks, along with many others, resist any such impositions and distinctions.

Writing of the Mayan Codices, Womack notes that "recent scholarship has shown that these books were used as a *complement* of oral tradition rather than a *replacement*" (2009, 16). Brotherston corroborates such a claim in broader terms when he aligns the "graphic conventions of the Nambikwara and the Tupi," the timehri of the Carib, and Cuna and Chibcah iconography. "As examples of visual language," he writes, "these . . . signs are typically said to have been fetched or acquired long ago, together with corresponding examples of oral language like the nation's store of songs and narratives, according to a dual grammatological model that inheres in the all-encompassing medium of rite and performance" (1992, 44). Having established these connections between mark/image and orality, Brotherston goes on to make a geographically bolder move by relating them to North American traditions. Placing these sign-systems in the context of a discussion of literary traditions in the New World, Brotherston's commentary on the nature of textual study is also useful here:

Traditional in literary criticism and recently resurrected in linguistics, text is no more (or less) than a particular or framed instance of language. Indeed, as a privileged example of discourse and the space in which meaning happens, a text may actually frame and define itself, reflexively, whether it consists of words or some visual sign system. As a result it may propose analogies between media, notably the verbal and the visual, that override the differences between them and thereby become an artifact or entity that is specifically and consciously literary. (45)

We risk losing sight of the specifically visual, or artistic; we risk, too, overlooking the embodied presence of the act and fact of mark making; but Brotherston's suggestion that breathed words "invoked within a textual frame . . . become the exact analogue of painted signs, and their respective sources acquire the same authorial identity" (45), offers a particularly interesting way of thinking about how the writers in this study invoke and engage with these same kinds of visual signs and the ways in which they employ or examine other kinds of images and expressions of the visual.

Such analogical deliberations take us in one direction, beginning with Brooks's linguistic linking and extending that connection to the full reach of Brotherston's analysis of textual modalities. Describing a more mediated position, Teuton's *Deep Waters* "demonstrates how crucial twentieth- and twenty-first-century literary texts develop a sustained and illuminating critique of the relationship between tradition and modernity through their conceptual and thematic explorations of indigenous traditions of oral and graphic forms of communication" (2010, xiv). Teuton's desire to "decenter the standard definitions of *orality* and *literacy* that provide a structuring binary common to Native American literary studies" (xv) is clear and places his book in conversation with other major arguments in the field. Like Brotherston, Teuton places emphasis, without theoretical obfuscation, on Derridean decentering of the "privileging of writing" and the devaluing of "context-dependent forms of signification" as "less culturally advanced," which have "contributed to the historical and political subjugation of Native communities" (xv).

Along with scholars such as Penelope Myrtle Kelsey, Teuton is among a group of critics recently producing book-length analyses of the relationship between speech, image, and text. These promise a compelling theoretical framework for an Indigenous image-text paradigm that intervenes in the common models proposed first (or most cohesively) by W. J. T. Mitchell. In his introduction to *Picture Theory*, Mitchell notes:

> Foucault's claim that "the relation of language to painting is an infinite relation" seems to me true, not just because the "signs" or "media" of visual and verbal expression are formally incommensurable, but because this fault-line in representation is deeply linked with fundamental ideological divisions. (1994, 5)

Mitchell's argument begins with the fundamental premise that "we live in a culture of images, a society of the spectacle, a world of semblances and simulacra" (5). Mitchell writes here in response to "anxieties about the power of visual culture," for the manipulability of televisual images, for instance (2). In framing this anxiety, Mitchell states a "primitivist" truism that we will reflect on briefly in chapter 4: "But then people have always known . . . that images were dangerous, that they can captivate the onlooker and steal the soul" (2). Moreover, he proceeds from the critique of a point of conviction, embedded in a 1988 report by the National Endowment for the Humanities, that "the tensions between visual and verbal representations are inseparable from struggles in cultural politics and political culture" (3). As my own argument progresses, I will attempt to show how tensions, but more specifically convergences, between word and image, visual and verbal representations are implicit interventions into cultural politics in the United States and Canada.[18]

As such, I have real sympathy for Mitchell's insistence that notwithstanding their differential capacities and means for conveying meaning, the verbal and visual are inseparable, that "all media are mixed media," and certainly for his desire to "trace their linkages to issues of power, value, and human interest" (5). Describing the antiocularcentric tradition, which produces a set of iconophobic and iconoclastic conventions, he reminds us:

> From Plato's banishment of the artist to Richard Rorty's "linguistic turn," . . . as Wittgenstein put it, "a picture held us captive, and we could not get outside of it." Heidegger thought that modernity had trapped humanity in an "age of the world picture," and that philosophy (or poetry) might find a way out of it. (Grønstad and Vågnes 2006)

Mitchell draws a distinction between "image" and "picture," the former signifying not a singular design so much as the way our understanding of people, things, culture is governed by the primacy of the image. The image is a conceptual, organic abstraction; the picture is its container. The texts I examine here often ironically invoke the visual image as a means of resisting the "image" of the *indian*,[19] reinscribing the latter figure with an image in which the visual plays a powerful role. That I invoke Mitchell and other contributors to the "pictorial turn" at various points in this study is testament to their work in relation to that antiocular tradition over the last twenty or so years that resounds in the various permutations of image/text (as problematic gap in representation), imagetext (as synthetic work), and image-text (as "*relations* of the verbal-visual") (Mitchell 1994, 89n9). These, in turn, offer ways of thinking about the relationship between image and text within the fiction and poetry under scrutiny here and between that contemporary work and Anishinaabe visual traditions.

That the antiocular tradition around and against which thinkers such as Mitchell write prioritizes the written directly implicates it in the imperialistic mechanisms that generated orientalism, double consciousness, and the duality of savagism and civilization, just three of many colonizing paradigms employed in and/or created by the oppression of non-Europeans by European modes and the political, cultural, and economic frameworks they produce and are produced by. All three of these paradigms have produced the Other primarily through the image,[20] fixing and ossifying vital and diverse cultures in singular representations (in both pictures and words). Mitchell's interpretation of Du Boisian double consciousness is highly pertinent to this notion, and reflects on the impact of images and stereotypes on Native peoples in the Americas: "Double consciousness, for DuBois," Mitchell writes, "arises out of a consciousness of being perceived as an image, through a screen or 'veil' of racist misrecognition, and the 'second sight' that the subject of the racist gaze receives as a result" (Grønstad and Vågnes 2006). For *indians*, this image begins and ends with the "primitive" or noble savage, a figure entirely available for inscription precisely because "he" (for he is usually gendered) is quintessentially antimodern, anachronistic: he lacks the tools to inscribe his own self-image.

Teuton argues that the subjugation of Native peoples is nowhere more in evidence than in the oppressive characterization of them as "oral, nonliterate peoples" (2010, xv). This singular fact of the prioritizing of orality as a singular mode of expressive life simultaneously serves to emphasize the fact of nonliteracy. It services, in other words, the imperialistic binary that has conventionally maintained notions that Native peoples had no literature. Most readers will doubtless find that an absurd statement, yet it often persists in common stereotypes.

Moreover, that characterization, Teuton argues, "has blinded scholars to the ways oral and graphic traditions function in interdependent ways in the expression of indigenous knowledge" (xv). These may be introductory remarks to Teuton's argument, but they are claims that, however well known in Native studies, are very rarely articulated, so it is worth repeating them here. That Teuton uses a metaphor of (lack of) sight to describe this particular critical lacuna is apt, given the theoretical starting point for visuality itself as a discursive framework. Rooted, as Nicholas Mirzoeff explains, in the work of nineteenth-century Scottish historian Thomas Carlyle, visuality and visualization as critical and interpretative tools are wholly bound up in the machinery of empire. Such a scenario generates a willful blindness that is effectively characterized by the bigoted closed-mindedness of the man himself: "As one typical description [from 1997] by a leading Carlyle critic ran: 'Carlyle's unequivocally antidemocratic spirit, stylistic self-indulgence, shameless racism and deeply felt sexism have dropped him almost absolutely from favor at the moment'" (Mirzoeff 2006, 54, qtg. George Levine). Recent revisions of the period recuperate Carlyle's legacy to a degree, revealing him in the following terms:

> Carlyle has emerged in this context as a key figure. Opposed to Chartism, pan-opticism and all the emancipatory movements that stemmed from the French Revolution, Carlyle imagined a moral imperialism led by great men in a visualized narrative that came to have considerable resonance in the period. (54)

Implicated in the modern production of what Mirzoeff calls the visual subject ("both the agent of sight . . . and the object of discourses of visuality" [54]), the link between majoritarian status (power) and subjectivity (autonomy) established in Carlyle's paradigm became instrumentally valuable to minority groups such as women and slaves. "Herein," Mirzoeff observes, "lies the contradictory source of the resonance of 'visuality' as a keyword for visual culture as both a mode of representing imperial culture and a means of resisting it by means of reverse appropriation" (54). As Denise Cummings puts it, "visuality concerns the field of vision as a site of power and social control," and as such we can understand visuality "as both a mode of representation and means of resisting as it pertains to the constructs, discourses, and practices of the colonial and postcolonial" (2011, xiv). While the image, and control of the image, paradoxically, becomes the means by which people as objects are "blinded" in the hierarchy of imperial visuality, it also becomes a significant means of resistance and reappropriation of autonomy.

Mirzoeff further riffs on Hal Foster's differentiation between vision suggesting sight as a physical operation and visuality suggesting sight as a social fact (Mirzoeff 2006, 55), emphasizing "a difference, many differences, among how we see, how we are able, allowed, or made to see, and how we see this seeing or the unseen therein" (55, qtg. Foster). I am most interested in the visual image, rather than in ways of seeing, but the significance of the image, the inability of colonial interlocutors to see images through anything other than their own terms of reference and significance, and, of course, the significance of vision in both literal and spiritual senses to the domain of the image in Indigenous societies means that these things are all imbricated. The operations of visuality also come to play in important ways in the contemporary relationship between art and Native American literature. This is amply supported in the sense that, in his treatment of Dante's *Divine Comedy*, which Carlyle described as poem, song, and painting, "from its very conception, visuality was a multimedia term, connecting art, literature, and music" (Mirzoeff 2011, 141). Of course, the ambivalent nature of its instrumentality is also clearly demonstrated in this comparison, aesthetically bound as it is to precisely the model of Christian heroism that drove empire. And as Mirzoeff further confirms, "In a sense, all visuality was and is imperial visuality, the shaping of modernity from the point of view of the imperial powers" (196).

Yet, and following Mirzoeff's own decolonizing project of "countervisuality," several of the authors in this study repeatedly demonstrate the degree to which Indigenous visual practices interrupt the imperial project and contribute to modernity. They do so in ways that invigorate active Native presence and destabilize the "transhistorical genealogy of authority marked by a caesura of incommensurability between the 'indigenous' and the 'civilized'" (Mirzoeff 2011, 196), not by erasing difference but by resisting the imposed taxonomies and hierarchies that write Indigenous agency out of history. Put more forcefully still by Dylan Miner, the destruction and occlusion of Indigenous texts through the colonial project has meant that "the reciprocity between seeing and being was simultaneously ruptured. It is from the colonial ashes of these oppressive acts that anticolonial visuality has emerged. And in many ways, it has continued to be modernist in scope" (2010, 179). In her video poem "Pre-Occupied" Heid Erdrich employs a range of popular and iconic imagery, including Langston Hughes's rivers (from "The Negro Speaks of Rivers"), maps, the Occupy movement, Pop Art, TV cartoons, stereotypes of Native Americans, environmental devastation, Superman, and much more, along with Indigenous iconography in the form of the spiral.[21] The extended video ends with a version of John Lennon's famous song "Imagine" ("G'pkwenmaag Noongwa"), translated into Anishinaabemowin by Howard Kimewon and Margaret Noodin (credited as Noori), and sung by Noodin. As I shall reiterate in chapter 3, this video captures and recalibrates the Occupy movement in relation to historical acts of occupation and oppression. In doing so, it examines questions of land occupancy and ownership, rights versus responsibility, popular vernaculars of heroism, and the competing countervisualities of Occupy and Indigenous sovereignty movements.

Insofar as the countervisual is about the attempt to change the perceived "real" in which it takes place, the video poem becomes a means of re-presenting Occupy as an inheritor of the logic of imperial visuality, revealing the disparity between an Indigenous "real" and the biopolitical spaces and rhetorics within which capitalism and its counters operate.

Visuality is only part of this discussion, but the images and visual aesthetics under examination here certainly speak to both ways of seeing and being seen, so adding this element to the critical framework enables further examination of the impacts and means of resistance both implicit and explicit in these authors' use of the visual. I do not, however, want to imply that visuality and countervisuality—the establishment of and resistance to dominance—are the sole emphasis of the visual in Anishinaabe literature. Over two decades ago, Thomas King forcefully made the point that

> while post-colonialism purports to be a method by which we can begin to look at those literatures which are formed out of the struggle of the oppressed against the oppressor, the colonized and the colonizer, the term [postcolonial] itself assumes that the starting point for that discussion is the advent of Europeans in North America. . . . And, worst of all, the idea of post-colonial writing effectively cuts us off from our traditions, traditions that were in place before colonialism ever became a question, traditions which have come down to us through our cultures in spite of colonization, and it supposes that contemporary Native writing is largely a construct of oppression. (1990, 11–12)

I have ample sympathy for those arguments that prescribe limitations to postcolonial theory's application to Indigenous issues, embedded as it ostensibly is in Euro-Western theory, in temporal notions of the postcolonial, however abstract they may be,[22] and in geopolitical, economic, and spiritual assumptions that do not necessarily map readily onto Indigenous North American communities and the questions that exercise them.[23] As Jodi Byrd has suggested in one of the more rigorous examinations of the relationship between Native and postcolonial studies, the resistance is bidirectional, where "the very idea of indigeneity can be too dangerous and xenophobic when combined with nationalism or anticolonial struggle in a world shaped by forced diaspora, migration, hybridity, and movement" (2011, xxxiii). Nonetheless, she continues, "bringing indigenous and tribal voices to the fore within postcolonial theory may help us elucidate how liberal colonialist discourses depend upon sublimating indigenous cultures and histories into fictive hybridities and social constructions as they simultaneously trap indigenous peoples within the dialectics of genocide" (xxxiv). My point is more simply that visuality, like the postcolonial, must not be permitted, in its emphases, to present or infer the fact of colonization, the experience of imperial exclusion, or to be the center around which postcontact Native literary and visual practices constellate. While bringing Indigenous critical theoretical questions to bear on both visuality and postcoloniality, the intention is to examine, rather than to endorse, the assumptions of both. If, in its imperial instrumentality, visuality implies powerlessness on the part of Indigenous actors, this book dwells on the ways in which that powerlessness is itself inscribed within the mechanisms of power that sought/seek still to render Indigenous peoples—and Indigenous power—invisible. It is an attempt to both peel back the veils of obfuscation and address the ways in which Native textualities perform engaged resistance while I ruminate on the power implicit in Indigenous sovereign aesthetics.

Let us close the circle: Louise Erdrich's claims for the common root *mazina* insist "it is the root for dozens of words all concerned with made images" (2003, 5). The connections she makes posit a "textual" tradition that long predates European contact and that both underpins and complements an oral tradition that constitutes one half of that "ideologically loaded" binary. Teuton deconstructs the oral-literate binary by calling on the graphic mode—by which he designates a range of material forms including wampum, beadwork, pictographic paintings, and petroglyphs. Naming the "dynamic relation" between oral and graphic the "critical impulse," Teuton goes on to describe a relationship "in constant flux," generative of "critical discourses that . . . disrupt static forms of power and dominance" (2010, 28). On the one hand, then, the prioritization of the visual and the seen, its reading through and against visuality, and the primacy of the made image in the texts under examination here embody the demand to take seriously Anishinaabe visual practices as different from but equivalent to textual, expressive, and scriptoral practices in the colonial/Euro-Western world. In "Bush/Writing," Peter Kulchyski writes of the "teaching rocks" of Peterborough, Ontario, that when "assimilate[d]" to "the category of literature," "retain a stronger destabilizing power" (2012, 262) relative to what he calls "the writing of the state" to which Indigenous peoples are asked to surrender. Inquiring what it means to call that which has "been compared to visual art" *literature*, in order to call up its power "to disturb the very being of literature," he asks "what kind of literature inscribes itself on rock?" (262). That question itself performs the kind of destabilizing work of Teuton's critical impulse, and it is a question implicit in many of the textual engagements with visual forms throughout this book. To think about the visual in relation to the literature of Native North America, then, is to engage with both this rich visual archive and the relational, ethical, and decolonial practices that are intimately connected with it.

Coda: Squatters, Poachers, Allies, and Advocates

James Cox has written about academic "poachers," who intrude on Native communities and resources in the interests of furthering their careers, retreating ultimately into the sanctuary of tenure and (tenured) white privilege (2009); Jace Weaver, meanwhile, extends the analogy to "squatters" who "lay claim to the field and remain to exploit it and the People" (2007, 237). The squatter-poacher par excellence may be none other than Henry Rowe Schoolcraft, whose career was founded on his embeddedness among the Anishinaabeg of the upper Michigan peninsula. It is with complete consciousness of the attendant irony that I follow at least partially in his footsteps as a white scholar studying the literary culture of the Anishinaabeg. Any such identification demands qualification of course: Schoolcraft actively mediated between Anishinaabe communities and his own audiences, tightly controlled the means of literary production, translated and rewrote his informants' stories, and worked directly as a self-interested servant of an occupying power. While I therefore occupy radically different ground from him, it is not without acknowledgement of my own privileged position and outsider status in light of that prior imposition that I have embarked on this project. With this awareness full center, I attempt/intend here to avoid what Sara Suleri calls the "will to cultural description" of the colonizer "reading" the colonized (1992, 7), which, as Patricia Yaeger explains, presents the flip side of the narrative of the "colonizer's terrified encounter with otherness (a terror that translates into the frightening 'unreadability' of the colonized)" (1996, 15). Suleri and Yaeger are describing the Indian subcontinent, but their point holds for those aspects of the earlier discussion wherein generations of white scholars have sought to *translate* the perceived inscrutability of Indigenous cultures in North America or, conversely, to treat them as differently the same through the general application of Western theoretical strategies. I do not—indeed, I could not—jump the cultural gap and read the texts under examination here through anything other than the eyes and the lenses of a white European male. But I attempt, as far as is possible, to read through the texts' own hermeneutic codes, ever mindful of Daniel Heath Justice's warning, quoted earlier, of the danger of eliding alternative textualities and illegibility to the mainstream. Although, as I will suggest in a number of scenarios, "illegibility" can itself be a viable strategic move, Justice's warning echoes Suleri's and Yaeger's concerns about the "inscrutability" of Indigenous cultures: conversely, the attempt to "read" can itself filter out difference. Balancing on that high wire while offering observations that can intervene positively in the development of discussion about Indigenous aesthetics and their politicization symbolizes the necessarily precarious position in which you find me.

Similarly, as I have noted, my focus on Anishinaabe literature represents an attempt to prioritize depth and definition of analysis over the potential for homogenizing moves across diverse tribal practices. Although I draw on a variety of secondary sources, I do so in the spirit at least of Kimberly Blaeser's call for Indigenous-centered theorizations, following Vizenor's engagement of a wide variety of theoretical texts in the interest of generating new "theories of tribal interpretation" (1993, 14), and with Anishinaabe material practices at its heart. Like Cox, Konkle, and others, I seek to prioritize Native scholarship. Like Kirwan, I do so "out of the conviction that Native American texts are, more often than not, expressions of tribal sovereignty in modern America" and in order "to examine the reverberations caused by the claims of indigenous writers to artistic, political, and cultural sovereignty, and [to] do so by engaging Native American contexts respectfully and meaningfully" (2013, 23, 37). That the endeavor risks homogenizing the incredible diversity of Anishinaabe cultures is, in some measure, mitigated by those points of commonality that are not pressed out of the "pan-Indian" mold. In his review essay "Against Separatism," Tol Foster describes the overreactions of non-Native scholars to the perceived essentialism at the heart of American Indian literary nationalism. Calling out Kenneth Lincoln's "blog-worthy rant against Womack and Warrior as 'purist bloods, ethnic nationalists or academic essentialists,'" Foster ponders, "perhaps an anxious expression of non-Native critics' reluctance to explain exactly why they are working in the field, Lincoln's fear has no *actual* basis in the work of literary separatism" (2008, 570). Foster's supposition is interesting. Among colleagues in wider literary studies, the self-positioning he describes—relating to political and ideological rationales as much as, or more than, aesthetic or historical ones—produces a certain amount of incredulity. It is, however, a common and real aspect of Indigenous studies more broadly. Yet, where once the major voices in Native literary studies were largely Euro-American and European, the significant areas of discussion in the United States and Canada are more frequently being led today by Native scholars, by the theoretical and historical structurings and restructurings of Native writers, and by those who would seek, self-consciously or otherwise, to produce work that serves the survivance of Native communities. Their work is varied, impassioned, and absolutely an engine-room for the future development of the field. This is not to suggest by any measure that the decolonizing work laid out by such thinkers as Devon Mihesuah and Angela Cavendar Wilson (2004), Linda Tuhiwai Smith (1999), or indeed in the recent recommendations of Canada's Truth and Reconciliation Commission has been effected in the academy. Indeed, beyond rarefied pockets, academic institutions and institutionalism remain resistant, and even deaf, to the need for greater Indigenous representation through not only the presence of Indigenous academics, but the acceptance of Indigenous knowledges, protocols, and pedagogic practices.

This scenario points toward affirming futures in which conversations in Indigenous studies are driven by those questions closest to Indigenous interests and that, most significantly, the products of those conversations are becoming ever more accessible to Indigenous communities, both in terms of disseminated research findings and in terms of opportunities for Indigenous graduate students to succeed professionally in the academy. Having control of the means of production is key to the development of literary cultures: as both Weaver and Foster clarify, so too is control (or at least a controlling stake) in the production and dissemination of literary criticism.

Whether or not this shift relieves non-Native critics of the need to explain themselves—beyond those aesthetic, historical, and theoretical questions most commonly driving the choices of critics and readers—remains moot. As Sam McKegney argues, "Critical interventions, even when they are flawed, can forward others' thinking by inciting reactions in which might be developed new avenues of investigation and new methods of inquiry" (2007, 44). This assumes that Native studies scholarship as benefit to Native communities is an incontestably desirable state of affairs. It is impossible to argue in favor of the continued critical colonization of Native cultures by envisaging it any other way. That it presupposes that non-Native scholars are at greater risk of producing "flawed" interventions is also inevitable. McKegney goes on to assert that "an ally, in my understanding, acknowledges the limits of his or her knowledge, but doesn't cower beneath those limits or use them as a crutch" (45). In the spirit of that disclaimer, I too "apologize for any weaknesses that might emerge in my analysis . . . but I don't apologize for analyzing" (44) although, unlike McKegney, I hesitate to claim the label of ally on my own behalf. Participation in Native literary critical discourse through "analysis, contextualization, and elucidation in the political, social, and creative objectives of the texts with which [we] engage" (44) is a warranted ambition and a necessary set of priorities in the work of decolonization. That such can be done without becoming unjustifiably polemical, didactic, or lacking in critical rigor is a given.

At the same time—and here, perhaps, is where I give in to the anxiety Foster describes by gesturing toward my own motives—the various blind spots in American studies and colonial and postcolonial studies that, once confronted, tend to draw non-Indigenous scholars to Indigenous works, as much with a desire to understand the causes as well as the content of such lacunae, render it necessary to participate in a way that does not simply leave one's colleagues wandering off incredulous. In Europe in particular, Indigenous studies has no true institutional home; Indigenous literary critical practitioners tend to work within schools of English or comparative literary studies, departments of American and/or Canadian studies, and, still, centers of anthropology. As such, the intellectual imperative to clarify those blind spots, to bring Indigenous studies closer—through elucidation and critique—to other disciplinary fields, becomes a means of academic survival as well as an intellectual motivation. To do so, however, does not necessarily mean to seek to incorporate or synthesize Indigenous literatures into these fields, or to present Indigenous writing as, for instance, "one thread within the developmental, and often triumphal, narrative of American literary history" (Madsen 2011, 357). Indeed, in her largely critical survey of Indigenous studies in Europe, Madsen points to Craig Womack's work, to claims such as "'Native American literature *is* American literature' and that all other literary production in the United States must be seen as an adjunct to Native American literature" as a means of reframing syllabi, which will "point the way forward to a more satisfactory and just representation of the originary status of Native American cultures and, also, of the canon of American settler-nation texts" (357). She might equally, though, point to the broad interdisciplinarity of Weaver, or to the influence of Edward Said on Warrior, or to the presence of key postcolonial theorists such as Said, Ngũgĩ, Memmi, Frantz Fanon, Michel Foucault, and others in the work of other leading Native scholars—Glen Coulthard, Audra Simpson, Chris Andersen, for starters—as models for the fuller engagement (and articulation) of Indigenous studies with-and-in broader conversations without simply being subsumed by those respective fields. Indeed, the aforementioned theorists tend to figure as affiliative markers, as intellectual path-breakers, as benchmarks, touchstones, and provisioners; they are consistently supplemented, complicated, and often drowned out by the increasing wealth and depth of Native "voiced" scholarship on offer.

In "The Text, the World, the Critic," Edward Said writes, "It is not only that any text, if it is not immediately destroyed, is a network of often colliding forces, but also that a text in its being a text is a being in the world; it addresses anyone who reads" (1975, 3). Ultimately, this project springs from the encounter between critic and text, an encounter that is characterized by the attempt to respond to Kimberly Blaeser's instruction to be "alert for critical methods and voices that seem to arise out of the literature itself" (1993, 53). I take as given, then, McKegney's insistence on the effort to become a suitably informed reader, while remaining alert to Said's point that "words and texts are so much of the world that their effectiveness, in some cases even their use, are matters having to do with ownership, authority, power, and the imposition of force" (1983, 48).

I take seriously Penelope Myrtle Kelsey's injunction that scholars of Indigenous literature ought to endeavor to learn Indigenous languages. I am not a speaker of Anishinaabemowin to any meaningful degree—and in making the argument that almost all the literature I address in this book is written in English by authors whose first language is English, I take a position that, though clearly caught up in the history of colonization, English is a language that has been molded by generations of Native peoples to serve a function that is capable of articulating concerns specific to Indigenous peoples. Yet Kelsey is clearly right when she notes:

Language lies at the core of the study of all literatures, and Indigenous languages—whether visibly present or no—influence the composition and worldviews of all tribal texts. . . . Underpinning these languages are unique tribal knowledges, epistemology, and philosophy, and Indigenous writers repeatedly and mindfully invoke and deploy these tribal worldviews in their English, French, Spanish, and tribal language publications. (2010, 1)

Waziyaṭawiŋ Angela Wilson, meanwhile, makes an equally forceful claim for the nature of historic identity: "The history of an Indigenous people cannot be cut from its roots. The Indigenous perspective is holistic and inescapably linked to language. Language is linked to systems of thought, which are linked to history and identity" (2005, 11).

I take these critiques of nonspeaker criticism very seriously and continue to make efforts to acquire a working understanding of Anishinaabemowin through the various dictionaries, linguistic studies, webinars, and websites that exist. These attempts are both essential to the larger development of Indigenous studies beyond not only Indigenous communities, but North America, and also integral to a fuller understanding of Indigenous literatures even when produced in non-Native languages. That said, it must also be noted that a too-ready assumption of the centrality of language learning to the understanding and development of Indigenous literatures risks, as I see it, two things. The first is that it potentially assumes a new gauge of authenticity. The question of who has the right to speak about a given body of literature—and we must make a clear distinction between speaking *about* and speaking *for*—has long been intertwined with the red herring of biologically determined notions of authenticity. If it is generally understood that well-reasoned—and sensitive—outside perspectives can be to the benefit of all, then, one might say, the prioritizing of language does not exclude outsiders who are equally at liberty to learn Indigenous languages. However, there are clearly always going to be limitations to the kinds of cultural immersion available to the non-Indigenous learner, not to mention no one single authoritative Anishinaabe dialect that would adequately encompass the geographical and historical range of this book. But that is beside the point; my hesitation here has far more to do with the potential exclusion, at this point in time, of Indigenous students and readers who happen to be nonspeakers.[24] The dangers inherent in a kind of hierarchization of authority based on degrees of linguistic immersion in respect of books written in English and marketed to—whether originally written for or not—a general audience are implicit. The second possible risk, very much extrapolated from the first, is that too close a focus on language, at this moment in history at least, risks limiting audiences and, more particularly, the critical conversation about particular literatures in unsustainable ways. With 2019 being designated the UN Year of Indigenous Languages, hopefully this will not always be the case.

I attend, then, to Simon Ortiz's widely endorsed assertion that "Indian women and men have carried on their lives and their expression through the use of the [colonial] languages . . . and they have used these languages on their own terms" (1981, 7). Working on the assumption that the texts under scrutiny here "perform" through the medium of English, I trust that my ability to read them, different though it will necessarily be from the insights a cultural insider and Anishinaabemowin-speaking reader might bring, is generally valid and useful. I acknowledge that when one critiques French texts, for instance, one generally reads them in French, so it is important to reiterate that I deal almost exclusively with texts written first—only—in

English.[25] More linguistically knowledgeable scholars than I are engaged in more comprehensive studies of Anishinaabe literature in which Anishinaabemowin plays its proper part, and to that end I have been at pains to avoid crass generalizations about language, and epistemological questions specific to language, except where those questions can be answered through the current scholarship. In other words, although I will, by necessity, discuss culture and language, I do not seek, here, to make authoritative or overarching claims about or on behalf of Anishinaabe people and heritage. My interest, rather, is in a specific aesthetic thread as it is elaborated through a range of texts by a diverse body of Anishinaabe writers and scholars and its relationship to ethical and political questions germane to Anishinaabe peoplehood. Nevertheless, on those few occasions where language comes to the foreground, I endeavor to work with the original, taking advice from scholars in the field where possible. And more generally, throughout this work, I pay attention to current Anishinaabe linguistic and literary-linguistic scholarship, drawing on the work of eminent and important linguists, including John Nicolls and Earl Nyholm, Anton and David Treuer, and Margaret Noodin, as well as discourse/narrative analysts such as Roger Spielmann.

CHAPTER 1

An Indian Well Versed

(Con)Textualizing Anishinaabeakiing—George Copway
and Jane Johnston Schoolcraft

his chapter picks up on a number of threads left hanging in the preceding
introduction. It represents only a brief foray into the work of two of the
best-known nineteenth-century Ojibwe writers, but it establishes early
engagement with many of the key themes and motifs that run throughout
this book. From George Copway's impassioned descriptions of both the form and
instrumentality of Anishinaabe pictography to Jane Johnston Schoolcraft's more
elliptical appreciation of traces left on rock and soil by nature, spirit, and human,
the examples I address here engage these motifs in the course of deconstructing the
hegemonic image of the "Indian."[1] The relationship that each author has to writing,
and that their writing has to intellectual and literary imposition by settler-colonial
modes of interpretation, is central to a disruption of the oral-literate binary that
governs that image. More significantly, though, these authors' interventions directly
establish a thread of continuity between Indigenous presence, Indigenous "writing,"
and their own status as writers.

In *Voices of the Marketplace*, Anne Rose repeats a truism in the course of both
analyzing and exemplifying the racialized discourse in which early Native American
writing was immersed and against which it agitated (see, for instance, Apess 1833).

Quoting Henry Louis Gates, who asserts that "fugitive slaves, deemed 'things' by law, used autobiographies to '*write themselves into being*,' performing 'an act of self-creation through the mastery of language,'" she affirms the essential novelty of such practice, claiming: "Native American cultures lacked alphabets and hence texts, and Indians who produced autobiographies did so in a spirit of asserting selfhood similar to that of blacks" (1995, 133). Despite the major differences in their circumstances, their generalized common experience of subjugation by (white) Europeans and the similarities in practice of achieving liberation through the act of self-narration render such comparisons between the endeavors of African American and Native American writers in the late eighteenth/early nineteenth centuries understandably common. Donald B. Smith, for instance, makes several allusions to Frederick Douglass in his discussion of Mississauga Methodist missionary, orator, writer, and entrepreneur George Copway, or Gaagigegaabaw, and his fellow Mississauga Maungwudaus (George Henry), offering up a conceptual affiliation, while explicitly suggesting that Copway's first autobiographical text "resembles the African slave narratives then available, texts written by individuals from predominantly oral cultures" (2013, 187; see also Brennan 2003, 53).

Lavonne Brown Ruoff, meanwhile, in the introduction to Copway's *Life, Letters, and Speeches*, points out that "Copway and other Christian writers, like the African-slave writers, undertook the dual task of demonstrating to their audiences the virtues of traditional tribal life and the capacity of their race to adapt to white civilization" (Copway 1997, 9). While such comparisons are both logical and cogent,[2] the irony implicit in such alignments is clear in that racial discourse itself. In his 1848 "Address before both houses of the legislature of South Carolina," for example, Copway himself makes clear a distinction between Native Americans and "the colored man" to whom "*Fanatics* have talked of extending universal suffrage," while "their being *silent* in reference to that which would elevate the North American Indian, proves that they assent to his downfall" (1997, 169). A rhetorical provocation—not dissimilar to those used by Apess—to point out the hypocrisies of a white audience, Copway's distinction nevertheless illuminates great disparities in racial differentiation.

Similarly, Paul Gilmore notes, "Frederick Douglass transforms the submissiveness of blacks noted *in Native American texts* into a positive mutability by arguing that 'the Indian, dies, under the flashing glance of the Anglo Saxon. *Not* so the Negro: civilization cannot kill him. He accepts it—becomes a part of it'" (2001, 204n47; emphasis added). Again, Copway's awareness of the very discourse at stake is evident in his address where he declares: "The wide world looks with wild intensity to our shores for a model—a noble example it finds in him who loved liberty, the father of liberty, GEORGE WASHINGTON" (1997, 169). He highlights the broad crossover between the antislavery rhetoric of liberty and the ideal of natural liberty both conjured by the Native American and articulated in the founding documents, and he effects the ironic inversion of describing the onlooking (white) European audience as "wild" in their search for a "model . . . of liberty," which very deliberately evokes both senses above, once again belying the hypocrisy of Euro-American attitudes. While Douglass—and almost certainly Copway—were undoubtedly opposed to the oppression of groups other than those they represented, their respective writings nevertheless elicit glimpses of the racial chauvinism of their time. That we can discern in both instances an internalization—and recitation—of an imposed racial rhetoric reflects the ways each writer attempts to get inside the structures and logics of hegemony in order to disrupt it in their own cause.[3]

In *Like the Sound of a Drum*, Canadian scholar Peter Kulchyski suggests "the state is a certain kind of writing," an anonymous, administrative form to which Indigenous peoples are asked to surrender (2005, 262). Presenting writing as the function of offices of bureaucracy, and embedding his discussion in the work of Nicos Poulantzas, Kulchyski quotes the latter's assertion that "there has always been a close relationship between the State and writing" and that writing, particularly under capitalism, represents "the articulation and distribution of knowledge and power within the State" (Poulantzas 2000, 59). Corroborating Poulantzas's argument, Kulchyski further argues that "nothing happens in the sense that no events take place unless they are inscribed in the sanctioned forms, no being is recognized as existent unless it has a signature or a written status." As such, "the written, the inscribed, is a material embodiment of the State" (2005, 262). For Poulantzas, "there has always been a close relationship between the State and writing, given that every State embodies a certain form of the division between intellectual and manual labour" (2000, 59). In both Douglass's and Copway's narratives, then, the accession to writing, demonstrated not only in the specific act of self-representation but in the apparent mastery of rhetorical forms associated with authoritative script—biblical, legal, and political—itself heralds a dialectical shift between "manual," codified in Copway's case through the figure of the precivilized noble savage, and intellectual labor. Thus, through writing, albeit not in the administrative register that records "the bureaucratic sites and mechanisms and [represents] the hierarchically centralized space of the [capitalist] State" (Poulantzas 2000, 59), they force admission to the nexus of knowledge, language, and power that the State controls and that the state consistently uses to *overwrite* the other's agency.

Precarious though it is, writing—self-representation—thus becomes a means of resisting those specific forms of writing of the state by which Native Americans and African Americans, ex-slaves and "Indians" were codified, taxonomized, and excluded, and which become naturalized in popular perception. There persists, though, a singular tension—one returned to repeatedly by critics—between the liberatory act that writing represents for the ex-slave and the Native intellectual, and writing as an assimilative move, a complicitous act, as they take up a "weapon of conquest" that can "effectively compromise a native culture" (Lepore 1999, 27). As such, they simultaneously resist and inadvertently risk becoming subsumed by the very apparatus they employ.[4] In *Sovereign Selves*, David Carlson avers that Copway "self-consciously aligned himself with the institutions of colonial governance," and describes him as a "colonial functionary" committed to "the joint endeavor of civilization and conversion . . . manifested throughout his autobiographical text" (2016, 75–76). As I will discuss shortly, such charges—entirely fair in the terms Carlson levels them—give way to forms of suspicious reading that, while well intentioned, often end up occluding the agency of the writing/speaking/asserting subject.

The above instances, then, suggest that the strategic alliance of Native and African Americans was not necessarily always either feasible or desirable in practice, and also that the specific ideological battles engaged on the field of literacy rendered each a useful rhetorical foil for their claims of liberty and civility. They conjure a hypothetical—critical—affiliation that in some measure belies a politics of divide and rule that was at least partially absorbed and rearticulated by the very people invoked by Rose, Smith, and others, even before we take into consideration the precarity of writing as a gauge of (de)coloniality. While significant work has been done in the reconstruction of literary lineages in the two decades since Robert Warrior's *Tribal Secrets: Recovering American Indian Intellectual Traditions* (1994), it is only very recently, and arguably belatedly, that scholars in Native American studies have begun in earnest to address the question of literacy more broadly, confronting the other assumption of Rose's that the concept of "writing"—with or without its attachment to selfhood—is an explicitly colonial act.

In his recent essay "Indigenous Writing" in Warrior's *The World of Indigenous North America*, Daniel Heath Justice asks:

if the colonizer's worst nightmare is indeed "an Indian with a pen," then what of
the Indian without one? What of the generations of Indians and other Indigenous
peoples who practiced other forms of textual expression in the past, and the
many who continue to do so today, or who are newly learning, revitalizing, and
re-employing these old ways for new purposes and new struggles? (2015, 292, qtg.
Betty Louise Bell)

Justice addresses precisely the "erasure of Indigenous literature" implicit in
Rose's assumption that the lack of an alphabet should equate directly to a lack
of texts—a figurative silencing with echoes of early assessments of Indigenous
languages, religions, governance, and even rational capacity. While ignoring the
contributions of roughly fifty years of development in material culture studies,
which has increasingly expanded our apprehension of what constitutes textuality
(see, for instance, Schlereth 1999), it more significantly reveals the legacy of one
of the major assumptions of colonial and settler-colonial logic. As Birgit Brander
Rasmussen explains, "colonial records and subsequent scholarship have elaborated
the notion that America's indigenous people had no writing. These material and
discursive practices have converged to link terms such as 'writing' and 'literature'
predominantly to alphabetic script" (2012, 2). More pointedly, she suggests that
"during the colonial process, literacy became a signifier, as well as the 'sine
qua non,' of civilization, and 'writing' became a crucial dividing line between
colonized and colonizer. The ways in which literary scholars have constructed
their object—and abject—of inquiry remain deeply entangled with the history
of European imperialism" (3). So long, then, as the alphabetic model remains the
primary means of understanding—legitimating—forms of literacy, "we uphold
that legacy by defining other forms of recording knowledge and narrative out of
existence" (3).

In fact, Copway's *Traditional History and Characteristic Sketches of the Ojibway
People*—a text Rose mentions in passing—is also revealing. To say that "mastery
of language" is evidenced only by writing—and writing in a European alphabet
at that—is, as Rose's context suggests, a discursive application derived directly
from African American studies. It does not take a comparative analysis of the
ruptures of slavery set against the ruptures of colonization to discern the kernel of
comparable truth in the will to exert agency through such forms. Yet, as this chapter
explores, the rupture Rose depends upon is incomplete: the moment of bridging
she describes represents the passage from a world bereft of texts to one in which

self-actualization through text can occur, and as such, it is as much representative of scholarly myopia as epistemological rupture. Buried deep within its heart is the myth of the white crusader: our very own culture hero who saves, enables, and empowers the beleaguered Other whose soul has been heretofore chained in the ignominy of silent, sentence-less irrationality. One wonders where oral tradition fits in this schematic—whether Native American, African, or African American. One wonders, also, whether Rose actually encountered Copway's descriptions of images painted on rock and etched into birch bark, or of shells set into patterns on belts and knotted strings: while not written languages per se, they certainly account for a "familiar[ity] with symbolic representation" (Monaghan 2005, 47). Copway describes therein a rich textual history, one that supported, elaborated on, and was accounted for by Ojibwe and other Nations' oral traditions. Of the pictographs he goes on to elucidate, he insists: "An Indian well versed in these can send a communication to another Indian, and by them make himself as well understood as a pale face can by letter" (1850a, 132).

Whether scholars are willing to recognize what Copway describes as a literate tradition or not, his claim is that the graphic tradition he describes is writing that precedes European contact and is commensurate with the act of writing that constitutes his *Traditional History*. Secondarily, his writing, in other words, stakes a claim of sorts to administrative competence prior to and outside the assimilative state instrument—a claim that complicates, if it does not exactly resolve, understanding of his complicity with the colonial administration. Moreover, it suggests an administrative competence that underwrites his bid—much maligned as itself an assimilative complicity—for a new territory, Kagega, on which his people (and other Native Nations) could settle and that might, in time, achieve statehood.

This chapter, then, will dwell on two brief instances, in the early nineteenth century, of "literary" reflection on Anishinaabe texts. In the context of a world in which the aspiration to the literary arts—history and poetry in Copway's case, poetry in the case of Jane Johnston Schoolcraft, or Bamewawagezhikaquay[5]—is read as demonstrative of the civilizable potential of Native Americans, the brief turns both authors make to alternative textualities, to parallel literacies, present significant moments in their claims to inclusion in the literary sphere and their resistance to total subsumption by the modes and models of that world, to a certain kind of writing of the state. For both writers, those modes and models are arguably best encapsulated by a single man, Bamewawagezhikaquay's husband Henry Rowe Schoolcraft, whose interpretative authority is writ large over nineteenth-century understandings of Anishinaabe lifeways. Although only fleeting moments in their work, this chapter will delineate and examine the ways their literal and figurative gestures to Anishinaabe expressive forms—the making of marks on birch bark and rock, in particular—participate in a broader resistance to the process of colonization that sees not only land, but the knowledge of the people themselves, circumscribed and calibrated by Anglo-American ethnographic instrumentalism. In so doing, they join with several other strategies through which Native writers, even as they make use of supposedly imported forms and languages, resist the closure and compartmentalism inferred by the "socially privileged forms of literacy" represented by "alphabetic script, Roman orthography, [and] books and papers in Euro-derived languages" (Justice 2015, 292). I propose here, then, in these two microcosmic snapshots, to introduce several of the major visual themes of this book, to highlight the potential in these early texts for interplay between graphic, oral, and critical impulses (see Teuton 2010), and to desuture ideas of writing as "solid materiality" (Warkentin 1999) from binary notions of human development.[6]

Textures of Connection and Continuity

Planting those themes in the earliest of an Ojibwe literary tradition in English and reflecting on that moment's relationship with an alternative, or parallel, literacy, I infer a speculative (loose) genealogy. In her essay *"Name"*: Literary Ancestry as Presence," Anishinaabe poet, playwright, and critic Heid Erdrich includes Copway and Schoolcraft among a list of Ojibwe literary ancestors. "I choose to be guided by a metaphor," she writes, "that involves a play between the notion of landmark literary works and the pictographic marks/signs/presence that Anishinaabe people left/leave/find on rock and elsewhere" (2013b, 14). The metaphor itself, she explains, "arises from an Anishinaabe-centered epistemology that relates writing with landmark, and marking with ongoing presence in place," through the "transitive animate" verb name' (14). In doing so, she draws attention away from the intense scrutiny of early Anishinaabe writers' assimilated qualities. Although the lines of connection may not always be self-evident, the embeddedness of these writers in a common epistemological ground and their common labor as writers in a period of great social and political change that involved the recasting and refusing of a host of pervasive images of *indian*ness along with the ethical deployment of the imagic, of a significant visual aesthetic, is, I believe, apparent. Erdrich's shift of focus from the absence of assimilation to the presence of landmark thus addresses more concrete markers of survivance:

> Ojibwe authors enact a traditional literary motion that I see embodied in the Ojibwe word *name'* (to find/leave signs of a being's presence), which is a stem word meaning "traces." . . . an Ojibwe-centered notion of literature as persistence and continuance, a presence that is at once new and at the same time based in an Ojibwe epistemology as old as petroglyphs. (2013b, 18)

Copway's place in this genealogy is significant, not least because it quietly troubles the assertions of a kind of abject splitting in his character made repeatedly in the scholarship on his work.[7] Erdrich, in contrast, writes that her "own reading of Kah-ge-ga-gah-bowh is of a remarkable author who managed, without denying the humanity of Ojibwe people or the culpability of the Europeans who brought pain to his people, to write both as a Christian and an Ojibwe" (2013b, 16). Where too little is known for certain about Bamewawagezhikaquay—the intervening hand and voice of her husband muddying the waters—in Copway's case we know almost too much. We know of his ambition and of his occasionally overreaching desire to make his mark. We know of accusations of vanity and egotism, albeit from men like William Boutwell, an Anglo missionary whose distaste for Anishinaabe customs and values was no secret (see D. Smith 2013, 174, 177–78). His speedy popularity and its equally quick souring has been well noted, as has his progressivism and the inevitable contradictions in what Cheryl Walker describes as the "agonistic tendency" in "the writing of many 'minorities'" to "juxtapose the fragmented experience of the individual with the dream of a significant polis or group, without being able to resolve the emergent contradictions" (1997, 106). This latter aspect certainly feeds into the ambiguity and apparently counterintuitive nature of some of his decision making, such as his relationship with the nativist Order of United Americans and his voicing of support for the American Party, or "Know-Nothings," the order's political manifestation.[8]

Other noted attributes of his entrapment betwixt and between such as the shifts in perspective in the records that declare him to be both a powerful orator and an incoherent rambler with a poor grasp of English are less readily corroborated, since a scan of the archive reveals that it was always thus. For instance, critics wishing to point out a general arrogance turn to critiques of his oratory such as that made by Elihu Burrit of his presentation at the World Peace Conference in Frankfurt in July

1850: "Chief Copway made a long, windy, wordy speech, extremely ungrammatical and incorrect" (D. Smith 2013, 199). Yet even positive early reviews made similar observations, making clear his limitations while remaining positive about his intent. A review in the *Baltimore Clipper*, for instance, states that the deficiency in his "knowledge of the strict rules which govern the English language . . . was more than compensated by his figures of rhetoric and his thrilling incidents" (D. Smith 2013, 189). His eventual decline into obscurity, the confusion around which is unpicked by Donald B. Smith, certainly evinces a loss of support, but critics too readily construct narratives of cause and effect.[9] If his story is incomplete, it is also inchoate, yet scholars pretend to know the man through his words. There is a marked contrast, then, between Erdrich's "remarkable author," who may be read as resistant to the implications of what Phil Deloria describes as "temporal Others, reflections of a primitive stage of cultural existence outside modernity" (1998, 137), and Walker's "personif[ication of] the incoherence of the American subject" (1997, 106).

I do not aspire to any kind of resolution here—indeed, the ambiguities and contradictions in his work and life are George Copway. If we can permit Ralph Waldo Emerson such intellectual license, why not his contemporary?[10] This latter allusion is not entirely specious, since running through Copway's antics appears to be a real desire to be a literary figure and an exemplar of adaptability. Inconsistently eloquent though he may have been, he performed the oratorical duties common to literary men of the era. He penned poetry, and in one famous instance put his name to the poetry of another, co-opting—in the interests of fundraising and with the author's permission—Julius Taylor Clarke's *The Ojibway Conquest* in 1851. He adored Longfellow's *The Song of Hiawatha*, several commentators confirm, dressing in his Ojibwe regalia to declaim its lines on many occasions in Eastern U.S. cities and naming his last-born daughter (b. 1860) Minnehaha (see D. Smith 2013, 204). Although Schoolcraft's *Historical and Statistical Information* was Longfellow's major source, Copway may well have contributed to its content. My interest, then, is served by the achievement that Heid Erdrich, too, shines a light on: "He showed national/tribal pride, and his work also asserts the longtime literacy of the Ojibwe by explaining the 'picture writing,' which he declared as useful as English writing" (2013b, 16–17). If, as Kulchyski argues, a "precondition for playing the game [of political participation] is surrender [to state writing]," Erdrich's "Ojibwe epistemology as old as petroglyphs" brings into play a form of resistance that represents "the many ancient modalities of writing deployed by Aboriginal peoples, especially modes of writing on the land and writing on the body [that] are being reconfigured and redeployed in creative ways" (Kulchyski 2005, 17). In Copway's account, this writing on the land—through a writing that claims the land—interrupts the hegemonic account of Native lack of writing with a symbolic communication that allows him to "perceive literacy as the same process in a different form" (Monaghan 2005, 47).

Writing in his *Traditional History*, Copway explains: "The records of the Ojibways have a two-fold meaning; the hieroglyphic symbols of material objects represent the transmission of a tradition from one generation to another. This refers more particularly to their religion, which is itself founded on tradition. Picture writing is most prevalent, and is used altogether in their medicine and hunting songs" (1850a, 126). Although Copway makes a clear distinction between writing as direct representation of speech (glottographic, or logographic writing) and picture-writing (semasiography, or iconographic writing), observing that "the Ojibway language has not yet been reduced to a perfect written form" (126), he simultaneously clouds that distinction in his explanation of pictographic forms. Presenting five distinct ideograms he asserts, "Here are figures which suggest sentences to be sung" (126). Clearly, it would be easy to overemphasize the significance of semantic choices, but it is interesting that Copway should choose to relate these images to "sentences" rather than to "phrases" or "verses" or "scenes," given his emphasis on his ability, "in imagination," to "see the enemy, though none were within a hundred miles" (128). Indeed, that distinction is further blurred a couple of pages later, where Copway introduces his transcription of several dozen more figures by insisting, "These are some of the figures used by us in writing. With these, and from others of a similar class, the Ojibways can write their war and hunting songs" (132). Even more pointedly, he emphasizes their significance, claiming, "An Indian well versed in these can send a communication to another Indian, and by them make himself as well understood as a pale face can by letter" (132). For Joshua David Bellin, "this roster functions . . . to proclaim the Ojibwas' ability to record events, to set down, as one observer put it, 'where they came from, where they are heading, and what they plan to do'" (2001, 193). Moreover, they convey in concert with the oral tradition the "whole story" of the tribe, rather than simply functioning as static, singular images, and in so presenting them, Copway "scorns the distinction between a transient orality and a permanent literacy" (Bellin 2001, 193–94).

Maureen Konkle, highlighting the same passage from Copway, affirms that "settlers therefore do not have exclusive claim to the technology of writing" (2004, 217). Although Copway does on occasion refer to these forms as "emblems," echoing

Schoolcraft's and others' comparisons to heraldry, he nevertheless repeatedly asserts their status as written record, most significantly in his recounting of the presence of secret mide documents: "There is a place where the sacred records are deposited in the Indian country. These records are made on one side of bark and board plates, and are examined once in fifteen years. . . . Most Indian Nations of the West have places in which they deposit the records which are said to have originated their worship" (1850a, 128–29). Again, for Bellin, Copway's invocation of the medicine lodge intentionally "invites comparison between his act and those of the Mide priests, who, he says, renew the 'sacred records' of the tribe to prevent them from 'decaying'" and, in consequence, "complicates Schoolcraft's claim that pictography belongs solely to those mired in myth" (2001, 193). Copway's own writing has long been understood within the tradition of conversion narratives, anywhere along the spectrum from assimilationist discourse to hybrid text and mediational document. At either end of the spectrum, whether Copway is perceived to be derogatory toward what he describes in *The Life, History, and Travels of Kah-ge-ga-gah-bowh* as his "savage" state prior to conversion, or whether he is understood to be reaching out to his white, Christian audience in terms they will readily comprehend, his reflections are often held to be inauthentically Ojibwe, evidence only, Cathy Rex suggests, of the "Noble Christian Savage" (2006, 2). Such dominance by a pejorative hybridization in the crude biological terms such hybridity evokes maintains that while the rootstock remains Indigenous, the newly grafted bloom is entirely European and objectively dominant in terms of agency and subjectivity. Though purportedly in the interests of critique of the dominant society, which is ever mournful for that "vanishing Indian" world whose absence is rendered in the presence of such interlocutors as Copway, such interpretations perpetuate an archetypal discourse that "Indians" and writing are always already contradictions in terms.[11]

One of its many net results is to present figures such as Copway as children in the world of letters. In fact, in spite of the acknowledgement most of his commentators make, that Copway was clearly aided in his endeavors by a writer attuned to Romanticist tropes (probably, consensus has it, his wife); in spite of his own very clear and frank admission that he was assisted, at least at a grammatical level (Copway 1847, v); in spite of fleeting comparisons of his autobiography to slave narratives (Rose 1995, 133), or his willingness to put his (Anishinaabe) name to epic poetry;[12] in fact, in spite of much evidence of a complex literary character, rhetorical complexity, it would appear, is the one thing his critics are unwilling entirely to afford him. Indeed, even Cheryl Walker, whose nuanced critique readily identifies Copway's complex voice, ultimately inadvertently reduces his narrative to a familiar "caught-between" binary, when she describes "an almost textbook case of subjugated discourse both in its evidence of political longing and in its disturbing implications of self-division and even despair" (1997, 84).[13]

If there is a resistant note in the passage of *Traditional History* text quoted above—an interrogative space that opens up around Copway's use of the word "us"—between Copway the Christian and the traditional spiritual beliefs of his people, it is arguably reflected in the tension between his *Traditional History* as a documentary record of Indigenous practices and customs, and picture writing as an example of Indigenous practice and, most significantly, "sacred records" (1850a, 128). With only few exceptions, and those largely related to his articulation of contemporary nationhood, Copway's use of the collective pronoun is anomalous in the *Traditional History*. Far more ubiquitous in his more openly autobiographical *Life, Travels, and History*, this instance of the second person punctures the objective stand Copway takes in his *Traditional History* in connection to matters of tradition. That tension possibly conjures a paradox: in the midst of a discourse that seeks to demonstrate the assimilative capacity of the "Indian," that seeks, in other words, to destabilize the pseudo-scientific efficacy of contemporaneous ideas about race, Copway (the writer) identifies directly with so-called primitive form in support of his argument against said primitivism.

While Copway's literary production undoubtedly reflects subjugated knowledge, making it a site of contest, to see it solely in those terms delegitimizes the contexts in which Copway is working, rendering this delineation of alternative literacy a textual element of Copway's bicultural split personality—a symptom, in other words, of rupture (those "disturbing implications of self-division"), rather than a reflection of intellectual sovereignty. But for that "us," which places the onus of interpretation, or even translation, on Copway, this scenario could qualify for that erasure of difference anticipated by Lepore. Copway, however, makes clear the contexts in which Ojibwe "writing" is used, rendering the cultural-specific and suggesting a keen awareness of the ways in which writing and speech establish a binarized paradigm that conflates European and New World cultures, modern and archaic, and so on. Indeed, a brief glance at Michel Foucault's second definition of subjugated knowledge, that which he refers to as "disqualified knowledges" or "local memories," might suggest that Copway's reflections on writing, far from exemplifying subjugated discourse and effecting erasure, makes another kind of claim entirely:

I believe that by subjugated knowledges one should understand something else, something which in a sense is altogether different, namely, a whole set of knowledges that have been disqualified as inadequate to their task or insufficiently elaborated. . . . I also believe that it is through the re-emergence of these low-ranking knowledges . . . that it is through the re-appearance of this knowledge, of these local popular knowledges, these disqualified knowledges, that criticism performs its work. (Foucault 1980, 82–83)

It suggests a discursive counter to subjugation, in other words, writing out the possibility of a local literacy with supposedly more sophisticated forms of symbolic communication that undermines the very terms by which writing as a "weapon of conquest" enacts that subjugation. The writing of authority that codified pictography at this point in history was largely produced by the protoethnographic writings of Schoolcraft; in insisting on his own access to the meaning and form of picture writing, then, Copway, who, incidentally, is consistently respectful toward Schoolcraft, nevertheless asserts a writing against authority that establishes a contest between Euro-Western and Anishinaabe interpretations of "picture writing."

The possibility of that contest is potentially reinforced by the most iconic—if also deeply ironic—iteration of Ojibwe "picture writing" that the nineteenth century produced. While Schoolcraft and Garrick Mallery furnished the most comprehensive "scientific" records of pictography, it is section 14 of Henry Wadsworth Longfellow's epic *The Song of Hiawatha* that etched them into the popular memory. That section opens by lamenting the passing of knowledge, wisdom, heritage, and craft "From the memory of the old men." It describes a writing-less world, one in which great speeches are lost to the winds of time and future children suffer the loss of great traditions and orations left unrecorded, in which the graves of forefathers are anonymous, and in which distance is untravelable by message and memory. Such notions, readily identifiable in Schoolcraft's ethnological analyses, depict the very antithesis of the civilization and settlement of the Americas. Indeed, Schoolcraft saw the legends and myths he collected with the help of his wife's family as "expressions of the Indian mind, 'the interior man,' as he termed it in *Algic Researches*," judging "the inability of a Native narrator of tales to relate 'a clear, consistent chain of indisputable facts and deductions to fill up the fore ground of his history' [as] evidence of the noninductive Oriental mind" (Swann 1996, xxiii). As such, as Brian Swann elaborates, he "thought of Indians as children" (xxiii). This was not an uncommon view, as evidenced by Lewis Henry Morgan's description of the "infantile condition of the Indian mind in its apprehension of the supernatural," which in its intractability and unchanging nature was "obtuse" (Bieder 1986, 239, 164). Meanwhile, the oral tradition was evidence for Schoolcraft of "the savage phasis" of the human heart (Swann 1996, xxiii). Out of this void comes Hiawatha's paint box:

> From his pouch he took his colors,
> Took his paints of different colors,
> On the smooth bark of a birch-tree
> Painted many shapes and figures,
> Wonderful and mystic figures,
> And each figure had a meaning,
> Each some word or thought suggested. (1898, 205)

While Longfellow appears to have taken something concrete from Copway's descriptions of pictographic meaning (although Copway is not named as a source), his representation of that art, following Schoolcraft's analysis (since he is stated as a source), is as the singular feat of a genius in the moment of his passing, eliding the description of ancient practice with the moment of postcontact eclipse. In a close examination of what she refers to as the "passage of one American language into another—of the na*tive* into the na*tion*," Virginia Jackson describes "Longfellow's borrowing of the first American ethnographer's depiction of Indian ideographic characters as cultural inscriptions that doom Indians to a prenational, prevernacular, prefigurative literature redeemed in Longfellow's own national, vernacular, richly figured verse" (1998, 478–79). Jackson goes on to note that "much has been made of Longfellow's bad faith in Europeanizing native traditions, but little has been said of the notion of Europe involved in *Hiawatha*'s translation of 'them' into 'us'" (479). While the "them" and "us" here are clearly Europeans and Americans, or a switch from a generally European to a specifically American poetics, the resounding echo of Copway's momentary switch from "them" to "us," which figures a movement from detached, objective register to the localized tone of cultural recognition, is highly suggestive. The opposing intent or direction of the switch is palpable, and yet both men lay claim to the same material—the picture writing, of course, but also *Hiawatha* itself, which Copway adored—in the moment of assertion of a form of cultural nationalism.

Jackson surmises that Longfellow's "discovery" of pictography in Schoolcraft's work "must have seemed a perfect illustration of the universally available composite he wanted European languages to look like to American readers" (1998, 481). All the better, since "according to Schoolcraft, the written language of these indigenous foreigners seemed to require no translation at all, since it was made not of letters but of pictures" (481).[14] Of course, Schoolcraft would note that understanding of these arcane images fades as with the people themselves; Copway, perhaps in that vein, accurately portrays them as highly context- and knowledge-specific, and he has the knowledge required to decode them. If literacy provides the major obstacle to civilization, then, Copway seems to be saying, two can play at that game. He consciously compares Anishinaabe literacy with European literacy as the same yet different, and then provides compelling evidence that the former is epistemically unavailable to the latter; that, like English for the Anishinaabeg, it requires translation.

Perhaps, then, the major, and certainly the most pointed, difference between Copway's and Longfellow's apprehension of pictography, consists of its relationship to oral tradition. "Lo! How all things fade and perish! / From the memory of the old men" Longfellow writes, reclaiming Pope's shorthand for the "plight" narrative for the American vernacular.[15] In *Hiawatha* the eponymous subject conjures pictography from an absence in order to "preserve the memorial trace, to create a history, to transmit a history, to claim an inheritance, to establish kinships, to disseminate presence across distance but also to keep communication private" (Jackson 1998, 482). In thus "inventing" picture-writing, Hiawatha creates the means to both transmit Ojibwe ideas and inscribe them in a way that secures their persistence as a kind of memorial, the closing line of the fourteenth section of the poem confirming his final lesson to the people as he teaches them to leave their mark "On the grave-posts of the village." "Thus," Jackson contends, "even as we watch Hiawatha make a culture, we are meant to decipher its undoing" (1998, 483) in Longfellow's poem itself, the act of translation that makes available what Schoolcraft describes as "the earliest form of the notation of ideas adopted by mankind" (1860, 341). Even as Longfellow writes "the epitaph . . . of forgotten men" (Jackson 1998, 483), he absorbs their own marks of presence into the universal composite of the American epic, perversely rendering them objects rather than subjects of that epic narrative.

It would be gratifying were we able to read Copway's explanation of pictography as a response to Longfellow's treatment, but the chronology is reversed. Any too easy anticolonial interpretation is also rendered impossible by the degree to which

Copway appears to have loved, and adopted, the performance persona of Hiawatha as one of his many means of making a living. However, if Copway is not writing back to Longfellow, he is at least in part writing back to Schoolcraft. The role he undertakes of translating series of pictographs for his Euro-American audience performatively underlines Schoolcraft's most fundamental error: as Jackson notes, "pictography does not pretend to contain its own interpretation. The metadiscursive and the discursive can be joined only by an interlocutor who translates blank lines back into oral tradition. The need for such a translation is what Schoolcraft finds wanting in picture-writing: it allows no vernacular literacy, since the system 'is largely mnemonic'" (1998, 485). Copway not only reveals an alternative knowledge, then, but he reveals it as knowledge, an attribute that heretofore the writing of the state has been methodically denying Indigenous peoples. That denial resounds in ideas of the stages of man—what we might tend to think of now as cultural evolution. See, for instance, Rousseau's *Essai sur l'origine des langues*, where he writes, "The depicting of objects is appropriate to a savage people; signs of words and of propositions, to a barbaric people; and the alphabet to civilized people" (cited in Derrida 1976, 3). Such ideas are incipient in Schoolcraft's presentation of pictography as a kind of protoalphabet—his "translation of American Indian inscriptions as old writing destined to become (already 'denoting') modern letters" (Jackson 1998, 487). Derrida himself declares the whole of history ("of writing and of knowledge") unthinkable "except within these two limits" of prewriting and writing proper, an "absolute pictography" and an "absolutely formal *graphie*" (1976, 285). The "collapse" Copway's inference induces, then, is not temporal but conceptual—articulating not an "advancement" into alphabetic writing, but a shifting from one epistemological format to another.

Writing about Cherokee script, Margaret Bender points out that "beliefs about writing systems in the Americas are powerfully connected to social ideologies because of the multiple associations between writing and colonialism, Christianity, indigenous knowledges, formal education, forces of both assimilation and resistance, and so forth" (2010, 179). Bender's explication that in relation to such systems as, say, Andean Khipu, language ideology reveals assumptions about intelligence, or morality, reflects in the long missionary history of Ojibwe country. There, questions about rationality, suitability for conversion, capacity for self-governance, and so on, have long played out in the literature, in which Schoolcraft's deliberations are central. To evoke alternative literacies is to bring into dialogue the false assumptions and Eurocentric logic that underpin the settler hierarchy.

In complete contrast to those familiar analyses of Copway's divided self, then, this one claim to a writing technology stands out for its emphasis on continuity rather than rupture. Where for Schoolcraft and Longfellow it spells a precolonial anachronism vanishing into the mists of myth and metaphor, for Copway, remember, it is a technology "used by us," very much a living form that is still understood and that, though by no means identical in intent or purpose, maps onto the writing technology with which he now describes it. In other words, as a writer in English, the emphasis might well be placed on his co-option of a foreign form rather than its assimilation of him. Rather than reading his writing as straightforward evidence of a colonized mind, he offers us one small glimpse into a mind in the process of resistance to total subjugation to the colonial hegemony's terms of reference.

Insofar as settler colonialism's "logic of elimination" depends, according to Patrick Wolfe, on an "organizing grammar of race" (2006, 387), Copway's implicit positing of a continuity between the graphic practices of his people and his own literary-historical endeavors here refuses that grammar. It resists, explicitly, the linear assumptions that place "Indians" at the cold end of an evolutionary spectrum, while implicitly teasing apart the preconceptions that underpin it, such as the absence of record keeping, the absence of complex language, the absence of sophisticated religious practice, and so on.

This is no reductive case of cultural relativism, in the sense that Copway makes clear the different nature of recording and (lack of) circulation in a capital sense of Ojibwe writing. Nevertheless, he stakes a claim, in the moment of describing a written tradition, to a literacy not understood as such by the hegemony (or even, he says, by many of his brethren), and which precedes the "western progressive discourse" (Walker 1997, 85) his entry into alphabetic writing represents: "These are some of the figures *used by us in writing*" (Copway 1850a, 132; emphasis added). The possible paradox, then, has its potential deflated by this alternative sense: far from identifying with primitive form, with something akin to the "simple rites and ceremonies by which the untutored Indian showed his faith in the Great Spirit" (134), that the white man, albeit wrongly in Copway's view, ridicules, he asserts and delineates a viable technology that is different from, but analogous to, writing.

This does not necessarily sit comfortably alongside the more usual perceptions of the oral tradition, particularly with regard to the idea of self-authoring. Walker's lament about the "disturbing implications" of Copway's *Travels* echoes this ambivalence. Comparing *Travels* with Black Hawk's "as-told-to" autobiography, *The Life of Black Hawk*, she remarks, "Whereas Black Hawk distrusts writing, and is driven only in extremity to preserve his Indian identity through the medium of a written text, Copway urges his reader to see him as a text, a personification of Indian progress towards acculturation" (1997, 84). And yet, in the course of addressing the infelicities—the incompleteness—of Copway's textual persona, she dramatically insists that "the very premise of the book, then, asserts the superiority of that monologism, that form of western progressive discourse, which the texture of the text will confound" (84–85). This contrast between the idea of writing as a tool for the preservation of identity and the construction of a specifically literary subjectivity is intriguing. That it implicitly endorses the temporal binaries that separate an authentic "Indian" past from a modern hybrid/degraded state is made more explicit in Walker's willingness to also characterize the text as dividing a "past which must be forgotten even as it is remembered, and the present which must be constructed as an overcoming and a forgetting" (85). And yet, the texture of the text confounds the very discourse to which he is aspiring. In other words, the text's dialogism, its polyvocality, refuses, precisely, his approximation of the Western subject. Rather than reading this as a form of strategic mimicry, as might other, later, scholars such as Deanna Reder who suggests that in choosing the autobiographical form, Copway may in fact be "expressing his culture's value in actions that increase personal honour" (2010, 157), and rather than reading that layered textuality as a counter to her argument of dissolution, she maintains the latter's psychoanalytic arc.

In Copway's *Traditional History*, that texture is further enhanced by his own juxtaposition of forms of writing with the literacy through which he allegedly seeks to self-actualize. Tracing genealogy in an inverse direction, we might, for instance, note that the textured textuality and polyvocality that Walker identifies as his literal undoing is echoed in the writing of numerous Native writers, and is particularly prevalent among contemporary Anishinaabe authors who not only favor such techniques as literary techniques, but exemplify them in the range of mediums across which they work. In direct regard to the juxtapositional quality of text and image, and the alternative literacies the latter implies, there is, of course, a contemporary analogue for Copway's assertion of Indigenous expression in Vizenor's own utilization of those same forms Copway reproduces, although it may seem counterintuitive both to readers of Vizenor and those readers more familiar with the binary terms of the oral-literate argument in Native literary studies. I will explore this further in chapter 5, in direct relation to Vizenor's work. Nevertheless, it deserves brief pause here. Adam Spry, in his essay in *The Poetry and Poetics of Gerald Vizenor*, writes that "the appearance of the Anishinaabe oral tradition in printed translations, such as those of [Frances] Densmore and [Theodore Hudon] Beaulieu, is deeply ambivalent for Vizenor" (2012, 23). Vizenor's own partial response, certainly in texts such as *Summer in the Spring*, is not only to reimagine the dreamsongs that Densmore, in particular, transcribed and translated, but to print alongside them a number of the pictomyths with which their original recipients recorded them. Further articulating that ambivalence, then, Spry continues: "At the time the songs and stories of *Summer in the Spring* were originally published, wrote Vizenor, 'Written languages and translations were contradictions in most tribal communities.' Yet, at a time when tribal cultures and languages were threatened with total annihilation, writing their traditional stories and songs in English provided the Anishinaabeg with 'chances to overcome tragic reason and the loss of tribal memories'" (23). Thus, the juxtaposition of inscribed forms with the imposed "contradiction" of written English narrative effects the same disruption as I have suggested Copway intends. In these terms, Copway's endeavors arguably demand that we modify Walker's emphasis: Copway urges his reader to see him as a textual producer, a personification of the "Indian's" readiness, through a literacy that was already his, for the very administrative demands he sought in his bid for an Anishinaabe territory that could, in time, enter statehood. For all that he repeats the common clichés about the inferior development of the Indian, his brief treatise on writing might suggest the pathway from forest specter to settler society to self-governance within the nation-state is not, after all, so long and treacherous to travel.

"In a certain sense," Poulantzas writes, "nothing exists for the capitalist State unless it is written down" (2000, 59). Referring to the mechanistic frameworks of state bureaucracy, Poulantzas's assertion nevertheless carries echoes of the philosophical and historiographical assumptions that attain to the "discovery" and settlement of the New World. It is precisely against that backdrop of discursive ahistoricism, and the ready dismissal of the oral tradition, that Copway's apparently naïve remarks about Ojibwe writing—and, whether intended or merely inferred, about administrative readiness for self-governance—are made. In "Bush/Writing," Kulchyski effectively asks what it means to describe the petroglyphs at Peterborough's teaching rocks as writing. Perhaps, in spite of my optimism here, Copway remains easily, readily assimilable? Certainly, as Bernd Peyer illuminates, "Copway and his fellow Mississauga missionary Peter Jones interpret Ojibwa history from a relativist Christian moral standpoint and are thus at pains to point out similarities between Ojibwa society and their adopted occidental ideals—namely, worship of one Supreme Being, notions of good and evil, democratic form of government, individual ownership of hunting territories, and so on" (1997, 271). The strength of that analogue may well transfer to his insistence on reading pictography as writing, evoked as it is in his descriptions of the copper mide plates, sacred texts whose secure knowledge is passed down through specifically selected lineages and used centrally in religious ritual. They are not liturgical, and in their arcane state, they are far from being the communicative "glad tidings" that the gospels represent. Nevertheless, the relationship between oral traditions, inscription and transcription of such accounts and direct revelation, and their interpretation and communication by select, chosen individuals may not have bypassed Copway as a useful analogue for the gospels. It certainly will not have been lost on many of his Christian readers. But as Kulchyski's gesturings to the rock paintings aver, those forms and images that Copway draws on are, themselves, "not so easily assimilated" in spite of their co-option by Longfellow. Indeed, their co-option by Longfellow, and the lengths of translation to which he goes, may even be evidence of their unassimilability.

Touring the Traces, Dwelling in Stone

I wish, in fact, to turn in another direction to consider this aspect further, not least because of Kulchyski's emphasis on the embodiment of these writings, which "overrules their powers of abstraction" and "point to the possibility of a different being of writing than that which is normally encountered, which is normally read: a writing in stone." The inevitable abstractions of Copway's transcription and translation of forms largely inscribed on transportable mediums like bark, wood, and copper necessarily result in a loss of the situational, of "their attachment to place" and, to a lesser degree, "their role in ceremony" that the teaching rocks embody for Kulchyski (2012, 262). Nonetheless, these and similar images recur throughout Ojibwe country, and it is to his less literal, more literary forebear I will turn for another cornerstone. I will not take for granted that Bamewawage-zhikaquay was intimately familiar with the pictographic sites described by her husband toward the eastern end of Lake Superior. Indeed, the pictographs at Agawa Bay, for instance, and Schoolcraft's broader understanding of pictography came to him second and third hand, from Shingwaukonce via his brother-in-law, George (Konkle 2014, 84). Furthermore, the first volume of his compendious *Historical and Statistical Information Concerning the Indian Tribes of the United States* (1851–57) did not appear until nine years after Bamewawagezhikaquay's death in 1842.

Nevertheless, Bamewawagezhikaquay's knowledge of the pictographic tradition is evidenced through various materials she supplied Schoolcraft and, of course, in the fact that her wider family were by far his best-excavated mine of cultural knowledge (see Konkle 2014, 84–85). Bamewawagezhikaquay's immersion in the kinship networks of her mother, Ozhaawashkodewekwe, and her grandfather, Waabojiig, gave Schoolcraft access to a vibrant archive and certainly indicates the likelihood of considerable local and cultural knowledge on her part, as did her family's place more generally at the heart of the fur trade, itself at the heart of Anishinaabeakiing in Sault Ste. Marie.

Writing in a piece titled "Historical Traditions of the Chippewas," Schoolcraft would note: "This people possess also the art of picture writing, in a degree which denotes that they have been either more careful, or more fortunate in the preservation of this very ancient art of the human race" (1991, 303–4). Ascribing the art of preservation to "this people," Schoolcraft's work, though often fairly conjectural, demonstrates that in the inception of the ethnographer's art in the Americas, discourse about writing, about the production of permanent records of historical events was foundational—although he would of course disavow their historiographical function. Contrary to later developing discourses that situated Native Americans as ahistorical precisely because of their lack of documentation,[16] Schoolcraft would suggest of picture-writing:

> Here, then, is the first element of transmitting thought. A bow and arrow, a spear and club, a sword and javelin, were no sooner made than they were employed as symbols of acts: for next to action itself, is the desire of perpetuating the remembrance of the act, however rudely or imperfectly it may be done. (1860, 341)

As such, Schoolcraft's words implicitly contradict the work of erasure that Long-fellow's poem is shortly to perform, albeit they very deliberately connote the earliest and most primitive form of inscription. While *Hiawatha* documents "picture-writing" as the anomalous and fading gesture of a dying race, Schoolcraft here presents both the people and the art as very much present in the present (if not of the present), with a clear capacity, nay urge, to record past actions. Although his comment similarly places the actual practice in the past, as a "very ancient art," and while he too makes claim to it on behalf of a universal order, his acknowledgement of its significance not just to the ethnographer but to the people who "possess" it is explicit. Schoolcraft's appreciation of pictography, then, gives us pause for thought not so much about writing as about reading. Roughly 125 miles west of Bamewawagezhikaquay's home lay the famed Pictured Rocks, a variegated sandstone formation on the southern shore of Lake Superior. Sometime in 1831 Bamewawagezhikaquay would pen a poem titled "On the Doric Rock, Lake Superior" referencing a pillared rock formation at the eastern end of the Pictured Rocks.

Dedicated *"To a Friend,"* "On the Doric Rock" is, Robert Dale Parker explains, a response to a letter from Melancthon L. Woolsey, "a printer of Detroit, a young man of pleasing manners and morals," whom Schoolcraft had engaged as a member of his retinue on a "Voyage Inland" to Prairie du Chien in the summer of 1831 (2007, 94–97). Accompanied also by Bamewawagezhikaquay's brother George Johnston, Lieutenant Robert E. Clary, and a small detachment of troops charged with the voyage's protection, plus sundry others, Schoolcraft headed over six hundred miles westward to take smallpox vaccinations to Native communities in what would become western Wisconsin,[17] and, while there, to both discuss treaty terms and conduct explorations. Opening as if to eulogize those men, the poem begins:

> Dwellers at home, in indolence and ease,
> How deep their debt, to those that roam the seas,
> Or cross the lands, in quest of every art
> That science, knowledge, pity can impart
> To help mankind, or guild the lettered page
> The bold discoverers of every age. (Parker 2007, 94)

Bamewawagezhikaquay—one such "dweller at home"—thus offers an expression of gratitude for the elucidatory function of Western knowledge, and the men of course who seek it.

Following Parker's lead, Bethany Schneider's incisive reading of "On the Doric Rock" suggests a caustic sarcasm on Bamewawagezhikaquay's part. The sarcasm is not misplaced, as, echoing its tone, Schneider explains that "Woolsey devotes much of his letter, remarkably, to describing the Ojibwe landscape to this Ojibwe woman, as if she had never seen it" (2008, 127). Perhaps, to be generous to the man, she need not have seen it necessarily to have known of it. What is more significant—more damning—is Woolsey's assumption that she might be ignorant of its existence and of its structure. At 125 miles away from home, he might have reasoned, she was unlikely to have knowledge of it. Whether the conclusion he draws is based on a generalized notion that women of his acquaintance did not tend to travel great distances, or whether he is making a more particular (and of course wrong) assumption about the static nature of Native life, its "mythic immobility" (Bellin 2008, 193), is hard to determine. That the latter would make him entirely ignorant of the migration, and of migration stories, of the Ojibwe—and it is worth noting that the Pictured Rocks appear in both—is no great barrier to its possibility. Bamewawagezhikaquay and the children had accompanied the menfolk part of the way and turned back, perhaps undergirding any associations about the limited domestic sphere of the female in the early nineteenth-century "Soo."

The Johnston family occupied a relatively elevated social position to be sure; John's connections in Ireland were "persons of rank." Schoolcraft's descriptions of his first encounters with the family indicate refinement: "[John Johnston's] family received us with marked urbanity and hospitality." Socioeconomically well placed, Schoolcraft also gifts them a mythical high seat, when, in a footnote, he suggests that "Mr. Johnston, by marrying the daughter of the ruling chief of this region, placed himself in the position of another Rolfe. Espousing, in Christian marriage, the daughter of Wabjeeg, he became the son-in-law of another Powhatan; thus establishing such a connection between the Hibernian and Chippewa races, as the former had done between the English and Powhatanic stocks" (1855, 77). He echoes, in fact, the superintendent for Indian affairs, Thomas L. McKenney, who "describes the Johnston family as a kind of ideal combination of the natural gentility of Europeans and Native people" (Konkle 2004, 168). Deftly inserting himself into that American aristocratic lineage, Schoolcraft nevertheless reminds us that "Miss Jane," the elder daughter of John and his own future wife, "received her education in Ireland" (1855, 77), cementing her educational stock even as he claims her most American of geo-mythical origins, the progeny of American Indian leaders and European gentry at the then center of transnational trade.

Such biographical detail is not entirely beside the point. Readers of Bamewawagezhikaquay's poetry will be just as aware as those cognizant of her biography that she was relatively well traveled: she traveled to Europe as a child, accompanying her father there in 1809, during which time she spent several months with relatives in Ireland; she also accompanied her father as an interpreter on trips to Detroit, Montreal, and Quebec (Konkle 2004, 167); and later, reluctantly, she traveled east with Schoolcraft. She was also very well read: to think that she would be either unable or unwilling to travel around in the lakes she loved so dearly is a counterintuitive assumption to make. Indeed, in Schoolcraft's own missive from the same stage of the trip, he tells Bamewawagezhikaquay that the arch they "saw in 1820, hs fallen down," while Parker reminds us that "HRS opened his 1821 *Narrative Journal*, which would have been familiar to JJS, with an illustration of the Doric Rock on the frontispiece, followed by a detailed description later in the book" (Parker 2007, 96, 95). Nevertheless, either Woolsey makes the assumption or, as Schneider asserts, he employs a "system of substitute and citation" to serve his own, ideologically bound, expectations (2008, 135).

We can assume the same knowledge of her brother, George. In Woolsey's letter, however, George's response to the sublime sight that greeted them at "the Doric Rock" is "Oh! *Oh!*" (Parker 2007, 96). Schneider observes that Woolsey's own "happy verbosity" belies his claim that "nothing more could be said," and that "his tongue runs on greased wheels up to and away from George's paradigmatically curt Indian grunt" (2008, 133). George, she continues, was "even more educated, by white standards, than his sister," suggesting that

> under Woolsey's logics of citation, the complexity of George's actual culture falls away, and his Indianness serves as *emphasis* . . . allowing Woolsey to make the tired argument that only Indians can express—through non-expression—the beauty of the landscape, while only white writers can interpret and thereby colonize that landscape through vast and iterative citational description. (133)

Close analysis of the poem itself speaks to just this issue, and I will turn to that presently. It is worth reminding ourselves, however, that this very question—one of both the languages and the image of "Indians"—is precisely up for contest in the work and worldly presence of the poet Jane Johnston Schoolcraft and others. When Schoolcraft shows his wife off in cities back East, for instance, it is precisely because she combines Native birth with eloquence and refinement that she is prized.

Her ability to render her poetry through the idioms and grammar of nineteenth-century Romanticism is, in this instance, one such site of contest over her *indianness*. It is a site reflected in Copway's writing, too, and even more so in the critical scholarship on Copway's writing, which, without major exception, returns repeatedly to the question of how much his English wife, Elizabeth Howell, edited or even wrote on his behalf. Donald Smith, historian of the Mississaugas, writes in his *Mississauga Portraits* that in 1851,

> George Copway published *Running Sketches*, his account of British and European travels. Elizabeth possibly helped to transcribe the spelling of the German and

French words that appear in the travelogue and helped to select many of its lengthy extracts from British guidebooks and newspapers. (2013, 197)

Indeed, Smith nominates Elizabeth the "chief suspect as George Copway's literary assistant" (194). As with his emphasis on writing, however, Copway is notable not only for the florid, derivative, citation-full quality of his English. If, regarding writing, he emphasizes the relational legitimacy of Ojibwe graphic forms, when it comes to language he pits Anishinaabemowin's efficiency against English's deficiency. In his *Traditional History*, he insists, "After reading the English language, I have found words in the Indian combining more expressiveness" (1850a, 123). More to the point, he proceeds: "A language, derived, as this is, from the peculiarities of the country in which it is spoken, must, necessarily, partake of its nature" (125–26). Did the multilingual George Johnston honestly have no words other than "Oh! *Oh!*" for the landscape he saw, a landscape to which his mother tongue was geologically adapted?

Copway takes it further: "Our orators have filled the forest with the music of their voices, loud as the roar of a waterfall, yet soft and wooing as the gentle murmur of a mountain stream. We have had warriors who have stood on the banks of lakes and rivers, and addressed with words of irresistible and persuasive eloquence their companions in arms" (126). So, Woolsey's George is neither orator nor warrior, the Ojibwe have lost their oratorical magnificence in the twenty years between Schoolcraft's journey and publication of the *Traditional History*, and Copway is prone to exaggeration? Well, while the latter may be true, it hardly disproves his claims. And while the second is clearly untrue, the validity or otherwise of the first point is hardly justification for Bamewawagezhikaquay of the reductive cliché served up by her correspondent. The result, in the poem "On the Doric Rock, Lake Superior," if Schneider is right (and notwithstanding Parker's reluctance to say for certain whether the poem responds directly to the letter, although he is willing to conjecture a crush),[18] is a veritable master class.

Readers who know the poem will understand that I have made a shift here, from Copway's writing about pictography to Bamewawagezhikaquay's reading of the landscape. In both instances, the counterstrategic move addresses those qualities of education, knowledge, and inscription that their interlocutors find wanting in the "Indian mind." It is not, then, a set of images inscribed on a landscape that Bamewawagezhikaquay reads in her poem, but the landscape itself; the landscape as inscription and, by implication, the associated images of nature, *indians*, and European exploration that describe it and, in describing, possess it. It anticipates and resists the withdrawal of the "Indian" into vestigial nature in the Romantic poetry and painting of the likes of William Cullen Bryant and the Hudson River School—such seeds well sown in the British tradition—largely by engaging their very terms of reference. It is no large stretch, for instance, to see in "On Doric Rock" the outline of Pope's most famous of Indian references:

> Lo, the poor Indian! whose untutored mind
> Sees God in clouds, or hears him in the wind;
> His soul proud Science never taught to stray
> Far as the solar walk or milky way;
> Yet simple nature to his hope has giv'n,
> Behind the cloud-topped hill, an humbler heav'n. (1891, 25)

The echo of those lines resounds in Bamewawagezhikaquay's poem, the final stanza of which reads:

> The simple Indian, as the work he spies,
> Looks up to nature's God above the skies
> And though, his lot be rugged wild and dear,
> Yet owns the ruling power with soul sincere,
> Not as where, Asia's piles of marble high,
> For idol gods the beast was doomed to die,
> But, guided by a purer-led surprise,
> Points to the great good sovereign of the skies
> And thinks the power that built the upper sphere,
> Hath left but traces of his fingers here. (Parker 2007, 94)

Bamewawagezhikaquay's response to Woolsey's allusions is curious, not least where the latter describes "a large urn of nature's own design and workmanship," which "might be a fit repository for the ashes of some of those mighty men, who before the children 'with a white, white face,' overran their country, strode through these forests, or, in their light canoes bounded over these vast waters" (qtd. in Schneider 2008, 127). The invocation of the Keatsian urn (published roughly eleven years earlier) tacitly conflates those "mighty men" with nature, evoking the analogous vessel but not the possibility of its Greek maker. Thus, as Keats reflects on the relationship between art and its audience, Woolsey declares nature effectively unobserved prior to the apprehension of the white man. The "mighty men" become as objects in nature in a scene properly appraised by the writer himself.

Bamewawagezhikaquay's response, therefore, relates that same natural scene through eyes capable of looking—of reading the landscape and discerning in it not a natural scene but a spiritual one. Moreover, Schneider comments, Woolsey imagines that the urn should "commemorate a sylvan culture" but that it ultimately "commemorate[s] the Indians' failure to produce memory" (2008, 127). Where the scene on Keats's urn offers "a portrait of libidinal and spiritual consummation almost" (128), witnessed by an artist, Woolsey's "mighty men" simply run and paddle with abandon, failing to anticipate the coming of the white man. The only "witness," apparently, is Woolsey himself, the ashless urn testimony to an abandoned, even unacknowledged, landscape idyll. In the ironic terms of acquiescent gratitude that she adopts, Bamewawagezhikaquay effectively goes on to gently refuse Woolsey's frame of reference and, in doing so, subtly—perhaps even unconsciously—those of the Popeian "Lo," as well.

Schneider's excellent analysis of "On Doric Rock" demands little by way of addition. She makes the observation—useful to my argument here—that "the Dorian invasion of Greece marked the transition in Greek culture from savagery to 'civilization'" (2008, 128). Doric Rock, named "La Chapelle" by French voyageurs, is recorded by Radisson as a "place of veneration and sacrifice" (Parker 2007, 95). While that name, which is still in use today, captures a sense of the spiritual, albeit Romantically inclined, Schoolcraft's nomenclature invokes the learning of the ancients.[19] Indeed, in his own *Narrative Journal* descriptions of the Pictured Rocks—where, incidentally, Longfellow sets *The Song of Hiawatha*—his lens is provided by Walter Scott's *Lady of the Lake*, a readerly mechanism that maps the Scottish Trossachs region onto the Lake Superior shore (see Olmanson 2007). This combination, self-evidently, functions as part of the process of settler colonialism: a sequence of naming and erasure that appropriates the landscape by emptying it of its inhabitants and, with them, its history. Thus, the moment of apprehension signals the arrival of civilization into the space from which "savagery" has already been eliminated. Bamewawagezhikaquay's poem acknowledges that "none but hunters trod the field before," but, unlike Woolsey, her "hunters" bear witness to the scene: "The simple Indian, as the work he spies, / Looks up to nature's God." Moreover, he recognizes its significance, or "owns the ruling power" that wrought it. Bamewawagezhikaquay's "hunter," then, has the measure of the Romantic poet in the presence of the sublime.

The purpose of Schoolcraft's party's journey—vaccinations and treaty discussions—similarly speaks loudly in this exchange. While the inoculations shade both the science of the travelers and the "primitive" capacity of the Natives, who have neither vaccines nor immunity, those treaty discussions will ultimately seek to displace and dispossess. Again, Schneider proposes that "Woolsey imagines he is 'help[ing] mankind,' but in fact his writing merely provides decorative underscoring to an old script, gild[ing] on the already 'lettered page' of European conquest disguised as beneficence" (2008, 129). The logic of elimination is writ large in that gilding, but Bamewawagezhikaquay's response cuts to the quick of his "condescending 'pity'" (129). Similarly, Schneider observes that Woolsey's presumptuous descriptions of the landscape, as if to a woman ignorant of them, are returned in the poem in deeply ironic terms. Undermining the fantasy of firstness, Bamewawagezhikaquay gestures to the fact that "none but hunters trod the field before." Those hunters will go on, as I have noted, to bear witness; in this moment, then, we may already begin to read them as unsettling the naïve ahistoricism of Woolsey's "mighty men." Furthermore, Bamewawagezhikaquay goes on to describe the wonder of this Superior setting, and "the grandeur of Superior's show / Where nature's forms in varied shape and guise / Break on the view" (Parker 2007, 94). This is, to all intents and purposes, a wonderfully evocative and poetic nod to the fact that Woolsey's correspondent is really quite familiar with the scene.

The poem, then, switches from the opening stanza's gratitude to a scene of "native knowledge" that echoes Schoolcraft's own letter (Schneider 2008, 129)—but which we might equally call Indigenous knowledge for its implicit assertion of a form of prior occupancy. The hunters trod this field before, and so did the poet. And this is a seen scene. Both of them saw it, bore witness to it and, if the poem is anything to go by, appreciated its "grandeur of design." There is an equivocation here that mirrors that in Copway's work—an easy riposte, let us say—in that I am imputing to Bamewawagezhikaquay's words an Ojibwe identity and a measure of Indigenous apperception of the landscape that might equally, and indeed more easily, be put down to the travels of an agent's wife. Again, I concur with Schneider who argues that "here, she is not métis, not even contemporary—she gladly takes on the fantasy of a lost and distant Indianness in order to model the preposterousness of placing *her* in a primordial past" (2008, 130). Her very contemporaneity, in other words, is Ojibwe, every bit as much as it is Irish-American; the latter does not consume and subsume the former. Her "Dwell[ing] at home, in indolence and ease" thus conjures a Heideggerian sense of remaining in place—not statically, but through belonging to and maintaining relationships in space and with place. Bamewawagezhikaquay's "dwelling" as a point of contrast to Woolsey's colonial witnessing reminds me in particular of Gregory Smith's suggestion that "when truly dwelling, [wo]man is constituted in relation to the indigenous, poetically revealed things that constitute h[er]" (1996, 265). So, if we remember Heidegger's assertion that "only if we are capable of dwelling, only then can we build" (1971, 160), we might seek to read Bamewawagezhikaquay's words again as countering the settler-colonial impulse behind Woolsey's assumptions. Her "dwelling" at home is both specific to the house she shares with Schoolcraft and general to the geography of Superior: a dwelling that connotes longevity, care, the right to "build." Tim Ingold explains: "the forms people build, whether in the imagination or on the ground, arise within the current of their involved activity, in the specific relational contexts of their prac- tical engagement with their surroundings" (2000, 186). Bamewawagezhikaquay's "dwelling," therefore, ironically expresses a highly dynamic spatiality, and a sense of belonging in which, "bound together by the itineraries of their inhabitants, places exist not in space but as nodes in a matrix of movement" (Ingold 2000, 219). In this persona, she is, works, lives, moves, reads in and through the landscape that, located at "home," becomes the home in which she—her Ojibwe ancestors, her neighbors and friends—dwells. In contrast, Woolsey and Schoolcraft's will to textualize and then read the landscape through which they move presents building (as coloniality; the construction and cultivation of culture prior to dwelling) in precisely the inverse terms that Heidegger critiques. Ingold again: "Building, then, cannot be understood as a simple process of transcription, of a pre-existing design of the final product onto a raw material substrate" (2000, 186). Dorian architecture, read through Romantic tropes, transcribed onto the Indigenous land cast as terra nullius of the Great Lakes shore: Bamewawagezhikaquay invokes a sense of dwelling in direct response to a description of architecture that connotes coloniality, majesty, a building on rather than a dwelling in the land. Although not advancing a sense of Indigenous priority in any explicit way, this possibility does, nevertheless, consolidate those questions about the uncritical presumptuousness of her admirer.

The combination of these effects is clear—the Doric arch as a signifier for the transition from one form of society to another, the poetic tropes that consolidate the pathetic and heroic roles of correspondent and correspondee. Schneider notes, though, that the litany of citation depended on by Woolsey is matched and indeed usurped by Bamewawagezhikaquay, who raises his Keatsian urn one "Ozymandias." More than this, though, she "trumps Woolsey's eternal urn with Ozymandias, then turns around and trumps Ozymandias with the eternally generative passion of nature" (2008, 132). Bamewawagezhikaquay's words—"These pillared rocks and castle pomps prevail / Standing, like some vast ruin of the plain"—evoke the pomp and might of the fallen empire, and yet "'Twas nature's wildest flower, that graved the rock" (Parker 2007, 94). "For [Jane] Schoolcraft," then, "the wilderness that buries Ozymandias is, in fact, the immortal masterpiece" (Schneider 2008, 132). That Bamewawagezhikaquay returns citation with citation, allowing both herself and her brother George to "inhabit the stereotype" (133) of hunter and "Lo" respectively, ultimately testifies to her readership, steadily undermining the authority of Woolsey's gaze by matching his learned referencing while insisting with increasing intensity on the fallacy and indeed the incongruity of his frameworks. Thus, again—and once more following Schneider's perceptive lead—where Woolsey criticizes the propensities of Natives' "pagan" religion to "make to themselves a Deity in the rushing stream of the beetling cliff," Bamewawagezhikaquay rejoins with a resoundingly clear theistic reference. Referring to that "nature's God" to whom "the simple Indian" looks, however, is no mere conceit; nor is it a theological pose. Rather, "the phrase 'nature's God' is itself a resonant citation, through which she quietly but firmly reminds readers that among those who 'act from the impulse of nature' are America's founding fathers" (Schneider 2008, 134).

Bamewawagezhikaquay rejoins with an incisive takedown of the paradox Woolsey's position presents: either the Declaration of Independence and its authors' deistic leanings implicate the very empiricism on which Woolsey's authority stands in the same kind of irrationality with which he imputes Native religions; or, well, those religions aren't so backward, naïve, and anachronistic after all. Schneider observes that Woolsey's dismissal is also a dismissal of Ojibwe belonging in Ojibwe land—a view that reverberates in his decision to lecture Bamewawagezhikaquay on the qualities of her own people's homeland. If Bamewawagezhikaquay reads the scenery citation for citation, it is in that deliberation on creation—on who, or what, besides European poets—wrote, made, or marked the landscape that she "hangs Woolsey out to dry" (Schneider 2008, 135). Schneider is concerned with origins—or rather with nonorigin, specifically in the ways Bamewawagezhikaquay's "'simple Indians' thought, that the creator leaves only traces of his fingers, disallows the sort of reading that can *interpret* origins as citational" (138). Thus, she negates Woolsey's catalogue of citations that disavow Native American possession as the already displaced and the never really in place. Schneider turns then to the Derridean trace, wherein "writing always refers back not to an author but to another trace, making impossible belief in a single moment of origin" (138). In doing so, she reads Bamewawagezhikaquay's anticitational citation, those "traces of his fingers" as "invoking a philosophy of the 'here' to which citational structures do not stick," which differs from Derrida's trace "which *is* citation" (138).

The convolutions of this position are understandable—in order to have Bamewawagezhikaquay undo the authority of Woolsey's citational origins, Bamewawagezhikaquay's own citational authority appears to be put under erasure, leaving only paradox. There are, perhaps, two ways out of this bind. At first-order level, the "Indian" who "Points to the great good sovereign of the skies / And thinks the power that built the upper sphere, / Hath left but traces of his fingers here" has his own pointing finger implicated in the finger-traces that mark the terrain—traces evidenced, presumably, in the marks by which "nature's wildest flower . . . graved the rock." Nature's engraving, an inspiration of divinity, whether "nature's God" or another "sovereign of the skies," and the pointing "Indian" are coimplicated in leaving "but traces of [their] fingers here." Metaphorical or literal (and we have no cause to read into these traces any actual images on the rock), the traces that mark the landscape as readable terrain are nominally legible to the poet, and to "Lo," for all his simplicity. That (anachronistic) philosophical anxiety aside, the authority of Bamewawagezhikaquay's citation is tempered in respect of the fixity of meaning assigned the system of traces she evokes. In *Red Ink*, for instance, Drew Lopenzina writes that "the purpose of these [pictographic] symbols was not . . . to cordon off spiritual or intellectual enquiry. They served instead to offer interpretations of events that could be told in a different manner by different interpreters and were not necessarily in need of absolute (authorized) versions to retain cultural validity" (2012, 38). The ethereality of Bamewawagezhikaquay's traces, then, and the merely gestural way in which they invoke the graphic itself, are entirely germane to their representative ambiguity. The question of origins, therefore, is secondary to the question of reading as a process of transposition, from a familiar textual landscape to an unfamiliar, or nontextual one, which is what we find Woolsey doing, and Bamewawagezhikaquay undoing, stripping back the citational impositions by revealing them as just that through her own systematic artifice. In that undoing, she reveals an already legible, already textual landscape.

At the second-order level, rather than choose to follow Schneider down deconstructionist pathways per se, we might return to Christopher Teuton's brief examination of Derrida's notion of "context dependency" and "the relational nature of signs [that] insists that they must be read against and within each other" (2010,

30). Teuton then turns to the ways "Native American forms of signification actively engage presence and absence through two interdependent and reciprocal modes of communication, the oral and the graphic" (30–31). To do so offers two further layers to the interpretation of Bamewawagezhikaquay's fingered traces, both of which contribute to the refusal of Woolsey's lamination. Firstly, if those traces represent the graphic, the readable sign, we might remember the ways in which other Native writers and non-Native observers have borne witness to the storied landscape. The best-known examples—Keith Basso's *Wisdom Sits in Places* and N. Scott Momaday's recounting of the formation of Bear Lodge in Wyoming in, for example, *The Way to Rainy Mountain*—explicitly reveal the textual environment that is only hinted at in "On Doric Rock." Nevertheless, the latter hints in its closing at a terrain that is already charted, storied, narrated, and read. Over that text, then, the explorer lays his imports, producing a palimpsest that of course fails to fully erase those earlier traces. Where the discoverer sees an "empty" space peopled by the already or soon-to-be removed hunters, the poet "sees," or more appropriately knows, the interdependent archive of natural marks and the oral stories that attend to the region. And if the superimposition of European tropes fails to erase those preexisting marks, the resulting palimpsest, its signifying forms ever in interdependent interplay, can expect to do no more than signify the mechanisms of colonialism. The prior traces of belonging, in other words, ever disrupt the present act of possession.

"On Doric Rock" does not depict petroglyphs per se, but it speaks almost ekphrastically to the immanence of knowledge marked into the landscape; and it speaks to the ability to read that landscape as a mark of indigeneity, contested by the colonizer through the will to declare it illegible. The question of origins—of marks, of stories, of persons—is irrelevant to that contest, since it asserts rights of belonging within the terrain not as a matter of priority but as a logic of dwelling. Woolsey can only move through, remark, analogize, and ultimately mark himself out as stranger. It is, after all, his own astonished apprehension of the arch for the first time that prompts him to write of it to Bamewawagezhikaquay. The traces of fingers in this landscape —both the sovereign of the skies and the simple "Indian," whose own fingers could well have traced forms on the rock—find further graphic form in the poem itself, where experiential and relational knowledge unavailable to Woolsey, and even Schoolcraft, reveal the essential fragility of the explorer's (trans)planted images.

"As scholars such as Walter D. Mignolo, Roy Harvey Pearce, and Gordon Sayre have argued," Teuton reminds us, "European colonizers in the Americas authorized their actions by their self-claimed entitlement as bearers of the word of God in the form of a book" (2010, 25). Both Copway, as a Methodist convert, and Bamewawagezhikaquay, as the daughter of a Scots-Irish father with a sizeable library, were acutely aware of the authority that "word" accrued to itself. Both had also been carefully educated in Ojibwe contexts—Bamewawagezhikaquay arguably more comprehensively than Copway, whose parents' Methodist conversion occurred when he was roughly nine years old. Writing of Copway in relation to his fellow missionary Peter Jones, Scott Michaelson says: "For both Jones and Copway, conversion becomes the central event of—*the centering event for*—Ojibwa history." In noting this, Michaelson posits the argument that they recall preracialized European anthropological models, "in which the method for distinguishing Amerindians rotates around the axes Christian/non-Christian and savage/civilized" (1999, 115). While Copway's comments about writing significantly disrupt the assumptions of those binaries, they also give rise to the question of whether, ultimately, conversion actually becomes the central event of the *articulation* of Ojibwa history. As Konkle argues of Jones's inability to wholly relinquish his "artefacts"—backed up perhaps by Smith's descriptions of Eliza (Field) Jones's resignation to Jones remaining "an Indian"—both he and Copway produce, through their so-called conversion narratives, a counterdiscursive strike against the ethnological assertions of the time, particularly as they regard intelligence and other markers of what are fast becoming racialized understandings of "Indian" inferiority. In other words, Christianity becomes the discursive site of entangled histories in which Ojibwe epistemologies, while not unproblematically recuperated, are nevertheless defended, respected, and/or acknowledged even in the course of their apparent rejection.

While Bamewawagezhikaquay's "On Doric Rock" does not confront these issues so head on, it nevertheless concerns itself with epistemological questions—questions that pertain to both the nature and implementation of knowledge-as-authority. The poem's persona then presents Jane Johnston Schoolcraft the "Indian" as a contemporary of Woolsey, with the same level of citational reference, the same apperceptions of nature and god, with the ability to read, and to read a different kind of writing—the landscape directly rather than the landscape through poetry—and, in doing so, to negate her correspondent's desire to dismiss that legibility. So, where Copway insists on the validity of a vehicle for knowledge that tacitly resists the claim of knowledgelessness (that infantile mind), Bamewawagezhikaquay examines the claim for knowledge itself and finds it wanting. Both, in doing so, "present traditional knowledge as capable of beauty in the literary-aesthetic realm and as representative of the truth in history . . . at a moment when Native peoples' traditional knowledge was being refracted, rewritten, and effaced in the invention of ethnology and reified in sentimental and popular entertainment" (Konkle 2004, 166).

To reiterate Konkle's assertion, "education provided a means—literacy—of resisting the colonial bureaucracy," and writing then became, for a host of nineteenth-century Native Americans, a "key strategy in resistance" (2004, 191, 193). Critiquing power through the means of its own enforcement is at once well understood in Native criticism and also well critiqued. As my opening pages to this chapter attempted to outline, the compromises and contradictions of such work are multiple. Here, however, these authors go further, critiquing power through the invocation of alternative mechanisms—mechanisms that neither correlate with nor substitute for the explicit purposes to which writing, particularly administratively, has been put, but that nevertheless constitute "hidden transcript[s]" and alternative literacies (Lopenzina 2012, 17, qtg. James C. Scott) at the root of both rhetorical resistance (Robert Warrior) and rhetorical sovereignty (Scott Lyons). In both instances, in other words, writing becomes the means by which other, prior, significatory, communicative, and graphic signs may be revealed, engaged, and deployed in the interests of both counterdiscourse and indications of continuities of knowledge and practice. Copway influenced Longfellow, whose Hiawatha forges picture writing—inscription on rock—at the Pictured Rocks. This puts him (here) in dialogue with Bamewawagezhikaquay, whose rock traces, however ethereal, evoke a graphic practice embodied in the relationship between the human figure and the land, in turn encapsulated by her own writerly trace. These are minor moments in the work of both writers, by no means dominant motifs, yet they express something of the transition between types of graphic inscription in their relation to the oral tradition, which initiates a search for form that persists to the present. For Konkle, again, Copway's "narrative consistently returns to the difficulty of finding a means of writing his experience that does not ultimately deny that experience" (2004, 194); for Bamewawagezhikaquay, meanwhile, the Romantic form her verse takes sits in productive tension with the ways in which Native knowledge or textuality undermine that form's assumptions and application in "On Doric Rock." In both cases, the ability to read, write, and recognize the literary and bureaucratic mechanisms of power becomes the very means by which those mechanisms are troubled. Underpinning this, Bellin explains, "the force of Copway's methodology lies in its suggestion that 'truth' is local, not absolute: that diverse stories generate diverse grounds of validation" (2001, 193). In both Copway's *Traditional History* and Bamewawagezhikaquay's "On Doric Rock," the act of writing and the claim for writing/reading unsettles not only the narratives mapped onto their discovery by the "discoverers," but also their very claims to authority, entangling them not with an absolutist alternative—an "enemy" that could be countered, "the former needing to be viewed through, and fated to be vanquished by, the latter" (Bellin 2001, 194)—but with systems of signification and expression that, embedded in land and language, cannot readily be erased from the settler-colonial ground.

CHAPTER 2

X-ing Boundaries

Transmotion, Transformation, and the Art of Engaged Resistance
in Contemporary Anishinaabe Poetics

J ust as Langston Hughes raises the specter of Walt Whitman in his "I, too,
sing America," so Heid Erdrich invokes or, in fact, samples Hughes in the
opening refrain of her video poem, "Pre-Occupied" (2013a): "I've known
rivers: / Ancient, dusky rivers. / My soul has grown deep like the rivers."
The video uses Hughes's sound recordings of the poem against a jazz bass line,
while simultaneously displaying the words, typewriter-style, on the background
of a riverside cityscape.[1] As the final line is reached the point of view drops below
the surface of the river, just prior to Erdrich's own voice announcing the title of
the poem. At this point, the backdrop switches to an abstracted block-pattern, and
as Erdrich declaims the opening words of her poem, they too appear on screen:
"River, river, river; I never, never, never." The words abut one another at right angles,
forming a spiral that rotates center-screen, diminishing in size as the point of view
moves back and the block-pattern is revealed to be a door in a graffitied brick wall.
The spiral continues to grow, as the author self-reflexively confesses: "I . . . never
etched your spiral icon in limestone." At this point, a chalk spiral forms on the brick
wall, corkscrewing between a pair of love hearts, one empty, one with the initials
"B+M" at its center.

Hughes's "I, Too" stakes an important claim to an African American's personal belonging in America (his country) as a full citizen of the United States (his nation). "A Negro Speaks of Rivers," meanwhile, both spiritually and mythically underpins that claim by transposing African blood from the cradle of civilization to civilization's new experiment at the dawning of the postbellum era. It signals the *re*clamation of the African mind, body, and soul from the Euro-American historiography that systematically excluded African history. In "Pre-Occupied," Erdrich too stakes a claim that enacts a reclamation in deeply ironic, powerful terms. It picks up geographically, so to speak, where Hughes's "Negro" leaves off, in the waterways of North America and, with no small sense of irony, in the "civilization" that has been built on their banks. In the final section of this chapter, I will briefly return to Erdrich's video poem alongside consideration of recent ekphrastic poems of Armand Garnet Ruffo and Margaret Noodin, along with Kimberly Blaeser's pictopoems, to consider the highly explicit turn to the visual in recent Ojibwe poetry. I begin by describing "Pre-Occupied," however, for two reasons: Firstly, it offers a powerfully arresting combination of the visual and verbal in which new forms such as the video itself both utilize and dialogue with ancient visual practices to produce an aesthetically rich interrogation of representation-through-image (combining comics, maps, star maps, photographs, cartoons, and more), of the spectacle itself, and of the grounding of the postcapitalist moment. In doing so, it implicitly examines how what Guy Debord described as the "social relationship between people that is mediated by images" (1994, 12) inheres in the coloniality of movements such as Occupy. Secondly, it represents a contemporary reflection on the making of marks—"I . . . never etched"—that is germane to much (though not all) of the poetry I will consider in this chapter. That Erdrich "never etched your spiral icon," then, places that action in dialogue with the poem itself, retreading the ground of the physical act as a gesture of what Dean Rader (2011) calls "engaged resistance"; the "never etched," both thought, spoken, and written/illustrated/seen, becomes the act of etching.

As such, the poem, like much of the poetry under scrutiny here, effects an interplay between an aesthetics of resistance and an aesthetics of sovereignty. In placing primacy on the act of marking the landscape, it also conjures both the alternative literacy and the marks of presence with which the examples in chapter 1 engage, a feature that will both recur here and forecast forward to the generating of X marks, treaty "signatures" that, as I will argue shortly, are drawn through a poetics of transmotion into that same dialectic. Transmotion, among the best known and now most commonly deployed of Gerald Vizenor's neologisms, is "personal, reciprocal, the source of survivance, but not territorial," and "an instance of natural reason . . . transmotion is motion and native memories . . . an ethical presence of nature, native stories, and natural reason." Finally, it is "an original natural union in the stories of emergence and migration that relate humans to an environment" (all Vizenor 1998, 182–83).[2] More recently, Vizenor has written, "Native transmotion is directly related to the ordinary practices of survivance, a visionary resistance and sense of natural motion over separatism, literary denouement, and cultural victimry" (2015, 65). Not slippery, exactly, the fluidity of Vizenor's own interpretation, and of course its primary quality of mobility, "the right to freedom of travel . . . the freedom to move across physical and conceptual boundaries" (Madsen 2015, 23–24), is directly engaged by the image of the river in "Pre-Occupied" and the spiraling icon as a figure of active presence. Elsewhere—and implicit again in much of what I will discuss in this chapter—David J. Carlson describes it "paradoxically" as akin to "the dialectical consciousness" of finding oneself "at home" through exile (2016, 160). In ethical terms, it might also be useful to think of transmotion as the condition of encounter in which connection does not lead to subsumption or absorption of the other. More prosaically still, Anna Brígido Corachán describes transmotion as "the ability to move between different territories—local, national, international—the ambiguity of not constituting a fixed category, the ability of escaping the construction of the passive, victimized Indian" (n.d.).

In her preface to an earlier anthology of contemporary Ojibwe poetry, poet-scholar Kimberly Blaeser similarly plays with associated connections, writing, "These poems are more than literature; they are tactile traces—in blood, bone, and stone" (2006, xvi). Those tactile traces resound in Erdrich's rivers and icons: the former Hughes's metaphor for bloodline; the latter, clearly, the literal ground on which the spiral icons appear and, simultaneously, a figurative evocation of the city and the land on which it stands. Meanwhile, Blaeser's statement echoes, at least distantly, Rader's sense of "contention, revolution, and continuation" in his "sites of engaged resistance," a theoretical location identified through his "attempt to understand how recent American Indian writers use the lyric poem as a mode of resistance that also participates in the cultural history of Native oral discourse" (2002, 149). Rader's position alludes to the deeply nuanced relationship between the written and the oral in Native American cultures, embedded in a complex network of transculturative modes in the postcontact era. Blaeser's language—the nouns blood, bone, and stone particularly—reiterates this connection and goes a step further, lifting the poetry from the page and placing it in the contexts of lineage, memory, and story, of formal histories of displacement and loss and, importantly, continuity. The stones she evokes point not only to the land but to the scenes and beings depicted in pictographs and petroglyphs in the northern Great Lakes and the vital presence of ancestors in the literature about which she writes. The tactile trace, meanwhile, evokes both the act of mark making itself and the materiality of the Ojibwe document, the birchbark scroll, on which a pictographic system records stories, myths, kinship, ideas, and sacred details, all of which surface frequently in contemporary writing, in multiple guises.

That the oral tradition centers a complex social relationship—between members of communities and between those communities and the spiritual and physical landscapes in which they reside—is a truism well known and often repeated in literary criticism. That it is sustained in many Nations' cultures in part through a vital material record has, until relatively recently, been largely neglected in critical renditions of "orality" in Native American literature.[3] To treat the verbal utterance as an abstract and immaterial manifestation of culture is to repeat the basic misperception that tribal communities had no formal or textual tradition, that the oral tradition leaves no physical trace. As I have already suggested in the introduction, however, the generative tales, personal and family stories, political agreements, and spiritual truths of Native America are not only born of close relationships between peoples and their ancestral lands or migratory passages, but also find visual, material form in other types of nonverbal representation. The traces of land, memory, and ancestry in stories and treaties are also traces left through artistry and artisanship, on bark and stone, a reciprocal immanence of "tactile traces."

While the texts themselves share a common complexity—the figures on rock, according to Rajnovich, for instance, do not mean one thing but several, and the observer must, like the poetry critic, have all the possibilities in mind when drawing conclusions about their meanings (1994, 20)—the modes and purposes of "textual" production between the scrolls and books, between the pictographs and literary fiction, clearly differ markedly, particularly those pictographs, "Kekeewonin" (Vastoukas and Vastoukas 1973, 44), intimately connected to the quest for medicine/power. Nevertheless, these kinds of ties offer a purposeful sense of connection across a span of time and space otherwise characterized, according to non-Native approaches to history, literature, and culture, by rupture. The real presences of these precolonial "texts" are essential, then, to Vizenor's central dialectic of absence and presence that "attests to the absence of a precontact, pregenocide tribal presence but at the same time calls for the imaginative re-creation of such a presence" (Mackay 2008, 259). It does so, more specifically, through actively calling into play the palpable physicality of the trace, the mark, the text itself in the "absence" of text, in explicit interaction with the abstractions of memory, story, including the ineffable and extralinguistic cues that accompany them. In so doing, he—and as I argue in this chapter, other Ojibwe poets also—engages the reader in a process that is at once visual and verbal, that mediates between the limits of visual and verbal communication, each emerging where the other fades. Far from simply rendering the oral in the written, as decades of Vizenor criticism avows, then, this process simultaneously invokes a textual continuum implicit in the materiality of the mark, and the primacy of a visual aesthetic.

These traces exist too in ironic relation to those other forms of mark making— the ethnographies, treaties, maps, Bureau of Indian Affairs files, and more—that both directly and indirectly have sought to contain, define, and efface First Peoples since European settlement, embodying the "metanarratives and other forms of representation that demand the disappearance of indigenous peoples—for example, Manifest Destiny, social Darwinism, and the inevitable plight of the tragic mixed blood" (Wilson 2007, xii). The tension between the presences that the aforementioned scrolls attest to and the historical elision-through-documentation of Euro-American bureaucracy finds its most apt metaphor in the "X marks" on treaty documents that represent the "mark and seal" subjoined to the signatories' names. Invocations of these figures and documents in contemporary writing speak to Vizenor's sense of the writers in his collection *Touchwood*, in which prose extracts are headed by reproductions of mide scrolls, "announc[ing] their names" (1987, v). Thus, the invocations of X marks, both literally and through other representations of mark making as a signature of presence, disconcert dominant narratives of absence, "announcing" those who went before, while disrupting the administrative writing of the state that seeks to subsume them (see previous chapter; Kulchyski 2005, 2012).

X Marks the Spot

At the beginning of *X-Marks: Native Signatures of Assent*, Scott Lyons states simply that "an x-mark is a treaty signature" (2010, 1). That he ironically underplays the political potency with which he invests the X mark heightens the sense of accumulative weight the mark acquires by the end of his book as, with each move toward defining it, he reveals the "prospect of slippage, indeterminacy, unforeseen consequences, or unintended results" (2–3) in its paradoxical nature. Lyons teases out the implications of that paradox, proposing that "The x-mark [is a] coerced sign of consent" to an imposed order that "signifies power and a lack of power, agency and a lack of agency" (2). Although here in this section I am trying to consider a particular kind of ethical-aesthetic engagement with the X mark rather than the specifics of the political history that Lyons elucidates—which is, though, implicit—some of my comments coincide with that double sense of the X mark as being both contained and codified within the document itself and resistant to that codification; a mark, certainly in its poetic re-presentation, of assertion rather than simply coercion, and of a writing against, through a sign of the writing of, the state. X marks reveal, too, a double poetic of motion and stasis, of migration and belonging-in-place. Writing about the "sovereignty of transmotion" Niigaanwewidam James Sinclair affirms the "historical sense of motion" that grounds Gerald Vizenor's particular migratory poetics: for Lyons, meanwhile, that sense of mobility is intrinsic to the X mark as "another stopping point in a migration that is always heading for home" (10). Sinclair nevertheless takes Lyons to task: "The theory offered by Lyons," he writes, "is totalizing. 'All Indian texts are x-marks,' he pronounces, 'acts coerced and influenced by hegemonic (and usually oppressive) forces'" (2013a, 88). Acknowledging Lyons's point that "every so often an x-mark can be seen escaping from the prison house of dominant discourse" (Lyons 2010, 30), Sinclair nevertheless illuminates his oversight of nindoodemag, or the pictographic "signatures" of clan markers also commonly found on treaties. Such absence from Lyons's consideration constitutes a "glaring gap" that prioritizes the "'contamination' and 'coercion' of Indigenous expression" in a "'pure vs. tainted' framework [such as] Craig Womack describes in *Red on Red*, a problematic and progressivist set of binaries" (Sinclair 2013a, 89). This particular argument arguably plays out more readily in the contexts of actual nindoodemag, X marks, and treaties as explicated by Sinclair. In the course of my discussion here, however, I emphasize the reiterative representation of this figure in a range of poetry (and some prose) as a highly mobile paradox. In so doing, I take both Lyons's assertions and Sinclair's objections seriously to consider the X mark as "a provocative attempt to recover an oft-cited instrument of colonization" (Sinclair 2013a, 89) and a signifier of alternative orthographies that carry with them modes of agency, modernity, and literacy that do not rely on binary reductions such as pure/tainted, traditional/ modern, or oral/literate, and that operate as both visual markers of intellectual and aesthetic sovereignty and indicators of engaged resistance that move beyond the idea that "'escaping from the prison house of dominant discourse' is all Indigenous expressions are and can be" (Sinclair 2013a, 90).

I would further like to propose also that that X mark and, by extension, the figure of inscription, the mark maker, the ekphrastic gesture that links word to image, and the visual more broadly, serve to generate an ethical-aesthetic engagement along the lines of Christopher Teuton's explication of the critical impulse. If, as a signifying trope for this chapter, the colonial document (both literally and figuratively as it is encoded in the X mark itself) represents "static forms of power and dominance" ripe for disruption by the critical impulse (see introduction; Teuton 2010, 28), the interplay between the oral and the graphic, or the Indigenous aesthetic implicit in that interplay and the settler-colonial imposition the document signifies, troubles its dominance and simultaneously unsettles colonial authority while re-presenting Indigenous space.

In Gordon Henry's 1994 novel *The Light People*, which will be more fully examined in chapter 3, Elijah Cold Crow, the prisoner of haiku, writes haiku on birchbark parchment, haiku that become the culmination of his political resistance. That resistance is predicated on art, on a relationship with images that works back from the smoke of his series of politically inflected arsons, through the murals he turns to in prison, to haiku and dreamsongs, imagistic inscriptions born of "a partial loss of language, new forms, old forms" (71). Those new-old forms—a poetic convention that, in being inscribed on birch bark, evokes Anishinaabe pictography—reflect on the inscribed, and ultimately proscribed, nature of personal and collective identities where he writes:

> Signatures, names, the
> undersigned, with marks and lines
> anglicized in print.
>
> Clan leaders, head men
> scripted identities so
> many with an x. (73)

Invoking the bureaucratic erasure of a pretreaty relationship between people and place, the X mark also echoes that linguistic erasure of unnaming or anonymity, the lived reality of "clan leaders" and "head men" reduced to "scripted identities," to a crossing out; at face value, then, the reference to the treaty document here evokes the processes of colonization, beginning with the theft of language—those anglicized marks and lines—and moving on through the theft of land. This is the terminal creed of treaty discourse, the treaty as document of containment, in which the land and the people it sustains are measured, arranged, and subdivided.

At the text's opening, meanwhile, Henry introduces a paradox that persists throughout the narrative, when the protagonist, Oskinaway, who is undergoing a ceremony to locate his parents, dreams of his father:

> At other times, in the space of a moon-struck room, he saw the man across from him, dimly lit, at the edges of a fire between sleeping and waking. Then at some point his father became unnameable, unreachable, the introspected absence of a conclusion, an allotted X of an intellect tangled in a village of stories and imaginative encounters. (3)

The "allotted X," signifying absence through inscription, becomes a repeated indicator in the novel of bureaucratic erasure, of physical loss and loss of identity. And yet the X is also an initial marker of written language. Literally and symbolically it is a lexigram or pictograph, indication of the ability to write, to make marks—whether it be by signing one's name, drawing a picture, or marking the proverbial "spot"—not simply a stamp of negation and anonymity but also the locus of discovery and mystery. As a mnemonic device it becomes a signifier, in other words, of presence and, if we connect it to other areas of American political life such as the civil rights movement, a symbol of political resurgence and reclamation of autonomy.

This "signified absence" may thus be seen to become potentially politically empowering, literally crossing out the colonial erasure of identity with a sign that renders the individual identifiable only in relation to a whole community. For members of the Nation of Islam, the replacement for the surname is at once a reclamation of identity and a refusal to yield that identity to European patriarchal norms. At a more philosophical level, in *Glas*, Jacques Derrida memorably writes of the artistic signature: "The emblem, the blazon open and close. . . . The signature is a wound, and there is no other origin for the work of art" (1986, 184). Early identifications of doodem with heraldry, as I shall elaborate shortly, suggest that the "signature" here is not the unique identifier of an individual but of a kinship community. Thus, in its fictional reappropriation, at least, the signator's X potentially does similar political work. Significantly, also, this trope returns toward the end of the text, where Jake

Seed tells Oskinaway to "Look for Abetung, *he who inhabits, like the X on a treaty document*," a legally (and ethically) mean*ingful* mark that is, of course, inherently mean*ingless* and available for appropriation, manipulation, and exploitation (Henry 1994, 174; emphasis added).

As the X mark circulates through *The Light People*, then, it increasingly resists closure. Indeed, it does so quite literally in the musings of the character Bombarto Rose:

> The validating party represented by the X signators may reside in the box of words for a while, but their resourcefulness and their refusal to be limited by the box space will probably generate deeper, more expansive interpretations of the articles of the document. (78)

Pressing beyond the "articles of the document," which represent the "parameters of residence" of reservation boundaries, the X marks recall the mark makers from their bureaucratic entrapment, displacing those scripted identities with the novel's slowly accumulating network of relations, in turn collapsing temporal and spatial boundaries between the generations of the novel's community. The X mark, then, connotes agency too, the space of subjectivity that Abetung inhabits.

The X mark thus comes to inhabit the center around which the narrative circles, which, as I will return to in chapter 3, anticipates Henry's own sense of a "center (or centers) [that] is always dynamic, never static, and thus invokes responses which might include return, forgiveness, healing, vision, or so on" (Blaeser 1997a, 557). In turn, Blaeser continues, "they might reflect the motion of the landscape, the motion of people, the motion of the seasons, or the motion of families or communities" (557). In *Fugitive Poses*, Vizenor writes that "native memories, stories of totemic creation, shamanic visions, burial markers, medicine pictures, the hunt, love, war, and songs are the transmotion of virtual cartography" (1998, 170). Subsuming the X mark into this virtual cartography is, among other things, a reminder that the mark as it represents the "signature" of ancestors, signatures of assent in Lyons's eyes, is not the static sign of permanence or symbolic consent to the entrapments of cadastral boundaries and dissolution of tribal sovereignty. Rather than allowing them to be understood within the context of the settler legal mechanisms that (nominally at least) bind and constrain, their circulation in the novel securely integrates them into the totemic traditions that were similarly often used in treaty signings as substitute "signatures."

In her analysis of such "Nindoodem pictographs" as appear on treaties like the 1701 Grand Paix de Montréal, Heidi Bohaker argues that they "functioned as the equivalent of seals, not signatures, on these documents" (2010, 17). Redolent of Henry Rowe Schoolcraft's claims that clan markers were equivalent to heraldic crests, the seal is a marker of authentication whose usage in the West has direct antecedents in the ancient world. Whether they were read in these terms by European countersignatories or not, more significant is Bohaker's suggestion that "particularly in the seventeenth and eighteenth centuries, Anishinaabe pictographs were as likely to represent a father and sons, or brothers, or an entire extended family 'clan segment,' as a single individual" (16).

In his own incisive analysis of nindoodemag, Sinclair writes:

> Using treaty markings of Nindoodemag . . . I argue that principles embedded in this system encapsulate an intellectual narrative tradition that gesture to different forms of relationships Anishinaabeg carry with other living beings in their territories. Modeled on animals and fauna in Anishinaabeg environments, these suggest ways in which Anishinaabeg nationhood are expressed and embodied. They also provide a basis, through individual doodems and the specific knowledges they offer their relations, in which Anishinaabeg narratives over the past three centuries can be understood. (2013a, 64)

While Sinclair admonishes Lyons for overlooking the significance of nindoodemag in the X-marked "assent" to modernity, his assertion of the principle and purpose of these signs further encourages us, I believe, to understand the X mark itself as a proxy for an alternative orthography than that designated the signature. In other words, though the X mark on treaties effectively erases or occludes the tradition of signing with nindoodemag, its circulation here, as a literary trope, re-presents the relationality inherent in the doodem marker.

Just as those X marks signify the absences I have described above, in other words, so they implicitly invoke connection, presence-through-relation, and carry connotations of a community relationship to land, not just the sense of a spatial bond. Likewise, their ambivalent status between oral (as signifiers of nonliterate or preliterate mark) and literate (as the "initial marker" I mention above) is further prefigured in the clan marker, in that "the artists who drew these images embedded significant information in line sketches, inviting multiple ways of reading: as text, as metaphor, and as art" (Bohaker 2010, 15). In other words, they both communicate as textual marks yet resist interpolation into Euro-Western taxonomies of form. Therein, also, lies their resistance to stasis, their transmotional essence, politically, linguistically, and aesthetically as "a spirited and visionary sense of natural motion and presence" (Vizenor 1998, 15).

In *Fugitive Poses*, Vizenor writes that "transmotion is personal, reciprocal, the source of survivance, . . . an original natural union in the stories of emergence and migration that relate humans to an environment" (1998, 182–83). In the course of *The Light People*, the X mark takes on this aspect through the personal stories of individual narrators who interact with the reciprocal, relational quality of the X marks they encounter, transforming the latter from their administrative origins to nodal points in the novel around which the community is mapped. This spatial arrangement, or sense of orientation, is consolidated in the haiku/dreamsong sequences of Elijah Cold Crow, the "prisoner of haiku," with whom I began this section. At the very end of his long sequence, retrieved from the poet's body as a bundle of birchbark pages by Bombarto Rose, the latter draws comparisons between his own references to documents and Cold Crow's "return to old forms," saying, "The dream *X* draws us on. I cannot speak for Cold Crow, but his words have forced me from the page. I see how he returns to old forms, and in my references to documents I hammer away at myself for thinking of myself" (Henry 1994, 80). Cold Crow's old forms—the dreamsongs and the birch bark—become, on the one hand, mnemonics: "I understand the dream songs, the haiku attempts. I understand this frozen road; the words will come back. They will return from the air and re-form on distant lips" (80). They represent, in other words, inscriptions that ensure the continuation of the felt experience of the spoken word. On the other hand, they also represent inscription-as-substitute for the spoken voice, in light of Cold Crow's muteness and, of course, his death.

Rose's interpretation of these events in turn figures the critical impulse of Teuton's triad, which Rose elucidates through metaphor when he recounts: "On the road a few memories wander away singing, their tracks filling with falling snow. This is who I am, a few photographs taken for a moment of truth, a few belongings wrapped in brittle paper, a few dead relatives away from my own road into the sun" (Henry 1994, 80). There is a dissolving of the contrast between the visual trails of memory—filling tracks, photographs, even Cold Crow's body—and the permanence of inscription: the manuscripts, the road itself. As if to underline this his hand, "pinched at the [finger] tips . . . as if Cold Crow stopped in oratory, gesturing to his heart as he referred to some deep truth without words," leads Rose to the final manuscript in his coat pocket. Through all of this, then, the trace of transmotion, both linguistic and personal, casts Cold Crow's words and gestures as inherently circulatory, relational. Again, this is spatially conceived, most explicitly in his "Final Dreamsong":

> a note to hold
> the eyes open a hole
> in the Fineday earth
>
> make an x in the snow
> where you saw me standing last
>
> I am on this road
> to town to find a gun
> for my lips
>
> make a circle in the snow
> a prayer offering of tobacco
> make this place
> a prayer place
> to each of the four directions
>
> put flags of different colors
> when the wind turns warm. (81)

The repetition once more of the spatial marker, X, here a ritual mantra, a suicide note, and a request, connects the inscription itself to ethereality, and to absence. In other words, the language, the inscription, returns primacy to the symbolic—the flags and the four directions—and the natural. Inscription and ritual action, the circle, the tobacco, imbue place with specific significance. The X, then, becomes not simply a signifier of absence and even negation but also makes that absence itself a site of reengagement, of radical revisualization of Native American subjectivity, and figures Native sovereignty through transmotion in the X that marks the spot as relational rather than possessive.

That relationality is implicit in the four directions, marked out by Cold Crow's instructions—to draw a cross within a circle, first and foremost, before making offerings to the four directions and planting flags of different colors, presumably of the four directions: red, white, yellow, and black. Similarly describing a compass in these terms—the cross within the circle, both literal and metaphorical—Louise Erdrich's poem "Turtle Mountain Reservation" from her first collection, *Jacklight*, begins:

> The heron makes a cross
> Flying low over the marsh.
> Its heart is an old compass
> Pointing off in four directions.
> It drags the world along,
> The world it becomes. (1984, 82)

As I argued in *Louise Erdrich* (2010a), the heron, clan totem for the Be-nays, on the maternal side of Erdrich's family, makes a cross in flight—a syncretistic allusion to both the crucifix and the cross that represents the fourth level of the mide, the highest rank in the Ojibwe midewiwin or medicine society. The cross becomes a compass, the heron's heart, a second double image that, pointing off in four directions, corresponds to both the pan-Indigenous sacred hoop and the navigational aid central to the work of empire that, metaphorically speaking, encompasses the land. Both of these readings clearly inflect differently on that last pair of lines, "It drags the world along, / The world it becomes." The former is suggestive of colonial usurpation, or the construction of social realities; the latter is perhaps more evocative of mythic transformation, or relationship with, rather than power over, the natural environment, the preceding and future generations, and all earthly and spiritual beings. In her discussion of phonetic consonance, Margaret Noodin includes her own bilingual poem "*Waagaamiitigoog*/Crooked Trees," the first five lines of which are

> *Anishinaabeg gii owaangawi'aawaan* / The Anishinaabe tamed them
> *Weweni owaagibizhaawaan* / bending them carefully
> *Waawiyebii'igankewaad* / making compasses
> *Aadisookaanag biskinaawaan* / of stories folded
> *Wiikwiiwin waamdaanaawaa* / of energy visible. (2014b, 183)

While Erdrich's poem does not offer equivalent linguistic scrutiny, "The world it becomes" resounds with a similar sense of the immanence of storied energy.

Simultaneously, then, we read an instance of navigation as alternately imposition on and fusion with (or fission in?) the "world." This dialogic interplay between the signs and symbols of two cultures and their relationship with the land and, therefore, between the transformational mode of myth and the enterprise of the colonial map makers, poses two ways of approaching the relationship between landscape and culture in Louise Erdrich's oeuvre: the first, a tribal-centered view of the intricate relationship between language, place, nature, and culture; the second, cultural geography's focus, following the likes of Keith Basso, on "place" as the realm of cultural meaning, identity, imagination, and significance, and more particularly on the means of documenting said place.

That syncretism, or perhaps the tension inherent in it, is not just spiritual, but political too. The emphasis on the cardinal directions also evokes—perhaps inadvertently—the U.S. Public Land Survey, which, Vizenor reminds us in *Fugitive Poses*, abandoned its metes and bounds approach on the eastern seaboard for survey lines that were "oriented predominantly in cardinal directions" (1998, 174, qtg. Norman Thrower). If (and that is a very tentative if) we read Erdrich's poem this way there's an interesting conflation of the personal and the historical that signals a tension between Western and Native conceptions of space. The reminder, through Noodin's poem, then, of the significance of the kind of geoglyphic importance of particular landmarks remembered in story/song such as the crooked trees again prioritizes the sovereign aesthetic implicit in that storied energy.

In *Fugitive Poses*, by way of illuminating that point, Vizenor's invocation of Norman Thrower—through the latter's work in *Maps and Civilization*—leads to a discussion of visually rich medieval mappa mundi alongside the cartographic productions, or "active creations, not passive reproductions" of the midewiwin (1998, 175). Writing of the pressure on mide practitioners to "reveal the stories and visions of this great society of healers to outsiders," Vizenor goes on to note that "that was a testy time in native stories, since the visual and aural were transcribed as the scriptural; and the transmotion of native memories, that sense of a presence in stories, was courted in the social sciences as cultural evidence" (175). In Erdrich's poem, the suggestive compass formed by the heron teases apart the cartographic certainties of settlement, its totemic connotations assuring priority to the Anishinaabe reading of its significance, which reorientates the reader according to a different understanding of mapping. In other words, and in inversion of the historical process, the cartographic X mark that redesignated the territory understood as Ojibwe country is placed under erasure, Indigenous space reemerging from the colonial palimpsest. As such, the poem represents the cross, a virtual X mark, as a site of survivance and engaged resistance, while the remainder of the poem traces a familial narrative grounded in the earth of Turtle Mountain, itself, of course, subject to the fragmentations of government survey, including allotment. The family that the poem goes on to describe, like the "*anishinaabe* and other natives . . . [endure] in virtual cartography, the certain mete of native sovereignty" (Vizenor 1998, 175).

If, to return to Vizenor's formulation, the heron's cross marks a virtual cartography, then that space and its habitus is mapped more intimately by the poem's persona, who moves outward through the poem's landscape from literal self-reflection and a consciousness of the traces she leaves in her movement, to the wider contexts of kinship and, through that kinship, to her relationship to place. "My face surfaces in the green / beveled glass above the washstand," she writes (Erdrich 1984, 83). Connoting a coming to consciousness in the space of home, rather than the narcissism with which the mirrored reflection might be associated, this image also conjures the illusory quality of presence-as-permanence, implicit in that sense of "surfacing"; as "real" as the face in the mirror appears, we know it will vanish, just as the fish that surfaces in the water will surely submerge again. Yet it is not to anticipate that absence, but to a presence-in-absence that Erdrich gestures in the following line, in which she observes "My handprint in thick black powder / on the bedroom shade." While the image of the face surfacing in the beveled mirror suggests a distortion, the apparition of something apprehended but not precisely seen, the handprint is a clear symbol of presence that, in keeping with the imaged tension aforementioned, generates conflicting ideas. It is a reminder, of course, of the traces we leave on the things we touch, the spaces we inhabit. It connotes a melancholy sense of permanence in that respect. There, like the fingerprints at a crime scene, presence is a stealthy, fugitive thing, as a figure moves through a space leaving a trail that either indicates her discomfort or incrimination.

If the fingerprint connection, though, is produced by the "black powder" in which the handprint is left, that same powder is reminiscent of the charcoal and ochre paints with which thousands of handprints have been left on cave walls throughout the world. There, the image of spiritual power, the signatory action of the artist, and the deliberate self-assertion of the maker come to the fore, again, drawing Indigenous presence from the deep shadows of colonial occupation. While the handprint certainly feeds into the poem's deliberation on time—which inevitably includes aging, death, and in which such marks are denotative of loss—in the context of the Turtle Mountains after which the poem is titled, it also expresses a sense of belonging in Indigenous space. That sense of belonging is traced through family connections, through three generations of relatives and their stories: the youthful Theresa preparing to face the boys in local bars; drunk Uncle Ray and his nightmares of nuns descending from the sky; and Grandpa, Pat Gourneau, to whom the poem is dedicated, walking home from bingo and St. Ann's Catholic Church, becoming one with the stones and animals in his senile old age. Apposing that heron's flight, then, with the materiality of earth, the poem concludes with the poet's observation of her grandfather's arthritically fused and twisted hands, "Hands of earth, of this clay / I'm also made from." Those same hands have left traces, both literal and metaphorical, just as the poetic persona's handprint marks the lampshade, and her face, surfacing like memory across time, inhabits—literally dwells in—the earth of the Turtle Mountains, mapped not through public surveys, but through clans and totems, families and memories, bodies and the traces they leave on the world they touch.

In an interview with Carmen Flys, Gordon Henry notes that "we have to keep remembering the people of our families" and that in remembering them, "it remembers those moments in time, to bring them back and give them another kind of force" (1996, 173). Evoking, and then displacing, that image of the survey map, then, the poem *re*maps its psychic terrain, an image of motion—the bird in flight—framing a powerful sense of connection through memory that Erdrich has evinced elsewhere. The poem recalls the "tactile traces—in blood, bone, and stone" with which Blaeser so evocatively introduces the work in her second poetry anthology (2006, xvi); recalls, in turn, the personal "traces / blood, bone, stone" of Vizenor's "Almost Ashore" (Blaeser 2006, 222). As such—and I will return to Vizenor's poem shortly—the poem itself effects another trace, or sequence of traces, that connect voice, place, and relations through words that evoke both the visual and material marks and the oral/aural of Native transmotion.

Erdrich's poem is not entirely unambivalent, however, as that evocation of haunting—the face in the mirror, the print on the shade—conveys. As I will suggest in chapter 4, Erdrich later acknowledges her sense of comfort in Minneapolis in *Books and Islands in Ojibwe Country*, an indicator perhaps of the degree to which "home" itself is differently constructed around heritage, extended and nuclear family, work, and so on. While "Turtle Mountain Reservation" thus offers a ground, quite literally, for identity, it is by no means an unequivocally "centered" space within the poem. Vizenor insists that "the notions of native sovereignty must embrace more than mere reservation territory" (1998, 190). The circulatory ethic of a poetics of transmotion describes Indigenous space wherever Indigenous relationality and "natural reason" persist. As such—and although they are often similarly ambivalent for obvious reasons—poems that map out the indigeneity of urban space also invoke the X mark. One such poem is Marcie Rendon's "Urban Rez."

In "Urban Rez," Rendon reuses those same signifiers of presence and absence— the rez, which becomes an almost conceptual alternative to the urban, and the cross and circle—to stake out a different kind of territory, while exploring several destructive and potentially destructive relationships. The poem begins with an incantation repeated several times throughout that is recognizable in the kinds of assertions of land and memory we recognize in the work of N. Scott Momaday, Paula Gunn Allen, and others:

> generational memories
> passed from body to body
> womb to womb
> to all the future
> generations
> sorrow and joy
> joy and sorrow. (Grover et al. 2002, 56)

It evokes Beatrice Medicine's assertion that women are the carriers of culture, a spider's web thread of responsibility that is paradoxically both infrangible and terrifyingly fragile. These few lines operate as a kind of frame to the poem. They are left-justified, where the poem's narrative is inset. They are repeated, a kind of chorus that creates rupture between the ritualized space this familiar incantation establishes and the "real" space of the urban scene the poem's narrative describes: one of violence, drugs, danger, betrayal.

Here again, X marks the spot, a different kind of territorial marker, first the "criss-cross / hip-hop" that "took over the whole damn 'hood," a different kind of cultural terrain from the one described thus far; then "X marks the spot / where santiago's dreams / joined / the neighbor lady's hollyhock roots" (57), a figurative signifier of the poem's tragic litany that fuses with the territorial markings of local taggers, which includes the persona's daughter. These tags, in turn, mark out yet another territory, like hip-hop, before it takes a literal step further away from the poem's frame:

they used to go under the 16th ave railway bridge
and tag the concrete
the O's on that same lady's garage
mark the bullet entrance holes
my Indian-born daughter tried to tell that young man
his snoop-doggy-dog t-shirt
was NOT some modern day ghost dance shirt
if you dare to happen under that bridge
and see her sniffin instead of taggin
(think she does a lot of that these days)
would you tell her to please come home
or at least tag the neighbor lady's garage
she can sign it with XXXX's and OOOO's
and I'll get the message. (57)

Here, those X's seem to describe a space entirely separate from that established by the poem's frame, by the poem's central lineage:

carried inside my womb
inside my mother's womb
inside my grandmother's womb
and my daughter's daughters
nestled inside of them
inside of me.

Yet they also refuse to deny the connections, drawing these scenes into the (ritual) frame of generational connectivity, performing a reconciling, creating a transformative space for the gap of generational experience that seems otherwise to merely dislocate and divorce within the urban space itself, where the Xs and Os clearly, if perhaps paradoxically, mark presence and absence, as agency and victimhood, both the assertion and the elision of the tagger/signatory.

Again, then, the cross and the circle combine in relation to an orientation within a given landscape that marks both space and relation, combined through story, that simultaneously speaks to movement and deferral—including linguistic deferral—as functions of that cartography. The X mark as a sign of presence described through absence and, thus, through the capacity of language to re-create and resituate spatially and temporally defined kinship networks, impacts upon urban as well as reservation terrain. In "Offering: words," from her collection *The Mother's Tongue*, Heid Erdrich comes at the relationship between language, belonging, and genealogy from another angle, but similarly reveals the mutually constitutive marks that leave their traces on mother and child. The poem's epigraph, "Gichimookomaanimo: speaks American, speaks the Long Knives' language," illuminates the nature of the reflection:

> Mother, if you look it up, is source,
> (fount and fountainhead—origin,
> provenance and provenience,
> root) and wellspring. (2005, 1)

She puns on language—tongue—itself throughout the poem, drawing on idioms, such as "mother-wit," "native wit," the verbal use "to mother," and forms of communication such as "sign language" and "contact language," to demonstrate the importance of acts of communication in the establishment of self and the metaphorical closeness of birthing and speech or language. On English and Ojibwemowin the poem continues,

> both spoke forwards our mother country,
> our motherland (see also fatherland,
> our home, our homeland, our land)
> called soil in English our mother tongue,
> our native language that is not my Native language
> not the mother language Ojibwe:
> wellspring of many tongues, nurse, origin, and source. (1)

Older sister Louise writes of the legacy of that language to her self-identity as an American writer in *Books and Islands*: "For an American writer, it seems crucial to at least have a passing familiarity with [Ojibwemowin], which is adapted to the land as no other language can possibly be" (2003, 85), a generative lexis located in the land. Rene Meshake goes further in his poem "The Grand Entry":

> The Spirits asked, "Who are you?"
> . . .

Finally, it dawned on me
and I proclaimed, "I'm Anishinabe,
Mz aye, indoodem
Dyoosh indanishinabe-biomaadiz."
One of the Spirits acknowledged,
"Biindigen, gichi Anishinabe.
Truly, any Anishinabe who still speaks the language
makes a grand entry in the prayer world." (Blaeser 2006, 137)

Meshake reinvigorates what often, inevitably, becomes a reductive politics of autochthony with a clear sense of tribal origin and national belonging. The poem pays homage to the relationality between the spirit and human worlds, the power of prayer, and moreover the abundant power of language as act of communication between humans, and between humans and spirits, place, form, and more: as a link to and as a conduit for knowledge. Nowhere is this more beautifully encapsulated than in the bilingual poem Margaret Noodin includes in her introduction to *Bawaajimo: A Dialect of Dreams in Anishinaabe Language and Literature*:

Pii Anishinaabebiigeyaanh	When I write in Anishinaabemowin
Nd'shkitoon	I am able to
nagamobiiyaanh	sing idea strings
nambiing, nibiishensing	of underwater leaves
wiigwaamigong, chigamigong	of birch places and deep spaces. (2014a, xviii)

Ideation, space, image, material object, song, all converge in Noodin's poem to convey a sense of written language as both oral/aural and visual. Echoing the potency and play of Heid Erdrich's poem, too, she describes the essential fluidity of linguistic form in the following terms: "The sound *bii* could relate to the *bii* of water, the *bii* of tree veins, the *bii* of a flowing *ziibii* (river), or the black on white *bii* of *zhibiige* (to write). Language can teach what it means to meander, bringing life through water, through lines of meaning" (xviii). Implicit in these X marks, in the "capture" of word in written form, is a nevertheless inherent resistance to fixity, indeed to that capture—an engaged resistance that again figures the legacy of transmotion, or "unceded identities and a way of looking at the world that resists stasis, defines existence and energy in motion, and requires constant observation for survival" (xx).

Elsewhere, this legacy-as-flow is located in material inheritance, for instance in "Quilts and afghans in a rainbow of colors, . . . the legacy left to me by the strong women in my family" (Blaeser 2006, 15). Extending the metaphor, this kind of legacy becomes another form of communication, the quilts, like the language, transmitting not only maternal connection but literally the history of a line, a family, a community, becoming communicators of and vehicles for continuity. There is an intimacy to this kind of vehicle, an intimacy that resists external imposition, that understands without naming. "Legacy," Blaeser writes of a similar scene,

> is not a word these sisters use. . . . Still they wear the strands of history like strings of colored trade beads. . . . Keep the names from rusting on the tongue. Teach their children to welcome the repetition of stories. (12–13)

Meanwhile, in her "Star Blanket Stories," Heid Erdrich tells a tale of the continuities of grandmother and granddaughter sewing sessions, which are also, tacitly, opportunities to educate about love and courtship through tales of star boy who "comes with an offering, / a neat logo design, free, in open use" (2008, 45). At once a mythological reiteration and an imagic moment, the poem ends:

> There's a reason they tell this story
> absent the mother. Better Grandma bear it.
>
> Astronomically distant from you, pretending
> you still greet us each morning,
> your face a blaze, nothing changed. (45)

Returning us to the image of cycles and repetitions, those connections between women and in turn between the generations, marked in language, in physical scars and traces, in specific material practices that map and carry narrative and memory, are a key thematic of these texts.

I want to draw some of these threads—traces, if you like—together before I turn to a more focused discussion of form and effect. I have used the word "trace" apparently unreflectively from the start of this chapter, but it is actually with the strong criticisms in mind of blanket applications of Euro-Western theory, or the powerful refusal of Penelope Myrtle Kelsey of "the theory of the trace" as a poststructuralist obscurant to tribal-centered theorization (see 2010), that I reiterate, as many have before me, its centrality to survivance and its recoverability in literature and language as a figure that, like the X mark as formulated here, resists the binary closures that permit the conditions for the wholesale "loss" of such things as "culture," "tradition," and so on. In that regard, I am particularly mindful of Derrida's evocation of the ashes of holocaust as the "ineradicable trace of eradication," the trace that "mark[s] the limits of the linguistic turn" (Mackay 2008, 256). However, as Mackay also points out, Vizenor, from whose usage the term most commonly derives in Native literary criticism, deploys the word "trace" for all its nuances. It is most usefully regarded in the full variety of its connotations, including the trace as actual physical presence on/in an environment; as a transitive verb used most commonly to speak of the search for origins, patterns, and development; and the tracing of history, including, ironically, the literal tracing of scrolls and pictographs in various anthropological studies. None of these senses alters the term's potential fluidity, or the ambiguity of the trace as discernible but essentially illimitable. On the one hand, then, articulating the multiplicity of "trace" is essential for keeping in mind its possibility and the potential in language to trace, in another sense of the word, those genealogies that precede, evade, and transcend colonialism. On the other hand, the deconstructive turn itself, while clearly problematic when deployed as a means to unseat "truth" in any facet—as dangerous to a counternarrative as it is to any master narrative—enables a more nuanced understanding of the operative relation of spoken and written language in contemporary Native practice. For, in respect of that sense of the illimitable, Michael Lewis writes in *Derrida and Lacan: Another Writing* that "[Derrida] is attempting to indicate the absolute beyond of determination, the other (of the opposition [between the same and the other]) that is always appropriated by the textual" (2008, 133). As I have explored thus far in this chapter, and as I hope the remainder of this chapter will underline, it is in resisting the foreclosures of textual appropriation—including the notion that the textual is itself inherently colonial—that this work finds both its engaged resistance and its continuities.

I turn, then, to another kind of document, another form of textual capture, in Blaeser's "Housing Conditions of One Hundred Fifty Chippewa Families" (2007, 82). Titled after Hilger's study in the late 1930s, Blaeser writes:

wigwam
peaked lodge
bark house

tipi
log house
tar-paper shack
frame house
u.s. rehabilitation house.
sister hilger
. . .
you graphed
photographed
measured dimensions
calculated cubic air space
enumerated every construction detail—23 with broken windows;
99 without foundations, buildings
Resting on the ground;
98 with stove pipes for chimneys.
house, dwelling, place, structure—home. Endaayaang (82–83).

Baraga translates that last word, spelled Endaiân in his *Dictionary* (1992), as a possessive form of the noun "home" or "dwelling." This repetition of home, reinforcing the juxtaposition of the material study of "houses" with the emotional resonances of "home," also performs more immediately in Anishinaabemowin, translating as "our home," confirming the bond between poet and the object of study, and subtly underscoring the objectification of Hilger's project.

The relationship between Blaeser's poem and Hilger's text (both formal responses to inadequacies but with radically different takes as to the nature of the problem) is testament to the relationship between Ojibwe writing and the official document. It demonstrates the gap between Bureau of Indian Affairs bureaucracy and the real lives of Native people, between the textual documentation of Anishinaabe lives and lived experience, between the often well-intentioned motives of those (self-)appointed guardians of Native welfare and the needs and desires of those they are intent on saving, and between the particular ideas that Anishinaabe people—Anna and Mary, their Métis neighbor, Mike, "a regular League of Nations," and his white wife, Jane (Blaeser 2007, 82)—might have about home and the American administration has about housing. The poem also highlights a basic difference in the nature of the text itself, in the official mapping of White Earth versus the artistic response to that mapping, that refutes both the lines of the prior document's own form—lines it lays down around the people, as if they are mere objects within a set of socioeconomic data. The final difference lies in a devotion to place, which includes the memories, the stories, and the bones of times past:

> And does the land remember you
> Sister Inez, of the tar-paper-shack dwellers?
> As surely it remembers Mary
>
> . . .
>
> did your BIA-commissioned sojourn
> in the land of white clay
> somewhere lay its soul mark
>
> . . .
>
> even as the measured drip of black ink
> might draw tabulations
> upon white pages? (82–83)

Tabulating white pages and other equivalent sign-making dominates, although it is clearly not exclusive to, much Ojibwe fiction. That Blaeser's free-verse rumination responds to the "ruled edges of report ledgers" (82) is one measure of the nature and degree of resistance to official records at both content and discourse levels; where Hilger's text tabulates and objectifies, Blaeser's poem reveals the people and their inhabitancy of the land. Chris LaLonde has argued that the turn to documents/texts to both highlight inherent inequities and reclaim ground speaks, admittedly in different ways, to the use of both text and language as an "effective weapon in the struggle for survival" (1997, 23). In Blaeser's poem, that core strategy is supplemented by the literal use of Hilger's text and Anishinaabe language to reclaim the substance of the ethnographer's documentation and resituate it in terms that evade capture.

Haiku, Dreamsongs, and the Pictomythic

Movement for the effacement of text is a governing metaphor in Blaeser's early analysis of Vizenor's haiku. It is also, presumably, key to her own use of the form. I will return to this point specifically, but I come to it through a query raised—and then in fact answered—by Karen Jackson Ford in "Marking Time in Native America:

Haiku, Elegy, Survival." Contemplating Vizenor's "birth" as a poet through haiku, Ford avers that "it remains curious that haiku, with its visual, imagistic focus, should be the one form of poetry Vizenor finds most resonant with his concerns. We might expect orality rather than imagery to be the foundation of his poetics" (2009, 345). Although, just prior to this, Ford has succinctly demonstrated the care Vizenor takes to avoid treating Native identity in his haiku, her desire to read the haiku through his Nativeness in these terms is understandable—possibly even desirable given his own discussions of form. In chapter 5 I will more directly examine Vizenor's use of and rumination on the dreamsong and what he designates "pictomyths" in his *Summer in the Spring*. In anticipation of that discussion, though, it is worth dwelling on the unarticulated presence of the image when Ford points back to his early work *South of the Painted Stones* (1963) as evidence that Vizenor "situates his own work in relation to an oral tradition" (2009, 345). Ford continues to quote Vizenor's elaboration of the essential orality of Anishinaabe poetics, where "in his introduction to *Songs of the People* (1965), Vizenor describes the oral tradition in distinctly imagistic terms: 'The anishinabe did not have a written history. The past was a visual memory and oratorical gesture'" (346). It would be unwise to disagree that orality is at the heart of Vizenor's own theorizations and motivations here, but what Ford ignores, despite her acknowledgement of his imagism, is the materiality of the image that accompanies the dissolution of words. In this section, then, I will pause on the haiku in two respects: firstly, I will revisit Blaeser's analysis with which I began this section; and secondly, I will look to the relationship between the oral songs and stories and the material marks from which Vizenor's haiku/dreamsong aesthetic (and that of both Blaeser and Henry) develops.

In identifying Ford's oversight, I do not intend criticism of her reading. Indeed, her reading of Vizenor's haiku is very much in keeping with that of others, building implicitly on the foundations established by Blaeser's early work and of course by Vizenor himself, who writes about haiku in precisely the terms Ford elaborates. In *Gerald Vizenor: Writing in the Oral Tradition*, her seminal study of Vizenor's oeuvre, Blaeser writes that the haiku form's transient quality "advertises its absences and requires the response of the reader to bring it to fruition," which in turn "engage[s] the reader in the process of 'unfixing' the text" and "break[ing] through the boundaries of print" (1996, 113–14). Such emphasis, clearly, speaks to Vizenor's articulations of transmotion, natural reason, and survivance in its connotations for breaking free of the rhetorical captivity of the *indian*. Haiku, thus, become a move toward the ultimate expression of the text that denies itself. Self-effacement in turn becomes a politically constitutive act,[4] a covenant, if you like, between writer as witness, text that bears witness, and reader who experiences the words as if a natural fact: "The reader," Vizenor explains, "creates a dreamscape from haiku; nothing remains in print, words become . . . traces on the wind" (1984a, 1). So when Blaeser writes, in the first haiku of "Haiku Journey," "the tips of each pine / the spikes of telephone poles / hold gathering crows" (2007, 48), she declares and transcends a presence—the poet's witness as well as the natural features of the scene. Repeating Vizenor's own words, Blaeser writes, "haiku 'ascribe the world,' . . . they 'ascribe the seasons,' are 'earth tones,' and . . . there 'is a visual dreamscape in haiku which is similar to the sense of natural human connections to the earth'" (1997b, 5).

In the course of discussing the adoption of the modernist "kaiko" form of haiku (a form that admits self-expression, Ford observes) by counterculture poets and interred Japanese Americans during and after World War II, Ford's observation that "most [American] poets since World War II . . . have employed haiku as a form uniquely suited to accepting rather than resisting the conquest of Native peoples" (2009, 338) adds a further layer to their (perhaps) ironic deployment by the likes of Vizenor, Blaeser, and Gordon Henry Jr., not to mention William Oandasan (Filipino/Yuki; see Ford 2009), Mary TallMountain (Koyukon; see Liang 2016), and Nora Marks Dauenhauer (Tlingit; see Stratton 2015) among others. Understanding that deployment attends in part on the contrast between "Anglo-American poets who take up Native America in haiku . . . to elegize the 'pitiful last days of Indians'" (Ford 2009, 338) and what Ford sees as their paradoxical service to Native writers in "doing just the opposite," becoming "central to their individual projects of tracing and maintaining connections to the indigenous past" (341). That Vizenor chooses a form that ties him to the modernist appropriation of Japanese form effects an indigenizing of the modernist project that is increasingly coming to the fore in his more recent fiction (see *Blue Ravens*; *Treaty Shirts*). Where those Euro-American poets (particularly Ezra Pound, Amy Lowell, and their inheritors) appropriate the form in a direct sense, Vizenor's relationship to it is more complex, stemming from his own immersion in Japanese literature and history following his time there in the early 1950s,[5] and secondly from the relationship he and others trace to the spirit of the Anishinaabe dreamsong, rendering it on the one hand an instance of "compositional resistance" (Rader 2011, 5) and on the other a repurposing of a written analogue for an oral form.

Blaeser observes that "both haiku and dream songs are tightly constructed poetic units with vivid images (often of nature) and with little commentary, meant to transport the reader beyond the words to an experience or what Vizenor calls a 'dreamscape'" (Blaeser 1997b, 8). The proximity of the haiku and the dreamsong is further illuminated by the close coincidence of both coming to high poetic consciousness in the early 1910s. The synchronicity of the moment—of dreamsongs and haiku entering the American literary consciousness—cannot readily be accorded anything other than coincidental status; both, to some degree, were products of the clamor for cultural preservation/revitalization of the late nineteenth and early twentieth centuries. Nevertheless, to understand the modern interpretation of the dreamsong as coterminous with the rapid development of modernist literary aesthetics in the second decade of the twentieth century is to acknowledge correspondence, at least. The story of modernist borrowing from "primitive" forms is well known; of course, the traffic was emphatically two-way, as Michael Castro explains that though the correspondence was "superficial at best and more apparent than real," it was also an inevitable consequence of translators "us[ing] imagist concepts and techniques to produce their English translations" (1991, 22). Nevertheless, Densmore's *Chippewa Music* was first published in 1910. Coterminous as it may be with the advent of imagism proper, Kenneth Rexroth importantly points out that Densmore "worked with the Chippewa many years before . . . Japanese translations and their imitations in modern American verse came into existence" (1961, 283; for a fuller overview of this debate, see Blaeser 1996, 111–13). That Vizenor began writing haiku shortly before he published his "reexpressions" of Anishinaabe dreamsongs is, however, more interesting, not least because it gives rise to connections independently arrived at by Gordon Henry Jr. some years later. In a sense, Vizenor reclaims Native subjectivity from the status, well entrenched in high and late modernism, of Native Americans being the objects of the modernist gaze through primitivist discourse. Fellow Anishinaabe artists such as George Morrison and Robert Houle perform similar tasks for the visual arts, through similarly minimalist lenses such as abstract expressionism and color-field painting. In his introduction to *Summer in the Spring*, Vizenor himself notes that "dream song pictures, or pictomyths, are sacred *and heard only by members of the midewiwin*" (1993b, 11; emphasis added), asserting in turn that "the *anishinaabe* stories and dream songs are heard as the voices of individual freedom; in published translations the songs are lyric poems" (13). The transition from oral to print, then, is not merely a translation from Anishinaabemowin to English, but from a sacred, and ostensibly secret, form to a demotic form, a cultural translation that transforms both meaning and context. In his turn to haiku, perhaps, he seeks form that transmits both elements—the lyrical, the written and the oral, the visual/visionary—without the transformation that, without meaning to imply loss or corruption, misleadingly conveys the untranslatable.

Ford stresses the fact that Vizenor undertakes this work without explicit recourse to cultural identity—or, as she puts it, of his contributions to Cor van den Heuvel's 1974 *The Haiku Anthology*, he "scrupulously avoids any reference to his ethnic identity or cultural heritage and seems to carry no burden of intimate heraldry from aboriginal America" (Ford 2009, 335). Nevertheless, his "haiku have also sustained what he terms his 'survivance,' a 'condition of not being a victim'" as well as to "represent" and "exceed" the complexities of Native American history (341). It might be sustained, in light of this analysis, that the haiku evoke the X marks, as "signatures" that mark Native agency while also embodying and evoking a wealth of apparently contradictory signification. If we return to *The Light People* briefly, we discern a similar process in the "prisoner's" journey from haiku to dreamsong. Elijah Cold Crow writes his haiku on birchbark parchment, which become the culmination of his political resistance.

That he details this process in the form of haiku reminds us of that emphasis on transience discussed above. In articulating his scripted captivity through the "vanishing" form,[6] he also symbolically resists, and even undermines, the power of text, invoking what Vizenor experienced as a form of liberation "from the treacherous manners of missionaries, classic warrants, the themes of savagism and civilization, and the arrogance of academic discoveries" (1994a, 26). The X marks both of and in the prisoner's haiku, then, return to language as markers of presence, evoking a speaker or actor in a process, rather than denoting the preliterate absence of an erasure, a nonspeaker, or silenced subject. The dreamsongs that he goes on to develop, in turn, are both explicitly linked to the haiku as a recovery of form and also to the birchbark pictograph by virtue of their reproduction in scroll form. In turn, then, as forms that both adopt and adapt through cultural encounter and that nevertheless evince continuity with earlier processes, they indirectly connect the prisoner to late nineteenth-century ledger art, which have already been partly evoked by murals that Cold Crow paints on his cell walls. The murals, in their turn, suggest a range of arts of protest, from the monumental murals of "Los tres grandes"—Mexican muralists David Alfaro Siqueiros, Diego Rivera, and José Clemente Orozco—to, closer to home, the art and text that came to adorn the buildings of Alcatraz Prison during the Indians of All Nations occupation of the island from 1969 to 1971. His various artistic acts, then, ground him absolutely in a visual grammar, returning him from his "partial loss of language" to an older mnemonic form of expression that finds its ultimate expression in a scripted form that is inherently imagistic and visual, as well as visionary.

In the introduction to *Summer in the Spring*, Vizenor writes, "The personal visions that were unbroken in the extremes of nature would seldom be heard in mere isolation. . . . Tribal relations were created in visions" (1993b, 12). In turn, he sees in haiku "a visual dreamscape . . . which is similar to the sense of natural human connections to the earth found in tribal music, dream songs" (1984a, 3). While Vizenor rarely explicitly alludes to the mark making that is ubiquitous in the haiku and dreamsongs of *The Light People*, the presence of the poet or observation of another intervention into the natural scene grounds his haiku's ethereal impermanence in the material actuality of vision. A number of poems in *Raising the Moon Vines* (1964b), for instance, articulate the signs of human presence in a natural scene and describe incidental interaction between the two:

> The nails leave lines
> On the old morning glory fence
> Dripping dew. (42)

> Old brown paths
> Through the weeds are brightly marked
> First Autumn snow. (82)

Or the imaged result of direct human and animal interaction in a landscape:

> Under the crossing log
> Fresh openings in the ice
> Haloed with footprints. (89)

> White leafless tree
> A shadow of little footprints
> Traced in the snow. (92)

In *Seventeen Chirps* (1964a), meanwhile, the more deliberate and deliberative making of marks on surfaces comes to the fore just twice, in both cases humorously describing interactions:

Maple beetle
Stood where I was writing
Watching the cat. (n.p.)

Haughty neighbors
Baying at the hopscotch marks
Just before it rained. (n.p.)

The latter example, in particular, evokes the imputed impermanence of the form itself, the hopscotch marks likely to disappear with the rain, as the words dissipate in their apprehension to give way to the imaged scene, the moment of remark itself.

The haiku, then, like the X mark, becomes that very "note to hold / the eyes open" of Cold Crow's final dreamsong, in which the "note" connotes both the materiality of the birch bark or paper and its inscription *and* the ephemeral transience of the aural/oral communication, which in combination produce the visionary experience of the viewer/listener/reader—whose eyes are held open in the act. Thus, in a quite direct sense, where "the oral tradition is a visual memory passed down from one generation to another in images, . . . haiku is particularly well suited to carrying those visual images forward" (Ford 2009, 347). And where the oral tradition is complemented by a graphic tradition, through which combination the ritual, spiritual, and intellectual practice and content that derives from the visionary tradition is secured and transmitted, the haiku is its own image in words, or combination of image and words, "'destined to *halt language*' . . . to 'act . . . on the very root of meaning, so that this meaning will not melt, run, internalize, become implicit, disconnect'" (Barthes, qtd. by Hein 2012, 116). Indeed, we remember here that while writing—as a mechanism for stasis and a tool of colonialism—is a recurring target in a variety of ways for Vizenor, it is not just writing; more broadly, his imagist poetics paradoxically drives toward the halting of language, the halting of narrative, such that the "moment [should allow] the reader to 'enter' into the perspective of the narrator, *see what she sees*, and hence participate in the experience" (Sarkowsky 2012, 103). What this articulates is a shift from language to form, from textual to graphic, that prioritizes sight and the thing seen. In a more recent essay this shift is discernible in Vizenor's use of quotations from Diane Glancy's *Designs in the Night Sky*. Early on in the essay he approvingly quotes: "But writing the words of a story kills the voices that gather in the sound of the storytelling" (2010, 47). Toward the end of the essay, however, he returns to Glancy to cite: "I begin to think the books want me here. They want me to hear what they say. They talk from the written word. Maybe writing doesn't kill the voice" (50). Thus, writing, itself a graphic form, paradoxically becomes the means of effacing itself, re-presenting the voice and, crucially, the vision of the witness; Vizenor, then, seeks a way of using writing that simultaneously functions as writing and channels a form of alternative literacy more closely associated with orality.

As such, the proximity of haiku to the dreamsong is matched by its proximity in Vizenor's descriptions to the pictomyth, where he writes in *South of the Painted Stones* that "the word pictomyth is used by the author of this book to mean the believable anishinabe pictures of myths or the believable anishinabe myths of pictures. The author believes a pictomyth has more sense than a song picture" (1963, 115). This "gloss," writes Ford "suggests that the image, not the song, is what renders the myth believable or at least what gives it 'more sense'" (2009, 346). Or, more accurately perhaps, it is the combination of song and image that produces, or re-produces, the momentary event. Vizenor has long had a term for this effect—"word cinemas," allowing for the "stacking [of] visual images" (Blaeser 1996, 182) in an aggregative mode that ensures "the image, the event, the action, or description is broader than what is grammatically allowed" (Vizenor qtd. in Blaeser 1996, 182). That such a methodology indeed works to break free of the limits of language, the limits of writing, is true. But as is repeatedly demonstrated throughout such theorization of his process, it is not solely to the oral that this movement proceeds, but to the visual, and it is not just the voice but the image on which it relies. The relationship between the two in Vizenor's thought is neither entirely separate nor wholly elided. Rather, to borrow from David J. Carlson's discussion of the "imagic moment" in Vizenor's "analogical" thinking in relation to Anishinaabe political subjectivity, the two exist "in a dialectical state of transmotion—relating, but not collapsing, the two locations" (2016, 73).

Vizenor alludes frequently to the power of the pictograph in his work: indirectly in his imagism; directly through description; and literally in the representations of pictographs and scrolls that appear in texts like *Touchwood* and *Summer in the Spring* (see chapter 5). His visual references, however, are by no means restricted to "traditional" or Anishinaabe-only forms. They include the calligraphy of Haruko Isobe and John W. Horns and the ink paintings of Judith Horns Vizenor in *Raising the Moon Vines*, for instance. Japanese Shunga paintings and woodblock prints, a host of European modernist painters and sculptors, the artists of the Santa Fe Indian School, and a number of twentieth- and twenty-first-century Anishinaabe artists such as George Morrison and David Bradley appear frequently across his oeuvre. Among these various references, I wish to pause briefly on one example of his evocation of ledger art.

Productive of imagic moments, ledger art is often read as bridging precontact traditions with emergent forms in what Vizenor might term literary or artistic modernity. Political prisoners held at Fort Marion in Florida in the 1870s were given used ledger books and a range of art materials—obtained through trade elsewhere on the Plains—and, on backgrounds of lined pages and even inventories, they painted and drew scenes in vivid colors. Taking traditional forms of expression and recording—the pictographic representation of events, encounters, brave deeds, visions, and battles—and new vehicles for their expression through the materials themselves, this art form is seen by numerous commentators as a transitional form to a variety of other, contemporary forms of visual expression.[7] One of those critics, Anna Blume, describes some of the drawings as "weav[ing] themselves in and project[ing] themselves over the logic and space of writing" (1996, 42), a description that has immediate resonance with the culturally palimpsestic quality of much of the material discussed above. Vizenor has claimed, in this regard, that ledger art "is the continuance of a new warrior tradition" (1998, 178).[8] While the form itself has continued to evolve in such a way that renders that definition limiting, Vizenor's stress on transmotion (rather than transition) as an ever-moving, ever-evolving sense of Native sovereignty remains implicit, complicating the conventional if equally ambivalent narratives that stress the ledger artists' gradual assimilation, teasing out the active Native presence in the trial run of Captain Richard Henry Pratt's assimilation program that would come to be vigorously pursued at the Carlisle Indian Industrial School in the following decades. David Penney outlines the process in terms that are worth highlighting here when, describing the commercial images painted by the Kiowa Zotom at Fort Marion, he notes that "the novel experiences and means of Zotom's expression . . . remain no less authentic than those of the many artists who inscribed images on the cliffs at Writing-On-Stone [in Alberta] centuries before" (2004, 117). Meanwhile, Leuthold explains that "as individual rather than tribal expressions, these paintings—often signed—coincided with Western assumptions that artworks should be unique and creative: that they should reveal the hand of their maker" (1998, 80–81). While Leuthold's general claim is true—in that signatures, often glyphic themselves, can be found in many of the books, Denise Low-Weso brings greater nuance to this phenomenon, explaining that "multiple artists worked in the same book, even sometimes on the same page, suggest[ing] that the production of drawings was a social event, with men working together and no doubt examining and commenting on each others' pictures. Several glyphic signatures appear in most of these early ledgers" (2006, 86). In other words, though now recognizable to "Western" art history, Low-Weso's intervention indicates far less of a "gap" between the aesthetic practice these men continued and the line of acculturation implicit in Leuthold's claim. Nevertheless, and in either iteration, these imagic moments, perhaps, describe a form that articulates the literary modernity with which Vizenor has long been occupied.

He addresses this complex set of historical and cultural transactions in a poem in *Almost Ashore*. Titled "Blue Horses," the poem references the bright blue horses that run through the pages of ledger books:

painted horses
prison riders
by morning
blue in the canyons
green and brown
western posts
forever mounted
in ledger art
. . .
ledger mounts
blue horses
ride again
with franz marc
chagall
kandinsky
and quick to see (25)

We can take at least two things from this poem in the context established here. The first is that the poem describes a form of resistance, juxtaposing the vibrancy and vivacity of the horses and riders in the first stanza with the sense of enclosure, imposition, and envy of the third, leaving the riders outriding the processes of nomenclature and classification that seek to fix the images and their creators in a static museum moment, indeed to write the Indigenous subject out altogether. As such, it manifests a form of "engaged resistance," which the phrase's coiner, Dean Rader, describes as "a fundamentally indigenous form of aesthetic discourse that engages both Native and American cultural contexts as a mode of resistance against the ubiquitous colonial tendencies of assimilation and erasure" (2011, 1).

And the second is to stress the transformational aspect of transmotion, understanding the process as reciprocal, seeing the motifs in ledger art and its traditional precursors as transcending ethnic or cultural boundaries, as possessing their own life. That life brings ledger artists such as Howling Wolf Honanisto and the contemporary Salish-Kootenai artist Jaune Quick-to-See Smith into contact with non-Native artists—clearly connecting the animal leitmotifs in the primitivist and spiritual enthusiasms of Der Blaue Reiter artists and the folk-art influence and heavy symbolism of Marc Chagall's work to a dynamic, possibly dialectical, continuum that contains the horses that appear in the work of both Smith and Honanisto. Writing of the ledger tradition among the Northern Cheyenne, Denise Low-Weso observes: "The actual images are to a degree mnemonic and are completed by historic documentation, oral tradition, and further, Gerald Vizenor suggests, an intangible 'fourth dimension,' or 'presence'" (2006, 85). Connoted in part by the color blue—an inescapably symbolic color in the Vizenor oeuvre, tied to transformation, spirit, energy—that "fourth dimension" also effects a connection between entities separated by time and space but nevertheless "present" to one another. In "'Wanton and Sensuous' in the Musée du Quai Branly," for instance, James Mackay quotes from Chagall's autobiography: "Perhaps my art, I thought, is a wild art, a blazing mercury, a blue soul leaping up onto my canvases" (2015, 176). The correspondence, not only in the color, but in the somewhat maverick jouissance, between Chagall's and Vizenor's expression will be picked up again in Vizenor's portrayal of Dogroy Beaulieu in *Shrouds of White Earth* (see chapter 5).

Indeed, in his insightful analysis of that relationship in *Shrouds*, David J. Carlson argues:

> We should note the connection between Chagall and Native Ledger Art (a link that comes up elsewhere in the novel) and its pairing with the connection between Dogroy and Euro-American painters such as Kandinsky, Marc (one could plug Otto Dix into the list), and, of course, Chagall. In this web of analogies, we see something of the dialectics of transmotion, as these figures are placed in mutually defining, constitutive relations where they enter into each other in fundamental ways without collapsing into each other. (2016, 167–68)

That sense of entering into without collapsing one another is evident in the poem above, too, wherein the titular blue horses become, themselves, that presence of the fourth dimension, caught in an imagic moment, where the latter, Carlson explains, "articulate[s] the relationship between [Vizenor's] own transnational aesthetics and his evolving understanding of Anishinaabe sovereignty" (161; see chapter 5 of *Imagining Sovereignties* for further discussion of these concepts). If we read the poem in terms of one such moment, through the mutual recognition across boundaries of space and time implied in the "meeting" of nineteenth-century Native artists, Franz Marc, Chagall, Wassily Kandinsky, and Quick-to-See Smith, it arguably generates an analogue to the haiku/dreamsong aesthetic described above, in which the ledger art, with its visual cues taken from Plains practices and its "textual" vehicle from materials on offer that mark an "assent to the new"—an X mark—echoes the transitions of Vizenor's own aesthetic practice. Vizenor's ironic use of the word "primitive," then, implicates both commercial and museum taxonomies in a transaction not recognized by the art itself. The poem, in other words, as Vizenor later explores in greater depth in *Shrouds of White Earth* and *Blue Ravens* in particular, refuses the temporal and inferred cultural hierarchy of "primitive" origins and "modern/ist" borrowings to suggest an affinity that recognizes Native agency in exchange and Native sovereignty and liberation in art.

Pictopoetry: Toward Ekphrasis

Another proponent of haiku, Kimberly Blaeser has turned in her recent work to two other vehicles for her own experimentation with verbal-visual transaction. In this final section of the chapter I will look at a couple of recent examples of Blaeser's "Pictopoems"—poems that effect conversation with, reflect, and reflect on photographs—before moving on to look more explicitly at her recent ekphrastic poems alongside Armand Garnet Ruffo's 2015 book of poetry *The Thunderbird Poems*, a collection that responds directly, ekphrastically, to the paintings of renowned Anishinaabe artist Norval Morrisseau. In ending with ekphrasis, I bring this chapter full circle to my starting point in the avowedly explicit visual turn of this recent Ojibwe poetry. While Heid Erdrich's "Pre-Occupied" is not ekphrastic in an immediate sense, I will also return to it because it sits well alongside those poems I look at here for the interplay of word and image—in this case including the river, the spiral, the city, stills of comic books including scenes from "Superman"—in ways that emphasize a derivation of meaning from their interaction. Where Erdrich's poem effects what Mishuana Goeman calls a "spatial intervention," troubling and even decolonizing such varied spaces as the urban landscape, the Occupy movement, and popular cultural depictions of *indians*, the examples offered here from Blaeser's and Ruffo's work perform a more subtle, formal intervention, in their similar sensory demand to read (the words), see (the images, both literal and described), and hear (the stories implicit in the interaction). Although they have neither the soundtrack nor the animation, these poems perform similarly to the way Blaeser discusses Native photography's ability to "disrupt straight representation and employ techniques to engage the viewer in the imagining of . . . meaning" (2015, 165). In other words, it is in the deployment and interdependence of more than one signifying or expressive medium and the vitality of their connection that "truth," "meaning," or "vision" is attainable and through which these works most resoundingly function as "figurative acts of liberation, recovery, and resistance" (Blaeser 2012a, 332).

Such a figurative act is explicitly performed in Blaeser's poem "Framing." Published as a copy of the photo followed by a prose poem in "Nexus of Connections," Blaeser has also produced this poem in a singular setting, wherein the photograph—an Irwin Brothers studio portrait titled "Mabel Mahseet, Comanche" from around the turn of the twentieth century—is literally framed by the words of the prose poem. The image features a young Comanche woman posed in an ornate chair, her body at an angle to the camera but her face head on. Her head and upper body are enclosed by a large wooden frame, which rests on the arm of the chair. Rather than entirely contained, however, her right arm and long hair project through the frame and rest also on the arm of the chair. In a discussion of the photo, Blaeser comments on the way the image "works against Native objectification by seeming to advertise Mabel Mahseet's subjectivity" (2015, 170). Intended, she says, to "disrupt the boundary between image and reality" (170) the photograph's ironic nod to its own artifice militates against the romantic portrayal of *indians* that renders Native subjects absent in their own presence. Blaeser might have gone further. She records Mahseet's "somber and unsmiling" visage, later again referring to her "solemn face" (170). Although I am wary of overreading such images—photos so often tempt a form of intentional fallacy, encouraging us to read in posed faces a whole range of affect that suits the critic's or viewer's own projections—I nevertheless see a brightness in Mahseet's visage that suggests recognition, if not even instigation, of the visual play. Indeed, to lay out other possibilities, her expression is also redolent of the kind of quizzical look that may be questioning the photographer's actions—a sense that she knows she is involved in something unusual, that the self-reflexive quality of the composition is entirely the photographer's and that his model is a consenting but not entirely complicit subject. The ambiguity of that knowingness (is her face solemn, self-assured, quizzical?) nevertheless belies what Blaeser sees as a bringing together of "both the practice of Indian tourism as manifested in the understood desire for romanticized representation and the act of resistance through ironic commentary that disrupts the possibility of such a consumable construction" generated through her own poetic reclamation (2015, 171).

In Blaeser's broadsheet version, the photograph sits squarely in the middle of the page, with the poem surrounding it—the title forming the top of the frame, the first line level with the top edge of the image, and the poem's text wrapped around the image to provide the other three sides.[9] The first stanza, ending "just another sepia memory with reality leeching away like a winding red stream from a cracked inkwell," conjures a lament for the museological *indian*, just "a file number in a Western History collection of classic invented identities," whose tragic lot sees her captured, "shot" dead by the projection of European fantasy. This stanza, however, is literally bisected by the photograph itself—such that it is impossible to read the lines without the eyes traveling over the image repeatedly. That the stanza is also exactly level with—and takes up the height of—the framed head and shoulders of Mabel Mahseet emphasizes that focal point as both that which is being described and that which contests the description. The second stanza, the first half of which is still bisected by the bottom half of the photograph, underlines this relationship, its first line cut into two halves that read "The irony of / American gothic: a." As a prose poem, the enjambment is arguably less significant than that bisection. "The irony" refers both to the preceding image-text relationship and to the American gothic of its second half. Gesturing both to the incongruity of the Comanche woman (the "American") and the ornate Victorian chair (the "gothic"), the phrase also cannot help recalling Grant Wood's satirical portrait *American Gothic*, underpinning that sense of knowingness and defiance in the subject's confounding of a viewer's expectation of portraiture. Just as Wood's title raises questions as to both the Americanness and the gothicness of its subject matter, so Blaeser's nod subtly envelops the scene in a host of intriguing questions, questions that tease apart the assumptions behind such portraiture, as well as behind the "salvage" agenda that drove so much ethnographic portraiture of the nineteenth and early twentieth centuries.

That salvage work, of course, stemmed directly from the ideological construction of the vanishing American, in which, in full gothic mode, the *indian* becomes specter to the invention of America—a haunting presence whose physical absence legitimizes American settlement producing what Vizenor calls "the apophasis of the native other in ethnographic portraiture" (1998, 155). The irony here, then, also pertains to the way Mahseet's agency refuses the narrative such portraiture conventionally invokes. As Blaeser goes on to write in the poem (with the double virgule indicating the break effected by the photograph), "this / *ogichidaakwe* // breaks out, her / wavy waist-length // hair, deliberately / draped over one // corner of a large / wood frame, reaches beyond the captured image." Again, placement enhances the resistant tone of that ironic commentary. "Ogichidaakwe," set alone on the left hand side of the image, means "ceremonial headwoman" according to *The Ojibwe People's Dictionary*. Set alone as it is, its emphasis on her power—in both the sense of political community and imaged agency—is analogous to her frame-breaking pose, where here it breaks down the oppressive frame that Vizenor calls the "ornamentation of interimage dominance" (1998, 155). Rather than "pos[ing] in silence at the obscure borders of the camera," Mahseet, as she is reclaimed in Blaeser's poem, breaks out of embordered obscurity, her defiant gaze rendering the event (both of the sitting and, more clearly, of the commentary on that sitting) an imagic moment in which she challenges, rather than submitting to, the "simulation of the other as the *indian*" to establish her own narrative presence (Vizenor 1998, 155, 158). Mahseet, Blaeser contends, "becomes a warrior woman in [Blaeser's] own native language" (2015, 171). Her hair and skirt "become the swift pony on which she . . . rides her escape. . . . Warrior woman. *Animwewebatoo*. Run away making noise" ("Framing"). As such, "the poem recounts both speaking resistance and symbolic escape," countering through the mutually interruptive interplay of image and text the visuality of the *indian* (Blaeser 2015, 171).

Another pictopoem, "*Ikwe-niimi*: Dancing Resistance," brings text and image together in the invocation of the dance itself. The commentary, its subject, and the image of the object invoked, a jingle dress, combine to actualize a fuller perceptual reality than either words or picture alone. In his "Envoy to Haiku," Vizenor writes that "oral stories must be heard to endure" (1994a, 62), a line that Blaeser uses as epigraph to "Nexus of Connections" (2012a, 331). In "*Ikwe-niimi*," Blaeser goes some way to demonstrating a method prevalent in what I have discussed in this chapter in which apprehension of the written text is rendered multisensory through each writer's ability to engage us in different ways of seeing as we read. There is, of course, a literalness to this process in the pictopoem, as image and text cross-refer repeatedly: as one reads, so one sees the image in the periphery; as one looks at the image, so are the words an inescapable object of vision. Before sense or meaning even intervene, then, the "picture" is made complete by that conjunction of the pictorial and the written.

They do not, of course, make a perfect analogue to the physical presence of the dress or dancer and the physical presence of spoken language, but in the sense that they invoke the performance, conjuring a resonant trace of the heard and enabling a specific view of the poem's object, they offer an oratorical gesture. That gesture, then, enacts the moment of engaged resistance to the static signifier, much like the interaction between ironic commentary and image in "Framing," and also recalls the multiple interactions of graphic, oral, and critical impulse in Teuton's formulations, wherein the juxtaposition and combination of visual and verbal destabilizes the "truth" capacity of either and calls on the reader-viewer to engage in a more complex act of reading. Blaeser herself insists that this kind of "attempt to throw language or image into connection . . . often characterizes the Native creative process" (2012a, 333). Echoing the deconstructive frames of Vizenor's processes, she continues: "Language leads us to the non-verbal. Image is sign, trace. Words and picture finally dissolve into gesture. . . . As readers, listeners, or viewers, we are invited into an experience that moves beyond the writing on the page, the image, or the spoken. We arrive at a dynamic nexus of connection" (333). This juxtapositionary form, then, echoes for Blaeser the function of haiku in its will to move the reader/viewer beyond the sign to the experience of the moment.

The actual text of *"Ikwe-niimi"* further gestures toward this paradoxically ethereal materiality in its first sentence: "365 jingles in rows upon my dress / turned by the hands of one who deserted / escaped a mandated Pipestone education."[10] Pipestone Indian School was closed in 1953, and the jingle maker in question fled "266 miles looking backwards for pursuit . . . migrating like *maang* relatives by moonlight."[11] A singular act of resistance in itself, this act establishes a triad of generational connection through continuance. In the second stanza, for instance, the ribbons that hold the jingles to the dress are "colorful strips cut tied and threaded / stitched by the laughing women of my childhood." Those women, we are told, "earned 2 dollars and 25 cents for piece-stitching geese aprons." Undaunted by such labor, their "stiff fingers tapped drum beats to sew by." In the final stanza, the flight, the laughter, and the drum beats give way to the swish and sound of *zaangwewe-magooday* itself, the jingle dress, "ancient medicine dress /

silver-coned legacy sounding the cleansing voice of rain." The photograph depicts the right-hand shoulder and chest area of the dancer, a V-shaped line of red and silver jingles hanging from red ribbon attached to an orange ribbon stitched in its own V shape shoulder to shoulder across the tan-colored dress. Above it, a red and a brown ribbon follow the same line. It has a lightness to it that belies the weight of its history; similarly the text carries a heaviness of emotion—though not without the lightness of laughter, and free of a sense of victimry—that belies the lightness of the image. Together, they connote survivance in, as the poem's closing lines have it, the "145th White Earth Nation celebration pow-wow / the weight of *anishinaabeg* history on my back / a dress made light by resistance—this healing an art."

In the two recent essays I have cited here, Blaeser explores her own engagement with palimpsest and, to a lesser degree, ekphrasis. Both techniques—the overlaying and collaging of elements, and the reprisal of one form of art (usually visual) through another (usually literary)—speak profoundly to the multilayered, multiperspectival, and multisensory elements that Blaeser identifies as core aspects of Anishinaabe literary-artistic sensibility. Further, she argues that "ultimately, we have survived as Native peoples partly because our literary traditions are embedded with our nationhood" (2012a, 336). That embedding, she continues, was unambiguously destabilized through the transcription and translation of Native oral performances. In the sense that such literary traditions pertained to "healing rites, our community structures, our relationships to place and subsistence economies . . . woven into the tribal stories, songs, and dances," they were also inherently deterritorialized, removed from their sites of embodied practice by the development of print culture. Thus, she suggests, the "colonization of orature and literature is as real as the colonization of land" and indeed bodies (336). Her own particular poetic gestures, then, like the haiku before them and the poetic and figurative X marks with which this chapter began, figure a decolonizing aesthetic through a reclamation of forms, from the static, alphabetic text-bound to the dynamic, relational, transmotional, and recursively reinterpretative forms described here. Its result, or, at least, one of its results, is an "artistic necessity in Native creative works as they strive to counter colonial discourse and image by writing over, writing through, or importantly, *writing differently*" (334; emphasis added), evoking an alternative literacy in the combination of graphic, oral (or at least invocations of the oral), and critical practice.

Such reclamation of form as decolonizing praxis carries us next to the reexpressions and translations of two key twentieth-century artists—Daphne Odjig and

Norval Morrisseau—in works by two vital contemporary poets: Margaret Noodin and Armand Garnet Ruffo. While it is Ruffo's book of poetry in response to the work of Morrisseau that brings me to this point, Noodin's poem is too lovely not to dwell on, at least briefly. "Waanimazinbiigananke / Writing Images in Circles" was presented at the Forty-First Algonquian Conference in 2009 (under her previous name of Noori). Part of a paper subtitled "The Way Daphne Odjig Writes Circular Images," the poem is, according to Susan Berry Brill de Ramirez "a journey poem about the powers of art and language to bring persons, times, and worlds together, as Odjig did in her art and as Noodin does in her poem." In full, it reads:

Maajamigad maage maajtaamigad
It is leaving or it is beginning

ezhi-dibaajimoying name giizis miinwa dibikigiizis?
the way we tell stories under the sun and the night sun?

Ezhinaagwaziyaang ina n'mishomisinanig miinwa nokomisinanig?
Do we look like our grandfathers and grandmothers?

Nd'shkitoomi waabmaa'angidwa ezhi waabmaa'awad
Can we see them the way they saw them

anzhenii gii miinigoig kina enaandeg ziigidiwiigwaas, waasawaaskone, miskopskido-skine biinojinsing?
the angels who gave us the colors of wrinkled birchbark, far lit flowers and pink elbows of babies?

Nd'shkitoomi waabmaa'angidwa ina
Can we see them the way they saw them

niizh-ochaakanag niimiiwag dibishko baapaaseog bakadewaad deakogewaad?
two spirits dancing like woodpeckers hungry and knocking?

Giisphin maamwi-sagajigaaboying oshki niizhing aakiiong.
If we walk together in these two new worlds

mii sa gonemaa ingoding wii depsiniying.
perhaps then we will be satisfied.

Nd'aawmi miigisag negwikeong, migiziag mitigwaking, anongansag giizhigong.
We are shells in the sand, eagles in the forest, stars in the sky.

Maajaayaang pane maajtaayaang pane.
We are always leaving, we are always starting. (Hele and Valentine 2013, 205–6)[12]

Unlike Ruffo's poetic tribute, Noodin does not draw on ekphrasis, but on a common spirit of Ojibwe arts in which the verbal (story-telling's) emphasis on the visual (vision, the visionary, the fact of sight, and art) conjoin in the act of "walk[ing] together in these two new worlds." That act of walking together in turn bespeaks connections between material and spiritual ("the angels who gave us the colors"), between the relational nexus of land and community in its fullest sense ("We are shells in the sand"), and between generations ("Can we see them the way they saw them"). Framed by that repetition of a movement that is both perpetual ("It is leaving" / "We are always leaving") and yet centered in space and time ("it is beginning" / "we are always starting") the poem addresses Noodin's own assertion that "Anishinaabe literature is that memory of collective motion shaped by the place in which it originates." Art—both the art of the poem and the art it honors, which we take to include both Odjig's and the ancestral forms to which it gestures—connote the "legacy that continues, the need to remember and connect in ways that mark the trail of the Anishinaabeg" (2014b, 176). Marking the trail in literature thus recalls, again in decolonial spirit, the marks on the landscape that embody the presence of Anishinaabeg.

"Mark[ing] the trail of the Anishinaabeg" configures Ruffo's *The Thunderbird Poems* (2015), a book-length tribute to Morrisseau published shortly after his biography of the artist, *Norval Morrisseau: Man Changing into Thunderbird* (2014). Collectively, they continue a pattern set in Ruffo's two previous books of poetry, *Grey Owl: The Mystery of Archie Belaney* (1997) and *At Geronimo's Grave* (2001). The former, a poetic biography, mixes fiction and historical fact in its examination of the Englishman turned "Native" Canadian's life and legacy. The latter, meanwhile, takes the life of the Chiricahua Apache leader as a launchpad into exploration of Native history and identity. In all three cases, the poet takes a single exemplary life as both touchstone and creative energy. The difference with Morrisseau, perhaps, is the sense of cultural affinity that develops in the engagement of one Ojibwe artist with another, albeit working in different media, and, of course, the directness of ekphrastic engagement of the poet with the artist, the poetry with the art. In *Norval Morrisseau*, Ruffo quotes an early article in *The Gazette*, in which Morrisseau reads how his thirty-one painting show at Galerie Cartier in Montreal in the mid-1960s affords viewers the privilege of "shar[ing] in a fading culture's last secrets" and the opportunity to "learn of a forgotten people's rites and dreams" (2014, 128–29).

While the tenor of the piece indicates a settler-centric (Canadian in this instance) vision of the vanishing *indian* there is an underlying echo in Ruffo's account of the artist's motivations. When, for instance, Galerie Cartier's owner Henry Schwarz proposes collaboration on a book of Ojibwe stories, "it is another chance to preserve more of his great culture on paper" (2014, 129). For Morrisseau, though, that process of preservation is neither for the titillation of non-Native audiences, nor is it in the service of a dying culture. Rather, he quotes "his grandfather Potan, . . . 'the time has come for us to write and to record the story of our people; not only for ourselves but also for our white brothers so that they will be able to understand and respect us'" (129–30). Ironically, and in stark contrast to *Legends of My People*, the book he produced with the aid of Selwyn Dewdney in 1965, *The Windigo and Other Tales of the Ojibways* (1969) positions Schwarz as "author," eviscerating "the voices of Morrisseau's grandfather and the other wise old men" and crediting Morrisseau himself simply as "illustrator" (Ruffo 2014, 130). That tension, then, between the art (and stories) Morrisseau created and drew from and the market—beyond the community and landed sources of origin—that the art circulated in is palpable. For Schwarz, Morrisseau's pictures illustrate an agencyless past, one whose "voices" are now best interpreted through the living present of a dominant culture. For Morrisseau, such ventures as exhibition and book-making represent an apparently always risky venture in continuity. He "became the conduit for cultural transfer," according to Gerald McMaster, "positioning himself as a new communicator or 'image-maker'" (2005, 146). As such, McMaster continues, "in Morrisseau's case we see a kind of post-reservation act, where tradition is transformed into a new strategy [that] maintain[s] a self-conscious link with the past and intentionally oppose[s] repeated efforts . . . to sever Native people from their roots" (146). And it is that continuity-that-is-also-resistance in Ruffo's account that comes to the fore in that moment. Where *The Gazette* suggests that he offers a "valuable ethnological document," or an artifactual illustration, Morrisseau is more interested in process and presence: "Now that imagery and composition are second nature to him, he has to go deeper. When he paints the shaking tent, it is *his* ceremony. . . . Just as when he paints a thunderbird, it is a thunderbird he has seen through *his* own visions. No more surface stuff. To paint a shaman he has to become a shaman" (2014, 129).

It is emphatically within that tradition of the visionary artist that Ruffo's *Thunderbird Poems* confirm Morrisseau's place. Ruffo describes his own process as a "natural and spontaneous response"—the writing of poetry in reflection of the art that "moved [him] in such a manner" (2015, front matter). In other words, and although Ruffo concentrated on "tying the paintings to events in Morrisseau's life and, accordingly, to the artist's sources of inspiration, including Ojibway epistemology," it is his own form of intuitive response, his desire to "let the paintings themselves determine the content of the poetry," that drove the work, echoing that intuitive aspect of Morrisseau's own process. In one painting from the late 1950s / early 1960s, titled *Ancestors Performing the Ritual of the Shaking Tent*, a composition that is somewhat different from those iconic images easily recognizable as Morrisseau's work, three figures—one seated and two standing—are set before a depiction of the eponymous tent. Ruffo's poem by the same name begins:

> You are standing outside the ceremony
> gazing upon three red-hooded members of
> the secret
> Midewewin Medicine Society
> in the midst of the mysterious
> and powerful Jeeskum,
> the shaking tent ceremony.

Going on to describe the figures—one drumming, one shaking a rattle (albeit the rattle is not immediately obvious in the picture), the third "presumably praying"—the first two stanzas of the poem thus describe, directly, the scene the viewer beholds. The viewer, Ruffo describes in a note, "seem[s] to be floating above the scene as though we are dreaming it or someone inside the tent is dreaming us," connoting that very visionary quality that Morrisseau would later take to the heart of his work.

Stanza three, meanwhile, moves into the cultural terrain of the image, sharing detail that the casual observer cannot see. It describes a fourth figure, a "conjurer" within the tent or wigwam, "the one who makes things tremble," while stanzas four and five go on to describe the ceremonial process itself, and stanza six its conclusion—if successful—as the spirits' responses to the conjurer's questions "lift[] the tent off the ground." Here, then, the poem transcends the common bounds of ekphrasis to explicate detail that the image itself does not yield. The painting, in its turn, articulates a sense of captivation on behalf of the viewer—including the sense of being outside the scene under observation—that the poem, in its ethnological "interruption," foregoes. The poem is as unusual as the painting, in that just as Morrisseau's better-known paintings tend to emphasize the content rather than the form of visions, stories, and ceremonies, so too Ruffo's verse tends to respond to the seen and felt, and to the life of the artist, rather than the known but arcane detail of such events.

In a moving instance of the former, Ruffo recalls one of Morrisseau's many paintings based on the Anishinaabe great migration—this one titled *The Great Migration, 1992*. The painting includes a depiction of the artist himself, with a family in one of four canoes, and Ruffo's poem reflects (on) both the detail of the painting and its cosmological journey and a point in the artist's life at which his years of alcoholism and his recent episode (in the late 1980s) of living on the streets have begun to catch up with his health (see Ruffo 2014, 250–60). While the opening stanza sets up the migration story itself ("A story told and retold long before the tidal / wave descended"), the poem's ekphrastic aspect is most direct in its second stanza:

What we see is canoe upon canoe heading
west on a migration
of centuries. Families and clans s-t-r-e-t—c-h-e-d
by the thousands, searching for a new life,
birth, rebirth, transformation,
a community of human and other-than—human,
Anishinaabek, birds, bears, trees, all
moving in unison, in beauty.

Further descriptive details of the painting follow in stanza three: "A yellow-eyed Medicine Snake swims alongside / Happiness is a bouquet of butterflies, the / ocean is emerald." Stanza three itself, however, draws us out of the painting and the stories it depicts to place the viewer in the real-time moment of a gallery viewing. This temporal shift has already been recorded by interstanza lines that gesture directly to the present-moment life of the artist himself: "By now his health is gone" between the first two stanzas, and "By now there is no room for darkness in his life" between second and third. The "By now" of these intervening lines itself evokes a storytelling form of temporal direction. "By now" connotes the present of the telling, as well as the "now" of Morrisseau's life in 1992. The moment of apprehension of the painting, then, becomes a continuous present to invoke both the story of the migration and the event of its painting, collapsing Morrisseau's life and the visionary document into a spiritual continuum. Add to this, in stanza three, the moment of the painting's exhibition, too, and, thus, the poet's apprehension of it and subsequent inspiration. It reads:

> In the gallery we speak so low the mice in
> the walls barely hear
> us. We watch navigation and wish we
> understood the signs
> that appear like rainbows before our eyes
> and open us to possibility.
> The great sweet-water ocean where the
> Pull of demi-gods is
> unrelenting. We dip our heads into its
> blueness and stare for hours.

Rendering that looking a moment that repeats the visionary moment of the artist himself, the poem closes with a pointer to the Anishinaabe migration and its documented legacy, wherein "We know the people stop according to plan / to paint / their journey on rock." As the poet finishes this stanza with recognition of what "We know" about the migration, and the separation of clans and ultimate survival of the people, he closes the poem itself with a line that further imagines that temporal elision: "Guided by the shaman-artist, we witness a / dream of faith." The shaman-artist—his dream of faith—in this moment describes the scene portrayed as well as its portrayal, marking the trail that leads directly from the pictographic document on rock to Morrisseau's own painting. In that instant, both artists, both moments, become present to the onlooker. It is precisely in that sense of continuity, contemporaneity, that the works perform their resistance to narratives of absence, yet they are not concerned with absence; they do not counter hegemonic portrayal so much as bear witness to survivance, participating in moments of exchange in which image and text cohere and create new meanings. Like the migration itself, these images and the words that frame and respond to them participate in the

circulation of Anishinaabe ideas. To address them, in word and in image, is to per-
petuate both an aesthetic and an ethics of transmotion that means movement itself
implicitly suggests return, and that displacement is implicitly framed by relation.

Like the returns I describe above, I will close this chapter by cycling back
around to Heid Erdrich's "Pre-Occupied." The poem appears in text form—with a
QR code that can be scanned with a smartphone or tablet that will take the reader
to the video form of the poem—in Heid Erdrich's 2017 book of poetry, *Curator of
Ephemera at the New Museum for Archaic Media*. The sections of the book are framed
as an exhibition—part material, part conceptual—that includes several links to
video poems as well as other examples of ekphrastic response to artworks, such as
"Incantation on a Frank Big Bear Collage," which takes in Big Bear's monumental
Time Zones (Red Owl) (2012); or "Manidoo Giizhikens / Little Spirit Cedar Tree,"
which responds to Hazel Belvo's *Spirit Tree: Survivor* (2013). *Time Zones* measures
over five and a half feet by over thirteen. Made up of ten rows of seventeen small
rectangular vignettes, each collaged onto six-by-eight-and-a-half-inch postcards,
with narrow spaces between each column and row, the overall effect, as Erdrich's
poem's refrain has it, is of a scene "cut by bars, stripes from the American flag"
(2017, 32). The poem's opening line, "Bar the windows, the Red Owl looming into
view," speaks firstly to that gridded format, its barred aesthetic literally disrupting
the "view," fragmenting the field of vision such that the whole cannot be fully,
cohesively apprehended. As one zooms in, however, that barring process continues
in the detail, as images are cut up, sliced, and exploded such that the "assemblage"
becomes a work of reassembling on the part of the viewer. "Looming into view,"
meanwhile, in the backgrounds of the individual barred windows, is the Red Owl,
the logo of the Midwestern grocery store that began life in Rochester, Minnesota,
and, excepting a few local stores, was phased out from 1988.

The piece's title, *Time Zones*, plays on the way Big Bear's collage transports a
myriad different iconic and artistic images as temporally and geographically diverse
as Picasso's *Guernica* (superimposed with photographs of Anne Frank), B. B. King,
nineteenth- and early twentieth-century photographs of Native men and women,
classical sculpture, Marilyn Monroe, Mickey Mouse, and much more, and some of
which elements cut across two or more sections. The mixture of fine art and popular
culture, ethnographic and iconic motifs renders a dazzlingly visually discordant
display that refuses, as much as it admits, comprehension.

The Red Owl logo, with a white-on-black "On Sale" banner below, features as
the one constant throughout the piece, understandable where it is most visible as

a billboard. The postcard, in fact, is an invitation to the solo exhibition of his son, Star Wallowing Bull, *The Art of Star Wallowing Bull* at Minneapolis's Bockley Gallery in 2008. Big Bear's collaging over the top of the original image, however, as well as the fragmented aesthetic, means that it only gradually reveals its full force. To focus in on just one "window," then, reveals that the billboard logo itself is disrupted on the left-hand side by a ledger-style drawing of a battle between Plains warriors and the U.S. cavalry. What it also reveals, subtly, is that there appears to be blood dripping from the bottom left-hand cheek of the owl on the Red Owl logo. Other windows confirm this fact, while in some—where again the owl is more visible than others—it becomes clear that the owl also sheds tears. Closer scrutiny still reveals that the logo is not for the store but for a Red Owl product sold by volume: between the white of the banner and the black of the "On Sale" announcement is a yellow band; to the right of it, four simple numbers illuminate the visual pun. It reads "1876 oz."

When Custer's Seventh Cavalry was decimated in 1876 at the Battle of the Greasy Grass, two key consequences (among many) were invoked. The first was the expansion of the U.S. Army with the express purpose of routing the Plains Nations from their hunting lands and onto reservations. The second was a consolidating of resolute determination among U.S. Army generals to achieve this end no matter the cost (to the Native population). Artistically, perhaps, 1876—or at least that era of the Plains wars—marks an imagic moment; military activity on the Plains is what led to the incarceration of those warriors who would go on to develop the ledger form, for instance. And, despite the success of the Oglala Lakota on those fateful June days, it also marks the escalation of U.S. hostility and the finalizing of the reservation era, a "job" completed by 1890. That sense of the modern is evoked throughout the collage through the multiple invocation of other artists, the photography that further rendered Native people captive, and the popular cultural iconography. That Red Owl both cries and bleeds bespeaks the capitalist despoliation, perhaps, of settler colonialism; the principles of property on which such enterprise is built depend, of course, on the logic of elimination and the notion of terra nullius. Yet this artwork is not a eulogy to victimry, per se. Rather, it conveys a mixture of anger and humor—implicit too in Wallowing Bull's original—which are further illuminated by Erdrich's "Incantation."

The "Incantation" proceeds through alternating line beginnings, between the words "bar" and "cut," its couplets and single lines clipped and terse, a heard echo of the ocular assault the collage presents. Those two words also precisely convey the piece's aesthetic, its bars and cuts producing the fragmented composition that, in turn, produces visual dissonance and series of ironic juxtapositions. Some of those juxtapositions feature in the poem: "Cut the Bog Man so he sits right on Custer's face" its voice incants; "Cut the Blue Period into the blues guitar." While the first speaks for itself, the second describes a vignette in which B. B. King and Picasso's *The Old Guitarist* sit side by side. The painting, then, speaks to the broad influence of modern culture at all levels, both American and international, through a series of visual signifiers that both speak to and limit the contemporary artist. Simultaneously, it illustrates the appropriative absorption of Native peoples through the transformation of the imaged *indian* into that visual grammar. On top of that, it highlights the engagement of Native artists such as Big Bear himself and of course his son, with that visual grammar as a form of resistance through which we glimpse the continuities of visual sovereignty—the power of the visual to tell such stories. The result, paradoxically, is part grim-faced defiance, part celebration, and it is again evoked in the closing of Erdrich's poem, the final six lines of which read:

> Bar the windows, the Red Owl looming into view,
> cut by bars, stripes from the American flag.
> Bar the lines in my poem, the lines of my smile.
> Cut clean with keen comment, slashed and clashed colors.
> Bar the windows, the Red Owl looming into view,
> cut by bars, stripes from the American flag. (2017, 33)

To bar the windows is to utter a call that evokes the image of a property under siege or in danger of criminal entry—or, of course, a prison. The Red Owl looming into view, in turn bespeaks a cultural motif—the owl, who "can be both a threatening sinister power and a benevolent advocate" appears ominous in this instance (Pomedli 2014, 101). Significantly, in the context of settler colonialism, which the association of the red owl with the Battle of the Greasy Grass in Wallowing Bull's postcard image suggests, the owl "is associated with sickness, grief, and death; it can thwart hunting; and it can signify a loss during a game of chance" (101). Just as the U.S. Army was clearing the way for settlement and, particularly, gold prospecting in Paha Sapa, so too the Red Owl figures the relationship between land and capital. An augury, initially, of U.S. losses, "the owl's menacing eye, eerie call, and predatory nature" can, Pomedli continues, "serve as a measuring stick for both individual and community self-examination and correction" (101). That self-examination arguably not forthcoming, one might argue that the augur "looms" again in Wallowing Bull's painting and Big Bear's collage, its blood and tears indicative of the implicit violence of barring and cutting; an extended metaphor, in other words, for the perpetuation of cultural forms of Wolfe's logic of elimination to which Erdrich's poem is an impassioned rejoinder.

Erdrich's defiance in "Incantation" matches the defiance in "Pre-Occupied." The provocative invitation—"Bar the lines in my poem, the lines of my smile. / Cut clean with keen comment, slashed and clashed colors"—reiterates the process of silencing and occluding Native title, self-determination, and even voice, while simultaneously daring the establishment/reader to attempt the feat in the face of ironic defiance. Like "Pre-Occupied," then, the poem's X mark is not so much a cross of assent as a statement of refusal. Lyons argues that "all Indian texts are x-marks," a "totalizing" theory, according to Sinclair, that renders them "acts coerced and influenced by hegemonic (and usually oppressive) forces" (Lyons 2010, 26; Sinclair 2013a, 88). While "every so often an x-mark can be seen escaping from the prison house of dominant discourse" (Lyons 2010, 30), "Pre-Occupied" does not so much "escape" as confront dominant discourse through a mixture of sonic, visual, and textual forms (which even the printed version makes use of through inclusion of the QR code—for those readers, of course, who assent to the technology), the combination of which resonates with Teuton's tripartite oral-graphic-critical impulse, or with the holistic "record" of treaty discourse championed by the likes of John Borrows, who, among others, calls for a revaluation of treaty agreements such as that represented by the Two Row Wampum and the later Treaty of Niagara (1764) through oral and alternative textual recollections of such agreements.[13]

Moreover, the animation in the film version of "Pre-Occupied," like the text itself, foregrounds the spiral as a sign of presence and marker of place: "River river river / I never never never / etched your spiral icon in limestone" (Erdrich 2017, 25). In articulating a negative, the poet nevertheless evokes its opposite, the poem—and certainly the video—itself describing the spiralized glyph as a signature of the river that flows through the poem; the poet, as mark maker, thus announces her presence as commemorator of an ancestry that similarly signifies as both located and mobile, which, like the river itself will "Flow flow flow both ways in time" (21). In doing so, she proclaims the right of the "pre-occupied," the "original 100% / who are also 1% more or less" to address that claim as a counterclaim resistant to the settler logic that underpinned the Occupy movement. In failing to adequately engage Indigenous people, or with Indigenous claims—whether land, resources, or laws and despite its methodological similarities to the later Idle No More movement[14]—Occupy rested on settler-colonial assumptions of rights and belonging that demanded, but did not receive, further scrutiny. Moreover, in doing so, it largely un-self-reflexively participated in what Déné scholar Glen Coulthard sees as "a colonial relationship" characterized by "*domination*," in which "interrelated discursive and nondiscursive facets of economic, gendered, racial, and state power . . . structured into a relatively secure or sedimented set of hierarchical social relations . . . continue to facilitate the *dispossession* of Indigenous peoples of their land and self-determining authority" (2014, 57). Ironically, then, in "occupying" Wall Street in the interests of the 99 percent and in protest at the elite, establishment, 1 percent, the failure to address the original occupation of Manhattan and, if you like, the original "heist" of the many by the few further perpetuated colonialist dispossession.[15]

Many Indigenous critics of Occupy called for a change in the movement's terminology to "Decolonize Wall Street," a gesture that would both force reflection on the ongoing nature of U.S. occupation and, of course, refocus agendas around Indigenous justice. The suggested name change implies complicity in a colonial project that many in the Occupy movement would have struggled to recognize. Erdrich's invocation of the 1942 Superman episode "Electric Earthquake" speaks in complex ways to this issue. As she says in the coda "Notes of Pre-Occupied Digression," "In the 1942 cartoon . . . an indigenous (but not stereotypically 'Indian') Mad Scientist is thwarted, of course, by Superman. At one point Clark Kent admits indigenous land claim as 'possibly' valid, but says there's nothing the *Daily Planet* can do about it" (2017, 23). The Native figure, in the course of the episode, kidnaps Lois Lane and effectively reoccupies Manhattan, attempting to topple its skyscrapers, having declared that "Manhattan / rightfully belongs to my people" (Erdrich 2017, 22). The 1930s and 1940s saw a number of Supreme Court decisions that applied the takings clause of the Fifth Amendment to the taking of Native American lands held in fee simple. *United States v. Creek Nation* (1935), for instance, saw the Creek Nation seeking compensation for the appropriation of lands granted in 1833 and lost in 1891 when unceded Creek lands were treated as part of the allotment package of ceded Sac and Fox lands, and distributed as such. Brought in 1926 and argued in 1934, the suit was decided on April 29, 1935, in favor of the Creek, with compensation determined to "include such addition [to the value of the lands at the time of the taking] as may be required to produce the present full equivalent of that value paid contemporaneously with the taking" plus interest of 5 percent per annum (*United*

States v. Creek Nation 1935). Just one of a number of similar high-profile cases in the 1930s, *United States v. Creek Nation* catalyzed further large-scale claims.

The "threat" of Indian land claims in early 1942, then, is expressed in the somewhat paranoiac vein of "Electric Earthquake," which seems at once to acknowledge the legitimacy of the villain's cause ("possibly," says Clark Kent), while everything in the visual and verbal semiotics of the character point to the endeavor to reinvent that "Ignoble Savage" as a thoroughly modern, technologically sophisticated, lone-wolf enemy of the state (Erdrich 2017, 22). While "assenting" to Indigenous modernity, the besuited character very particularly making reference to the persuasive force of "*modern* science" (Fleischer 1942), his portrayal nevertheless recalls and revalidates colonial narratives of settlement. Implicit in Kent's "just what do you expect us to do about it?" is a sense of inevitability on the one hand—a subtle invocation of manifest destiny, perhaps?—and historical weight on the other: the notion, in other words, that whatever legitimacy the complaint may carry, Native people need to accept the current state of the United States and either assimilate or retreat. Both highly pessimistic positions for the all-American hero—an immigrant himself, of course, throwing in his lot with the good (settler) people of the United States (his "what do you expect *us* to do" connoting the people as much as the *Planet*)—his response evinces a whitestream culture of domination that forces us to reflect on the power balance of the later Occupy movement. For Superman is saving Manhattan for the people from a megalomaniac scientist; he acts, in other words, on behalf of settler culture in opposition to the threat of Indigenous land claims. The jarring juxtapositions Erdrich provokes with this alignment of the Superman episode with Occupy is furthered in two ways: the closing dialogue of the cartoon, for instance, sees Clark and Lois aboard a ferry sailing past the Manhattan skyline. "You know Lois," Clark intones, "the old island looks just as good as ever," punching through the irony of that atemporal "ever" or implying that its "goodness" is entirely inherent in its colonization. Lois's reply, meanwhile—"That's right, Clark. Thanks to Superman"—once more implicates the bebriefed superhero in the occupation.[16] As is common to most Superman storylines, this is a tale of two outsiders, one a threat, one an acceptable accomplice co-opted into the state apparatus; neither "American," but one apparently self-serving (that the unnamed villain acts on behalf of his people is not returned to after the opening line), while the other's altruism frames him in the exceptionalist mold. Well, that and the fact that, here at least, he saves that icon of capitalist potential, Manhattan. And the second way in which Erdrich heightens this juxtaposition is in her invocation of the Crash

Test Dummies' "Superman's Song" (1991), which features in text (in italics) and the film (as a sound clip) as a brief interlude: "*Superman never made any money,*" Brad Roberts croons (2017, 21). The clip stops there, but the song continues "For saving the world from Solomon Grundy / And sometime I despair the world will never see / Another man like him," which altruism Erdrich documents in her "Notes."[17] This interjection further aligns the hero with the vexations of the 99 percent, representing a postcapitalist model of altruistic labor that in this case explicitly shores up the wealthy domain of the 1 percent.

Erdrich's underpinning of her critique of both capitalism's and Occupy's colonialist blind spots, and her double deconstruction of popular cultural imagery, with the motifs of the river and its petroglyphic spiral icon, places the poem and indeed the poet both spatially and historically. It simultaneously refuses to assent to modernity in its sociopolitical, settler-colonial pose, eschewing one particular kind of demand for land, resource, and recognition, through an entirely different kind of claim, while proclaiming its modernity precisely through its assertion of continuity with ancestral practices and presences. That latter claim involves the reassertion of forms and values that themselves constitute an X mark as a metaphorical line drawn in the sand. Not the X marks of federal documents that define cadastral boundaries, but as placeholder for nindoodemag evoked by, if not present in, the spiral icons. Further eschewing artificial breaks between tradition and modernity, "Pre-Occupied" reinforces the implied narrative form of the river, indicating both deep time and cyclicity in such lines as "Flow flow flow both ways in time" (21), "River river river Our river / Map of the Milky Way / reflection of stars / whence all life commenced," and finally:

Sorry somehow now I've too much time
Flow flow   flow both ways   story-history-story
There's a river that considers us after all

All time   all hours all decades   all millennia. (22)

X marks, linguistic traces, natural reason, the marks of presence, and their visual cues forge a trail through this body of poetry that itself spans several decades and a vast geographical terrain. The resulting circulatory poetic maps an ethical relation between speakers and specters, spaces and their inhabitants. While Erdrich begins "Pre-Occupied" by noting that she has "never etched your spiral icon in limestone" she closes it with an echo: "River river river / I never never never—but that is not to say that I won't ever" (23). That is, she leaves us with an alternative history as well as an alternative cartography, a history that is cyclical rather than teleological, that is told in the mode of presence—story—and that remains unclosed, unfinished, not so much open to interpretation as open to participation. Countering the negativity of the depiction of Occupy as a facet of capitalist flow, the river image gestures to what artist Dylan Miner calls a "radical migration" highlighting the connections in Anishinaabeakiing rather than the disruptions of history. Moreover, such connection threads through the poetry here, both urban and rural, close to and distant from ancestral lands, reminding us that "a geography of belonging can extend far beyond the limits of tribal origination, ancestral homelands, and childhood homes" (Ramirez 16). And while Clark Kent's response to the "villain's" initial demand reminds us that the settler-colonial/capitalist nexus has neither space nor can it make allowance for the full reality of Indigenous land claims, Erdrich's "that is not to say that I won't ever" unsettles the teleology from Marx's precapitalist Indigene to Occupy's postcapitalist stance. Like the marks of presence and resurgence in the poetry that precedes it, she asserts a defiance born of knowing, understanding, and deploying the storied connections that bridge the colonial rupture without facilely asserting an unbroken continuity or reinforcing the binaries that render Native expression an aesthetics of "'contamination' and 'coercion'" (Sinclair 2013a, 89).

CHAPTER 3

Reckoning Beyond the Crossing/X-ing

Formal Diversity and Visual Sovereignty in Gordon Henry Jr.'s *The Light People*

Where, in the last chapter, I briefly looked at the presence and purpose of haiku and dreamsongs in Gordon Henry Jr.'s 1994 novel *The Light People*, in this chapter I return to that novel to more fully consider the variety of its aesthetic engagements. The narrative relay of *The Light People* gives way repeatedly to different forms of written and spoken narrative and different media from plastic and visual artistic practice in combinations that level the distinction between written, visual, and oral/aural.[1] Although the story is ultimately presented in novel form, it lays heavy emphasis on nonwritten narrative and forms of communicative material production other than writing to drive the critical function of its set pieces. The novel's structure itself contributes to that sense of testing the limits of fiction to give form to Teuton's tripartite relationship between oral, graphic, and critical impulses in the construction of Native narrative. Indeed, by drawing on and seeking to represent both, it speaks directly, as I will elaborate here, to Teuton's insistence that "the oral and graphic are not opposites, but interpenetrating media that, brought into concert by the critical impulse, allow for a flow of ideas that may account for tradition as well as innovation, individuality as well as community, memory as well as record" (2010, 34–35). As such, Henry's novel dexterously reflects two intertwined—and at face value, apparently oppositional—strands. The first very immediately reflects Teuton's own sense that "crucial twentieth- and twenty-first-century literary texts develop a sustained and illuminating critique of the relationship between tradition and modernity through their conceptual and thematic explorations of Indigenous traditions of oral and graphic forms of communication" (2010, xiv). As such, he continues, "Native American literature . . . continues a sophisticated Indigenous critical practice that explores the roles of the individual and the community in the context of survivance, balance, harmony, and peace" (xv). The second effects a dialogue with the Western theoretical tradition, reflecting Henry's interest in European, especially French, philosophy in the latter part of the twentieth century. In doing so, Henry demonstrates both the intellectual richness of an Indigenous visual aesthetic—prioritizing sight, vision, and the visionary as key thematic vehicles—and reorients the assumed hierarchy of critical theory and literary text, which has tended to mean that Native studies scholars have, to paraphrase Henry, privileged the influence of Western theory even as they seek to dismiss or decenter it (Henry, Soler, and Martínez-Falquina 2009, 3).[2] Testing the limits of fiction, then, becomes a test of the limits of culturally specific modes of reading (and writing) and of the relationship between theory and story within Native storytelling traditions. Taking this one step further, it also participates in the process of what Chadwick Allen calls "Indigenous languaging," in which "a single work [creates] different kinds of meaning for different audiences through a combination of visual and aural cues" (2012, 170). That "test" begins and ends with the novel's structure—the "narrative relay" between storytellers and their tales, and between different kinds of narrative praxis.

The careful reader is rewarded with the realization that the "story" as such begins roughly in the middle of the text, providing a backbone in the form of a long string of haiku—some of which were mentioned in the preceding chapter—and in the subsequent "Story as Payment to Bombarto Rose" of the prisoner Elijah Cold Crow's mother, Old Woman Cold Crow. Those haiku correspond more or less loosely to the stories that precede and follow them, effectively creating a circular structure framed by the quest of Oskinaway and his later return to the Fineday reservation. That the core of the novel is provided by that set of allusive and elusive haiku—the so-called prisoner of haiku's interpretation of the Ojibwe dreamsong form—with the stories circling around it reflects Henry's own characterization of Native storytelling, repeated by Kimberly Blaeser in "Native Literature: Seeking a Critical Center" (1993), as a pattern of "sacred concentricity" (57). Part of what

Niigaanwewidam James Sinclair refers to as "a call [to develop] rather than the delivery" of Indigenous-centered critical theory (2013a, 15), Blaeser's brief reference to Henry's otherwise unpublished notion nevertheless speaks volumes about Henry's development of narrative structure and its challenge to conventional novel forms not merely as an act of resistance or "writing back" but as a distillation in novel form of what he sees as key Indigenous narrative and aesthetic characteristics. Blaeser's footnote in another essay, "Writing Voices Speaking," maintains that Henry's coinage "describe[s] the complex dynamics of circularity present in many Native stories" and that he "recognizes in Native life and work a sacred center from which emanate ripples of power and connection." This notion of a sacred center, which she also describes in more profane terms as a "mobile center of consciousness" (1999, 66n2), is entirely apposite for Henry's concentric device. That said center would be "dynamic and thus invoke responses such as return, forgiveness, healing, vision" (66n2) seems further to describe the effective motion of much of the plot that ripples outward just as it relays forward, generating a plot structure that presents differently in both temporal and spatial terms, and figuring narrative "wholeness" both in series, as one would read a conventional written text, and in array, as one more usually expects to apprehend a visual medium.

Furthermore, this notion of concentricity anticipates core Anishinaabe values of "rebirth, motion, presence and emergence" described compellingly by Leanne Simpson (2011a, 144). Sharing the teaching of Maria Campbell, she recounts:

> acts of resistance are like throwing a stone into water.... There is the original splash the act of resistance makes, and the stone (or the act) sinks to the bottom, resting in place and time. But there are also more subtle waves of disruption that ripple or echo out from where the stone impacted the water. These concentric circles are more nuanced than the initial splash, but they remain in the water long after the initial splash is gone. Their path of influence covers a much larger area ... radiating outward for a much longer period of time. (145)

From the initial act of telling the story, then, or putting pen to paper, brush to canvas, the creative act echoes the act of resistance in its dynamic relation to the stone on the river bed and the ripples on the surface. *The Light People* both catalyzes and portrays such action.

All of these images pertain to what Jesse Peters sees as the flux at the heart of Henry's novel. In "'Remember the Last Voice': Motion and Narrative Flux in Gordon

Henry's *The Light People*," Peters notes that "the reader travels through layers of stories towards an understanding of the lineage of the character Oskinaway" and that "the stories move the reader through space and time and connect so that the answer [as to who Oskinaway's father is] becomes much more than simply a name" (2008, 1). This continuous movement and the developing arc of Oskinaway's own self-understanding suggest for Peters that "seeking the knowledge becomes more important than the knowledge itself; it is the movement through the stories which cause the stories [to] become a part of Oskinaway" (1). The accretive aspect of this narrative flux—the gradual aggregation of personal and communal detail, community relationships, and collective history—is itself figured through a number of devices that both serve a practical function in the narrative and evoke the graphic practices of Anishinaabe textual traditions. This chapter will focus largely on three such devices and, in the case of two of them, the artists whose work they introduce us to. The first is a painted stone that crashes through the studio window of Rose Meskwaa Geeshik, a painter whose artistic quest to record and interpret her dream experiences produces paintings evocative, although not imitative, of a range of mid- to late twentieth-century Anishinaabe painters. The second is the visual sovereignty associated with the prisoner of haiku himself, whose artistic activism prior to his jail sentence leads to the re-creation of significant historic moments in the smoke of serial arsons of federal buildings. The third, meanwhile, although not directly associated with an artistic figure as such, involves the recurrence of images of a river and its association, to echo Peters once more, with narrative flux, community cohesion, generative possibility, and travel, or passage more loosely. The river, then, becomes a shifting marker on a map through the real and storied world of Oskinaway's development, featuring as both the site from which his journey begins, when he must loosen his anchor-like grip on an immovable stone, and as a site of struggle over Indigenous and other knowledges, and Indigenous and other technologies at the end of the novel.

Stories, Sculptures, Scrolls

The prominence of the ode'imin—strawberry or heartberry—motif in the closing episodes emphasizes the river's connotations as a mapping fixture in the narrative. While the heartberry is a very common motif in Anishinaabe beading patterns, it is also highly visible in what Selwyn Dewdney famously titled the "Sacred Scrolls" of the Ojibwe and in the numerous stories connected with the midewiwin religious society. In one such example, William Warren explains that the first step in the afterlife involves stopping at "the great Oda-e-min (heart berry), or strawberry, which stands on the roadside like a huge rock, and from which he takes a handful and eats on his way" (1885, 19). Although such connections arguably confirm Blaeser's "sacred center," I have no intention of exploring the possibility here of mide-specific detail. On the one hand, Henry, mentored by Francis Cree at Turtle Mountain, is not about to give away sacred information. On the other hand, even if he were, the inappropriateness of my examining it is clearly a given. What is significant here, then, is that invocation of the birchbark scrolls in the metatext of the novel itself, echoing the ceremonial structure of the quest, which includes the healer Jake Seed (a loose anagram for Jessakid, the shaking tent healer), stories of vision quests, the prisoner of haiku's birchbark poetry, and a variety of dream sequences, all of which ensure the dramatic interweaving of spiritual and material accounts. Meanwhile, completing the various dreamlike sequences that narrate Oskinaway's origins, Jake Seed visits a cave and tells of a boy and his father—almost certainly Oskinaway's father—who sits in a cliff-top location sculpting human figures from clay, which the pair then drop into the ravine below. The red color of the clay evokes the red figures on pictographic sites such as Lake of the Woods, where paints, or atisikan ("eternal paint"), were ground from the blood red roots of a lakeshore plant and bonded with sturgeon oil (L. Erdrich 2003, 79). While some of the figures catch in the cliff face and others shatter below, most make it to the river below, where they float off to be collected and, as the collection the reader encounters earlier at Strawberry's bar has suggested, traded. As a metaphor for both the artistic venture and the act of creation itself (not least in its evocation of one of many interpretations of "Ojibwe" to mean "whence lowered the male of the species" [see e.g. Gross 2014, 251]), its enmeshing of colonization and commodification of the spiritual and aesthetic practices of the people—and, indeed, of the people themselves—thrusts a political dimension into the heart of the novel's deliberations on the creative.

Returning us to the figure's spiritual and relational function, in Old Woman Cold Crow's story to Bombarto Rose, meanwhile, she tells of a man who "liked to look at himself when he was / young," eventually seeing in his own reflection alternative versions of himself (Henry 1994, 86). "This looking grew in him," Old Woman Cold Crow tells Bombarto, until "he saw different things each time" (86–87). Far from being a Narcissus, this looking opens up other possibilities for the man, leading him eventually "far away in an academy full of strangers" where he learns to sculpt (87); he gives the sculptures away as gifts, gifts that continue to appear even once he himself has disappeared. One of those gifts, a sculpture of a man on a red horse, leads into "Abetung's Story" with the closing line from Old Woman Cold Crow: "Before he went away he said, 'This sculpture tells a story'" (88). The layers of connotation here are multiple and nuanced. The story Abetung, Oskinaway's father, then tells is of the time he rode Old Man Geeshis's horse Chabai ("Spirit") against the old man's instructions. That ride ends in the death of Franklin Squandum and the horse, and the coming together of Abetung and Mary Squandum. The ripples of meaning connect Abetung's looking and its outcomes to the novel's examination of the relationship between story, knowledge, material (including graphic and textual) production, and belonging. For instance, Abetung's looking, particularly his ability in time to see things other than his own immediate reflection, reflects not only his own visionary/interpretive abilities but also connects to a later statement by Old Man Kinew on the ability to see past the self, to move beyond the self's reflection or projection to what lies beneath.

The vehicle for his lesson—ironically ignored by the community—is the river and, more particularly, fishing:

> A long time ago, people knew the power of rivers, not just the power of the movement of water, but the way the river drew life forward. So in our learning, we learned about creeks before we learned about bigger streams. When I was young, my great grandfather took me to the creek at night to learn to spear, to fish that way. He had his way, a way that goes beyond even your remembrance. But he took me at night. We had torches, and he told me to walk into the water and stay until I no longer disturbed the water; then he said, "hold your torch over the water and the light of the torch will stop a fish right in front of you like light stops many animals. When the fish stops," he said, "spear it." That seemed simple, but when you fish this way, the fish always stops under the water in a place where the torch spreads the reflection of your own face on top of the water. So to fish this way, you had to put the spear about eye high into your own reflected face. If you did that you could get a fish every time. For some reason, many people can't do this; at first I couldn't do this. (219–20)

The lengthy quotation is worth repeating in full for its resonance with Abetung's story, as well as for the self-absorption that failure to learn to fish this way implies. Old Man Kinew delivers his lecture in response to alarm at the serial drownings of the reservation's children in the river, after their being drawn to Strawberry's bar. The suggestion that the youth cannot return from the "other spaces and other contexts" to which they have been drawn (Peters 2008, 7) because they have not learned to see past their own reflections—to understand the wider implications of stories and relationships—is further reflected in part by Kinew's cane, which carries carvings of the major clan doodems of the Ojibwe, a visual and physical reminder of the centrality of kinship. It illustrates the very values the children have lost, in other words, which both the cane and Kinew's story teach to anyone capable of listening and seeing. In this case, it appears, the first person witness Oskinaway is the only one who does—a result, perhaps, of the training regime his narrative relay has performed. The old man's remarks also recall Geeshis's earlier comment about Abetung's abilities, when he similarly castigates Abetung's youthful impetuosity. "Sometimes it seems like words have no meaning to you young people," he says: "You go in the direction you want whenever you want without thinking, without believing anything but what your simple passion suggests" (Henry 1994, 94). Like the young who cannot cross the river because they have forgotten how to negotiate what is in front of them and instead respond to their self-gratifying impulses, Geeshis impugns Abetung's self-control. At the same time, however, he reminds us that knowledge does not reveal absolute truths, but assists in navigating the contingencies of experience, where he accedes, "But who knows, maybe you took that horse for a reason. Maybe you saw these Squandum people in the eyes of the horse. I don't know. Only you can judge what happened" (94).

Of course, as we discover, the reason is Mary, who saves the frozen Abetung with her own body heat, a moment that then turns to passion and procreation. The point, ultimately, of Geeshis's concession is not so much the suggestion that Abetung knew this was going to happen, but that the line is very fine in the balance between learning how to be in the world—how to read events and understand success through skill, vision, and intuition (which Peters astutely sees as an encoding of survivance acts [2008, 7])—and acting on impulse. In other words, knowledge cannot deny chance, but it can furnish the individual with the skills necessary to take the gamble. Chance, thus, becomes potentially productive, not only in the encounter, but in the story that both produces it and that it leaves as its legacy.

Illusions and Allusions

Abetung himself comments on the visual and visionary aspect at the heart of his story by entreating the reader to look carefully—to learn to read/hear the story closely for the knowledge it imparts: "As for the sculpture and the story of the sculpture, if you look closely at the horse you see that the rider doesn't really have control, and that is part of what the story means" (Henry 1994, 89). The relationship between looking, learning, telling, and listening (or in this case, reading) this describes is at the core of the transmission of knowledge in Niigaanwewidam James Sinclair's insightful discussion of "Wenabojo and the Cranberries." In his essay "A Sovereignty of Transmotion," Sinclair revisits the version of the story told to anthropologist Victor Barnouw by pseudonymous Lac du Flambeau resident Tom Badger.[3] In the story, which Sinclair describes as "*aadizookaan* ('sacred,' 'traditional,' or 'classical' story)" (2009, 124), Wenabojo (Nanabozho) mistakes the reflection of cranberries in a lake for the real thing and makes several unsuccessful and increasingly humiliating and painful attempts to retrieve the fruit. For Sinclair, this opens a wealth of possibility for discussion and learning, from having his students consider the social and ethical contexts of story collection, to exploring a range of "high" theoretical readings (he mentions Platonic allegory, Baudrillardian simulacra, Lacan's mirror stage, and semiotics), before turning to the late Basil Johnston's "three interconnected meanings of Anishinaabeg 'traditional' stories" (Sinclair 2009, 124). Johnston's three layers—the surface, the fundamental, and the philosophical meanings—allow Sinclair to establish a complex understanding of the apparently simple story's significance.

The surface meaning of Abetung's story is perhaps not so dissimilar to that of Wenabojo's, since for both of them desire overcomes rational instruction: "What's most upsetting for Wenabojo is his inability to recognize the trickery embedded in the images on the water. . . . While this is an educational moment and one full of possibilities, it is also a reminder that 'reality' not only exists but comes with responsibilities and consequences (like carefully thinking, looking, and considering before acting)" (125). A turn to the fundamental meaning, which "considers the many constituent parts that make up a story, its surrounding universe, and the web of relationships actualized by its telling" (125), in the context of the novel produces a reading far closer to Geeshis's caveat. The "universe" of the storied relay and the relationships that amplify Oskinaway's own presence are very much actualized both in the telling of the story and through its consequences. Thus, the individual and the story that might be used to caution against the reckless expression of individual desire, and the communal in the web of relationships that is spun out of the encounter and within which the story is already woven, effect a balance that highlights the symbiotic embrace of chance and situated knowledge, over and above human projections such as order, irreducible fact (as opposed to subjective experience), and absolute truth. The mutuality of story and theory that Sinclair's treatment of "Wenabojo" reveals, and that Henry and his coeditors invite their contributors to deliberate on in *Stories through Theories, Theories through Stories*, is absolutely germane to *The Light People*. What Henry emphasizes is the equality of vision to sound, imagination (and the visionary) to voice, and graphic to oral in the construction of story as a vehicle for the critical impulse.

To refer back to the patterning of chapter 2, then, the ultimate act of mark making, the X that marks the spot on the story-map, is the individual present to himself as a mobile site, not a fixed or predetermined and static entity, a "personality," but as being-in-process, part of a wide web of connections, relations, and circumstances. The stories that revolve through the novel's many cycles are both that web and resources for the means to navigate it and understand the self within it. If the plot and its entanglements, as well as the huge cast of characters and subject positions, only some of which I have outlined in these opening pages, sound confusing and elusive it is, quite frankly, because they are. That they force an active reading is testament to the way Henry demonstrates narrative's fluidity, which, like the river that flows through the book, is at once life-force and hazard. One can move through the captivation of one's own reflection to find the substance beneath, as the ripples of punctured surface emanate out from that center; or one can become caught up in the waters like Oskinaway at the start, unappreciative of their power, or the children from Strawberry's at the end, blind to its dangers and, like Wenabojo, unable to discern in the images of sustenance (whether berries or bars) that "what they really hold are absences as unsatisfying, empty, and ultimately inedible 'fakes'" (Sinclair 2009, 125).

Dream and Image: Rose Meskwaa Geeshik

In his transitioning between examination of "Wenabojo and the Cranberries" and his discussion of transmotion, Sinclair quotes Gerald Vizenor on the trickster, noting first that "Naanabozho . . . wanders in mythic time and transformational space"

(2009, 128). While *The Light People* presents numerous possibilities for trickster interpretations, Henry avoids rewarding indulgence by effectively putting trickster everywhere and nowhere. While many characters could be viewed through that particular lens, none is explicitly more or less tricksterish than any other. Thus, while the book is infused with attributes commonly accorded to the figure—such as a will to disorder and fragmentation, roles of teacher and healer, from deceiver to comic liberator, and more—any determinative claim to his appearance is more persuasively made for the narrative itself rather than as a specific character. In this respect, Henry avoids any too-easy reduction of his complex social and cultural canvas to a single often clichéd and certainly much-misunderstood trope (see Reder and Morra 2010). Nevertheless, the narrative itself, with its frequent hops into mythic spheres, dream spaces, and historical abstractions, very much presents that ground in which Vizenor's Nanabozho wanders—if nothing else, actualizing Vizenor's contention that Nanabozho is, in essence, a disruptive sign in a language game. Without specifically, or in a limited way, being a "trickster narrative," then, *The Light People*, like the "trickster narrative[,] situates the participant audience, the listeners and readers, in agonistic imagination: there, in [often] comic discourse, the trickster is being, nothingness and liberation; a loose seam in consciousness; that wild space over and between sounds, words, sentences and narratives" (Vizenor 1993a, 196).

The transformative possibilities of language (and narrative) and the transportative potential of story are nowhere better figured in the novel than in the relationship between artist Rose Meskwaa Geeshik's share of the story, one of her paintings, which itself tells a story, and Franklin Squandum's death dream—a dream space rendered as theatrical dialogue that partially realizes Rose's painting, rendering the latter a visionary work. That Franklin's dream sequence begins in the reflective surface of the eye of the horse—that same horse's eye that drew Abetung to his future—further enmeshes story, sight, and vision. So, three types of narrative vehicle (story, painting, play) reflect three different forms (orality, art, drama) to produce a larger visionary drama in which apparently unrelated people and events are shown to be in relation. More importantly, perhaps, Rose's story begins with commentary on visuality—with the primacy of, and the will to deconstruct, stereotypical imagery of *indians*—but moves quite powerfully into the embracing of vision and art, interrupted by her grief over her husband's absence, before being returned to her work as she returns to the reservation. That latter move all starts with a stone; but first, the image.

In the early section "Rose Meskwaa Geeshik's Monologue on Images," Rose begins: "Everybody on the outside . . . they claim to know us" (Henry 1994, 25). That "knowledge," sustained as it is by "sincere singers of sorrow and guilt," few of whom "can fathom the cryptic nature of their own concern, genuine or otherwise" (25), is demonstrably oppressive in its blindness to the gulf between what they "know" and the way Native people live in the present moment. That settler-colonial society is dedicated to appearance—to the primacy of the image as reflective of a quantifiable singular reality—is very much reflected in Rose's commentary on the effectiveness of the image in the maintenance of the colonial power dynamic: "Then there were the images, the cowboy killings, the product faces, figures giving authenticity to their smoke, their Sunday heroes. And for a long time I swallowed it all and grew sick with anger, knowing the images inside can kill you and put faces on you that you can't get off" (25). Taught by her father—Jake Seed himself—and mother "different, greater things about images, about the imagination, and growing toward healing," Rose "found [she] could turn images inside out from the mind to the hand, and the images in turn could replay healing images inside someone" (25). This switch from feeling the burden of the image as a tool of control and oppression, to understanding its power for healing and survivance reflects a deconstructive approach to the simulated *indian*—in exegetic terms. In other words, as Vizenor's craft has always shown, there is power in switching that which is a damaging burden to that which can be wielded as a productive tool, to producing what Mirzoeff calls a countervisual strategy. That said, Rose's is not a subversive art; nor is it postmodern parody. Her turn to the image is not an ironic reversal of the image of the *indian*—she is no James Luna or Fritz Scholder—but a movement into a style that combines a kind of contemporary reflective vérité with the medicine painting of artists such as Norval Morrisseau, Daphne Odjig, and others, whose practice developed in contemplation of traditional representative and visionary practices among the Anishinaabeg.

In her master's dissertation, Goretti das Neves Moreira astutely delineates the "progression" of Rose's thematic—from her "turtle period" where her paintings focus on creation, to her "eagle period" where they turn to the message: "In Anishinabe culture the eagle establishes the link between the people and the Creator. It carries prayers and messages. The same is the case with Rose's paintings" (Moreira 2007, 49). In the main work of this period, *The Nest and the Mind*, eggs hatch symbols of technology and consumption, while dead eagles—or unheard messages—pile up at the foot of a tree. Meanwhile, a white-haired old man at the foot of the tree paints an X-ray painting of an upturned nest inside which people are engulfed in steam; in the sky of his painting, eagles fly. Recalling the so-called Woodland School's aesthetic, itself partly inspired by the pictographic tradition on birchbark scrolls, and the sweat lodge, this painting within the painting speaks to ancient praxis linking ritual, art, and healing.

In "Horizon Lines, Medicine Painting, and Moose Calling: The Visual/Performative Storytelling of Three Anishinaabeg Artists," Molly McGlennen observes that "the artwork (painting, sculpting, drawing, performance, etc.) of Anishinaabe people in the twentieth and twenty-first centuries can be viewed as a vibrant continuation, adaptation, and creative expression of . . . traditional modes of storytelling [typified by birchbark scrolls] that helped (and still help) Anishinaabeg understand the world around them and how to 'be' in that world" (2013, 342). Rose's paintings take their place in this history, both as commercial objects for sale in the Twin Cities and as vehicles (in her case produced by dreams and visions) for narrative and healing. Rose describes a number of her paintings, but most notable among them is the award-winning *The Nest and the Mind*, in which a nest sitting at the top of a tree is "full of waste, garbage, and the eggs of the eagle . . . were hatching glowing signs, advertisements, human legs and arms, body parts, rusting machinery, flowers on fire, liquor bottles with warped human heads inside . . . mangled airplanes, plastic guns, boys with needles in their necks, girls choking on pearls" (Henry 1994, 26–27). Elements of this painting are revisited explicitly in other parts of the book, such as "Franklin Squandum's Death Dream" and Oshawa's story (where he dreams a similar dream), while its overarching sense of desperation in the face of human (capitalist/consumerist) self-destruction palpably colors the reservation community's dilemma at the end—that dilemma figured in the question of knowledge and right action as a result of seeing and hearing the stories.

While Rose's painting is arguably more immediately contemporary in subject matter than the "legend paintings" of the Woodland School's most famous practitioner, nevertheless, like Morrisseau she draws on both her own dreams and visions as well as inherited (gifted) stories and artistic forms to "create[] a visual language whose lineage included the ancient shaman artists of the Midiwewin scrolls, the Agawa Bay rock paintings and the Peterborough petroglyphs" (Houle 2007). Acknowledging the often complex differences in operation of both ancient ritual art and contemporary fine art, Amelia Trevelyan nevertheless argues that the milieu of the New Woodland School represents a cultural corollary to the "bursts of artistic and ritual activity [that] developed in response to cultural crises," in what A. F. C. Wallace designated "revitalization movements" in the 1950s (Trevelyan 1989,

196). Arguing that "conditions within the Native cultural milieu at the inception of the New Woodland School corresponded in many ways to those associated with precontact revitalization movements," she explains that for Wallace, "revitalization in response to cultural crisis was always initiated by individuals and was strongly associated with the personal visionary experiences of its leaders" (qtd. by Trevelyan 1989, 197). Furthermore, "the art and the message it carried always involved a reconciliation of old ways, symbols, and ideas with realities . . . a catalyst for reconciliation between diverse political and cultural entities" (Trevelyan 1989, 199). Tying back through the Woodland School, then, to older practices, Rose's art both depicts cultural crisis and instantiates the site for its addressing, through a form commonly associated with intra- and intercultural reconciliation.

As just one minor example of the aesthetic connection, then, Rose's "X-ray" image of the nest is highly evocative of the Woodland School style in such paintings as Carl Ray's *Medicine Bear*, in which the bear's heart, stomach, gall bladder, and more are visible attributes of the overall composition or, with even more explicit reference to pictographic forms, Morrisseau's *Ojibwe Midewiwin Sacred Bear*; Morrisseau's style, of course, has often been referred to as X-ray painting. Perhaps even more pertinently, the latter's friend and contemporary Salteaux artist Robert Houle continues, "he invented an interior color space where the imagination with its paradigms, viewpoints and methods was in complicity with the potent traditions of critique and resistance" (2007). Not quite in tow with Morrisseau's explicitly spirit-driven aesthetic, Rose's critique of consumerism, waste, and other forms of degradation are not necessarily entirely out of kilter with the commentaries of Odjig, Blake Debassige, and other members of the school, who were renowned for incorporating more immediately political, social, and domestic narratives into their work. Rose's "glowing signs, advertisements . . . rusting machinery," and so on are similarly suggestive of more recent painters who draw heavily on artifacts of popular culture such as film characters, famous coffee chains, hood ornaments, and so on, in the celebration of the diversity of Anishinaabe cultural reference as well as the critique of modern consumption. Thus, artists such as Frank Big Bear (especially, for instance, his *Chemical Man in a Toxic World*) or his son Star Wallowing Bull come to mind for their combinations of primarily decorative Anishinaabe motifs with contemporary signifiers of popular culture, technology, and conspicuous consumption. I have suggested elsewhere that their depictions draw those signifiers into the broader aesthetic scope of Anishinaabe artists, rather than simply acting as critique of avarice or waste, but in their implicit commitment to a form of engaged resistance their work similarly works to reconcile in a mode of revitalization (see Stirrup 2013).

Presenting another instance of the shift from self-perception to something more outward-reaching (marking the difference, perhaps, between inspiration as a signature of artistic "genius," that Romantic stream of the subjective interpretation of vision, and as a quality of the visionary-as-conduit for external phenomena), Rose's new studio practice back on the reservation is interrupted by the appearance of Oshawa's stone, which shatters the picture window through which she gazes. Looking up, her face covered in blood, she "realize[s] my own image in the glass was gone" (Henry 1994, 29). Effecting an altering of perception that evokes the perceptual exaggerations of Cubist abstraction, she notices pieces of shattered glass scattered on her sketch of an old woman: "Those pieces magnified parts of her face: one of her eyes appeared larger; part of the shadow on the bridge of her nose whirled out wider and darker; the closed part between her lips opened a bit more" (29). Vision and image in this sequence forge a complex relationship. The window—that which reflects, mirrorlike—has also already been shown to be dangerously transparent, since, "One day as I sat at the desk nodding off to sleep, a sparrow hawk flew into the window and broke its neck" (28). As a division between spheres (in this instance the inside and outside), the glass window thus becomes a metaphor for projection and deception. As Rose strives to find more images to paint, she is caught in the tension between phenomenological perception, imaginative or intuitive apprehension of the noumenal world, and spiritual intercession. That tension levels out any perceived gap between subjective and objective modes of "seeing," as the window itself emphasizes the ways in which physical vision itself is rarely free from distortive—and potentially destructive—mediation. The apparently transparent window is therefore revealed as a barrier between the perceiving self and the world; shattering it alters Rose's perception, reveals its distortion, and levels the perceived gap between "real" and "imagined" spheres. In *Phenomenology of Perception*, Maurice Merleau-Ponty observes science and philosophy's "unquestioning faith in perception," wherein "perception opens a window on to things" (2002, 62): Henry's description of the window explores the gap between the primacy of perception as an empiricist lens and the essential intersubjectivity of animate entities, in which perception moves beyond the five senses to dream-, death-, and myth-world dimensions, wherein, as for Merleau-Ponty, the spheres of dreaming and waking are ultimately inseparable (see Merleau-Ponty 1968). If the window represents a division between the discerning subject and the material object, its shattering by the stone—and particularly the damage that shattering does to Rose's visage, and the subtle way it alters her perception even of that which she has only intuited—removes the distance between subject and object/self and other and reminds us of the multiple ways of seeing at work in the novel.

Such philosophical exploration—not at all out of keeping with Henry's intellectual interests—is emphatically interrupted by the presence of the stone, literally shattering the artist's contemplation of external objects as a source of *in*sight and positing itself in the middle of this reflection of the Western practice of art. That practice is partially reflected in Rose's situation: a solitary artist in her studio awaiting inspiration to produce a commercially viable product, her participation in the capitalist fetishization of art-as-object is inherently ambivalent given the history of appropriation and objectification that dogs Indigenous material culture. If the dream aspect of her painting already avows the visionary or spiritual—already, in other words, underpins its authenticity (in philosophical, not anthropological terms)—the stone and its markings take a turn toward the sacred, and toward the "art of the old ones" (Moreira 2007, 51). The stone's animacy is infused through its circulation: "The stone felt different in my hands too, like someone had touched it many times before, like it had a human purpose attached to it" (Henry 1994, 29). Rose ascribes that purpose—or at least the clue to its nature—to the symbols painted on it. "A thin band of green paint divided the stone in half," she describes. "On one half of the stone was an image of a blue man painted against a yellow background; on the other half a white bird rested on its back against a red background" (29). These markings make clear that the stone has a sacred origin and purpose, suggesting a link between human and animal, earthly and divine.

It is again in the dream realm where the communicative power of the stone manifests, and it "speaks" to her, beginning: "Dire Seer / You of a broken window / Descendant of a finer day / Daughter in search of a greater image" (30). The painted stone also departs demonstrably from the artistic transaction (from dream to commodity) that she was involved in, presenting emphatically as a function as well as a product of creativity, a means to produce rather than an end in itself:

This is a creation stone
A stone from the beginning of time
You may use this stone to create
to sing as a song stone

to tell stories as a story stone
to write as a poem stone
to paint as an art stone. (30)

A literal source of inspiration, within the dream in which the stone talks to Rose it also generates both prolific activity in the studio, which, in its turn, sees all of Rose's new sketches linked one way or another to stone ("I sketched a stone bust of every American president, and each bust had Indian clan symbols emerging from the backs of the presidents' heads" [31]) in ways that continue to link Indigenous symbolism (the stone, as well as clan markers and so on) to a narrative of resistance to a range of images of hegemony, from Renaissance art to the commodification of women in strip clubs, to treaties and more.

The stone, however, also demands reciprocity (which it describes as a "short-coming"), telling Rose "You must care / for a stranger / at your door" (30). In the dream, Rose's charge arrives shortly afterward—a little person, or bagwajiwinini,[4] with "a dark complexion, long wild black hair, and thick powerful arms" (31). Rose completes her sketches only to find the little man, prone to mischief anyway, "in another room . . . surrounded by bottles and cans . . . up to his neck, wild and drunk" (31). Becoming destructive, the little man ends up smashing the stone to dust before being stabbed through the chest with the broken leg of her easel by an enraged Rose. The dream ends with Rose's sketches being transported out of the window to the top of the giant maple, where the little man, on a death platform, was "wrapped up in red material as eagles, vultures, crows swirled about and above him . . . some even singing with human voices a death song I will remember and will carry with me to the end of my life" (33). In her waking hours, four days later, it is actually Oshawa who comes to Rose's door, to apologize for shooting the stone through the window. The stone's further generative and reciprocal function becomes clear as he explains that he received the stone from his uncle Oshawanung after it was passed down through the generations, having originally been given to the family by the little people, the ancient ones: inverting that sequence, responsibility for the next story is passed on to him, and then to Oshawanung.

Although the stone is taken by Oshawa for strength following his humiliation by classmates, and used by him for hunting, Oshawanung had already promised it to him as the keeper for his generation. In doing so, he explains, "Some stones carry earth histories, stories, songs, prayers, so their stone faces hold memories of the existences of other eras; other beings of the earth, air, fire, and water live on, embedded in shapes, in esoteric formations of strata and substrata, in scopic design and microscopic elementals we can only imagine in our limited view of the exterior stone" (41). So Oshawanung begins with part geological explication, part invocation of reverence for what the stone represents in the animate and inanimate worlds in Anishinaabe cosmology, where it features as older brother of semi-deity Nanabozho as well, of course, as source of materials for multiple functions, from madoodoowasin (sweat stones used in sweat lodges) to cutting implements to surfaces for drawing and carving. Its mnemonic, or memory, function is also vital: "A person can use this stone to remember, or turn it over and use it as a weapon. Remembering with the stone will keep you safe in creation, since remembrance opens you up to forms of creation" (41). While the stone's paintwork relates to these two functions—remembrance and battle—its utility as an object in the narrative also serves as a mnemonic tool, in that "your safety will reside in your willingness to understand the story of the stone and use the story in the stone to understand and create your own story as you remember the stories of our family, our people" (41). Thus, the stone itself becomes the object dropped into the river, emblematic of the heart of the novel's story cycle that generates the ever-increasing ripples of concentricity.

Oshawanung's story leads to the story of the Four Bears family, which in turn brings in Bombarto Rose's ruminations on blood and identity, the prisoner of haiku's tales, and a court case over the repatriation of Moses Four Bears's leg. When the storytelling responsibility returns to Oshawanung and Oshawa, on the other side of the stone's ripple effect, as it were, Oshawa confesses to his uncle his misuse of the stone, which consequently explains the raging destruction of the little man in Rose's dream: "'But I may have misused the stone,' Oshawa said. 'I shot at someone once, tried to kill, I put anger in the stone'" (163). The circulation of story here—that narrative relay from Oshawanung onward—is thus made a metaphor in the form of the stone, painted to remind its holders of its sacred significance and to embody a symbolic, as well as to imprint and thus pass on the legacy of its original holder, the painting's originator. Just as story demands responsible handling, so too does the stone, which becomes a weapon in the wrong hands. The ethical imperative implicit in both the inheritance and passing forward of the stone and the stories is figured both in the human contact required for both (hand to hand, mouth to ear) and in the presence signified by the painting on the stone itself. Thus, each step in the relay bears responsibility to each preceding step back to its originator and his or her original intentions; Oshawa's moment of anger marks not simply an act of disrespect for a potentially sacred object, but the breaking of a covenant chain that connects an unknown number of individuals across an ageless time span.

In "The(st)ories of Ceremonial Relation," Silvia Martínez-Falquina suggests that "Native writing has a primary ceremonial motivation, broadly understood as an opening of the possibility of transformation for the participants in the process" (2009, 192). While this arguably evinces a set of assumptions most pertinent to what Paula Gunn Allen called the "second wave" of Native American fiction, it certainly resounds in *The Light People*, about which specifically Martínez-Falquina is writing.[5] She discusses the court case for the repatriation of Moses Four Bears's leg, about which the Four Bearses' attorney Catullus Cage says, "We apprehend the truth as we become part of the story, and the story always brings the truth back to us in some form. In this case, the form is the leg of Moses Four Bears" (Henry 1994, 128). As Martínez-Falquina puts it, "According to this Native voice, truth lies in stories and their capacity to integrate, for human reality has to be conceived of as related, and not in isolation like the limiting point of view of the museum" (2009, 195). The form of truth, the form of story, then, takes many shapes, whether spoken or written word, painted stone, or leg with legging and moccasin; the apprehension of that truth depends on understanding one's relationship to its form of delivery.

While the museum's witnesses rely on abstract, theoretical understandings of knowledge (Martínez-Falquina 2009, 196) to justify their case, the Four Bears case, and indeed Henry's engagement with theory, repeatedly returns us to genealogies, webs of connection, and intersubjective relations. Like Rose's paintings' place in the capitalist cycle, then, the museum's abstraction of knowledge depends on the commoditization of individual "genius," and the perceived value of the rareness factor—whether that rareness be the material object or the expertise of the anthropologist, curator, historian, lawyer, or critic. The latter not only produce and reproduce what Vizenor calls terminal creeds, but they render particular markets, spaces, and discourses exclusive in order to contain and control value. In contrast, and notwithstanding the role and status of specialist knowledge holders such as mide elders in Anishinaabe communities, knowledge in Henry's novel is presented as a relational field. As a result, responsibility rests not solely with the knowledge holder/storyteller but with the audience, too, to interpret not according to external facts or principles but according to the internal logics of relation of the story chain. Again, Martínez-Falquina reads this difference in ethical terms: "By centering our interest and attention on listening to the voices speaking in the text, we not only hear their own definitions of themselves and the other . . . but we can also creatively redefine an ethical relation of responsibility towards the Native text as other" (2009, 197). We must also, as she herself affirms, recognize that that ethical relation of responsibility will differ depending on our relationship to the Anishinaabe text—"in awareness of our positioning" (192).

Transience and the Transitional Text

While we "listen" to and read Henry's novel, the thrust of my argument differs little from Martínez-Falquina's. It is essential, however, that we recognize the ways in which the novel's portrayal of the "Native text" forces the non-Native reader out of her Eurocentric preconceptions of what does and does not constitute "text" or even story. In the first instance, stone and leg constitute forms of both—forms that apprehend truth more immediately than the written or spoken word in the context of the courtroom. This is, in part, attributed to the mark of presence of a "scribe"—the little person who painted the stone, for instance, or, more explicitly, Willow Four Bears who made the moccasin—rendering that originator and others in the chain of relation, as well as their intention, their gift, their memory, and so on, present to the occasion; or, as in Vizenor's oft-repeated story of Charles Aubid, the obviative (fourth person proximate) presence of Four Bears himself. The passages that describe Rose's own paintings, however, speak to the multiplicity of textual form more directly, in two ways. Firstly, they hint at a nonverbal narrative form capturing the quality of dreams more accurately or adequately than narrative description; and secondly, as if to prove that point, the descriptive passages themselves reveal the inadequacy of language—or at the very least, English[6]—to fully capture the visuality of the dreams.

Vizenor cites visual neurobiologist Semir Zeki, who argues that "language is a relatively recent evolutionary acquisition, and it has yet to catch up with and match the visual system in its capacity to extract essentials so efficiently" (Vizenor 2009, 195). Vizenor's own imagist aesthetic is one means of linguistic apprehension of the visual or envisioned subject. Literary ekphrasis—the "verbal representation of visual representation" (Mitchell 1994, 109)—is another. Yet in Rose's descriptions of her paintings, we have neither, leveling heavy emphasis on the blunt instrument that language becomes in the absence of either the image or the sight of the image, which communicates in a way the prose cannot; in this instance, the descriptions are neither adornment nor narrative vehicle, nor instrument, serving in the role "as a 'servant' of narrative" (Mitchell 1994, 109). Rather, the paintings are the first means of documenting and interpreting Rose's dreams, evoking a modern-day counterpart to the ways seekers of visions would mark their dreams on rock face before recounting either the dream or the process of its reception.[7] The net effect, perhaps paradoxically in the case of a novel, is to lay stress on the pictorial and the visual as both necessary precursor to and integrated element of the oral. The insufficiency of description to capture the visual quality of both paintings and dreams emphasizes the significance of the seen image. This, ultimately, is further underlined in the ekphrastic quality of "Franklin Squandum's Death Dream," which appears to dramatically re-create aspects of Rose's painting (particularly the tree, the upturned nest, and the eagles), irreducibly binding together Rose's dreams, her art, and performance generally as well as *the* performance of the stories and messages his vision communicates. In the end, it is in the combination of effects that the narrative finds its completion.

As I discussed in chapter 2, the prisoner of haiku makes the transience of the linguistic trace his trademark—not just in terms of the absent presence of the author in the text, but more directly in the form of his poetry, designed, like Vizenor's haiku, to "include what is absent by allusion . . . to break through the boundaries of print" (Blaeser 1996, 114). Writing of Vizenor's engagement of his readers to create "a dreamscape from haiku" wherein "words become dream voices, traces on the wind, twists in the snow," Blaeser quotes a famous line from Vizenor's *Matsushima*: "The *nothing* in a haiku is not an aesthetic void; rather, it is a moment of enlightenment, a dreamscape where words dissolve; no critical marks, no grammatical stains remain" (117). The dissolution of print, then, extends to the dissolution of words entirely, wherein "haiku seek to slide back down the chain of signifiers, eliminating the final stage and, by eschewing most literary tropes, creating an illusion that it has evaded the first stage of signification" (Lynch 2000, 212). Prior to arriving at haiku, however, and indeed the cause of his incarceration, the prisoner, Elijah Cold Crow—"a silent man of hands, a sculptor, then a political artist, an invidious communicator of visual forms" (Henry 1994, 62)—creates a devastatingly violent form of artistic activism by setting fire to federal buildings. As the buildings burn, the smoke clouds they produce replicate iconic forms that speak to mythical and historical moments in the past of the people.

Once more, Tom Lynch's discussion of Vizenor's haiku aesthetic offers a pertinent entry point to consideration of this "art." Under the subheading "Shadows," Lynch quotes Vizenor's assertion in *Manifest Manners* that "the shadows are the prenarrative silence that inherits the words" (2000, 213). "When the words dissolve," Lynch proceeds, "only their shadows remain" (213). Furthermore, "he related the concept of shadow explicitly to haiku in which the dissolved word is replaced with a shadow in the evoked sensation" (213). In this instance, our interest is in the smoke formations of Cold Crow's fires, which suggest the shadows of events and peoples committed to memory through story in some cases and text in others. Before I elaborate, it is worth remembering that Cold Crow is mute, his "tongue" stolen from him by cruel teachers at residential school. Before he refinds his "voice" through haiku and dreamsongs, his expressive medium is a prelinguistic, prenarrative, and impermanent visual medium. So, where Lynch explains that the shadow in haiku "inheres in the sensation that precedes and postcedes language" (214), that sensory—and above all affective—turn presents in the wholly visual forms that dispense with language to communicate moments in space and time. In both cases, they demand a phenomenological embrace of imagination and vision.

Elijah Cold Crow's arsons, then, invoke an apparition of a face, interpreted by onlookers as that of the "first bringer of light, or of one who floated in a stone white canoe"; the illuminated words "The Treaty of 1837"; and "on the night of his greatest political burning . . . an old lodge, ancestors within the lodge, throwing melted clocks into the air, burning the country-and-western ambiance of chairs and wall hangings, pointing to the melting jukebox, singing instead healing songs through that wasting machinery" (Henry 1994, 63). That last is Cold Crow's seventh fire, evoking the Anishinaabe migration story. In *The Mishomis Book*, Lac Court Oreille elder Edward Benton-Banai's famous retelling of the Seven Fires Prophecy, the seventh fire reveals a dilemma conventionally interpreted as that between technology and spirituality, paths derived from the technological developments presented by the light-skinned incomers and a return to the traditional ways of the Anishinaabeg. While the first and final of Cold Crow's fires reflect the prophetic history of the Anishinaabeg as well as their migration from the Eastern seaboard to the western Great Lakes, the middle one, "The Treaty of 1837" addresses their political history, becoming a metonym for their relationship with and treatment by the settler colonial government since the decline of the fur trade, explicitly framed by the visionary history of the people.

The Treaty of 1837, or "Treaty with the Chippewa, 1837," was concluded at St. Peters in Wisconsin Territory on July 29, 1837.[8] Among many controversial aspects of the 1837 treaty between the Ojibwe of east-central Minnesota and northeastern Wisconsin and the U.S. government was the ceding of thirteen million acres of land at an equivalent of seven cents per acre. The agent at the Mackinac Island-Sault Ste. Marie Agency in Michigan at the time, one Henry Rowe Schoolcraft, himself "wondered 'why it was that so little had been given for so large a cession, comprehending the very best lands of the Chippewas in the Mississippi Valley'" (qtd. in Satz 1991, 23). Selling it on at $1.25 an acre, the government finally conceded its fraudulent nature through the Indian Land Claims Commission in 1971. The impermanence of the protest intriguingly underscores the permanence of that earlier damage. Perhaps even more pertinently, the transfer of millions of acres of timberland to federal holding in the treaty arguably catalyzed close to a century of manipulation of Anishinaabe timber rights. While the Ojibwe signatories believed their retained rights on the ceded land would enable them to maintain their way of life, upholding the written terms of the treaty has been anything but straightforward.[9] Like their right to continue using the pine, the right to hunting and fishing resources, which Satz explains translated into Anishinaabemowin with a "word meaning 'general foraging' with *any* kind of a device for *any* purpose" (1991, 24), have continued to be contested—most controversially through protests and counterprotests at Mille Lacs—with a series of court cases running from 1974 to 1991, just a few years before first publication of *The Light People*. Furthermore, as is true of countless treaties throughout the New World, the background to the treaty signing is replete with instances of bribery and corruption, lack of adequate ground surveillance, and the influencing of certain bands and leaders to the detriment of others; in this case, Satz reports, the Pillagers under the leadership of Chief Hole in the Day and one other unnamed leader fell under the strong influence of lead negotiators. Again, Schoolcraft comments: "the Pillagers, in fact, made the treaty. The bands of the St. Croix and Chippewa Rivers, who really lived on the land and owned it, had, in effect, no voice. So [too] with respect to the La Pointe Indians" (qtd. in Satz 1991, 23). Colonial institutional manipulation and the erasure of voice are, needless to say, matters close to Cold Crow's own heart.

The Treaty of 1837 has further significance in relation both to the novel in general and Cold Crow's art in particular. The 1837 document closes with the statement, "To the Indian Names are Subjoined a Mark and Seal," a readily recognized preface to the X mark and totemic symbols with which Native signatories often recorded what Scott Lyons calls their assent to the new. To recap my discussion in the preceding chapter, notwithstanding their equivocal signification—as Lyons argues, "The x-mark is a contaminated and coerced sign of consent made under conditions that are not of one's making . . . signif[ying] power and a lack of power, agency and a lack of agency" (2010, 3)—those marks are marks of presence, made not solely as individuals but on behalf of their families, clans, and bands (see Bohaker 2010).[10] For all the potential damage the document does, the X mark is thus a claim, simultaneously an acceptance of terms and a refusal to be rendered absent, or erased, from the negotiations. The X mark, and indeed the totemic marker, are interesting in this regard in being both a proxy signature and not a signature at all—that is, they both endorse or accept or assent to the terms of the document and refuse (or fail) to participate in the precise terms of its Euro-Western construction. They signify, then, the very "prospect of slippage, indeterminacy, unforeseen consequences, or unintended results," not to mention the unacknowledged (by those in power) possibilities implicit in the process (Lyons 2010, 3).

Those markers, too, remind us palpably of the spoken negotiations that precede the treaty signing—negotiations that countless Indigenous commentators note are far more significant to the Native signatories than is the written record. Anishinaabe legal scholar John Borrows, for instance, writes compellingly of the verbal negotiations that preceded the largely forgotten Treaty of Niagara of 1764 and the earlier Royal Proclamation of 1763—parts, he insists, of the same treaty. "First Nations," he remarks, "were not passive objects, but active participants, in the formulation and ratification of the Royal Proclamation" (1997, 155). Their understanding of such negotiations, he continues, means that "contextualization of the Proclamation reveals that one cannot interpret its meaning using the written words of the document alone[, which] . . . conceal First Nations perspectives and inappropriately privilege one culture's practice over another" (1997, 156). Rather, First Nations negotiators "chronicled their perception of the Proclamation through other methods such as contemporaneous speeches, physical symbols, and subsequent conduct" (1997, 156). Those "signatures of assent," then, also remind us of alternative epistemologies; they are markers not of the "primitive," which was the lens through which their interlocutors read them, but of that different recollection of events and means of documenting them.

In the specific context of the Treaty of 1837, then, Satz avers that "since oral rather than written communication was the typical mode of Indian negotiations, the final written document to which Indians affixed an 'X' or their symbols was not as important to them as their understanding of the verbal agreements made, a direct contradiction to most white people's assumptions" (1991, 25). To take the inference that the written document can be entirely dismissed in this instance is misplaced, since it assumes the negative—a lack of power or agency—rather than acknowledging the substantive agency of both the mark making and the oral negotiation it affirms. Similarly, the binary proposed by such a reading—"although most whites would see written words as taking priority over spoken, this is not true in Chippewa culture" (Satz 1991, 25)—while not without truth, reductively fails to acknowledge the significance of the mark making as written signifiers of active presence, legal and political agency, and even engaged resistance. The image— literally and figuratively—of Elijah Cold Crow's "Treaty of 1837" fire tacitly recalls this implicit ambivalence. An imagetext in essence, it simultaneously signifies the silencing of oral testimony in Euro-Western law while also, in being a written phrase that nevertheless dissipates as vapor, illustrating the illusory permanence (and authority) of language and text. In doing so, "Treaty of 1837" visibly commemorates the traces of the treaty process itself inherent to both text and oral memory, validating and valorizing neither except as part of a larger, mutually completing whole—visual sovereignty in very explicit, distinct terms. As if to underpin this resistance to the authority of the written text and commemoration of the erasure of silencing, his final firebrand act is to paint the words "guilty" and "not guilty" on a T-shirt, creating another imagetext in which the visual and the verbal-textual conjoin, before taking off the shirt and burning it with an offering of tobacco (Henry 1994, 64–65). Since the words "guilty" and "not guilty" are present in the courtroom either as pleas (by the accused), accusations (by the attorneys), or verdicts (by the jury) and thus are spoken in the first instance, the symbolic significance of their being written and that writing then destroyed returns us again to the contextual dependence of process and perspective with which his earlier ironic art has also been engaged and an act of engaged resistance to the linguistic authority of the settler judicial system.

Following his arrest and incarceration, "for years prison meant a series of drawings to this artistic warrior," Elijah Cold Crow (64). Painting historical murals on the walls of his cell, Cold Crow joins a long tradition of Native political prisoners documenting historical events while in prison. On the one hand, then, that aspect recalls the work of the Fort Marion prisoners in Florida in the 1870s onward, who began drawing with pencils on the pages of used ledger books given to them by their guards. Part artistic resistance to their incarceration, part a new form that nevertheless recalls long-standing traditions of painting and drawing on hide, ledger art leaves a distinct trace through Native art and literature broadly. The form of Cold Crow's art—his murals—also evokes the activism of Latin American artists such as José Clemente Orozco and David Alfaro Siqueiros. Since we are not told anything about the content of Cold Crow's murals, we must I think assume that it is these cultural and political inferences that embed him in long-standing traditions of visual resistance that are paramount.

As I noted in the last chapter in discussion of the haiku themselves, Cold Crow's visual art is supplanted when he encounters the haiku and the dreamsong. Like Rose's art prior to her return to the forms of the stone painter, these activities preface his attempts to find a new vehicle—the haiku in his case—for older aesthetic/ritual practice that will bridge his present experience. Where Rose, as David Callahan puts it, "has to go through layers of story before being able to use her vision usefully" (2005, 194), Cold Crow has to experiment with form before finding the right interpretive vessel for his memories and visions. Both instances invoke Leanne Simpson's sense of the need to reclaim the fluidity around tradition (2011a, 51)—in other words, their attempts represent necessary elements of revitalization rather than dislocation. Cold Crow's non-Native instructor who first taught haiku before introducing the class to "translations of traditional dream songs" (Henry 1994, 65), "hoped to make a connection for the prisoner [wherein] . . . a culturally, politically appropriate act could be generated in a foreign form, from language to language, image to form" (65). Well intentioned, the instructor's hope is nevertheless belated. In *Native Liberty*, Vizenor insists that "analogy is an active, aesthetic, creative connection in the visual arts" (2009, 195). Moreover, "in the sense of natives, analogy is a desire to achieve a human union in visual images, rather than a cultural separation in language" (195). Anticipating that desire, the narrator of "The Prisoner of Haiku" suggests that "what she hoped the prisoner would understand in the relationship between haiku and dream songs was deeply embedded in the prisoner's history. A partial loss of language, new forms, old forms were part of his existence" (Henry 1994, 65). Although the text does not make explicit whether this is intended as a personal or a cultural quality, it certainly suggests an analogical equivalence not just between haiku and dreamsongs, but between the prisoner's former work and "culturally, politically appropriate" aesthetics more generally.

There is a certain consonance between Christopher Teuton's focus on the necessary balance between oral, graphic, and critical impulses, and W. J. T. Mitchell's brief but useful summary of what he calls the "pictorial turn" in twentieth-century European philosophy. Mitchell places emphasis on the picture as a point of friction (1994, 12–13) between the visual and the linguistic in Anglo-American philosophy. His focus, Richard Rorty's "determination to 'get the visual, and in particular the mirroring, metaphor out of our speech' . . . [echoing] Wittgenstein's iconophobia and the general anxiety of linguistic philosophy about visual representation," demonstrates for Mitchell the "pictorial turn" that reflects a "need to defend 'our speech' against 'the visual'" (1994, 13). All of this manifests—for Mitchell—in such developments as Charles Sanders Peirce's pursuit of semiotics, Derrida's decentering of "the 'phonocentric' model of language by shifting attention to the visible, material traces of writing," Adorno's and Horkheimer's excoriation of the culture industry, and so on (Mitchell 1994, 12). Said theoretical stakes, as I have lightly touched upon here, reside almost spectrally in *The Light People*, where the linguistic trace, or the Foucauldian exposure of "the rift between the discursive and the 'visible,' the seeable and the sayable," is implicitly refracted through the novel's tableaux—as actors and producers in an Anishinaabe-centered, storied world rather than as foils or respondents to the postimperial hegemony (Mitchell 1994, 12).[11] Yet that theoretical shadow elicits other responses, chief among them a view of a world in which image and language are communicative (and communicating) links in a chain, ripples in a stream, parts of a process in which content dictates form (multiple forms) and knowledge is gleaned from the patient accumulation of and meditation on narrative variety—like Rose, the reader must work through layers of story to achieve clarity of/for vision. It is a scenario that resists any too-easy "privileging of writing as recorded speech," which Teuton, after Derrida, insists "has led to the perception that context-dependent forms of signification . . . are less culturally advanced" (2010, xv). The challenge to "the way writing as recorded speech has been valued as the most technologically advanced, clearest, most efficient mode of signifying" (xv) is not to displace writing as a valuable technology, but to use it to incorporate other formal possibilities, including varieties of oral performance—drama, courtroom speeches, tape recordings, and a talking bird—and graphic and visual forms such as painting, photography, treaty making, sculpture, and more into "writing" as a formal category.

These ultimately textual maneuvers correspond to Teuton's three shared "basic commitments" of Native cultures and literature, themselves concordant with the interplay between oral, graphic, and critical impulses: "(1) to develop new knowledge in relation to a dynamically changing group experience," which at the very least describes the forging of a memoried community for Oskinaway, developing new knowledge in several spheres for both him and his readers in the context of at least three generations' worth of change. Teuton's second commitment, meanwhile, more explicitly and immediately embodies the story cycle, its "relay" of knowledge, and Oskinaway's reception of the stories: "(2) to maintain necessary knowledge for posterity and to share that knowledge." At the same time, "(3) to critique both the contents of and the process leading to that knowledge," speaks resonantly to Peters's argument that knowing, and understanding that knowledge, is key to future decision-making, which in turn echoes through the novel's closing sections, in the community's dilemma over the watercourse, in particular (Teuton 2010, xvi). In explaining the balance inherent to his understanding of the oral and graphic impulses, Teuton argues that without the counterbalancing effects of the graphic impulse, "where once an oral tradition represented a group's fluid intellectual engagement with the world, it now risks becoming mystical dogma disconnected from the contemporary lived experience of a community." Meanwhile, "when cut off from the oral impulse the graphic impulse may overreach its cultural roles and become abstract, theoretical in the narrow sense, freezing community knowledge in objectifying, unchanging, authoritative forms" (xvii). If we accept Teuton's judgment here, we can certainly understand *The Light People* as a text that consciously inter-weaves and balances the visual (graphic) with the oral in ways that consistently and persistently undermine the authority of the written representation. Indeed, the text itself, even as it seeks to represent both the content and connective web of the oral, and even as it contains the critical impulse in the complicating tension between form and content, becomes simply another instance of the graphic impulse. Where "writing has been a tool of both colonialism and survivance" (Teuton 2010, xix), this model demonstrably favors survivance, decentering writing's ability to carry the whole message by consistently and repeatedly reminding its readers of the immediacy and possibility inherent in other media.

Teuton turns to Vizenor, and specifically to Vizenor's *Bearheart: The Heirship Chronicles*, to address the dominance of alphabetic text and the wielding of docu-ments in the settler-colonial suppression of Indigenous knowledge. As is commonly asserted—and abundantly clear—in Vizenor's work, writing as a tool of oppression comes under regular fire: writing that works toward the erasure of writing's authority is, thus, central to his haiku aesthetic. As I will argue in the next chapter, and as is highlighted here, the graphic impulse—visual forms that preexist the imposition of alphabetic literacy and generate alternative literacies that interact with, support, preserve, and predicate the oral tradition—is nevertheless central to that same aesthetic. Indeed, when the haikuist seeks the haiku's dissolution, it is to a range of other sensory apparatus it appeals, including sight, sound, and sensation, through the evocation of the scene/seen, the felt element, and the season. The haiku, in being a written form itself, thus emphasizes the place of the graphic—whose marks are "permanent" even as they insinuate the "impermanent" or momentary—in a compound process, a deferral through form as well as language, and a means of avoiding "capture by text" (see Cox 2006).

In no small measure, then, *The Light People* speaks to Teuton's reminder that "how American Indian literary studies defines *oral tradition* and *writing* matters deeply, for these terms carry an intellectual genealogy into their critical usage today" (2010, 8). While Henry's novel resists any too-easy conflation or elision of alphabetic text and other forms of mark and image making, it nevertheless posits a series of reminders of alternative textualities. In the Strawberry Inn bar, for instance, a curiosity cabinet of trade goods including "photographic prints and drawings . . . a variety of red pipestone pipes . . . carved into animal shapes of eagles and buffalo" or otherwise ornamented, adorns the trading establishment's walls. "On both sides of the mirror" behind the bar's liquor stand, "simulated treaty documents covered the wall in glass cases. Human clay figures, about a foot tall—each unique, in facial feature and physique, each marked with an engraved pictograph on the forehead—lined shelves above the treaties" (Henry 1994, 68). Besides the textuality of the objects themselves—what material cultural studies understands as their witness to events, above and beyond the relationship of purpose and form—the juxtaposition of treaty documents and sculptural figures is highly suggestive. The semiotics of this scenario are highly nuanced, but I read them in the following way. While the treaties appear to take pride of place and, furthermore, are "preserved" in their glass cases, there is a clear significance to their being simulations—not even facsimiles, but simulations, that is, not the copy of a form but its imitation—that renders this image of enshrinement ironic. Given the gap—already discussed here—between the process the treaty represents and the effects (and indeed affect) of the document, the encasing of simulations of those documents mocks their relationship to the real while also mocking the valorization of the written text as manifestations of truth, fact, or reality. Further, as simulations, they have not been touched by the hands that forged them, unlike the other "texts" in the bar, which, whether photographic prints or modeled pipes, bear the "presence," in a manner of speaking, either of their referent or their maker.[12]

This seeming displacement of the document, then, is further encoded in the novel's use of the X mark as a mobile site—the X that marks the spot where culture, community, identity, whatever entity it is that the seeker seeks, stands—rather than as a fixed point in time or space. The treaty that marks out the territory through the dots and dashes of cadastral boundaries, that lays out the "claim" that enables the agency, or in this case the trader/bar, to establish its "legitimate" trade on the boundary, and that codifies the rights of the people without due recognition of how they recognize those rights, the document—a minor part of the process that nevertheless represents the whole—is shown to be partial, artificial, a sign that "dissimulate[s] the fact that there is nothing behind [it]" (Baudrillard 1994, 5) other than the pure image of the settler-colonial display of power. Set as they are behind glass, however, they ironically represent artifacts or even art works, their X marks the marks of makers neither less authentic nor pregnant with possibility than the pipes and clay figures. On the one hand, then, it is a scene of commodity fetishism, a diorama of cultural cannibalism in which the legitimacy of the bar is underpinned by the false legitimacy of the rapacious and mendacious treaty process, its self-image of belonging bolstered by its collection of objects, and its trade dependent on a doubly debilitating exchange—culture for alcohol. Reminiscent, perhaps, of *Moby-Dick*'s Pequod, that "cannibal of a craft, tricking herself forth in the chased bones of her enemies" (Melville 1851, chap. 16), a synecdoche for empire or, here, settler colonialism itself, it also has echoes in the images of Tatro's collections described by Louise Erdrich in *The Painted Drum*.

In their turn, though, the "human clay figures" look down on the simulated treaties, the pictographic engravings on their foreheads a reminder both of the maker's intent and the relational dynamic into which they fit. Those pictographs, however arcane they may appear in the abstract, are readable signs, tied to a human community and embedded—as they are in the novel—in a story chain that charts the complex history of that community and the relationship between the material, experiential, and spiritual spheres. Writing of the creation story, Leanne Simpson, for instance, explains that "after Gzhwe Mnidoo has lowered me to the earth . . . [Gzhwe Mnidoo] put her/his right hand to my forehead and s/he transferred all of Gzhwe Mnidoo's thoughts into me" (2011a, 42). If we return to that earlier description of Abetung dropping his clay figures to the ground, we might read these figures, their foreheads marked, both as sculpture and as simulacra for the people themselves, sitting above those simulated treaties. Further, Simpson recalls that "the thoughts . . . spilled into every part of my being. . . . This tells us that in order to access knowledge from a Nishnaabeg perspective, we have to engage our entire bodies: our physical beings, emotional self, our spiritual energy and our intellect" (2011a, 42). Taking account of this detail, the figures, then, conjure a distinct contrast to the way the treaties themselves "embody" the spirit of the agreement by, quite literally, stripping away the physical being, emotional self, and spiritual energy, leaving only dry discourse and privileging the intellect over and above embodied knowledge.

As artifacts, the treaties, like Moses Four Bears's leg in the thrall of the anthropologists, are susceptible to meaning being projected onto them. That meaning differs markedly between the storied context the novel depicts—a context that represents the relational network that the "bare language of the document" obscures (Borrows 1997, 155)[13]—and the legal discursive framework from which treaties derive. If the stories provide the means, as Peters suggests, to recover or acquire the knowledge required to navigate and, as Teuton suggests, furnish the critical impulse to balance the graphic and oral—if the stories, in other words, complete their own hermeneutic circle—it is through multiplicity of form and perception that their meaning is to be recovered. The simulated treaties have no greater authority in determining the status of the community or its future, and certainly communicate no more of its past, than the other "texts" alongside which they sit and through which the stories Oskinaway is introduced to circulate.

The prominence and priority of these alternative textualities is ultimately inscribed in the very name of the bar itself and held in the foreground by the centrality of Elijah Cold Crow's haiku. That Cold Crow delivers his "writings . . . drawings" to Bombarto Rose in the form of a birchbark bundle evokes a continuity of tradition that takes in the mnemonic pictographic scroll, that early form of "oral tradition" the dental pictograph or birchbark biting, song scrolls, and mide map scrolls. The latter are particularly brought to mind by that scattering throughout the novel of strawberries—in the Strawberry Inn, and Oshawa's first crush Marie Strawberry—which feature notably in the sacred scrolls of the Ojibwe as presented by Selwyn Dewdney. I take their presence here as semiotic indicators—readers cognizant with the mide scrolls may, of course, infer more—and do not wish to dwell on the potential spiritual significance of the mide scrolls, other than perhaps to suggest that their function (for select initiates rather than general consumption) as documenting, teaching, and sustaining knowledge accords neatly with other arguments I have made here about the nature of story in the novel. The strawberry—or heartberry—is a delicious, sweet treat that in many versions of the story of its origin, such as that told by Lillian Pitawanakwat, "teaches forgiveness and peace" (2006). In the major instances of its occurrence in *The Light People*, however, its effect is inverted. Jealousy and bullying drive Oshawa's enemies to humiliate him in front of the Strawberry girl, whose favor they all seek. The Strawberry Inn, meanwhile, symbolizes the temptation that draws all of the children in—doubtless anticipating a form of freedom that turns out to be destructive. It is not, then, that these motifs indexically link Henry's stories to specific traditional stories, so much that their presence reiterates and sustains the recurrent emphasis on narrative and form—on the availability of forms of textuality—that predate, persist in spite of and alongside, and resist the domination of alphabetic script.

The visual aesthetic of *The Light People* speaks directly to Teuton's sense, drawing on Barthes's *Degree Zero*, of the processual and relational nature of the image-text, for which Henry's image of the flowing river, whose secrets, like those of the stories themselves, may be understood by those with patience and the ability to transcend self in order to garner them, is apposite. Solutions not forthcoming, the appeal of the engineer's idea in the community meeting toward the end of the novel speaks directly to the dualistic, literalist epistemic structures in which they have become caught: he suggests that they simply divert the course of the river—that, effectively, and in the absence of understanding, they simply force from narrative the meaning they desire. *The Light People* directly addresses, through dream, vision, multiple, experimental form, performance, and so much more, the need for the imagination and understanding to escape what Leanne Simpson calls "the cognitive box of imperialism" (2011a, 146). Mitchell addresses collective philosophical anxiety about the "pictorial turn"; that anxiety is shared by many who comment on the dominance of the image. Above, I quoted Baudrillard's thesis on simulation and simulacra in precisely that vein. If, there, Henry exposes the flimsiness of the document in its own right, elsewhere in the novel the relationship between the image and the actual, the simulation and the real fails to provoke a similar sense of anxiety—its X marks less phantoms than waymarkers in the increasingly unnavigable waters. Thus, what may seem at first aesthetic or even theoretical abstractions are firmly grounded in the ethics of relation that the network of visual images forms, and the specific relationships of creation and perception thread through the novel. Channeling Vizenor's account of Quanah Parker's photographic portrayal, vision and the visual in *The Light People* symbiotically resist the illegitimate textuality of the *indian* image and generate the tools of reconciliation through agency: "His eyes are the presence of the pictures; the stories of resistance, and traces of native survivance. His eyes dare the very closure of his own fugitive poses" (Vizenor 1998, 160).

Picturing Absence
and Postcolonial Presence

Unsettling a Colonial Grammar in Selected Works by Louise Erdrich

Since publication of her first novel, *Love Medicine*, in 1984, Louise Erdrich has regularly engaged with a variety of texts and images—documents such as maps and treaties, paintings, sculptures, objects and artifacts, popular stereotypes and Indigenous cultural forms—by way of both examining the cultural logics of colonization and exploring the various levels of resistance to and survivance in spite of its impacts. In so doing, she both invokes and disrupts what Mishuana Goeman (writing of the visual and political artwork of Seminole-Muscogee-Navajo photographer Hulleah Tsinhnahjinnie's photographic memoir) describes as "the forms that have constituted a colonial grammar and the forms that are manipulated . . . to make legible the power relations within them" (2014, 239). While none "of the elements that compose Tsinhnahjinnie's visual memoir are in themselves tribally specific" (239), Erdrich's work has long been understood as emanating from an Ojibwe ground and perspective, although the dominating focus of critics over the years has been its hybrid, cross- or bicultural, and postmodern patterning. The cultural demands thus placed on it—as site of sought authenticity for some and evidence of the (im)possibility of cultural authority for others—often detract from its literary qualities, but Margaret Noodin aptly summarizes the finely balanced texture of Erdrich's work when she insists that "certainly one can read each [of her works] for perspectives that are broadly indigenous, clearly postcolonial, and in many instances specifically Anishinaabe, but the dominant voice is that of a mother, a woman trying to manage the balance of caring for herself and her own sanity while also taking care of others" (2014a, 47). In beginning my discussion here with an examination of Erdrich's second memoir, *Books and Islands in Ojibwe Country*,[1] it is explicitly with the overriding ethic of parental (or kinship) responsibility, and a sense of tracing/writing a way back into Anishinaabe practices, and as liberation from the static signifiers of "Indianness" generated within Goeman's "colonial grammar" that this chapter is framed.

This chapter, then, is formed of two parts. In the first section, my exploration of Erdrich's trip into what she calls "Ojibwe country" in *Books and Islands* focuses on the self-reflexive interplay between reading, writing, and culture in that text. As such, her journey into marked terrain—marked in the sense both of the painted rocks of Lake of the Woods and in the sense of the colonial cartography signified in various ways throughout the text—effects a process of unmapping and remapping: as Chris LaLonde puts it in his description of the text's relationship to the printed map of the Canada-U.S. border on its cover page, "the effort at apprehension and orientation which is at the heart of all maps is immediately supplemented in Erdrich's narrative by a certain disorientation and reorientation" (n.d., 8). That reorientation—a navigation of sorts between ancestral spaces in the north and the vibrant network of connection the author enjoys back in the Twin Cities—unsettles and reimagines maps both real and metaphorical, maps that navigate landscapes and story-maps that navigate phenomenological and political understandings of self, of community, of culture and nation, while resisting totalizing interpretations of any of those terms. As such, the journey "back" into Ojibwe country generates a space of deep cultural immersion, a space out of time, that then refigures itself intermittently in the more quotidian routines of daily life, furnishing textual markers of those land- and context-dependent writing practices to which scholars such as Lisa Brooks have turned in their discussions of landed sovereignty.

In the second part of this chapter, I turn away from the literal ground of Ojibwe country to consider the more abstract realm of interplay between visual practices and (counter)representations of the *indian*, whose image, arguably, is a primary function of the visuality that sustains settler colonial logics, rendering Erdrich's portrayals largely acts of engaged resistance. While Erdrich engages in various ways the cultural rhetorics of specific Indigenous forms of image making and picture writing—the painted rocks of *Books and Islands*, birchbark inscription in her series of young adult communication to another Indian, and by them make himself as well understood as a pale face can by letter.

There are over two hundred figures in general use for all the purposes of correspondence. Material things are represented by pictures of them.

THE CHARACTERS USED IN PICTURE WRITING.

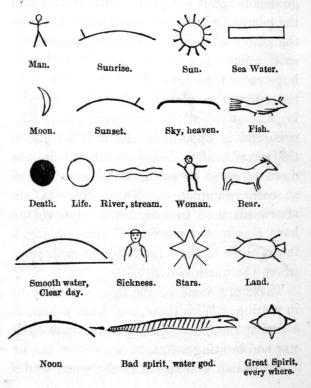

1A. Pages from George Copway's *Traditional History and Characteristic Sketches of the Ojibway People*. Screenshot. (pg. 134).

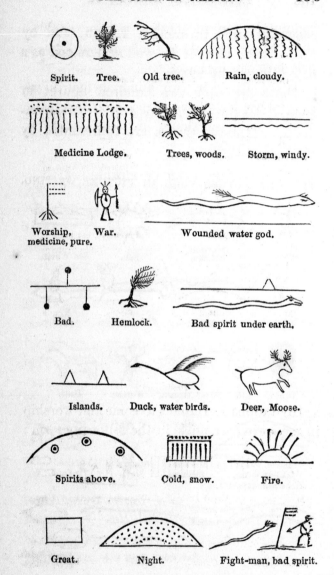

Spirit. Tree. Old tree. Rain, cloudy.

Medicine Lodge. Trees, woods. Storm, windy.

Worship, medicine, pure. War. Wounded water god.

Bad. Hemlock. Bad spirit under earth.

Islands. Duck, water birds. Deer, Moose.

Spirits above. Cold, snow. Fire.

Great. Night. Fight-man, bad spirit.

1B. Pages from George Copway's *Traditional History and Characteristic Sketches of the Ojibway People.* Screenshot. (pg. 135).

Bear killed. Spirits under water. Stand.

Animals under ground. Ran. Walked, passed. Hand, did so.

See. Speak. Sea Monster, eat man.

Mountains. Bad Spirit, Medicine. Scalps, number. Young warrior,

Dream.

Invitations to Indians to come and worship in the spring are made in the following form :

Medicine House. Great Lodge. Wigwam, woods. Come.

Great Spirit. Canoe. River. Lake.

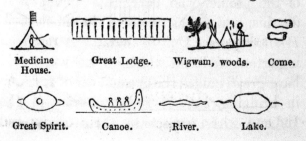

1C. Pages from George Copway's *Traditional History and Characteristic Sketches of the Ojibway People.* Screenshot. (pg. 136).

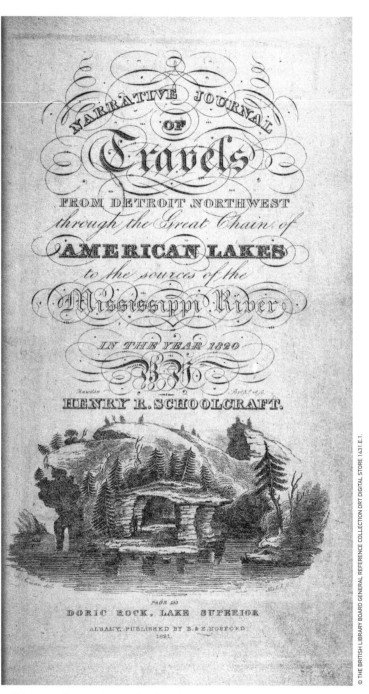

NARRATIVE JOURNAL OF Travels

FROM DETROIT NORTHWEST

through the Great Chain of

AMERICAN LAKES

to the sources of the

Mississippi River

IN THE YEAR 1820

Rawdon *Script sc*

HENRY R. SCHOOLCRAFT.

PAGE 155

DORIC ROCK, LAKE SUPERIOR

ALBANY, PUBLISHED BY E. & E. HOSFORD
1821.

2. Title page of Henry Rowe Schoolcraft's *Narrative Journal*, 1821, depicting the Doric Rock.

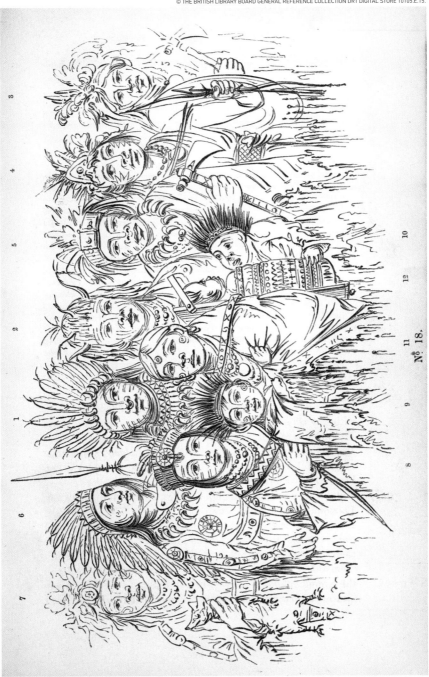

3. George Catlin, Maungwudaus's troupe.

Nº 21.

4. George Catlin, the canoe race.

No. 23.

5. Say-say-gon's sketch of Pane-way-ee-tung crossing the River Thomas.

№ 24.

6. Say-say-gon's sketch of On-daig meeting a white man for the first time.

7. Screen capture from Heid Erdrich's video poem, "Pre-Occupied" (0:37), with thanks to Heid Erdrich for permission to reproduce a still from the video poem.

8. Irwin Brothers, "Mabel Mahseet, Comanche," Irwin Brothers Studio Collection #45.

9. Frank Big Bear, *Time Zones (Red Owl)*, 2012, detail, collage on found paper.

10. The Indigenous "villain" from "Electric Earthquake" (DC Comics), screen capture.

11. Carl Ray, *Medicine Bear*, 1977. Collection of Sunita D. Doobay.

12. Patrick DesJarlait (1921–72), *Red Lake Fishermen*, 1946, watercolor on paper, 14 × 18 inches.

13. George Morrison, *Flight*, 1956.

14. A. Y. Jackson, *Terre Sauvage*, 1913, oil on canvas, 128.8 × 154.4 cm. Acquired 1936. National Gallery of Canada, Ottawa.

15. Marc Chagall, *A Pinch of Snuff*, 1912.

16. Lascaux cave paintings.

17. The most famous of the Agawa Bay rock paintings.

18. José Clemente Orozco mural.

19. Theodoor Galle, "Allegory of America."

20. *Maun-gua-dous* (George Henry), oil on canvas, 1849–51; Paul Kane (1810, Mallow, Ireland—1871, Toronto, Canada).

WITH SPECIAL THANKS TO CAROLYN LEE ANDERSON.

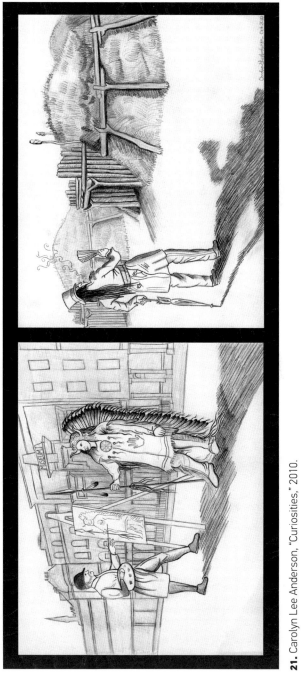

21. Carolyn Lee Anderson, "Curiosities," 2010.

22. Robert Houle, *Paris/Ojibwa*, 2010, Installation View 2—Art Gallery of Peterborough (2011).

23. Bonnie Devine, *Letter to William*, 2008.

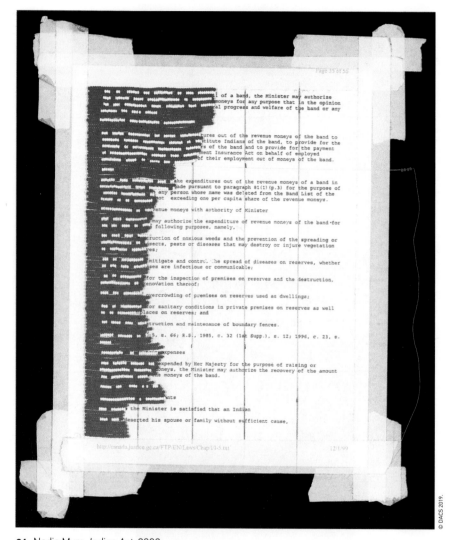

of a band, the Minister may authorize
moneys for any purpose that in the opinion
al progress and welfare of the band or any

tures out of the revenue moneys of the band to
titute Indians of the band, to provide for the
rs of the band and to provide for the payment
ment Insurance Act on behalf of employed
of their employment out of moneys of the band.

ake expenditures out of the revenue moneys of a band in
ade pursuant to paragraph 81(1)(p.3) for the purpose of
any person whose name was deleted from the Band List of the
ot exceeding one per capita share of the revenue moneys.

venue moneys with authority of Minister

may authorize the expenditure of revenue moneys of the band for
following purposes, namely,

ruction of noxious weeds and the prevention of the spreading or
sects, pests or diseases that may destroy or injure vegetation
ves;

mitigate and control the spread of diseases on reserves, whether
ses are infectious or communicable;

for the inspection of premises on reserves and the destruction,
enovation thereof;

vercrowding of premises on reserves used as dwellings;

or sanitary conditions in private premises on reserves as well
laces on reserves; and

truction and maintenance of boundary fences.

5, s. 66; R.S., 1985, c. 32 (1st Supp.), s. 12; 1996, c. 23, s.

expenses

expended by Her Majesty for the purpose of raising or
oneys, the Minister may authorize the recovery of the amount
the moneys of the band.

nts

the Minister is satisfied that an Indian

eserted his spouse or family without sufficient cause,

24. Nadia Myre, *Indian Act*, 2002.

novels, the visionary aesthetic and technology of the drum in *The Painted Drum*, beading in *The Antelope Wife*, and so on—she also evokes iconic artistic images and uses art and artists to explore a range of questions. From the limits of fiction as representative medium to the function of the arts in the oppressive machinery of the settler state, visual media, and art in particular, offers a lens on both microsocial relationships between couples and macrosocial relationships between Indigenous and settler societies in her work. Touching briefly on the first instance of this—the setting up of Nector's *Plunge of the Brave* pose in *Love Medicine*—this section will move on to consider two relationships between two female protagonists and male artists in *The Painted Drum* and *Shadow Tag*. Insofar as the two forms speak at once to intersubjective acts and to the difficulty, if not impossibility, of communication across what Jean Wyatt sees as epistemic difference central to Erdrich's work (2011), these themes also address "the fact that writing," and, I think we can add, art more broadly, "is necessarily about absence; it is a monument to loss. More to the point, writing can inscribe death, can mark the tomb of the Native" (LaLonde n.d., 5). Erdrich's work, then, grapples with both the ineffable loss inherent in the act of representation and the necessary acts of reclamation of, for instance, presence from absence, to which the writer/artist is called.

In *Books and Islands*, Erdrich avows directly that "books have been written around here ever since someone had the idea of . . . writing on birchbark with a sharpened stick" (2003, 11), evidence, as LaLonde points out, "of the centrality of writing and representation to the People" (n.d.). Published for a mainstream audience by National Geographic, Erdrich's words gained traction in literary academe through Lisa Brooks's insightful study *The Common Pot: The Recovery of Native Space in the Northeast*. There, in an incisive exploration and explication of the spatial—and scribal—praxis of the Abenaki and neighboring nations, Brooks notes that "just as Native writers spin the binary between word and image into a relational framework, they also challenge us to avoid the 'oppositional thinking that separates orality and literacy wherein the oral constitutes authentic culture and the written contaminated culture'" (2008, xxi; qtg. Womack). Alternatively, Peter Kulchyski describes the colonial logic embedded in the "violence in the letter" where he explains that "'we' from western culture have writing: 'they' have none; 'our' writing proves our cultural superiority: 'they' lack" (2012, 254). That oppositional thinking underpins a secondary form of colonial violence in the long-standing assumptions—inherent, still, to many forms of Native literary scholarship that invert the primacy of relations between orality and literacy that is itself reinforced through colonial grammars of purity and authenticity—that for a Native individual to write is to take one step away from their community and its traditional practices. As such, Drew Lopenzina argues, the early Native intellectual schooled in alphabetic literacy who often worked tirelessly on behalf of their communities has nevertheless been historically regarded "as a figure standing in isolation, an exception, or a genius of unusual talents who, by mastering European literacy, had in effect embraced colonial norms and turned his or her back upon Native peoples and traditions" (2012, 6). Such attitudes are not merely historical: "Even now, when so many Native people are writing and publishing," Brooks avers, "a belief persists that literacy is a mark of coercive colonialism and modernity inherently antithetical to Indigenous tradition" (2014, 536). This monolith has been challenged powerfully over the course of the last twenty or so years, not least in Native literary studies, through works that recover or reveal intellectual traditions that, in their celebration of Native praxis, refuse a priori demarcations of "Indigenous tradition." These demarcations amount, often, to reductive projections of assimilation.[2]

Intervening in that conversation, Erdrich's bold statement is rooted in linguistic (rather than material, mechanical, or functional) similitude. Reflecting on the prefix *mazina*, "the root for dozens of words all concerned with made images and with the substances upon which the images are put" (2003, 5), she then claims, "People have probably been writing books in North America since at least 2000 B.C. Or painting islands" (5). As such, she continues, "the Ojibwe people were great writers from way back and synthesized the oral and written tradition by keeping mnemonic scrolls of inscribed birchbark" (10), "*mazinibaganjigan*" or dental pictographs forging an early ironic bridge between Oral and literary traditions.[3] That at first glance Erdrich insists on a seemingly exhaustive understanding of the materiality of the "book" is not to elide the specific technologies she is referring to here. Indeed, it reminds us firstly that the "book" itself can refer to anything from a work of fiction to a set of legal documents; from a printed memoir to a hand-scribbled journal; from a textbook to a bound volume of printed images; and from the content of the object, of course, to the object itself. That, strictly speaking, it always refers in the contemporary vernacular to a portable, bound set of papers is in itself an evolutionary indicator of the book's function in modern societies, rather than any static, "natural" delimiter to what the book can be. Etymologically speaking, long-standing discussion of the relationship between the modern word "book" and the archaic German base of the word "beech" hints at an unexpected corollary even in Western understandings of precisely what a book is.[4]

What is more significant here than the materials, however, is Erdrich's deliberate move from the making of books to the fact of writing, inferring a relationship between her own status as writer and the traditional mark-making practices that she writes about in her examination of the landscape and painted rocks of Lake of the Woods. I have suggested elsewhere that this constitutes a claim to continuity, embedding contemporary Anishinaabe writing in a set of practices that precedes colonization (see Stirrup 2010b). That connection, in the embodied context of her journey, leaves the abstract realm as she describes female ancestors traced back by her mother and sister to Madeline Island: "Baupayakiingikwe, Striped Earth Woman, was one of those ancestors, as was Kwasenchiwin, Acts Like A Boy. . . . I can't help but imagine that these two women . . . walked where I've walked, saw what I've seen, perhaps traced these rock paintings. Perhaps even painted them" (2003, 80–81). Erdrich's own preference for the term "Ojibwe" over the now common autonym "Anishinaabe" to designate the People reinforces this because, as LaLonde puts it, "she pictures that the former is derived from the verb which means 'to write': *Ozhibii'ige*" (LaLonde n.d., 14; L. Erdrich 2003, 11).[5] The decolonizing implications of both the author's connection to prior forms of writing and the linguistic implications of the verb ozhibii'ge speak very directly to the politics of recovery and refusal outlined above. "She would have her reader see," LaLonde explains, "that the identity of the People is connected not merely to place and to language, but to writing" (n.d., 14). Writing becomes a sovereign act rather than an action indicative of assimilation.

Of course, it is not the tool but the manner of its use that remains paramount. Book history, then, which conventionally excludes the Indigenous peoples of the Americas until the eighteenth century at the earliest,[6] is beginning to take account of the fact that, in Germaine Warkentin's words, "the choice is not between objects that are books and those that are not; rather, it is the much more interesting difference between cultures that exhibit 'bookishness' and those that don't" (1999, 18). If, thus, "it is the individual culture that determines, inflects, and reinvents what it wishes to be its books" (18) then the apparent dichotomy of books and islands (or their painted rocks, at least) dissolves in the face of questions of function rather than form. As textual surfaces that demand to be read, the painted rocks of *Books and Islands*, which, as elsewhere, "represent the complex ecological and spiritual systems embedded in particular places" (Cariou and Sinclair 2011, 8), exhibit a "bookishness" that, functionally, is intimately tied to the oral cultures of the region, to the many stories and spirits immanent in the landscape. Some of those stories colonialism has erased from the collective memory, while others are retained and recalled by knowledge keepers like Tobasonakwut (who was himself involved in a project of reclamation of Ojibwe country), hunters like Nancy Jones, and language teachers such as Basil Johnston (through language tapes) and fellow language-learners in Minnesota. Still more, meanwhile, are forged through contemporary engagements with such spaces by Native visitors/readers/writers such as Erdrich herself. If, as Justice argues, "cultural investment in the idea of Indigenous peoples being consigned to the realm of the oral" embodies a move to "locate[] Indigenous knowledge outside of the sphere of legitimized cultural capital and thus relegate[] Indigenous intellectual and creative productions to the realm of fanciful prehistory" (2015, 293), Erdrich's intervention in *Books and Islands*, significantly, subtly unsettles the "bogus hierarchy" (Lopenzina 2012, 19) of written to oral and their assumed corollaries: modern/premodern, permanent/transient, universal/local and arcane, and so on.

It would be misleading if such a conclusion were read as a singular intent in *Books and Islands*. Like her earlier memoir, *The Blue Jay's Dance: A Birth Year* (1995), *Books and Islands* is partly an intimate reflection on motherhood, as Erdrich introduces her youngest daughter, Nenaa'ikiizhikok, to the land of her ancestors—those Ojibwe from whom Kiizhikok's father, Tobasonakwut, is directly descended.[7] In doing so, she also describes her attempts, through the doctoring of board books, to teach her daughter Anishinaabemowin as an infant, giving her knowledge and connection to the language that she herself has sought to learn as an adult. Furthermore, in doing so in the surrounds of both the painted rocks of Lake of the Woods and the isolated library of the ethnologist Ernest Oberholtzer on Mallard Island, Rainy Lake, she effects a rumination on the relationship between kinship (including with ancestral and spirit women), language, environment, literature/writing, and legacy or heritage. As such, the memoir is very far from being an ideologically driven assertion of continuity and connection, albeit its understanding of Ojibwe "textuality" effects engaged resistance to definitions of writing that specifically exclude nonalphabetic forms. Rather, it highly self-consciously engages with a sense of being out of place that accompanies the journey back into place through that combination of place, language, text, and kinship. This tension is reflected indeed in the apposition of books and islands, as Erdrich celebrates her lifelong love of the literary (including Laurence Sterne's *Tristram Shandy*, George

Eliot's *Middlemarch*, W. G. Sebald's *Austerlitz*, Jim Crace's *Quarantine*, and others, as well as nonfiction tomes like *A Concise Dictionary of Minnesota Ojibwe* and others she "sucks in" on Rainy Island such as the works of Ben Johnson, Chesterton on Blake, and the voyages of Radisson [L. Erdrich 2003, 111]), while acknowledging a general *il*literacy with respect to the painted rocks when she expresses her hope that Oberholtzer's "magnificent collection of ethnographic works on the Ojibwe" might "help explain the book-islands of Lake of the Woods" (3). As Brooks attests of those forms of awikhigan mentioned in my introduction, such images "are not always easily read" (2008, xxi). The implicit hesitancy, and indeed the responsibility of reading that accompanies such difficulty, ought not, as Justice abjures, to affix the rock paintings to an evolutionary arc on which "'alternative' textualities are those that are illegible to a mainstream audience" (2015, 302), but rather remind us of the context-dependent and community-specific nature of their creation. This intent is further underpinned as Erdrich describes the picture books she has "doctored" for her daughter this trip, overwriting their English text with Ojibwemowin. As such, Erdrich's text implicitly grows out of the very tensions Goeman's articulation of a colonial grammar generates, while her means of navigation combine the colonial ethnography with embodied experience, and personal connection, to quite literally recover the means of reading (and thus rewriting) Ojibwe country that settler-colonial statecraft has sought to erase.

Indeed, as Erdrich herself comments, "One thing certain is that the paintings were made by the ancestors of the present-day Anishinaabeg, for the ancient symbols . . . are as familiar and recognizable to Tobasonakwut as are, say [iconographic] signs to contemporary Americans" (2003, 49–50). In fact, earlier on in the book she claims, "in truth, since the writing or drawings that those ancient people left still makes sense to people living in Lake of the Woods today, one must conclude that they weren't the ancestors of the modern Ojibwe. They were and are the modern Ojibwe" (6). In claiming affiliation with the Anishinaabeg of Lake of the Woods and their historic practices, while simultaneously acknowledging a personal distance from both the forms and their meanings, Erdrich establishes a readerly relationship that necessitates translation through Ober's library, interpretation through Tobasonakwut's knowledge and memory, and the affective impact of her own apprehension in order for the author to fully comprehend the islands. From commentary on Tobasonakwut's childhood to that palpable sense of distance between Erdrich's present and the present-pastness immanent in the islands, "we see in no uncertain terms that Erdrich turns to writing in the face of loss," which haunts the text in all manner of ways. Nevertheless, as LaLonde continues, in so doing, rather than rehearsing a narrative of victimry or dwelling on the impacts of that trauma, Erdrich "returns to the connections that are articulated in the writings she finds, especially, on Painted Rock Island" (LaLonde n.d., 15). Those connections, moreover, articulate a sense of continuity that, like Noodin's description of the movement of Anishinaabe stories "like metamorphic rocks" into English, create "an indigenous modernity, still centered in the space of the Great Lakes" (Noodin 2014a, 22), and resound through the broader diaspora of historic Ojibwe migration, including vital fur-trade locations between the Great Lakes and the West such as Lake of the Woods.

The personal connections Erdrich threads together in *Books and Islands* speak in a variety of ways to the broader concerns of "Indian country," in all its forms and variations. That the books and book-islands she explores embody Ojibwe country every bit as much as the physical geography and geo-spiritual history she describes quietly resists all of the pejorative corollaries to the oral tradition noted above, instead fully complementing and interlacing that memoried archive while emphasizing the contemporary relevance and resurgence of those practices most closely related to it, such as language and spiritual revitalization, environmental/ medicinal knowledge, and more. Moreover, it "spins the binary" in Brooks's terms, between oral and written, by both emphasizing the long literary history of the Ojibwe and by introducing what Christopher Teuton sees as the third term, a "critical impulse" deeply connected to the relationship between the oral and the graphic traditions (as connoted by the painted rocks). "The privileging of writing as recorded speech," which, ultimately, has "contributed to the historical and political subjugation of Native communities by characterizing them as oral, nonliterate people," has, Teuton argues, "blinded scholars to the ways oral and graphic traditions function in interdependent ways in the expression of Indigenous knowledge" (2010, xv). Literally marking terrain, communicating geographical information, and capturing, translating, and perpetuating the visionary experiences and their legacies of Anishinaabeg intermediaries, the ancestral marks within the fabric of Erdrich's own documenting signal what Molly McGlennen calls "a heart-center that supplants colonial and tribal mappings of territory with storied and peopled 'mappings' of territory" (2015, 3). As it does for McGlennen, that "heart-center" places Erdrich in the city, but it is no less formed by the Anishinaabe spaces she explores and the fluid, migratory connections she embodies. As LaLonde notes, in reading the book-islands, "Erdrich asks that we pay particular attention to the 'lines drawn between things' in the pictographs 'for they express relationships'" (LaLonde n.d., 15; L. Erdrich 2003, 56).

In his thought-provoking essay "Bush/Writing," Peter Kulchyski asserts that when the famous "teaching rocks" of Peterborough, Ontario, are "assimilate[d]" to "the category of literature," they "retain a stronger destabilizing power" relative to what he calls "the writing of the state" to which Indigenous peoples are asked to surrender. Inquiring what it means to call that which has "been compared to visual art" *literature*, in order to call up its power to "disturb the very being of literature," he asks, "what kind of literature inscribes itself on rock?" (2012, 262). This same question is implicit in Erdrich's alignment of books with islands. As Kulchyski describes it, the writing of the state encompasses acts that seek to displace or erase the original embodied presence of the people, by removing, collecting, labeling, and otherwise controlling/destroying the residual agency that inheres in inscription. We might add to this notion as simple a definition of the literary that excludes non-Western understandings—an argument that readily encapsulates debate around the status of the oral tradition for much of the twentieth century, and in which Warkentin's interrogative suggestion that "the European definition of the 'written' in fact may involve some kind of category mistake" (1999, 12) takes its place. Writing in critique of the ways in which the state "as a totalizing structure" seeks "to ensure that time, space, and subjectivity are reconfigured in a manner conducive to the expansion of the commodity form and the accumulation of capital," Kulchyski argues that "writing is one of the key mechanisms that the state deploys in this field of activity," calculating, observing, measuring, reporting, "creat[ing] its own referent," and ultimately producing "linear, phonetic notation, individualized through the guarantee of the signature, [as] the form of writing associated with state power and [that] becomes defined as the only form of writing that exists" (2012, 253). It demands a counter and, as a Native woman well versed in its "culturally embedded" protocols, but with explicit connection to alternative literacies, Erdrich is well placed to engage a form of writing "against" the state (Kulchyski 2012, 253).

For Kulchyski, one manner of articulating "writing against the state" is a form of "embodied deconstruction," wherein embodiment marks "the movement of meaning away from universal abstraction toward situation, context, the body of land and people, individual or social" (266). Kulchyski's use of deconstruction here, meanwhile, "refers to a writing that insistently displaces certain hierarchical dualisms associated with a metaphysics of presence that ground western philosophical thought and practice" (266). It is not hard to understand Erdrich's journey into—and return from—Ojibwe country through such a lens. Exploring the relations that bind her to terrain somewhat distant from the open prairies of her native Minnesota and urban maze of her home city Minneapolis, Erdrich's return to the city community that provides a very different kind of solace—"Now, as I merge past Cloquet . . . the little cell phone I've taken, silent all along, makes a triumphant tootling sound. . . . All of a sudden I am back in the web of connection" (2003, 130)—carries with it the traces of her narrative of northerly venture, further participating in the "writing against the state" that questions the colonial history and its continued legacies in both settler states and for the Anishinaabe diaspora.

Erdrich thus orientates through Anishinaabe terrain and Anishinaabe understandings of that terrain without—and this is her genius—either obscuring Ojibwe modernity (in the form of diverse contemporary experience of both urban and rural spaces with differing notions of center that are all culturally and politically valid) or taking on herself the mantle of insider cultural knowledge that could render her text an artifact of bearing witness to authenticity. Instead, it presents a highly individual experience of what it means to be Ojibwe on a spectrum that takes in the full span of that terrain, the full compass of those centers. McGlennen avers that Vizenor's poetry "offers a blueprint for Anishinaabeg definitions of nation and citizenship marked *not* by states' attempts to regulate movement of people across borders, but rather by the people themselves determining the locales and ideals of the nation" (2015, 2). That Erdrich's concerns with Ojibwe country in *Books and Islands* share affinity with such an agenda is perhaps most evident in a literal border crossing. That crossing at the international border—wherein Erdrich's maternal relationship to Kiizhikok is questioned by aggressively zealous border guards—serves both to illuminate the precarity of the nation-state, its vulnerability producing a paranoia at the boundaries that has come to characterize the post-9/11 era,[8] and to remind us of the historical interruption that the settler-colonial state and its imposition of arbitrary boundaries presents to Indigenous communities. Even more evocatively—and painfully—Erdrich discusses her relationship to Kiizhikok in light of her reading of W. G. Sebald's *Austerlitz*, declaring her daughter "a light" (2003, 135) in contrast to the "chasm into which no light could penetrate" (134), which is how the narrator of *Austerlitz* characterizes the Holocaust. Recalling her term of study under Dan Jacobson at University College, London, in 1976, she writes of his childhood experiences of the Kimberly diamond mines in South Africa: "I can almost see him describe how it was terrifying to see such emptiness open up a foot away from firm ground, to realize that there was no transition, only this dividing line, with ordinary life on one side and its unimaginable opposite on the other" (134). Thinking of the Ojibwe people, she then ruminates, "it is as though when I look past a generation or into the past of Tobasonakwut's world there is a lightlessness, too, for nine of every ten native people perished . . . leaving only diminished and weakened people to encounter . . . the aggressions of civilization" (134–35).

Although Erdrich does not make the link explicit, this dividing line evokes the international border or, more specifically, what that border represents with respect to the imposition of spatialized markers onto Indigenous space. As Goeman observes, "The development of modern nation-states depended on sending out official mapmaking expeditions as a state tool to find information that would enable the assertion of political force over territories and all contained within" (2013, 401). For Indigenous peoples, the border survey was a different but no less damaging form of production "of the knowledge from which conquest could flow" from expeditions designed specifically to map the future of "territorial accumulation" (410). In this respect, I follow Chris LaLonde's assessment, as he "[takes] the measure of representations in and of the text, especially as they are connected to what [he] read[s] as a tacit critique of Euroamerican and Eurocanadian authority" (n.d., 17). For LaLonde, this finds its clearest expression in the reproduction of a simple line-drawn map in the front matter, which clearly labels the United States (Minnesota specifically) and Canada (represented by portions of three provinces) and "purports to help the reader get a handle on place by locating it in space and orienting it in relation to nations and borders" (5).

While the map conventionally presents a bifurcated continent (North America), we receive a classically dichotomous sense of the United States and Canada through the scene described above, wherein Canada signifies welcome while the United States is hostile even to its own citizens; and wherein Canada's cultural landscape offers an image of Indigenous preservation (despite acknowledged political oppression and suppression), set against the author's metropolitan American "home." Rhetorically (and somewhat ironically), Erdrich evokes the random distinctions of the settler-colonial nation-state to both emphasize the ways in which historical legacies and political concerns differ either side of the line and further emphasize the ways in which they remain deeply connected despite that history. Where many have read fragmentation in a kind of cultural dilution implied by Erdrich's fictional communities, her interplay as insider-outsider, as she examines her relationship to her daughter's ancestors in ways that make her own belonging apparent while simultaneously acknowledging her alienation, draws together these apparent divisions.

Dean Rader explains that "one of the stories maps tell is of the collaboration between the verbal and the visual. Pictographically, maps represent a space, and linguistically, language narrates that space" (2011, 50). Exploring the map essentially laid out by the painted rocks (as territorial markers, as guides for hunters, and as sites of spiritual significance), and by the historical continuities of ancestral Anishinaabeg and their contemporary descendants in what Erdrich designates Ojibwe country on her prefatorial map, the author effectively superimposes a countermap that does not simply erase but massively complicates the erasures of colonial cartography. Her assertion that in order to write about the landscape she apprehends requires a working knowledge of Native languages—"For an American writer, it seems crucial to at least have a passing familiarity with [Ojibwemowin], which is adapted to the land as no other language can possibly be" (2003, 85)—engenders an engaged resistance to the colonially bound spatio-linguistic terms of conventional mapping. Meanwhile, Margaret Noodin's description of petroglyphs and painted rocks presents an alternative map, which resounds in the spatiotemporal expansiveness of Erdrich's descriptions. "Traces of stories on stone extend back in time," writes Noodin, describing the discovery of petroglyphs at Lake of the Woods's Mud Portage. Buried under layers of archaeological deposit up to five thousand years old, these petroglyphs are thought to have been made about two thousand years ago (n.d., 4). The oldest alphabetic records of the peoples and their languages and stories—the *Jesuit Relations*, in the mid-nineteenth century—embody, along with the images on rock, "evidence of continued cultural practice, a group of speakers who adapted a shared system of symbol, sound and meaning to communicate essential information, preserve communal knowledge and celebrate the sustainability of their culture" (Noodin n.d., 4). The shift from rock-text to alphabetic diary, then, signifies for Noodin, as it does for Erdrich, a complicating of existing cultural forms, rather than fracture.

LaLonde suggests a form of reclamation of the map in the visual as well as the narrative elements of the book. He argues that "in labeling the larger map Ojibwe Country, *Books and Islands* produces a supplement to the nation, be it the United States of America or Canada, and thus calls the identity of both and their authority and power into question" (n.d., 8). As a form of engaged resistance, *Books and Islands* certainly "performs" in this way. At the same time, however, Erdrich's movement through the land with her daughter very much echoes Kulchyski's apprehension of the Peterborough Rocks as a form of writing against the state, where he writes:

> these places have something, some things, to teach. they are sacred places and speak of deeply spiritual and social matters. they are sites of art, of the expressive power of images. they are sites of remembrance, of social being, of reflection. they recall the expressive powers and inspirations of generations past. they are writings and stories. they are inscribed on rock. . . . they challenge not only the grammatical structure that underlies our literature—the form by which an inscription contains and expresses its meaning, the framing devices and internal rules of order that ensure self-consolidation, totality, and coherence—but the very mode of inscription that founds the being of euro-western writing. . . . they demand remembrance of the ethical charge of embodied writing, that subjects make their own interpretations and retain their powers of situational judgment, all within a strong social context. (2012, 263–64)

In apprehending the pictographs of Lake of the Woods herself, Erdrich highly self-consciously "fails" to read them, evincing her unfamiliarity and discomfort in their company. Yet their reading is also in itself a form of writing, a retracing of the "situational judgment" Kulchyski describes, within a social context that extends from her friends and family in Minneapolis to her maternal ancestors at Madeline Island, and the ancient ancestors of Tobasonakwut's forebears—all channeled, ultimately, through the next inheritor of this verbal-visual heritage, Kiizhikok, who, ironically, appropriately, Erdrich is teaching Anishinaabemowin through board books, appending image and text, and immersing her in the landscape of her ancestors. Thus, the map of Ojibwe country and the book's own remapping of connections "mediate[s and complicates] the maps of colonial and national imaginative geographies" by taking account of "Native-made spaces that are too often disavowed, appropriated, or co-opted by the settler state through writing, imagining, law, politics, and the terrains of culture" (Goeman 2013, 508) and alternatively maps an embodied geography that refuses the palimpsestic writing of the settler nation-state even as it explores and acknowledges its impacts.

Despite—or even perhaps because of—her explorations of the pictographs of "Pub-be-kwaw-waung-gaw Sau-gi-e-gun" (Tanner 1830, 48), or Lake of the Sand

Hills,[9] Erdrich does not reach to that figural tradition in her fiction, with the odd minor exception when, for instance, Nokomis in *The Birchbark House*, Erdrich's first young adult novel, compares the "tracks" of writing to picture writing. In fact, she does so in deliciously subtle and ironic terms, when Nokomis, watching the white girl Angela's demonstration of her writing practice responds to her explanation that "they're letters. . . . One follows the next. You look at them, just like tracks. You read them. They have a meaning and a sound," by exclaiming, "'Howah! That's a good idea! Like our picture writing" (2000, 178). Although, as I have suggested in chapter 2, Erdrich evokes totemic signs and the traces of human marks on surfaces in her poetry, Erdrich's fiction differs from most of what I have covered in this book for the absence of such signifiers. Such marks of transient presence, from the handprint on a bedroom lamp to the bitten incision on birchbark, become one of a number of means of reenlivening the directness and the ephemeral brevity of the "relational and experiential engagement with the world" that Teuton identifies in the "oral impulse" (2010, xvi). Erdrich's prose fiction, meanwhile, takes a more explicit and categorical turn toward the documentary and to the relationship between speech and writing, the oral and the written, as key determinative factors in the negotiation of what I will call a colonial dynamics of agency—or a centuries-old contest over rights of belonging, of belief, and of self-determination.

There are two texts in which more specifically continuous material practices occur—that is, practices that persist in relatively unchanged form from pre- to postcontact times—developing a cultural rhetoric around beading rather than painting on or carving into surfaces. In *The Antelope Wife*, for instance, the motif of beading takes both a metaphorical as well as a literal place in the novel, encapsulating material change (in the substance of the beads, for instance) while grounding both the characters and the broader community in traditions that reflect both precolonial practices and adaptation during and after contact. In *The Painted Drum*, meanwhile, beading Simon Jack's moccasins becomes a task over which Anaquot and Ziigwan'aage bond, sewing their revenge into a form that forces Jack to literally dance himself to death. Combining a material practice with powerful medicine and a narrative of female solidarity, Erdrich reveals little of the aesthetic practice beyond its medicinal potential. As such, it becomes an exemplary instance of what some commentators have categorized as magical realism in her work—a reading that bears more toward the postcolonial than the Indigenous/decolonial aesthetics I have engaged thus far. Vizenor's own insistence on understanding the "magical" in his work as, in fact, "mythic verism" arguably speaks to Erdrich's intent in her fiction; such a distinction is ultimately peripheral to this conversation, of course, but it is worth absorbing the way in which Erdrich's express acknowledgement of ethnographic material—while also a caveat against revealing sacred knowledge—insists on an authenticatable verity regarding the material object itself.[10]

Thus, while the drum in *The Painted Drum* represents arguably the most significant moment in Erdrich's adult fiction where dreams, visual aesthetics, and creative spiritual practices intersect in a narrative that, according to Jean Wyatt's reading, recalls the emphasis of Nationalist critics such as Warrior, Weaver, and Womack on "the value of works that adapt traditional practices and metaphysics to the complexities of contemporary life" (2011, 15), Erdrich's acknowledgement of its ethnographic basis underlines the general absence of such representation from her work. Although Wyatt uncritically invokes a "divide" in Native American literary studies that a number of critics, including Jace Weaver (see Weaver 2013), have done much to unpack, her reading offers a perceptive understanding of the drum as both narrative device and material artifact; what is arguably most interesting here is that the repeated use of Anishinaabe oral stories in Erdrich's early work are not given the same kind of caveat (although doubtless the same rules about sacred knowledge apply), thus generating a clear demarcation between content and form—between orality as narrative substance and material object as narrative device. I will draw on Wyatt's analysis, but my purpose is not to follow her into a discussion of the oral dynamic in Erdrich's writing, so much as to consider the way in which Erdrich's careful attention to both the manufacture and spiritual (healing) utility of the drum emphasize particular attributes of the novel's depiction of Kurt Krahe's sculptural practice. Alongside this, I will consider the more recent *Shadow Tag* for its depiction of both the artist Gil and his work, and the relationship he shares with his wife, Irene America.

If, as Noodin observes, "in *Books and Islands in Ojibwe Country* [Erdrich] writes of a place where the United States and Canada recede in relevance" (2014a, 47), in *The Painted Drum* and *Shadow Tag*, the framing nation-state—or more particularly the interlocking legacies and ongoing processes of what Patrick Wolfe calls the settler-colonial structure (2006, 388)—become significant again, particularly in that latter novel. In both books, Erdrich uses the figure of the artist (including the drum maker) and his relationships with women, children, and the wider community to examine a host of issues, from ecological and spatial engagement to intersubjective relations, visual acuity, and questions of representation and power. The function of the image in Native and Euro-Western societies, as well as the commodification of material culture, is fairly central to overlapping themes in *The Painted Drum*. In *Shadow Tag*, meanwhile, my emphasis will be placed on the novel's underlying examination of and resistance to the controlling dynamic of reification of the image. Both novels, in implicit and explicit ways, carry the historical weight of colonization, and in both instances their female protagonists bear their Ojibwe identities in different ways. Faye Travers, as noted, remains cautious about the deeper spiritual implications of Bernard Shaawano's stories, anticipating "years of prudent thinking and financial juggling to actually change the circumstances of our life" (L. Erdrich 2005, 269). She nevertheless accepts the inevitability of change. Irene America—more secure perhaps in her Ojibwe identity—takes to political rather than cultural concerns, developing layers of historical interest that, while largely subtextual, inform what Padraig Kirwan's incisive analysis reveals as sovereigntist themes; in spite of this, her fate is finally decided by her inability to change, to relinquish the passionate antagonisms that, as fast as they destroy her and Gil, are those same forces that forged them as an adult couple.

In *Books and Islands*, the intriguing insider-outsider position Erdrich takes up as both member of the Ojibwe diaspora and stranger to this particular Ojibwe community, and as both student and interpreter, reflects what Benjamin Markovits, in his *New York Times* review of *The Painted Drum*, describes as "her ability to inhabit, with utter conviction, the characters on either side of the culture gap, not to mention those caught in the wide no-man's-land between" (2005). *Shadow Tag*'s author, Kirwan elaborates, is even more explicitly resistant to occupying any single or unified subject position, being uninterested "in writing from *one* discrete space, be it as a member of the Turtle Mountain band of the Ojibwe, as a woman, or as a universal artist" (2013, 165). As such, the depiction of and relationship between artists and writers (and collectors)—and there may be a close relationship between the latter two in the sense that in making her own trip back to Ojibwe country Faye, like Erdrich herself, produces narrative—opens up both questions of representation itself as well as the form and function of art in both traditional and Euro-Western/Euro-American societies in the specific case of the drum itself.

The contrast between the cultural "pilgrimage" of *Books and Islands* and the postcolonial scenario implicit in Erdrich's engagements with the figure of the artist are writ large in *The Painted Drum*'s two versions of "art" as well as in her engagements with representation that bear somewhat on the metatextual commentary on her work—commentary that plays repeatedly off the polarity that sees her as both a "tribal storyteller" and a "postmodern technician." That those positions connote on the one hand a notion of insider-authenticity that values tradition, community, and orality, and on the other a deconstructivist undoing of all of those notions does not preclude the possibility of both, as studies of Erdrich's negotiation of that authorial task attest. Drawing on seminal essays such as Nancy Peterson's "History, Postmodernism, and Louise Erdrich's *Tracks*" (1994), which he recalls in his more recent analysis, Kirwan explores how *Shadow Tag* in particular "presents the reader with the fine balance between testimony and various twists and turns (radical changes in narrative perspective and so on), which appear to be in keeping with Erdrich's oft-noted engagement with the 'fluidity of identity that has come to epitomize so much postmodern self-conception,' and her construction of any number of structural, temporal, or story-bound 'ambiguities'" (2013, 157). That "fine balance" in fact inheres also in the relationship between artist and writer. The fluidity itself—not least in the apparently postmodern resistance to capital-t Truth—similarly echoes in what Gross and others see as an inherently Anishinaabe hermeneutics, tolerant of diversity, multiplicity of truths, and ambiguity (Gross 2014, 252). In that respect, Gil's paintings are as fundamental to the "truth" of Irene as are her own, already multiple (and multiplicitous) writings, expressing something ineffable—perhaps even unbearable—that her own prose cannot capture.

As many commentators have noted with varying emphasis, Erdrich's fiction has drawn inspiration in a variety of ways from the oral traditions of the Ojibwe, whether it be in her use of culture heroes and spiritual figures such as Nanabozho and Misshepeshu or practices such as games of chance (see e.g. Brehm 1996, Gross 2005, Pasquaretta 1996, Peterson 1994, Sarvé-Gorham 1995, Stokes 1999, Van Dyke 1992, for instance); or through the representation of storytelling, multivocality, and the contingencies of orality in novels such as *Tracks*, which juxtaposes Nanapush's narration to his granddaughter Lulu with the narration of Pauline Puyat, for instance (see e.g. Jacobs 2001, Schultz 1991, Sergi 1992, Wong 1999, among others); or in the representations of the documentary record in the form of Bureau of Indian Affairs files, treaties, and so on, which emphasize the power of orality by contrast and establish a site of resistance that leads to difficult and often damaging choices for characters like Nector Kashpaw (see e.g. Allen 2000, 2002; Rainwater 1990; and Wyatt 2011 among others).

By contrast, Erdrich's direct engagement with the visual image in her fiction is almost unremarked, certainly prior to *Shadow Tag*, in which, with its focus on the relationship between an artist and his muse, it can hardly be ignored. The priority of the visual, however, has its most memorable introduction in *Love Medicine*, where the aforementioned Nector takes a job as an artist's model. Wearing a toweling breechcloth Nector is painted leaping to his demise from a cliff in the portentous, Cooperesque *The Plunge of the Brave*, shortly after his stint in Hollywood performing the quintessential *indian* role of falling dead from his horse. The comedy of these scenes underpins a critical commentary on the ideologically powerful role such visual images have played in the (continuing) colonization of Native peoples. While the Hollywood satire is obvious, the painting is evocative of the American Romantics, as well as the legends that fed them such as the real-life Uncas's leap across the gorge above Yantic Falls at the spot now known as Indian Leap in Norwich, Connecticut. Equally, the staged traditions of "Indian capture" in the art of Paul Kane, George Catlin, Karl Bodmer, Edward Curtis, and others resound in the artifice of Nector's "leap." In multiple formats, Native presence—its agency intact despite the image's occlusion of it—becomes the stuff of *indian* myth. Erdrich's engagement with such motifs through Nector, as Barbara Pittman explains, offers "a picaresque as well as postmodern engagement with the canon" (1995, 781). Although Pittman concentrates on Erdrich's subversive dialogue with literary fiction, *The Plunge of the Brave*, and Nector's cinematic role, suggests a broader undercutting of Native people's absorption as noble/tragic victims into American culture in its formative texts, be they literary, visual, cinematic, folkloric, or cartographic. In this sense, the visual joins the literary in a dual process of both exposing and thus undermining the mechanisms of indigenization (by which the settler-colonial state self-mythologizes through appropriation[11]) and reclaiming agency—not least through Nector's tricksy elusiveness (see Stirrup 2010a, 73–75)—for Indigenous actors.

Nector's "escape" from *The Plunge of the Brave* is a quintessential captivity narrative. That the old painter's attempts to represent the *indian* ultimately fail to capture the Native nonetheless forecasts his interpellation into a system that works against the interests of his community. His progress into tribal politics becomes, like Flandreau Indian School before it, a possible means of securing Indigenous complicity in statist models of governance. Several readings of Nector's eventual madness, accompanied with the inevitable comparison between Nector and Eli, propose the argument that his dementia is itself symptomatic of those forces of captivity. In *Shadow Tag*, Erdrich more explicitly—or at least more directly—returns to this image of captivity, grounding it, again, in the artistic practice of a painter. This time, Gil is an "American Indian artist" (2010, 38), and the captive dynamic operates at first-order level as a critique of a particular kind of tormented marriage and the damage of what we might see—albeit reservedly, acknowledging the intersectional demands placed on the story—as patriarchy. The patriarchal model is in microcosm, of course, focused as the novel is on the family unit, but the mental and, to a lesser degree, physical violence manifest between husband and wife are located largely in Gil's actions. To see Irene's response—a deliberately misleading set of diary entries in a second, "secret," diary that she knows Gil is reading—as a secondary reaction is not to deny what Kirwan describes as her complicity and culpability; the fact is that while Irene wrestles back power and agency through her subterfuge, she does so under Gil's surveillance. Beyond this, and notwithstanding Gil's own claims to Native identity (claims generative of some of the tension between them), I want also to examine the ways in which Erdrich's depictions of this patriarchal manipulation become allegorical of colonialist mechanisms of control.

This allegorical potential is flagged early on when Irene, a stalling academic who has switched from writing her thesis on Louis Riel to writing on George Catlin, tells Gil the story of Mi-néek-ee-súnk-te-ka, or the Mink. One of the "Indian painter's" most famous Mandan subjects, Catlin painted her in her village in 1832.[12] A number of women in the village had already railed against Catlin for the power of his "medicine paintings," which they saw "as an agency of oppression" according to Joshua David Bellin (2008, 54). Describing the coercion of his subjects, Bellin argues, too, that Catlin's "cherished pose of championing the Indians by capturing their similitude is revealed as the means by which he furthers and sanctifies—or furthered *by* sanctifying—the violence he claims to despise" (54). When Mink began bleeding at the mouth, a party of Mandan intercepted Catlin on his onward journey, exclaiming that she was "dying! the picture which you made of her is too much like her—you put so much of her into it, that when your boat took it away from our village, it drew a part of her life away with it" (Catlin qtd. in Bellin 2008, 55). Bellin is rightly wary of affording Catlin all the power in such circumstances, denying his painterly subjects agency in the negotiation of their own likenesses and cultural arts. The intercultural dynamic he proposes, then, arguably echoes the intersubjective dynamic in the marriage. Where Mandan (and other tribal) sovereignty and agency inheres in those areas Catlin simply cannot or will not access, Irene perhaps retains her autonomy and demonstrates a willful co-construction through her maintenance of her second diary, a secret document that contains her "true" thoughts.

In the context of Irene and Gil's marriage, that co-construction connotes mutual capture not specifically by one another so much as by a process. If this is, indeed, an indictment of the role of representation in the "agency of oppression," its implications are, as Ron Charles suggests in an early review, universal in import.

Persuasively contesting too reductive a reading of universality, though, Kirwan points to the political specificity of Erdrich's standing as a Native American writer of global reach, while the novel itself drops a number of hints at the ways this politics plays out.[13] While Gil's frustration that he cannot be received as simply an artist echoes some of Erdrich's own statements of desire to be read as an *American* artist—"He was still classified as an American Indian artist, or a Native American artist, or a tribal artist, or a Cree artist or a mixed-blood artist or a Métis or Chippewa artist" (2010, 38)—his characterization does significantly more than merely express dissatisfaction with commercial classification.[14] His acknowledgement, for instance, that "although . . . in the depiction of Irene, he had not always been gentle, he thought that he had used her humiliation as something larger—as *the iconic suffering of a people*, one critic had said," though "chokingly reductive" (45), nevertheless knowingly implicates him in the exploitative "economics of colonization" (Kirwan 2013, 187). It implicates him, also, as a captive, his reputation established by and through his subject in an inescapable symbiosis that is as much the cause of the corrosive relationship as any other factor in Gil and Irene's marriage. Where Catlin manipulatively told the Mandan that "he had also put himself into the picture [of Mink] by using his own spirit in the making of it" (L. Erdrich 2010, 45) in order to deny their request for the painting's return, in Gil's case their stark warning that "such a thing [as Catlin had produced] that could diminish two persons really should not exist" (45) bears consequences. The implications of the destructive economics of colonization, particularly in the realm of the image, are further emphasized in the faint echo between Gil's lament that he had not kept any of "the earliest, the best portraits. They were selling for more" (8), and Catlin's confession in his letters that "my father says the value of my paintings of the Mandan will surely increase now that the nation has been devastated by smallpox" (qtd. in Denzin 2013, 13). While the latter may seem more explicitly cynical, both commodify and objectify their human subjects and their real and symbolic suffering. Gil suppresses the implications of patriarchal objectification through his self-identification with a number of artists whose relationships with their wives/muses, though purportedly mutually desired, ranged from the questionable to the outright abusive: "Hopper had painted Jo, Rembrandt had painted Saskia, then Hendrijcke. Wyeth had painted Betsey and of course Helga; Bonnard had painted Marthe; there was the limitless and devouring Picasso; de Kooning and Kitaj and John Currin painted their wives" (L. Erdrich 2010, 36).[15] While Gil fantasizes about his relationship to those artists, whose reputations he aspires to, it is the connection to Catlin that resounds most in Irene's assessment of their present-day relationship. Thus, although in the early days the work is very clearly collaborative, its mutual nature has become less clear. Meanwhile, it remains the case that, as "Gaby Wood has argued . . . Hopper would never have produced his beguiling series of 'shadow-faced, round contoured ciphers' without Jo's presence or their shared fantasies" (qtd. in Kirwan 2013, 175).

As Walter Mignolo remarks, "Commercial and artistic motives are indistinguishably embedded in the colonial matrix and therefore in the imperial imaginary through which a new sense of civilization began to be narrated" (2011, 175–76). Although Mignolo focuses on the sixteenth century, his assessment of the "colonial matrix" clearly inheres for the import of Catlin's work. While Gil's painting, for its attempted subversion of colonial narratives and Old World forms, vaguely gestures toward what Mignolo calls the "decolonial gaze,"[16] his early association in the novel with Catlin, and the increasingly violent nature of his relationship with Irene, renders any such optimistic reading difficult. Both Catlin and Gil, then, are implicated in the colonial violence such imagery enables, while in Gil's case the picture is somewhat—and necessarily—complicated by the questions his relationship with his wife and the similarity to those other artists mentioned raises. Those questions operate on several levels, and many of their answers, to a degree, are self-evident. Can a relationship that begins mutually become asymmetrical and destructive? Can one voluntarily participate in that destruction and still be considered to be under manipulation? It of course introduces questions about representation at all levels, from the generalized representation of the other, to the particular representation of women by men, to the specific representation of Native women and Native bodies. In light of the critical assumption that Gil's portraits represent the "iconic suffering of a people," there is a certain self-reflexivity in which Erdrich's own endeavor becomes implicated in the visual construction of images under critique. Many critics have pursued that "chokingly reductive" line of enquiry in relation to the fiction; none more bitingly, perhaps, than David Treuer who in *Native American Fiction: A User's Manual* writes, "And Indians in fiction—from the books of Simms and Cooper up to Erdrich and Alexie—function as knowing ghosts whose presence alone speaks back in time to the crimes committed against them" (2006, 16). The portrayal of the artist as a commentary on the authorial relationship to her material, then, generates questions of responsibility (to one's material, to the community that furnishes it, and, in this case of course, to the individual whose image is expropriated) that are subsumed under Gil's solipsistic desire to use his wife's image knowing how critics will interpret it, yet complaining when, in doing so, they impute a particular ethnic and political agenda to him.

The self-reflexive element of this reads as a knowing nod to the academic invasion of privacy in which the purported object of scrutiny—Erdrich's fiction—has turned only too frequently to speculation about the author herself, her private life, her complex life with her late husband Michael Dorris, and so on. Again, Kirwan explores this latter issue insightfully, arguing that the conceit of the double diary combined with the revelation of the novel's retrospective and posthumous construction by Irene's daughter, Riel, means that "rather than presenting the reader with 'glaring similarities' between her own life and that of her protagonist, and providing the reader with an 'imperative' to read deeply into her back pages, Erdrich's apparent directive *for* interpretation possibly serves to remind the reader of the perils of interpreting Native American fiction as verbatim" (2013, 155). Erdrich's self-awareness in that self-reflexive gesture contrasts wildly with Gil's complete lack of percipience, of course. In that sense, the depiction broadens out to a more general statement on the need, when investigating Indigenous subjects, to recognize responsibility to Indigenous peoples whose images have historically been obscured by deliberately damaging, or merely ignorant or ill-judged, representations. When the result is not merely lack of understanding, but social, physical, and psychological violence, the need for accountability in both the nature of the imagery and the uses to which it is put is incontestable. Erdrich, then, conjures two further specters that significantly complicate those earlier questions. When it comes to the question of voluntary participation, Erdrich's portrayal of the largely psychic violence visited on Irene forces reflection on colonial and feminist critiques that further perpetuate colonial and/or patriarchal violence. Beginning with the assumption of no or limited agency, Irene's complicity in her own entrapment, as she literally "gives away" her own image, is essential to that dual critique. "Over time," Kirwan explains, "it has slowly dawned on Irene that Gil's portraits are inspired by both the desire to pay homage to her beauty *and* the desire to frame and control her life" (2013, 159). Subject to a colonizing male gaze, Irene's culpability in the creation of the damaging images is both clear and usurped. In other words, her role is not that solely of victim: she has agency, just as many early subjects of European portraiture and later American photography were instrumental in their own compositions. Just as much of that agency was then eroded over the course of time, as the assumptions of later spectators were laid over the original exchange, Irene's control over the nature and reception of her image is gradually eroded through a kind of self-interest and duplicity that she simply does not see coming. She turns to rumination on the corrosive effects of the gaze: "It seemed that people had forgotten what a terrible thing it was to be looked at, and then she began to imagine that in giving away her image, to be looked at and looked at, she was somehow killing herself of disgust" (L. Erdrich 2010, 173). A Foucauldian (i.e., entrapping, possessive) imprisonment, Irene's compromising position certainly evokes a feminist critique of the male gaze. Yet it also evokes analysis of the role of looking in the establishment of colonial power by the likes of Stephen Greenblatt and Nicholas Thomas. Indeed, Jodi Byrd cites Thomas early in *The Transit of Empire*, noting, "Not content with the boundaries imposed by gravity, oceans, or ice, Europeans sought possession of all their eyes could see. 'This act of looking,' Nicholas Thomas writes, 'was the chief purpose of [James] Cook's voyage'" (2011, 2). Thus, the voyeuristic gaze of the artist becomes deeply implicated in the fetishistic gaze of the colonizer despite, or perhaps even because of, his own anxious relationship to indigeneity.

Such a reading possibly returns us to the question not just of representation but representativeness. As Kirwan suggests, on the one hand "this book is, to a large degree, about the unique treatment meted out to tribal writers, who must deal with the expectation that their literary work is, fundamentally, about truth telling" (2013, 156); on the other, "even though Irene's diaries may be culturally void, at least in terms of the *types* of stories they tell, they can still suggest why tribal peoples must find 'a way to connect with what [they] don't know, or are missing, and might learn as a result'" (207–8, qtg. Greg Sarris). Although he astutely avers that Ojibwe heritage in the novel "is neither exotic nor overlooked, but simply *is*" (211), Kirwan—perhaps counterintuitively given his comment on the culturally void nature of the diaries—urges a relatively culturally specific reading of what (who?) Irene represents. I concur with his reasoning in the sense that the ground of Irene's experience and of course the kinship connections (particularly her mother, whose absence she sorely misses and whose influence she feels might have saved her from her present torment) are very firmly presented as those of a contemporary Ojibwe woman. Yet the broader sweep of her interests as a historian—in Métis leader Louis Riel and then in Catlin's Indian Gallery and his work with Mandan and Dakota in particular—and, more significantly, her name suggest a wider symbolic significance to her characterization than the tribal specific allows. A misnomer, after the "accidental" naming of the continent after Amerigo Vespucci, Irene's name emphatically marks her as metonymic for the colonial relationship between the Indigenous female body and the land. A mythical attachment on the one hand,

Indigenous feminist scholars such as Audra Simpson and Mishuana Goeman have illuminated the explicit relationship between the domination of women and the seizure of land. "America" has been represented as a woman in art since early images such as the famous engraving by Theodoor Galle (after Joannes Stradanus), variously known as "Allegory of America" and "Discovery of the New World." Made in the early sixteenth century, the engraving depicts Vespucci, holding sextant and flag, waking a female and clearly Indigenous America from her slumber. A classic encounter of New and Old Worlds, the archetype for depictions of America as a woman comes often with headdress and spear. Central to a visual grammar of discovery, the ways in which early portrayals of Native peoples established the pathways for colonization and dispossession are well mapped. Gil's art, at least in its intent, seeks to deconstruct its logic, as he "consciously challenges and interrupts the image of the indigene as 'Edenic innocent, uncivilizable savage, noble savage, infantilized adult'" (Kirwan 2013, 197, qtg. Jimmie Durham and Jean Fisher). Indeed, "he'd been working on a mythic level with the portraits," we're told; "her portrayals immediately evoked problems of exploitation, the indigenous body, the devouring momentum of history" (L. Erdrich 2010, 11). There is an air of neutrality to that statement, however. On the one hand, it could reflect Gil's intent, which is thus ironically and even tragically undermined by the effect of his ultimately rapacious gaze—or the gaze it enables. Alternatively, it could reflect a more objective view, in which case the "problems" the painting evokes implicate the artist himself as much as their putative object of critique.

Such implication returns us to Catlin. Declaring the Mandan extinct after the 1837–38 smallpox epidemic that reduced their village populations to roughly 8 percent of their original number, Catlin actively participated in vanishing the very people his project purported to be preserving. There is a clear colonial logic, of course, in the act of preservation being simultaneously an act of disappearing, regardless of smallpox, since the production of a static image (and thus an "authentic" gauge) whether in art or ethnography, literature or cinema, enables the ongoing gradation of assimilation. This reflects on Gil only in the sense that it mirrors the ways he too becomes implicated in the violence his work is understood to undo. To suggest that he is caught up in the same colonial logic as Catlin is, arguably, to push a provocation too far, and yet Catlin's sorcery functioned as a form of self-promotion insofar as "Catlin relied on the illusion of representational totality to pull off his effects, and such an illusion could not be validated if the original bearers of the medicine he was vending [through his paintings of sacred performance] had *not* vanished" (Bellin 2008, 24). Although the violence of Gil's art carries different implications—and intent—from Catlin's, the increasingly graphic and aggressive nature of the work, manifesting in the physical act of rape as Irene resists the painterly gaze more robustly, speaks to the need to capture and retain for himself the essence of his wife. On the surface, the dependence of his own reputation on his subject gives ample explanation of that controlling dynamic. Yet in the early pages of the novel another potential factor is brought to bear, a factor that, while neither expanded nor explicitly corroborated, strengthens the thread of connection between Gil's art and Catlin's project.

Whether or not Gil can be seen to be complicit in the colonial project (and one might suggest that in the patriarchal asymmetries of his actions, he is certainly implicitly, if unintentionally, corroborating), there is a colonial logic underpinning his personal anxieties (about his masculinity and about his wife's fidelity) that resounds in an allegorical reading of Irene's surname, her body as commodified object, and questions of indigenization and land acquisition. Very early on, these anxieties are introduced through his fear his wife is having an affair—or more particularly, the ground for his suspicion about her lover's companion. First, we are told: "Germaine . . . was more Indian than Gil, three-quarters as opposed to one-quarter, and so Germaine had him by a half quantum, which was a big plus as mixed-blood women are generally suckers for darker men" (L. Erdrich 2010, 13). A concern presented only in thought, it is impossible to declare it unfounded, but the narrator is careful to note that if, as Gil suspects, "Irene probably was [a sucker for darker men] too, *she was careful not to say it*" (13; emphasis added), before Gil acknowledges that in a period of high anxiety around tribal enrollment, treaty rights, and so on, the fact that Irene had children with him ought to appease his paranoia. Nevertheless, even that is couched in a layer of additional anxiety: "Irene must have loved him very much to have his children when his tribal roots—a mishmash of Klamath and Cree and landless Montana Chippewa—weren't recognized" (13). As a result, he had no casino per-capita payment and "had to live by his art" (13). In other words, his livelihood, his reputation, his success, are intimately tied, just as Catlin's were, to his subject. But more to the point, there is an investment, a claim to the land (America) through Irene's (*America's*) body that underpins his own self-proclaimed tribal rootlessness, the landlessness of his displaced Montana Chippewa background, as a descendent of Little Shell's duped band. All of these things are consequences of and corollaries to colonization. Gil's anxieties, destructive and painful as they are, then, inadvertently participate in the colonial grammar of authenticity that rendered blood quantum and other biological and cultural markers a measure of identity, and that separated the people from the land in doing so (see, for instance, Meyer 1994 and Horse Capture, Champagne, and Jackson 2007).

Provocative as it is, this reading is arguably further complicated by early mention of Gil's technical mastery, which "allowed him an almost limitless authority" (L. Erdrich 2010, 11). Furthermore, while "abstract expressionism had been the tyranny of the day . . . he'd stuck defiantly with figurative painting and now his control of old master techniques looked almost radical" (11). While initially one is reminded of using the master's tools to dismantle the master's house, the fine line that pertains to colonial mimicry renders Gil's apparent subversion much more ambivalent than it first appears. That his own identity as well as his livelihood is so heavily invested in his *America* images mitigates against a reductive reading of resistance—engaged resistance instead inhering, I would argue, in Erdrich's depiction of that ambivalence. Moreover, Irene's name adds one more layer of irony to the scenario, underscoring the colonial legacy implicit in these representational traces.

That imagery of America as a Native woman persists through American self-representation in the revolutionary period, too, with Lady Liberty herself often appearing seminude with clear signifiers of indigeneity. Whether it is possible for Gil to extricate himself from that legacy even as he seeks to undermine it is perhaps indicated by the irony in Irene's name.[17] Irene, from the Greek Εἰρήνη, means "peace." Irene was, in fact, the Greek goddess of peace, equivalent to the Roman god Pax. That this connection hints at the mythical role the Indigenous female has been absorbed into in the settler-colonial syntax is ironic in and of itself, but the name Irene America—so resonating with connotations of the Pax Americana and echoes of "ˈaɪrəni America"—adds further layers of insinuation. Again, its connotations are not simple. The equation of peace and America embodied in an Indigenous woman carries a raft of trace inferences, from a kind of Rousseauian sense of natural (wo) man onward. At this level, it could be understood simply as ironic, given the gap between the idea of natural man (i.e., free of the vices of political society) and the will to violent possession that went into settling the New World; and, of course, given the gap between Irene's name and the lack of peace in her marriage also, arguably, driven by Gil's will to possess her. An equally insidious connotation lurks in that proximity to the Latin phrase Pax Americana, or American peace, a label applied to the post–World War II attribution of relative stability in the Western hemisphere to U.S. power. In this respect, the Indigenous woman symbolically embodies the land-based resources on which U.S. hegemony is built, literally subsuming the indigene as "resid[ing] in the supplement, in the radical alterity of the deferred" (Byrd 2011, 9, paraphrasing David Kanzanjian) into America's imperial transit. Just as British power (Pax Britannica) was based on its imperial exploitation of bodies and resources, American power rests fundamentally on the exploitation of African and Native North American bodies, and the expropriation of land and resources.

———————

The function of art and the artist in *The Painted Drum* is very different from what has been discussed above, although it is no less finely balanced on a colonial binary. That binary, though perhaps not the primary plot insofar as hierarchies can be discerned in Erdrich's multistranded novels, attends to two views of art, or artistic practice, and I want to dwell on this doubling as I draw this chapter to its conclusion. These two views in turn elicit understanding of epistemological difference around the value and function of material culture, the role of the artist in community, the relationship of the artist to the wider environment in which they work, the role of dreams vs. inspiration, and, according to Jean Wyatt, relationship to the dead as well as the living. Although the initial sense of opposition remains intact and indeed comes perilously close to establishing an essentialized view of cultural difference, the novel nevertheless portrays a form of exchange that enables Faye Travers's experience of Ojibwe community to alter the pattern of her relationships back home in New Hampshire.

That this scenario effectively opposes East and (Mid)West suggests a symbolic geography echoed in a range of related juxtapositions: relative wealth in the New Hampshire neighborhood compared with considerable poverty out West; New Hampshire as location of the collection in which Faye finds the drum, as opposed to the Ojibwe community as its origin and the symbolic source of such collections per se, and so on. Thus, although these narratives are highly localized, and certainly offer specific local detail, they connote broader imagery that figuratively engenders a spectrum of the modern/colonial world, spatially separated (at least initially) but temporally coincident. Revival Road suggests a somewhat dysfunctional community. It is not, as is a stereotype often cast at European and Euro-American cultures, devoid of community per se, but relationships between individuals are very clearly characterized by silences and secrecy. Faye and her mother, Elsie, for instance, are unable to fully and honestly confront their feelings about the death of Netta, hindered by the painful truths of Professor Travers's cruelty and Elsie's affair; Faye is unwilling to allow her mother to know about her relationship with the sculptor Kurt Krahe; and Krahe's own relationship to his daughter, Kendra, is difficult to say the least.

In the parallel story, Old Shaawano's grief at the loss of his daughter—a tragedy that was itself in part caused by his hurt pride, which resulted in his giving up on his wife, Anaquot, who leaves him for Simon Pillager—manifests in considerable cruelty against his remaining son, who runs away as a result, violent thoughts of self harm, and drunkenness. A retrospective narrative recalled by his grandson, Bernard Shaawano, the tale of loss and mourning, including long-term visitations by "tiny skeleton children" and "shadowy, dull figures" (L. Erdrich 2005, 150), reverberates in the present-day stories of Revival Road's traumatic losses of children, despair, and the inability to come to terms with the grief. That process of coming to terms begins for Old Shaawano when he has a dream-vision of his daughter, who "gives him a task that was meant to keep him here upon the earth" (155). Reluctant as he is to take on the responsibility of making a drum "that would attract the spirits in a powerful communion" (160), from wood seasoned specially for generations for just this purpose, Shaawano is encouraged by the old woman Geeshik to follow his daughter's instructions. Recalling his own father's practice of making tobacco offerings, he "found the birch stump . . . opened the bag and took some tobacco out and said to the twitching leaves of a popple tree or to anyone or nobody or to the Creator, 'Thank you for my existence'" (162). His furniture making—an artisanal streak that both ties him to his drum-maker father and indicates his suitability for the task at hand—combines with his offerings to draw him slowly from his melancholy to begin the next in his series of tasks, that of rebuilding a birchbark canoe loaned to him by a fisherman, Albert. He finds his way again to the ways of his grandparents by drinking a cleansing brew of cedar tea just as his grandmother had done. Being joined by Albert, who has also been visited by Shaawano's daughter, and Albert's son Chickie, Shaawano is told "[Geeshik] knew you were going to find your way towards this. . . . This was the fourth generation, this is the time, and it was said that our drum would be brought to us by a little girl" (168).

In clear comparison to Kurt Krahe's attempts to find his way through his grief for his dead daughter Kendra via his artwork, Shaawano's endeavors begin in communal fashion. Where Krahe employs young local men to assist with the "massive project of [the] execution" of his "assemblages of stone" (6), Shaawano works alongside Albert, Chickie, and of course his daughter. And making the drum is a process of self-actualization for Shaawano, and a form of coming into community—at least initially—that will, after a period of forty years, also forge a return to community.

Krahe's art, however, connotes a more solipsistic enterprise, aesthetics-driven and fundamentally ornamental. Furthermore, Krahe is led by a form of appropriative idealism of Japanese art and philosophy, reminiscent of several major movements in Western art history.[18] Though undoubtedly sincere in and of itself, Faye punctures the self-regard of the pseudo-fetishistic and culturally relative "high art" philosophy when she tells us: "He says that the Japanese have a word for the essence apparent in a rock. I ask him, why don't the Germans?" (7). More to the point, Faye also hints at Krahe's limited perception, a facet of the single-mindedness of his focus, when she continues: "I suppose that I love Kurt for his ability to see that essence, the character of the rock. Only, I wish sometimes that I were stone. Then he would see me as I am" (7).

Having once had success in the marketplace, Krahe, like many of those artists drawn to New Hampshire's lack of income tax, is inclined to solitude, a recluse both trying to make new work and working to overcome his grief (for his "not-so-recent loss of his second wife" and, ultimately, Kendra). Like Gil, he exhibits a habitually repetitive strain in his work, numbering his output such that when we first meet him he is pondering the still unfinished *"Construction Number Twenty* . . . commissioned many years ago by a large Minneapolis cereal company" (10); and, like Gil, he exhibits a "self-satisfaction" and pomposity that caricature the artist: "I have in mind a perception of balance, although the whole thing must be brutally off the mark and highly dysphoric" (9). I would argue that the characterization of Krahe and even Gil, particularly if set in contrast to the portrayal of the Little Girl drum's manufacture, deliberately evokes a set of common assumptions about the status of the artist as visionary, as genius, as solitary obsessive, and so on, and about art itself as product of said genius, caught by turns between commodified object and spiritual artifact. As John Berger infamously puts it in his vituperative summary of capitalization through reproducibility, both artists thrive on the "bogus religiosity which now surrounds original works of art" (1972, 23).

Again, there is no reason to suspect Krahe's sincerity—just as Gil's commitment to his work and his passion for his wife, though damaging in scale and consequence, is indubitable. Krahe, however, serves as a kind of foil to alternative conceptions of art (and art's function) in ways that also draw our attention to the relationship between aesthetics and politics in the novel itself. One line in particular crystallizes this possibility. Having revealed the desire of a chain restaurant specializing in "false folksiness" to buy their barn boards for added authenticity, Faye counters the Gatsby-like, cosmetic artifice by observing the webs of the orb spiders that live within the boards: "Of their means of survival they've made these elegant webs, their beauty a by-product of their purpose" (L. Erdrich 2005, 77). This observation, in turn, "causes [her] to wonder, [her] own purpose on so many days as humble as the spider's, what's beautiful that I make? What is elegant? What feeds the world? / Today, my art is blackberry jam" (77). The direct relationship between aesthetics and ethics here—through application to a wider community, through the function of the made object as well as the desire for it to be beautiful—articulates the comparison of forms in a way that reflects the novel's own self-conscious deliberation on art.

Jean Wyatt's positive reading of the drum's significance to the novel offers a point of reflection on that deliberation:

> Erdrich's portrait of the drum makes a gift to the Ojibwe community outside the novel as well. *The Painted Drum* contributes to the imaginative dimension of Ojibwe tribal sovereignty by, as American Indian Nationalist literary critics advocate, "return[ing] to Native ceremonies and traditions." . . . But such a return . . . can best demonstrate the usefulness of tradition by adapting traditional means to the challenges of the present." (2011, 24–25)

Like so much of Erdrich's work, then, the drum represents innovation on rather than straightforward repetition of tradition, "providing new meanings that are 'continuous with, but not circumscribed by, Native traditions'" (Wyatt 2011, 25). While the return to "Native ceremonies and traditions" can frequently itself take the place of the fetishized object, Erdrich avoids rendering her text artifact by, paradoxically, invoking the drum as anthropological artifact in research terms, in order to give the object textual life. While the sense of ethnographic detachment inheres in its descriptions, then, underlined by her acknowledgement of Thomas Vennum's *The Ojibwe Dance Drum* and her insistence that "as in all my books, no sacred knowledge is revealed" (2005, 277), she shores up Wyatt's observation that "Erdrich avoids depicting a traditional drum ceremony of healing [but] gives the drum personal power, so to speak: its interactions with people change those people's lives" (2011, 25). That said interaction, and indeed the relationships that are forged as a result of it, is central to the comparison of art forms—a comparison that Wyatt sees as resolutely epistemological, although she does not specifically ground her discussion in the art form itself but in apperceptions of death and the dead—is present even in its implicit medicine's negative outcomes. For instance, although it ultimately produces his destruction, even Anaquot's and Geeshik's beading of

Simon Jack's fateful outfit with a kind of fearsome, spikey woodland pattern forges significant bonds between them, arguably saving *their* lives. The drum, for its part in that sequence, finds itself in forty-year exile, as Jack dances the wrong way around it until his heart gives way. That, in turn, leads to its discovery by Faye and her reconciliation with her ancestral community.

One comment made in an NPR interview throws a spotlight, perhaps, on the nature of this self-reflection. Discussing the book's focus—"*The Painted Drum* is about relationships"—Frances Washburn recalls that interviewer Martha Woodruff "remarked that it is difficult to think of 'relationship' without thinking about the Erdrich–Dorris connection, a public closeness that Woodruff claims Erdrich says she 'fostered in part *to atone for her devotion to her art*'" (Washburn 2013, 90; emphasis added). Erdrich's devotion to her art—her solitary working practices as described in *The Blue Jay's Dance*, for instance—is a deeply necessary quality for an author who has produced as prolifically as she has. It is hardly unusual, either, but it offers an analogue here—and in *Shadow Tag*—for that aspect of the modern artist whose endeavor draws them away from their relationships, and whose art, in consequence, risks self-enclosure. In what could be read as a highly symbolic sequence, then, we witness the reconciliation of Faye and Krahe (from whom she has become alienated since the death of his daughter and his pruning of her ruined orchard, a kind of memorial to her sister) amid a scene of destruction: "Someone has broken into [Kurt's] studio, the renovated barn behind his house. That person has used all of the power equipment that Krahe keeps in the barn to demolish *Number Twenty-one* and all else that he has worked on or produced . . . since Kendra's death" (L. Erdrich 2005, 272). More significant than the damage is Faye's declaration that "I have no idea why this particular act of vandalism frees the two of us" (272), before driving to the studio, where "he seems more excited than horrified by the trashed scene. He seems more thrilled than bereft" (273). Coining a German neologism, "*Frohlockendzerstorung* [*sic*]," which would translate as a kind of exultant (Frohlockend) destruction (zerstörung), the two "link arms eagerly" (273) before spending the night together.

It is as if a tyrannical burden has been lifted; simultaneously, a new "work" has effectively been created—a work that recalls the pictography of Lake of the Woods: "All of the broken stuff and the pieces so massive they could only be nicked are scrawled with loops of spray paint. The paint is an intense blue, that blue my mother loves, and in its twizzling energy it is like an obscure but brilliant form of writing. Some new language is at work. The blue is everywhere" (272–73). While in color it evokes the blue of Vizenor's vital hue, which connotes transformative power and transmotion, its "writing" communicates the presence of a third party whose intervention in this landscape (it may be a studio, but this is writing on rock, after all) communicates, albeit in a tiny way, the wider web of connection of which they are a part. That the damage was likely done by Davan Eycke's mother further brings their attention back to the living, by reminding them that their own grief is shared beyond their private sphere. In turn, it is revealed by Faye that the simple gravestone Krahe makes for Kendra's grave, "the simplest emotional form, a concave circle of Carrara white," is the only piece of his that has ever moved her (275). His craft, in other words, in this most intimate moment of connection, takes on function beyond manifesting his "inspiration," becoming a communal marker of memory.

As Erdrich returns to her city home in *Books and Islands*, she discovers that the giant elm—Old Stalwart—that sits in her front yard has been marked for removal, its diseased state presenting a danger to the neighborhood, both in the threat of transmission of Dutch Elm disease and the possibility of falling branches as the disease progresses. It has been painted with a red "A" and a circle and, shortly after Erdrich's homecoming, is limbed and felled, the stump ground out until nothing but a trace remains in memory. That trace finds its way into *Books and Islands*, the manuscript of which is finished just as the last chip is ground by the city stump grinder. As I have already noted, LaLonde insists that "we see in no uncertain terms that Erdrich turns to writing in the face of loss and in so doing returns to the connections that are articulated in the writings she finds" (n.d., 15). Those "writings" of course include the rock paintings of Lake of the Woods: "Because they are alive," LaLonde continues, "because they are evidence that the material and symbolic practices of the Anishinaabe are alive [as Erdrich herself says,] the rock paintings counter the story of doom foretold in the bright red circled A" (15). The first pictograph she sees—a great sturgeon floating over a divining tent—LaLonde recounts, "remind[s] her and us of the need to recognize, honor, and learn from those connections and to put those connections and what is to be learned from them into writing, into books" (16).

"Books," rocks, diaries, artworks, the engagement with the creative act as a means of navigating the contingencies and ambiguities of life—as a means of forging, maintaining, recognizing, and negotiating the tracks and networks, connections and maps—is central to Erdrich's work. The visual functions in this process as both analogue for the written and its epistemic foil, as both analogue for the potentially alienating power of (mis)representation and as measure of relation. As is most explicitly played out in *Shadow Tag*, there is a writing that seeks to deceive (even to deceive the self), and a form of writing that seeks to connect, reconnect, and reconstruct: a writing to or for the self (manifest, arguably most clearly, in the "inspired" artworks produced by Gil and Krahe, and implicit in Irene's diaries), and a writing of the self, or of the self's relation to environment, kin, and context. The difference between them inheres, perhaps, in the difference between Krahe's destroyed creations and his gravestone for Kendra—a heartfelt piece that speaks not of his soul but of hers—or in the interplays between Irene's two diaries. Kirwan identifies the precarity of truth in *Shadow Tag*, but truth persists in the interstices, the traces, untangled by Riel in the course of her reconstruction. As it was for the modernists, that truth is glimpsed, if not grasped outright. The process of reaching (for) it, again most soul-baringly revealed in the relationships between artists and writers, and in those artists' journeys, bespeaks its own necessity as further "evidence that the material and symbolic practices of the Anishinaabe are alive" (LaLonde).

CHAPTER 5

So, How Can You Hear Stones and Pictures?

Gerald Vizenor's Imagic Returns

I n conversation following a panel at the 2015 meeting of the Native American
Literature Symposium, Anishinaabe linguist and poet Margaret Noodin com-
mented that "our idea of making books is embodying images." In the previous
chapter I looked at a particularly literal understanding of that notion in Louise
Erdrich's *Books and Islands in Ojibwe Country*, but it is no particularly giant leap
to see how such an idea might be at work in Gerald Vizenor's output. Indeed, as
I have already discussed in chapter 2, the imagism of his poetry holds the image
(and what he calls the "imagic"), or the seen and felt moment at its center, while his
early retranslations of Ojibwe dreamsongs celebrate vision and the visionary both
internally and through relationship with the "pictomyths" scattered throughout
Summer in the Spring. The primacy of the visual manifest in Vizenor's novels,
too—from early evocations of traditional visual and material cultural objects
such as copper bowls and birchbark scrolls, to transitional forms like ledger art,
and on to modern and contemporary painting by European, Euro-American, and
Anishinaabe artists—has roots in his recursively insistent destabilizing of the
authority of printed text. Commonly understood as an exhibition of postmodern
technique, recent writing on distinctions between alphabetic and alternative
literacies offer a parallel to understanding Vizenor's notorious slipperiness—and

certainly to appreciating the prevalence of visual forms in his writing. For instance, Daniel Heath Justice writes:

> "In the contestation between Eurowestern settlers and Indigenous peoples, writing has always been located at the privileged apex of the socio-political hierarchy, wherein oppositional notions of literate European 'civilization' were pitted against oral Indigenous 'savagism.'" Writing, then, has been central to the coding of privilege on the one hand and deficiency on the other; its imposition through structures like residential school education, whilst liberatory in one sense, has tended to reinforce the power imbalances implicit in that binary. Thus writing, or more specifically, alphabetic writing in colonial languages cannot easily shrug off the ambivalence of that colonial process. (2015, 295)

Vizenor, it would seem, is caught precisely in the jaws of that ambivalence. To describe his literary aesthetic as liberatory is to willfully understate the degree to which liberation features in the critical assessment of his work to date. That liberatory drive pertains to writing, to alphabetic literacy in the terms Justice outlines above, to the discursive means by which language is shaped to impose ideology and, more specifically to Native Americans, the terminal creeds that determine, restrict, circumscribe, and enforce identities, and to the linear narratives that constrain understandings of Indigenous epistemologies. A brief rifle through a recent volume of essays dedicated to Vizenor's work, for instance—Deborah Madsen's *The Poetry and Poetics of Gerald Vizenor* (2012)—reveals repeated versions of this principle. Writing of his epic poem *Bear Island: The War at Sugar Point*, Kimberly Blaeser suggests that "Vizenor's attempt . . . is to find a way in the age of written text to challenge the colonial constructions of meaning and liberate tribal story" (2012b). In a different iteration of his deconstructive gymnastics, translator Carme Manuel suggests that "Vizenor wants to move the original oral tradition of tribal communities into the written culture with acts of imagination and literary expression" (2012), shortening the distance, if not erasing the binary, between oral and written forms. Meanwhile, Adam Spry insists that "healing and liberation are Vizenor's ultimate goals in publishing *Summer in the Spring*," the collection of "reexpressions" of Ojibwe dreamsongs that seek—just as subsequent revisions emphasize—to free the sense and sensibility of the original songs from Frances Densmore's translations (2012). Vizenor's emphasis, throughout his oeuvre, on transience or impermanence, on contingency and risk, reflect precisely this approach to writing that seeks the present and presence of the oral event, including its digressions, repetitions, aporias, and variability, by mining the "slippery spaces of signification" (Moore 2012).

The ambivalence implicit in the apparent paradox of "writing in the oral tradition," to echo the subtitle of Kimberly Blaeser's comprehensive early study, resounds with postcolonial implications: the theme of "writing back," developed by Helen Tiffin et al. and adopted through tropes such as writing in and "reinventing the enemy's language" by such writers as Beth Brant, Gloria Bird, and Joy Harjo is one such example. As Audre Lorde famously asserted, "the Master's tools will never dismantle the Master's house" (2018). Far from presenting an impasse, however, Vizenor more than any other writer has rendered that ambivalence a productive, generative, and transformative space, but to date the focus of critical examination of that space has prioritized Vizenor's engagement with the linguistic turn. Eschewing, while resonating with, many of the gestures of the postcolonial, Vizenor's work reveals what Sinclair calls the "sovereignty of transmotion," implicit in the productive tension between tribal concerns and global discourses. While I do not underestimate the significance of theories of orality, of poststructuralist aesthetics and postmodern linguistic method, to Vizenor's development as a writer, this chapter seeks to add to that body of work consideration of Vizenor's own pictorial turn. In every sense, visuality,[1] I argue, has been central to Vizenor's exploration of cultural heritage and the place and role of writing in both decon-structing imposed ideologies, countering terminal creeds, and translating—without stagnating—orality, both literally and in spirit.

I return, naturally, to the relationship between the oral and the graphic as described by Christopher Teuton, and to the echo of that relationship manifest in literary apprehensions of the visual arts. Understanding this exchange to reflect an array of "intellectual traditions and textual technologies" that form the "com-municative repertoire" of Native American modernity, this chapter will explore the ways in which Vizenor's writing makes use of the image, of the visual arts, and of visually bound aesthetics as means of engaged resistance to the "ongoing illiteracy campaigns" of settler colonialism (Justice 2015, 299). In addition, I examine Vizenor's own exploration and reorientation of Anishinaabe graphic practices and knowledge in the contemporary world, and his illumination of Anishinaabe visual literacy. The two, in many ways, perform a symbiotic enactment of literary sovereignty, first refusing imposition and then rearticulating Indigenous modernity. Elizabeth Hutchinson has noted that "early historians of Native American art privileged artistic traditions that seemed untainted by Western influences" (2001, 740). In the Vizenorian oeuvre, "tradition" often signifies a condition of stasis and a provisional object of the terminal creeds that govern a whole host of authenticating mechanisms. Yet "hybrid artforms," in Hutchinson's terms, "were dismissed [by art historians] as inauthentic, assimilationist, or even degenerate" (740), frameworks against which Vizenor has long railed. Hutchinson further asserts that more recently, art historians "have become interested in how indigenous material and visual culture can express the transcultural situation of American Indian people" (740). Although this chapter focuses in large part simply on the interrelation of written, oral, and visual or imagic in Vizenor's work, it moves toward a similar articulation of the ways Vizenor's investment in the visual traditions of European modernism and Anishinaabe graphic practices and visual forms that both precede and intersect with modernist endeavor express his own transnational situation. It is a situation that resounds in his assertion that "by original styles, imagic scenes, and conceptual art, many contemporary *anishinabe* artists have reached beyond the bounds and obvious cues of tradition and culture" to produce art in which, as in the paintings of David Bradley, Natives "are always the active players in their own history" (Vizenor 2000, xii, xiii).

Some recent writing has begun to explore Vizenor's engagement with modernist art, not least since the publication of *Shrouds of White Earth* and *Blue Ravens*,[2] both novels set partly in France and focused on the relationship between a writer and a painter. In a paper presented at the Western Literature Association conference in 2015, David J. Carlson observes that "in recent years, Gerald Vizenor has made a strong pivot towards the visual arts in his writing," identifying the double move of a strong narrative relationship between a writer and painter, and the increased engagement with European modernist painting. Broadening the scope, Vizenor's nonfiction has increasingly included essays on Anishinaabe painters such as George Morrison and David Bradley, both of whom are featured in chapters in his 2009 *Native Liberty*, as well as in articles in journals such as *American Indian Quarterly*, and, of course, in passing references in his novels; in addition, chapters on "Ontic Images," and the photography of Edward Curtis, in *Native Liberty*, as well as lectures and articles on what he calls "cosmoprimitivism" further emphasize the degree to which the visual—particularly but not only painting—has come to the center of his work. Even taking the original publication dates of those *Native Liberty* chapters—between 2000 and 2009—this would appear to be, if not a "recent" turn, certainly a postmillennium one.

While that pivot may be more demonstrative in recent years, however, it is hardly a bold claim to suggest that the visual and the visual arts have long been at the heart of Vizenor's work in one form or another, both in terms of its philosophy, its aesthetic, and its source influences. Two publications among many suggest a starting point. In 1981 and 1987 respectively, Vizenor published *Summer in the Spring: Anishinaabe Lyric Poems and Stories* (a reworking of the 1965 *Summer in the Spring*) and *Touchwood: A Collection of Ojibway Prose*. The former, "reexpressions" of dreamsongs and stories recorded by ethnomusicologist Frances Densmore, resonates strongly with Vizenor's imagism and haiku more broadly, which he was publishing twenty years earlier, from 1960 onward. Translations though they may be, nevertheless they cohere fairly straightforwardly with his poetics. To say that they are at the heart of his work, it is worth remembering that *Summer in the Spring* brought together the two publications released as *Anishinaabe Adisokan* and *Anishinaabe Nogamon* in 1970; a third earlier poetry publication, 1963's *South of the Painted Stones*, further reminds us of his early investment in image. Interspersed with the songs of *Summer in the Spring* (words only, unlike Densmore who transcribed notation, also, fixing tunes in the single instance of her subject's performance), Vizenor includes a number of "pictomyths," pictographic drawings also gleaned partly from Densmore's collecting and again echoing that earlier titular nod in *South of the Painted Stones*. Vizenor "relies on Densmore to depict in a 'pictomyth' the spirit in the heart of a Mide singer," according to Michael Pomedli (2014, 144). It is a reliance, in a sense, not unlike the prisoner of haiku's, who also finds his way to dreamsongs via the interventions of a white cultural interpreter. Unlike Densmore, however, Vizenor's depiction is not separated out from the songs, abstracted in the interests of ethnographic accuracy. Although this is not to say that it is not abstracted—at least in the sense that, as images, the pictomyths in *Summer in the Spring* are difficult to read to those outside their visual vernacular, "deceptively simple" yet "demanding as much contemplation ... as the written material" (Weidman 2006, 250)—it serves an aesthetic, rather than informational, agenda. Vizenor depends on Densmore, then, in the sense that her collecting furnishes a resource, but in intent as well as form their projects diverge dramatically.

Touchwood, meanwhile, represents a very early (and highly selective) survey of Anishinaabe intellectual heritage in writing. First published seven years before Robert Warrior's *Tribal Secrets: Recovering American Indian Intellectual Traditions*

(1994), it anticipates both that book and Warrior's later *The People and the Word* (2005). Just as Warrior seeks to build connection and historical and intellectual heft across eighteenth-, nineteenth-, and twentieth-century nonfiction texts, Vizenor compiles extracts of the work of seven nineteenth- and twentieth-century Anishinaabe (Ojibwe) writers, suggesting the skeleton of what Heid Erdrich calls an Anishinaabe literary ancestry (see 2013b). Accompanying these texts—indeed, heading the titular page of each extract—Vizenor (or the book's designer at least) prefixed printed facsimiles of mide scrolls, like banners to the proceeding text.[3] There are two ways of reading these images—besides their illustrational value, that is. The first, and arguably the less generous, reading is that they perform a kind of authenticating function, bridging the gap between a visual cue to *indianness* and the alphabetic texts that follow, including texts by Christian missionaries such as Mississauga preacher Peter Jones, which fail by their nature to satisfactorily tick the ethnographic boxes of authentica. Such a reading not only assumes a cynical spirit; it also stands in stark contrast to Vizenor's career-long refusal to play a banal game of identity politics with his nation's cultural heritage.

That juxtaposition of pictograph and alphabetic text demands, however, that we consider the relationship between oral tradition, graphic practice, and the written tradition that begins for the Ojibwe in earnest in the early nineteenth century. Whether that relationship is suggestive of continuity or divergence becomes irrelevant to the potentially productive interplay between what Chadwick Allen refers to as "Indigenous customary forms" and the normative expectations of Euro-Western textuality. That interplay is further heightened in that one of Vizenor's core nineteenth-century selections, from George Copway's *Life, History, and Travels*, includes his explanation, described and discussed in chapter 2 of this book, of Ojibwe writing. Albeit a very different production than Māori poet Rowley Habib's "When I of Fish Eat," nevertheless both *Touchwood* and *Summer in the Spring* are worth considering briefly in light of Chadwick Allen's inspired examination of "Indigenous languaging," in which Habib's poem is the object of complex juxtapositional analysis. Of Habib's poem,[4] "written entirely in English and augmented by contemporary, 'modernist' line drawings," Allen writes that it "can—for certain audiences—produce bilingual and bicultural effects that enrich the poem's potential meaning and amplify its aesthetic power" (2012, 146). Such a claim can certainly be made of *Summer in the Spring*, and although the illustrations in it are far older than the time period ascribed to modernism, their documentation by Densmore in the early 1910s coincides with the turn to "primitive" aesthetics by writers and artists in the Americas and Europe. They may not be modernist in any temporal sense, in other words, but like the imagistic dreamsongs they accompany, they certainly appeal to a modernist sensibility. Perhaps, in that sense, and as I shall discuss in greater detail later in this chapter, they ground Vizenor's own modernist visual preferences.

Like the context, the dynamic of interchange in Vizenor's text to that of Habib/ Hotere's is different, but Allen's perceptive observations on the latter can illuminate some of the power of the former. For instance, where Allen writes that "'When I of Fish Eat' stages a scene of emotional, psychological, and, especially, spiritual connection between the speaker and his Indigenous ancestors" (2012, 171), we may be minded of the plethora of relations implicit in *Summer in the Spring*. Driven ostensibly by a sense of the spiritual, personal, and sensual, the often prophetic incantations of the Ojibwe songs "reexpressed" in Vizenor's translations carry a similar connective effect (and affect), quite literally so in those cases that were first transcribed by Vizenor's immediate ancestor, Theodore Hudon Beaulieu. That the songs are interspersed with the pictomyths—and Vizenor's designation of them as pictomyths forcefully reminds us that there is more to these images than meets the eye—serves to significantly emphasize those connections, creating what Allen calls a "visual empathy" that binds lyric and image even where the links are not explicitly obvious. Unlike "When I of Fish Eat," however, the images also remind us of the "unsignatured" aspect of such original forms, just as Vizenor's reexpressions signal the appropriated and repeated nature of the songs. Thus, those connections become more complex, indicating in the first instance a wide network of relations—those who received the songs and visions; those who repeated them and changed them in repetition; and those who passed them on to Densmore and others for transcription—among whom Vizenor becomes simply the latest (for an important examination of this process, see Henry 2017). Their life beyond *Summer in the Spring* further attests to this fluidity since, as Adam Spry explains, many of the songs have changed each time Vizenor has republished them. In the second instance, they also recall then that act of transcription, of Densmore's intervention, whose presence is acknowledged even in the act of reclamation. Presented as songs and stories of the Ojibwe, then, this complex dynamic sets in tension the notion of authorless iteration and collective authorship with those instances of "capture" and interpretation by the likes of Schoolcraft and Densmore, with contemporary and later, secondary, reinterpretations and reclamations by figures such as Jane Johnston, Beaulieu, and of course Vizenor himself.

The ethnographic abstraction of previous studies of the mide scrolls is arguably made even more explicit through their reuse in *Touchwood*, since outside their primary (and protected) use in ceremony, mide scrolls have only been reproduced in anthropological and museological contexts.[5] That abstraction is emphasized and unsettled here as the images of the scrolls are taken out of both ceremonial and anthropological contexts and aligned with this set of written historical, autobiographical, and fictional accounts. As such, they are explicitly aligned with writing—not, perhaps, to encourage the reader to think of them as such, so much as to illustrate both literally and figuratively the long heritage of Anishinaabe knowledge—to illuminate the archive, as it were. In anthropological context, plainly speaking, such objects are quite literally removed from the Anishinaabe archive and appropriated into the Euro-Western one, as artifacts of the latter's historical resource. Reprinting them in this fashion, then, serves two possible objectives: firstly, it nominally repatriates that material to the Anishinaabe archive; and secondly, it presents an analogical challenge to the notion of writing as evidence of assimilation, or writing in English as a mark of deficiency, inauthenticity, or cultural dislocation.

Further to these possibilities, the image-text relationship proposed by this assemblage, as with "Hotere's pictorial frame" to Habib's poem, "offers the potential of a synchral experience of English and Indigenous languages and cultural connotations" (Allen 2012, 171). While, as in the poem-picture interface, Anishinaabemowin is not explicitly represented, since pictographic writing is ideographic rather than logo- or phonographic, the scrolls themselves and the pictomyths in *Summer in the Spring* link explicitly in two directions, both to the oral stories that they intersect with and act as mnemonic identifiers for, and to the graphic tradition in which both contemporary Anishinaabe visual and literary arts participate. Thus, they explicitly recall alternative linguistic and extralinguistic contexts for their production and reception. Allen insists that in "When I of Fish Eat," "the speaker experiences a vision of the Māori past, as well as a deep understanding of how that past exists in the present" (171). In very different circumstances, and with quite different connotations, Vizenor's two texts nevertheless offer a similar temporal collapse across different media, demonstrating the ongoing capacity of older graphic forms to influence our understanding of written text. Understanding all of these texts, then, whether sacred or secular, history or prose fiction, to contribute to that larger archive of Anishinaabe knowledge anticipates another critical category in Native American and Indigenous studies—LeAnne Howe's concept of "Tribalography." In its first published iteration, Howe explains that "I am consciously using the terms story, fiction, history, and play, interchangeably because I am from a culture that views these things as an integrated whole rather than individual parts" (1999, 118). That rhetorical space she calls "Tribalography" demonstrates, Howe asserts, that "Native people created narratives that were histories and stories with the power to transform" (119). Throughout this book it has been and will continue to be implicit that "narrative" must include the graphic, pictorial traditions that precede and continue alongside alphabetic writing, and Vizenor's *Touchwood* arguably furnishes a prime example of how including such images—authorless, collectively authored, or however else one seeks to designate their origin—potentially transforms our perception of the written text as well as introducing (or reintroducing) those who are familiar with postcontact tribal literary cultures to those literacies that preceded and transcended the arrival of the Roman alphabet on Turtle Island. The scrolls, then, fit into the schematic of Anishinaabe communication as mnemonic "scripts," and song markers, along with maps, messages, and illustrations accompanying, and made in the course of, the telling of a story.[6]

As is perhaps already evident, Vizenor is more generous toward Densmore than some (see my discussion of Rendon's *SongCatcher* in the next chapter). He suggests, for instance, of Thomas Vennum's congratulatory gratitude to Densmore for "rescuing [the oldest songs of the tribe] from certain oblivion" that "Densmore would doubtless eschew the notion that her studies of *anishinaabe* music were rescue transcriptions" (1998, 171). Implicit in this rebuttal is a sense that Densmore's project, flawed though it certainly was, was something other—something less implicitly destructive—than the more expropriative forms of salvage ethnography. Certainly, he seems to afford her more sympathy than he does her distant predecessor among the Ojibwe, Henry Rowe Schoolcraft. This sense of sympathy is reflected too in her own view of the mide images, a view that bears certain echoes of Vizenor's own standpoint. Quoting her, he reiterates: "all the songs are recorded in mnemonics on strips of birch bark. . . . This record serves as a reminder of the essential idea of the song and is different in its nature from our system of printing" (1998, 171). As he will attempt to portray in *Dead Voices*, this "essential idea," which I will discuss shortly, "serves as both record and illustration, visual cue to verbal narrative"; it also, in doing so, plays a central role in ritual memorialization and performance—an active, transformative, transmotional role. "The Indian picture preserves the idea of the song" Densmore continues, "while our printed page preserves the words which are supposed to express the idea but which often express it very imperfectly" (qtd. in Vizenor 1998, 171). A figure for the gap between the literary and the oral—the impossibility of the fleeting visuality of memory to be adequately captured (or perhaps because it can only be "captured") or represented in print—the picture is far more intimately and integrally related to the story process than the story's reproduction as text can possibly be. And Vizenor goes on: "Song pictures are the creations and the memories of the music, a virtual cartography" (1998, 171). That "virtual cartography"—Native transmotion in story, song, and image—is at the heart of Vizenor's own fictive remapping.

In *Another America* Mark Warhus points out that "Native American maps were pictures of experience"—not material documents but "mental map[s]" augmented by the documentary record (1997, 3). As such, they function, as Vizenor explains, as mappa mundi equivalents, "comparable to the spiritual inspiration of cathedral windows" in the form of "native stories of creation, totemic visions, and sacred documents" (1998, 175). "The sacred *midewiwin* documents," he continues, "were active creations, not passive representations," which is key to understanding their interaction with both oral and literary tradition—their place not as static signifiers but as functional vehicles for transformative poetics. Dean Rader, responding to Vizenor's assertion that "maps are pictures, and some native pictures are stories, visual memories, the source of directions, and a virtual sense of presence," observes in turn that "one of the stories maps tell is of the collaboration between the verbal and the visual" (2011, 50). That collaboration represents both a narrative ethic and an aesthetics of sovereignty in Vizenor's work. For Rader, "Vizenor locates in mapping the semiotic toolbox of sovereignty, which for him is all about communicative action made manifest" (50). Such communicative action is both implicit in and made manifest through the interrelation of vision, sound, and text: just as communication relies on cues both visual and verbal, so too does Vizenor's poetic depend on the seen to augment and elaborate on the heard, to trigger the visual memories/associations that supplement thought, heard, and remembered narrative.

Native mapping—the virtual cartography of orality and its mnemonic and ritual accompaniments—like narrative itself, is transient, impermanent, scaled to need, not to the observances of cadastral markers. To that end, Vizenor's emphasis on mapping parallels his engagement with writing itself, with the ways in which such tools have been instrumental to colonial dominance and erasure and, therefore, the degree to which resistance to "the advances of colonialism and dominance" (Rader 2011, 50) is necessary in and through those very mechanisms. The intersection (rather than juxtaposition) of text and image in the texts above, then—particularly in *Summer in the Spring*, where their interweaving very clearly invokes the interrelationship of (mnemonic) pictographic texts and the songs and stories that accompany them, and the "map of the mind" to which that interrelationship contributes—speaks closely to Vizenor's ambivalence about writing. They serve partly to defuse the potency of the colonial hierarchy and to complicate the often-reductive misperception of Native cultural production prior to contact. That such a possibility may, mishandled, produce exactly what Daniel Heath Justice warns against is clear (see my discussion of Justice's argument in the introduction; Justice 2015, 302). And yet, it also suggests alternative audiences, as well as countercolonial strategies for unsettling the assurance of settler-colonial interpretations. There are those who can "read" such texts, whether or not that is the intention in including them in *Touchwood*. There are also those to whom, whether readable or not, they offer a sense of familiarity. And, of course, there are those whose sense of understanding requires, and indeed benefits from, the challenge to accessibility that such textualities provoke. We might, then, read their inclusion as another facet of Vizenor's attempts to "writ[e] in the oral tradition" (Blaeser 1996).

If this scenario suggests a typographical encounter, it does so not because Vizenor is given to stylistic gimmickry, but because the juxtaposition between forms of graphic production suggests the ways they complement, contribute to, and build on Anishinaabe oral literacy. In another literal example of deliberate mutual suggestion, Vizenor's *Earthdivers: Tribal Narratives on Mixed Descent* was interspersed with illustrations by renowned artist Jaune Quick-to-See Smith, whose work is acknowledged elsewhere in Vizenor's oeuvre. "Her artistic imagination," Vizenor writes in the preface, "is a special voice which soars through mythic time and sacred tribal memories," again attaching the visual to the heard and remembered in ways that connect his own and Smith's enterprises to tribal transmotion. Perhaps even more pertinently, he quotes Smith herself, who says among other things that "I place my markings onto a framework in homage to the ancient travois: in a sense, piling my dreams on for a journey across the land" (1981, xxii). Suggesting to the artist herself both aboriginality and prehistoricity, her "smears and stains of pigments with the crudeness of charcoal" (Vizenor 1981, xxii) anticipate what Vizenor will later say about cosmototemism.

So, in spite of his mantle as a postmodern innovator, stylistic experiment is generally eschewed by Vizenor, and where images occur, such as the photography in his *The People Named the Chippewa*, they do so only partly for illustrative and illuminative means. Moreover, such images become, at various points, the object of his own analysis. In his essay "Anishinaabe Pictomyths," for instance, Vizenor begins:

"The *anishinaabe* created by natural reason a sense of imagic presence and mythic survivance in the painted and incised pictures of animals, birds, and miniature characters on birch bark, wood, and stone. These images, or pictomyths, were venerated and carried into every native season, experience, and sacred histories" (2009, 179). He returns again to Densmore in his discussion of the pictomyths, "created by visions and sustained by stories," noting of "drawings [that] were also made in the soft, dry ashes of a fire or on the dry earth" that they "were usually a map, an illustration or a narrative, or a delineation used in the working of a charm" (179). Without lessening the emphasis on the transmotional qualities of pictomyths, though, Vizenor also suggests that "some photographs of ancestors are stories, the cues of remembrance, visual connections, intimations, and representations of time, place, and families, a new native totemic association alongside traditional images and pictomyths" (179). And he reiterates: "The *anishinaabe* pictomyths, transformations by vision and memory, and symbolic images, are totemic pictures and not directly related to emulsion photographs; yet, there is a sense of survivance, cultural memory, and strong emotive associations that bears these two sources of imagic presence in some native families" (180). First published in 2006 in the introduction to Bruce White's photographic history of the Ojibwe between the mid-nineteenth and mid-twentieth centuries—*We Are at Home: Pictures of the Ojibwe People*—this essay draws together graphic and photographic forms, bringing in the expressionist paintings of Anishinaabe artists George Morrison, David Bradley, Frank Big Bear, and Patrick DesJarlait, too, to examine "familiar cultural pictures" (180), those that "Native homes" (Vizenor's words) find space for.

What Vizenor terms imagic presence, which he defines as a common factor between pictomyths and photographs of ancestors, is further illuminated in the essay "Ontic Images," first delivered as a lecture titled "Imagic Moments: Native American Identities and Literary Modernity" in 2000. Here, he asks the reader to "consider the analogies of native visionary, totemic images, and the photographic representations of *postindian* identities, or those ontic, imagic moments that follow the invention and occidental simulations of the *indian* in the Americas" (2009, 159). "Analogies in this sense," he continues, "are visual," drawing on the work of Barbara Maria Stafford, whose emphasis on the analogical "as the creative and tentative weaving together of individuated phenomena" in counter to the "elevation of atomistic difference" (2001, 61) has obvious thematic appeal for Vizenor's work and its resistance to singularities and static determinants. So, too, can one see its appeal at a formal level, with the alignment of image and text as means of both unsettling absolute authority (implied by the written text) and bridging the divide between them, enabling a fuller, or richer at least, apprehension of the perceived object, as, in Stafford's words, "a practice of intermedia communication" (qtd. by Vizenor 2009, 159).

I want to turn, however, for the remainder of this chapter, to the ways in which the visual plays a prominent role in Vizenor's writing even in the absence of indexical, or literal, images. Again, Stafford's agenda suggests a vital entry point to this consideration. Where, thematically, the analogical emphasizes "ways of seeing sameness-in-difference," it formally and theoretically enables a "bridging process by which one can persuasively show that something is *like* something else or *participates* in that which it is not" (Stafford 2001, xvi). While the first part of that equation suggests a means of understanding the kind of transcultural exchange in which Vizenor has increasingly participated—particularly focused on the relationship between Anishinaabeakiing and France—the second offers a very clear means of beginning to consider the relationship between art and literature, and between the artist and the writer, and, by further analogy, between both art and literature/image and text and the wider cultural world in which they circulate. In his earlier novels, that relationship exists in interventional capacity as a means of both directly evoking presence and bridging the perceived gap between oral and literary. In turn, that maneuver unsettles the dominant stranglehold of the written while simultaneously resisting the elevation of the oral "tradition" as itself a pure or elevated form detached from other processes of exchange.

So, tying together Vizenor's discussions of photography to his treatment of what he calls "cosmototemic primitivism" and to his use of made and marked/imaged objects in the novel *Dead Voices*, I want to briefly explore his realizations and theorizations of Stafford's claim that "images analogically perform incarnation" (2001, 24). Moving on from there, I will join Vizenor in his leap slightly further into abstraction to explore the very explicit relationship he establishes between visual art and writing in the two more recent novels, *Shrouds of White Earth* and *Blue Ravens*. In doing so, I want to shift the discussion slightly to consider the relationship between literary aesthetics and visual sovereignty in Vizenor's work. Analyzing the transmotional moves of the latter two novels into the domain of French (and outsider) modernist art while maintaining a sense of Vizenor's earlier engagements with visuality and pictomythic transformation extends our analysis of what David Carlson suggests is Vizenor's treatment of "visual processes as allegorical representations of the writing process" (2015a). As such, it fundamentally challenges the notion that the Native state, as figured in colonial grand narratives from first "discovery," is somehow deficient, that Native peoples must "attain" the standards by which colonial settler ideologies measure "civilization," while simultaneously contributing to the career-long project of undoing the cultural dominance of *indian* simulations, which "denies real native pictures, cultural variations, conversions, and modernity" (Vizenor 2009, 165). Whether understanding the artist/writer (artist-writer) as exilic (Carlson 2015a) or outsider (Mackay 2015), Vizenor's sense of corollary in the process of interpretation of the spiritual to the imagic forges a strong connection in his work and in what he identifies as a "literary modernity." Thus, just as the image (not the portrait) connotes the continuity of survivance, in that "the imagic moment is the creation of an ontic sense of presence" (Vizenor 2009, 170),[7] so, too, his stories: "My father, grandmother, and other native relatives are a presence not an absence in my stories, and now that sense of presence is in the book. The creation of my native identities is in the book. My resistance to simulations and cultural dominance is in the book, and that is the ontic significance of a literary modernity" (163).

Making a concrete distinction between image-as-myth, the manipulative form invoked by Barthes, Mitchell, and others indicative of the pictorial turn, or the "age" of the image, and the image as manifest here, Vizenor notes that "Catlin and other painters created fugitive poses, ethnographic simulations of *indians* with vacuous eyes and barren hands. The *indians* in most portraits were interimage simulations" (1998, 162). These are precisely the "eternal contradictions of *indian* portraiture . . . the *presence* of the *indian*" that connotes "the absence of the native" (165). As is frequently seen elsewhere in his oeuvre, Vizenor's narrator Laundry in *Dead Voices* reasserts a truism about the relationship between the oral and print culture, when he reports the insistence of Bagese, the bear woman, that "tribal stories must be told and not recorded, told to listeners but not readers, and she insisted that stories be heard through the ear not the eye" (1992, 6). Blaeser's reading of the novel asserts that "Vizenor sets up an opposition between eye and ear . . . with the clear intention of breaking open the confined visual space of the text" (1996, 194). While this is undeniably the case, Blaeser's further suggestion that "it is alive, quick, quicker than the text that caters merely to the eye, and not to the ear, the oral, as well" neglects the significance of sight to the novel's narrative as "ongoing event" (194). Thus, the proposition that "the magic of Vizenor's *Dead Voices* is the disappearance of the text from the page" (Blaeser 1996, 194), while rightly paying attention to the ways Vizenor unseats the dominant authority of alphabetic text, understates the presence of the image-text itself as catalyst to the narrative and, perhaps more crucially, the connection Laundry makes between image, story, and written text at the end of the novel.

Dead Voices dissolves between spheres that we might designate the real and the spectral. Reflections and shadows dominate more palpable materiality. They unsettle perception and determine phenomenological apperception through the mingling of senses and insight—that intermingling constituting selfhood in the absence (or rather in the presence of the shadow) of the body. In spite of Bagese's injunction that stories should "be heard through the ear not the eye," in other words, "she was very determined about the ear in spite of the obvious inconsistencies" (Vizenor 1992, 6). Early in the novel as we are, those "inconsistencies" are not fully revealed as anything other than the necessary inclusion of other senses in embodied and spiritual experience, flagged by Laundry when, having noted the strong smell of the bear woman, he suggests, "The tribal world was remembered in the ear, but she never said anything about the nose" (6). Ultimately, it is of course the ear that plays the larger role, although the merging of embodied experience and memoried performance means that the olfactory trigger—as he is "in her scent"—speaks both to the scent-trace that holds him captive to her ("television soap" as it happens) and the trace memory that will forever make her present to him as a sensory specter.

The prominence of the eye, however, emerges through Vizenor's optical metaphors, which are by no means unique to this novel. Having told Laundry that stories must be heard in the ear not the eye, inducing his promise not to publish her stories, Bagese then tells him that "the tricksters in the word are *seen* in the ear not the eye," indicating the visual manifestation of the imagination, whether conjured by image or oral tale (7; emphasis added). Furthermore, the abiding metaphor for the traces of presence inherent to the stories in the novel is "shadow," where "echo" might seem more readily to cohere with the ear. The presence of mirrors, too, invokes a reflective (and deflective) quality to the traces, shadows, and images that populate and catalyze the stories Bagese tells. In foregrounding the optical illusion, Vizenor dissolves the distinction between the physical and the metaphysical, between the realms of story, spirit, and materiality. Those shadows themselves are multiple. On the one hand they recall the second of three epigraphs to the novel, taken from *Black Elk Speaks*: "It is hard to follow one great vision in this world of darkness and of many changing shadows. Among those shadows men get lost" (Vizenor 1992). Those dark, disorientating spheres are mapped through story; the means to navigate them with foresight and clarity are furnished through the ear. On the other hand, Bagese maintains, "the best listeners were shadows, animals, birds, and humans, because their shadows once shared the same stories" (7). So, while "written words were the burial ground of shadows," they are kept alive to the mind through the ear (7).

While not specifically images in and of themselves—I will get to that—this transition between spheres also evokes a specific aspect of Ojibwe belief. Notwithstanding Vizenor's aversion to ethnographic stasis, these connotations cannot plausibly be neglected, given the visionary trail from Black Elk's Flaming Rainbow (Neihardt 2014, 157) to Bagese's spatial and physical transformations. So, Christopher Vecsey draws on earlier scholars of Native religion such as Åke Hultkrantz to describe the dual souls of the Ojibwe self, wherein the "traveling soul, sometimes called a free-soul . . . resided in the brain and had a separate existence from the body, being able to journey during sleep" (Vecsey 1983, 60). Moreover, "it perceived, sensed, acted as the 'eyes' of the ego-soul, seeing things at a distance" (60). At death, while the ego-soul traveled to the afterworld, "the free-soul, or shadow, became a ghost" remaining for a time in the physical realm (60). This intercessionary capacity, implicit in the shadows and reflections of *Dead Voices*, thus invokes the spiritual domain, while it simultaneously calls into question empirical certainties. Forging such a strong relation between the visual and visionary rather undermines Bagese's insistence that the ear—and the oral/aural metaphor—alone is paramount.

There is one further connection through Vecsey to consider: "The Ojibwas," he writes, "considered a person's image, including the external shadow, as an integral part of the person, like a name. Drawing another person's picture was a means of influencing that person, just as injuring a person's external shadow might injure the whole person" (1983, 61). Just as, as Niigaanwewidam Sinclair has shown (2009; see also chapter 3), lessons about reflections and optical illusions feature in the Anishinaabe archive, similarly Vecsey recounts a story of Nanabozho in which he plans to avenge the death by drowning of his wolf-brother by shooting the shadows of the underwater manito, indicating a storied source for the power they carry. In fact, forgetting in the heat of the chase and shooting their bodies, he fails in his attempt (1983, 90). Again, whether Vizenor has the ethnographic explication in mind or not, the power of the shadow, both seen and unseen, is established in story and, in turn, that power links in various direct and more subtle ways to themes of sight, vision (including intercessionary vision between material and spiritual worlds) and the pictorial. Elsewhere in his oeuvre—"Shadows at La Pointe" in *The People Named the Chippewa*, for instance—shadows imply the traces of continuity and the insertion of self into (hi)story through the recounting. It also recalls Vizenor's embrace of "visual thinking,"[8] and his insistence that "the Anishinaabeg did not have written histories. . . . The tribal past lived as an event in visual memories and oratorical gestures" and "tribal leaders were dreamers and orators, speaking in visual metaphors as if the past were a state of being in the telling" (1984b, 24).

The visual metaphors that simultaneously convey and enact the oratorical event, as a collapse of the moment of telling into the moment recalled in *Dead Voices*, then, find themselves planted firmly in this domain. Yet Vizenor also confirms the graphic element in the relationship between vision and orature, writing that "the poetic images were held, for some tribal families, in song pictures and in the rhythms of visions and dreams in music: timeless and natural patterns of seeing and knowing the energies of the earth. The Anishinaabeg drew pictures that reminded them of ideas, visions, and dreams" (1984b, 25–26). That relationship persists in the novel in the centrality of the wanaki card game—"his fictional adaptation of an Ojibway dish game" (Blaeser 1996, 192), which is implicit in Bagese's name[9]—a game of chance and stories. Similarly, the card game is framed by the presence of a copper dish, which is equally significant.

In his first description of his encounter with Bagese and her later transformation and disappearance, Laundry informs us: "She became a bear and carved her image on a sacred copper dish the night before she vanished. She seemed to leave her mark, a signature, and that ended the game" (Vizenor 1992, 8). At the end of the novel, when this moment is repeated, a little more is divulged about the dish.

> Bagese became a bear, and at last she became a picture of a bear. She sent me a copper dish with several figures marked on the wide circle. The copper was once a sacred record of the woodland tribe. The first figure was the trickster at creation, and the other figures were tribal generations at the great river. Then there was a man with a high hat on the circle. He was taller than the others and must have been the first white man to reach the tribe. . . .
>
> The last figure was a new mark on the copper, the incised outline of a bear. . . . At last the bear in the cities was heard in sacred tribal histories. (143)

Again, the elision between the seen and heard, the oral and the visual, in the form of the self-made mark that renders Bagese a "heard" presence in sacred stories suggests a performative function for the image that significantly exceeds Blaeser's proposed opposition of eye and ear.

Where for Blaeser the novel stakes a claim for the primacy of the oral/aural, establishing a series of oppositions including that between ear and eye, the multiple authors of "Textual Interstices: Mirrored Shadows in Gerald Vizenor's *Dead Voices*" see its "defense of the aural" as of a piece with the way "the existence of the text as artifact and its construction through the voice of the narrative 'I' points to and criticizes the accepted fabrication of tribal life in books" (Dix et al. 2000, 179). There is clear merit in these arguments, and I will return to points in turn, but Arnold Krupat has taken a more tentative line, suggesting that the book effectively pursues a doubt, or a question, that more directly illustrates the tension in Vizenor's work between the "romantic position" of "loyalt[y] to speech as primary" and his "admiration, here and elsewhere, of a certain Derridean poststructuralism or Lyotardian postmodernism for which writing is privileged over speech" (1996, 81). The issue, he writes, "is whether stories can perform their healing function only as voiced or oral stories or whether they can retain their power—whether they can avoid simply becoming 'dead voices' when they are in written form" (70). The apparent dichotomy between Laundry (who "assert[s] that 'written words are pictures'") and Bagese (who "responds: 'Printed books are the habits of dead voices'" [Krupat 1996, 76]) mirrors the shift between "an orality traditionally associated with collective or 'tribal' identities and ancestral homelands," to which Vizenor is "deeply attracted," and the fact that he is "also absolutely and unsentimentally clear about the present necessity of writing the oral tradition in the diasporic solitude of the cities" (Krupat 1996, 81).

The mutuality of emphasis on the visual and the oral enables, I think we can argue, a reading of writing that supports rather than threatens the oral tradition. Like Bagese's dish, which evokes copper script kept by members of the midewiwin, the stories we read are heard in the pictures on the wanaki cards. Vizenor's writing around and between these pictures is itself a form of shadow writing. Krupat argues that it represents a hunt for the pronominal. We could also, however, consider it a hunt for form, or for an engagement with both language and visual thinking that either actively mediates between the seen and heard world or repeatedly invokes the visual as a sensory proxy for and complement to the aural. As Krupat observes, it reflects a transition, first observed by Elaine Jahner, from seeing "'all writing as an act that destroys the life of the oral exchange,' claiming as late as 1984 that printed stories alter tribal experience" (Krupat 1996, 81, qtg. Jahner) to understanding writing as a more nuanced tool, and one with true decolonial potential, "provided, of course, that the writing be of the type that, in a phrase of Julia Kristeva's 'breaks out of the rules of a language censored by grammar and semantics'" (Krupat 1996, 82).

Indeed, Kristeva's own focus on the "dialogism of Menippean and carnivalesque discourses" (1986, 55) has particular resonance for Vizenor's fiction—it resounds, in fact, in Blaeser's emphasis on the work's dialogic quality. In turn, Kristeva's sense that, in "translating a logic of relations and analogy rather than of substance and inference," that dialogism "contradicts [formal logic] and points it towards other forms of thought," meshes with the "politic" of Vizenor's aesthetic (1986, 55). There is one further coincidence with the language of Kristeva's anti-Aristotelian (antiteleological, antibinary) take, evoked if not fully explored by Krupat. This is her assertion that the dialogic novel is bequeathed what she calls "Menippean ambivalence," consisting of "communication between two spaces: that of the scene and that of the hieroglyph,[10] that of representation *by* language, and that of experience *in* language, system and phrase, metaphor and metonymy" (55). The "ambivalent literary structure" (59) that Vizenor's novel represents, then, takes the "two tendencies of Western literature: representation through language as staging, and exploration of language as a correlative system of signs" (59), and embeds in them a third system of expressive communication that neither explicitly seeks to represent language, nor functions fully (or indeed directly) as writing. That further layer, in other words, renders the literary ambivalence a tension of systems that supplants binarism with dialogism not simply as a heteroglossic, cross media, or intertextual event (yet it is all of these things), but across distinct epistemological forms.

By way of closing comment on this epistemic question, Krupat's distinction between Vizenor's "romantic position" vis-à-vis the oral tradition as a point of tension with his "admiration . . . of a certain Derridean poststructuralism or Lyotardian postmodernism" (1996, 81) may well be germane to his use of a certain kind of visual literacy. Citing Wolfgang Hochbruck, Krupat footnotes the distinction between "'Lyotard's harmless language games' and Vizenor's '"word wars' between different cultures," reiterating his own suggestion that Vizenor's "postmodernism, to recall [Kwame Anthony] Appiah, may be an antagonist as much as an ally of Western postmodernism" (81n13).[11] This, I think, is a leading point, which speaks also to the possibility of the ambivalence of Vizenor's own writing—in *Dead Voices*, at the very least—toward the inherent logics of the very poststructuralist play that fuels his method. Derrida's deprioritization of speech—in his deconstruction of the "violence" of "that dangerous supplement," that is—is integral to his articulation of *différance*, which in turn articulates the seemingly endless play of signifiers that typifies (and vivifies) Vizenor's trickster hermeneutic. It is, in other words, in part disavowal of that privileging of the oral that Vizenor's "writing in the oral tradition," to quote Blaeser's title, takes its force.

Interrupting and deconstructing both elements and the binary relationship they have tended to reassume in the context of Native American literary criticism, Vizenor's use of visual images, particularly those associated with alternative literacies, suggests a third relationship between signification and language that is distinct from the metaphysical shift in the French intellectual tradition toward the linguistic turn.[12] It also—ironically—recalls the tripartite understanding of writing that underpins Rousseau's formulations, the distinctions between "two pictographies," one that "proceeds *directly* [such as Mexican glyphs or Egyptian hieroglyphics as then understood] and the other *allegorically* [such as Chinese ideographic characters]," and alphabetic writing itself (Derrida 1976, 291).[13] Thus, in his invocation of speech/song and image, Vizenor engages all of those elements of Rousseau's treatise and joins the deconstructive process wherein, "in the play of the supplement the demand of metaphysics for an unequivocal, unilateral, and universal positioning of song, writing, metaphor, and poetry is undone" (Tomlinson 1995, 354). Even more pointedly, Gary Tomlinson explains that "the working of logocentrism, which would make those things familiar by setting them in fixed, immobile relation to speech—a relation, usually, of devalued accretion—is replaced by a different operation of fluid interrelations between speech and its others" (354).[14] In the course of *Dead Voices*, then, it is precisely that "operation of fluid interrelations" that Vizenor moves toward—what Tomlinson calls a "supplementary mobility."

I will turn shortly to the modern(ist) contexts of Vizenor's most recent fiction, in which the relationship between writing and painting becomes even more explicitly drawn. *Dead Voices*, though, closes with a gesture that renders my reading above even more directly. As each card is drawn, in each round of the wanaki game, it conjures the appropriate, related story about the figure depicted on it. Animals and tricksters, the cards of the wanaki game were created by stone—"a game that remembers him in stories . . . his war with loneliness and with human separation from the natural world" (Vizenor 1992, 29). In conversation about the cards—the conversation that sets up what is easily read as a polarized discourse around the defense of writing (Krupat 1996, 2002; Dix et al. 2000) and the priority of the oral/aural (see Blaeser 1996, for whom the novel is Vizenor's attempt to reattach language to experience)—the two proceed:

I was more than eager to remind her that the wanaki cards were an obvious contradiction to what she had told me. The pictures on the cards were the same as written words and could not be heard. I was certain she wanted me to ask obvious questions. "So, how can you hear stones and pictures?"

"The bear is painted not printed, and the praying mantis is seen as the president, this is a shadow, a chance, not a word," she insisted.

"Written words are pictures."

"Printed books are the habits of dead voices," she said and turned a mirror in my direction to distract me. "The ear not the eye sees the stories."

"And the eye hears the stories."

"The voices are dead."

"So, the wanaki pictures are dead."

"There are no others, these are my picture stories, no one sees them but hears my stories." (Vizenor 1992, 18)

Establishing this conversation between the old bear woman, who unequivocally signifies the oral, the mystical, and the tribal, and the young interlocutor who, as an academic, seems destined only to add to the dead voices of published tribal stories, Vizenor necessarily complicates that relationship. In closing the novel, in fact, he leaves the reader with a statement from Laundry that, though not entirely unequivocal, would nevertheless seem to absorb the spirit and ethos of Bagese's painted shadows into the printed book, enabling the possibility in reproduction of the ear seeing, and the eye hearing, and no one seeing but that "hears [her] stories." "Bagese," Laundry says, "these published stories are the same as the wanaki pictures and the stones that you placed in your apartment to remember the earth, the traces of birds and animals near the lake. I am with you in the mirror, and hold a stone in my pocket, the stone you left for me on the table, to remember your stories. We must go on" (144). There is, of course, a literal claim here—one that we perhaps cannot take too literally, knowing Vizenor's penchant for the tease, although Molly McGlennen avers that "Native peoples creatively engage the imaginative means of writing as a continued version of recording oral documents" (2015, 23n7). Whether or not we read Laundry as referring to form, or even to function precisely, he certainly tacitly suggests that effects, in the form of the visual affect engaging the ear and vice versa, coincide. He justifies his actions relative to Bagese's own: "she made the first record and published the first mark for the eye not the ear. The figure of the bear on the copper dish would have been silent if we had not published the stories she remembered . . . the mark on the copper was incised as a record of tribal creation and stories. That copper has become a written record of the return of the bear" (Vizenor 1992, 143). Nevertheless, that "these published stories are the same as the wanaki pictures and the stones" depends on the narrator having invoked the eye and the ear in equal measure. This, unequivocally, is one of the effects of the visual cues, metaphors, and images the novel employs, which, interrelating with the dialogism at the heart of Bagese's re-presenting, conjures that multisensory experience. In so conjuring, the incision cuts not only into the surface of the copper, the substance of the page, but into memory, returning the bear again with every telling/reading.

All of this relies, of course, on the play of signifiers Vizenor has long embraced. Thus, the presence implicit in the linguistic trace—"The secret, [Bagese] told me, was not to pretend, but to see and hear the real stories behind the words, the voices of the animals in me, not the definitions of the words alone" (1992, 7)—and the persistent misdirection of deferral, which ultimately unsettles the absolute authority of any single medium, are vital elements of this sensory equation (reminding us, perhaps, that just as the pictures require the interpreter to vivify the stories, so the stories and the interpreter require the pictures, and the game's chance value, as their catalyst). This latter notion is signaled quite directly in the text by the use of mirrors and the evocation of narrative maps. Dix et al. open up the optical and cartographic threads of the novel, writing: "The trick to the narrative lies in the elision of both tellers—beneath the containing texts of Laundry's translations are Bagese's own representations of fragments of an aural matrix of stories: the 'shadow' Vizenor sees uncovered in 'the ruins of representation.' Vizenor's own use of the Earthdiver myth serves as a model for this process: the aural appears as recoverable through the construction of the printed text as fragments of the old world form the seed of the new" (2000, 179). In a sense, then, and just as the narrative contains its own misdirectional trails (see Dix et al. 2000, 184), the printed narrative provides a map to the "aural matrix"—a map that is neither straightforward nor easily legible, but nevertheless enables the navigation of heard presences rather than containing and muting dead voices. The shadow is the trace reflected in the mirror that reveals Bagese's bear self, and that continues to reveal the bear, and the animals whose stories are catalyzed by the wanaki cards, to those with the optical acuity to see. Like the book, then, the mirror reflects (and deflects) depending on the attention of the looker/reader. Both maps and mirrors are of course themselves representations of the real, and as such they both cast illusions that what is seen bears indexical relationship to a real referent, further building up the complexity of the interplay of multiple supplements to the original presence. It generates, in the view of Dix et al., a palimpsest (2000, 180), in which no single text, no single layer, claims sole authority or complete or original presence, and in which all presences, glimpsed though they must be, are traceable.

If this does not immediately take us back to Teuton's insistence that "Native American forms of signification actively engage presence and absence through two interdependent and reciprocal modes of communication, the oral and the graphic," it is perhaps simply because there appears to be so much more in play than his triad suggests. Yet all of the signifying forms invoked, all of the layers of representation that stack up, come back to the relationship of represented form to optical metaphor to memory made present in oral story. Let us finish with an acknowledgement that the equation sketched out here is neither easy nor unequivocal. Indeed, Dix et al. observe the implicit threat in the novel's optical illusions, in Laundry's "antagonistic" first encounter with the tabernacle mirror: "his fear of the reflection (not *his* reflection, though) reflects his uneasy position within the map of the story. . . . For Laundry, the mirror is initially the site of an antagonistic exchange; the reflection simultaneously being what he most desires to ingest and that which he cannot face" or understand (2000, 184). Yet the depiction Bagese leaves on the copper dish is "framed with rosettes," a representation of the tabernacle itself, rendering the mirror integral to its own textuality: a metaphor, in other words, for the book. Learning to "read" dialogically, through and with a variety of media, becomes both the content and the message. What is ultimately evoked is a particular kind of relationship and a particular kind of instruction in how to understand the interconnections of multiple forms and senses. Laundry tells us, "I was never sure how to hear the stories she told me. I could see the scenes that she described, but meaning escaped me" (Vizenor 1992, 10). On the one hand, he speaks of language's capacity to recall visual scenes—the incredible intersubjective magic of visual thinking; on the other, he reminds us almost of a *symboliste* tenet that poetry is less about the meaning of experience (or language) and more about the experience of meaning (or, indeed, language).

Black Elk described the world in which we live as a shadow of the spirit world, noting that shadows can cloud our vision. In *Dead Voices*, however, Vizenor challenges the ability of Laundry to perceive the world in which he lives prior to his encounter with Bagese's stories. As he first approaches her city dwelling, he "casts himself in the role of a voyeur looking through a glass darkly" (Dix et al. 2000, 181) as he describes looking through the rain that "came in bursts . . . and blurred the window" (Vizenor 1992, 15). As Dix et al. note, it is ultimately in his looking "slant" at the mirror's reflection, entering the spatial frame of its "mythical discourse" that he really begins to see/hear (2000, 181). In other words, it is only through engaging multiple senses, through the affective possibilities of phenomenological experience, rather than passive observation from the outside, that he begins to gain any true insight. The result is by no means ideologically neutral or politically unproblematic, but in actively seeking to unsettle narrative centers, in opting for a play of multiple languages and literacies that place the viewing/seeing subject at their heart, he also gestures toward the decolonial aggravation of the authority of alphabetic text or its antagonist's reductively binaristic face-off with the spoken word. "In contrast to the narrations of traditional anthropologists," Dix et al. continue, "Laundry's self-reflexive accounts are more representative of what he (and he only) sees in the mirrors than of what he wants to see through the window" (2000, 181). As the reader is drawn into the text through its own multisensory invocations, they too are forced to confront what it reflects, rather than rewarding the suppositions they might place upon it.

This relationship between writing and pictures, and between the writer and the picture-maker, becomes far more explicitly rendered in Vizenor's more recent work. Indeed, *Shrouds of White Earth* proceeds from the vantage point of Dogroy Beaulieu, a contemporary Ojibwe artist, as he tells his story of banishment to a writerly counterpart. As is not unusual for Vizenor's work, but seems to become ever more personal, this novel invokes a wide range of his interests and touchstones, from the family name—Beaulieu—to his own early career as a journalist; from his essayistic interest in Anishinaabe artists such as George Morrison and David Bradley to a politically acute and ongoing analysis of the intersections between state ideologies and tribal politics, and much more. That Vizenor locates parts of the story in Paris reminds us of both his affection for the country of France and its intellectual heritage, and the transnational arc of much of his writing, which eschews both nation-state containment and the core/periphery binary of empire.

The relocation to Europe under conditions of banishment also conjures an early to mid-twentieth-century echo of mobility in the face of fascism, as well as invoking the enclave of "Lost Generation" artists and writers in interwar Paris and other expatriate artists after World War II. The former mobilized in response to what became mortal threat, but their banishment began with the revocation of their rights as citizens, becoming what Hannah Arendt would go on to describe in "We Refugees": "A refugee used to be a person driven to seek refuge because of some act committed or some political opinion held. Well, it is true we have had to seek refuge; but we committed no acts and most of us never dreamt of having any radical opinion" (1994, 110). There is an ironic inversion here in Dogroy's exile, as he briefly travels the opposite way across the Atlantic to Arendt and her fellow "Americans of German language" (110) after his nominally (and not really) subversive acts, and unlike Arendt there is no question of his relinquishing his homeland "after four weeks in France ... pretend[ing] to be Frenchmen" (111), but nevertheless the specter of the mid-twentieth century lingers in his European exile. He may seem, though, to have more in common with the expatriate writers, who escaped demons of other kinds, from rigid cultural tastes to social disillusionment to, in the case of James Baldwin and other African American, politically radical, and/or queer public figures, the extreme prejudice of American society in the 1940s and 1950s. The curtailment of individual freedoms in and by the machinery of state (and its withdrawal in the form of overzealous exercise of sovereign power) resounds in both scenarios. And yet Dogroy's sojourn in Paris is contemporary with our own moment, and he neither comes across as seeking a bohemian bonhomie or freedom from social oppression, nor as the broken example of Arendt's refugee; nevertheless, his exile is not entirely self-imposed as he occupies the position of scapegoat relative to the constitutional arrangements of his homeland.[15] In many respects, invoking recent Jewish history in Europe conjures a number of banal and problematic comparisons that are not necessarily helpful, but it is difficult to read Vizenor's depiction of banishment without such an analogy at least faintly, ironically, coming to mind. Certainly, Vizenor's notion of survivance resounds in Arendt's insistence that "very few individuals have the strength to conserve their own integrity if their social, political and legal status is completely confused" (1994, 116). And while this holds true to communities—to those tribal communities who have resisted and continue to resist colonial oppressions—it gathers a different, more implicit force in the context of the individual artist banished from the particular citizenship of his tribal nation in the wake of—and in contravention of—its new constitution.

In the more recent novel, the pair of brothers—Aloysius Hudon Beaulieu and Basile Hudon Beaulieu—who front *Blue Ravens* retreat to a Paris of the historical moment I describe above, arriving in France during the early weeks of U.S. involvement in World War I and later returning to postwar Paris to mix with the artists and intellectuals of the Left Bank scene. The result is in part an elegy to the cultural vibrancy of that city, as the protagonists relax in cafes frequented by American expatriates, dine with famous Parisian and Paris-based thinkers, artists, and writers, and make their mark in salons and galleries. While Native presence in Europe in the first quarter of the twentieth century is hardly unheard of[16]—indeed, Joseph Boyden's *Three Day Road* precedes Vizenor's as a fictional account of Anishinaabe soldiers in France in the 1910s—fellow Ojibwe (Red Lake) Patrick DesJarlait "is often cited as the first Native American modernist painter" (Anthes 2006, 91). DesJarlait's moment ticked into instance after World War II, making Aloysius a seriously early innovator in this mold. That said, George Morrison, the abstract expressionist painter about whom Vizenor has frequently written, tacitly expressed his difference from his fellow students in a life-drawing class, noting that "European modernists such as 'Cézanne and Renoir were regarded as . . . extreme, even though their works were fifty or so years old by then'" (Anthes 2006, 105) and affirming that his own understanding of art "as a creative and expressive activity" was engaged by a 1939 exhibition of Picasso at the Minneapolis Institute of Art, which was nevertheless "very extreme for Minneapolis" (105). Again, although later than Vizenor's time frame, the experimental Ojibwe artist is presented as already in accord with a modernist aesthetic.

The daring of Vizenor's design, then, is multiple, as he places his Anishinaabe writer and painter in a spot that is apparently geographically, historically, and culturally distant from the "center" of their homeland and not only sees them thrive but witnesses their intervention in the European avant-garde. They are neither exotic interlopers nor objects of enquiry, but cultural producers, innovators, and commentators in their own right and of their own volition. Bear in mind that this is the period when Densmore was investigating Ojibwe song—and, thus, Anishinaabe cultural production is in process of renewed objectification and interpretation by the anthropological gaze—and that human zoos, common in European cities in the nineteenth century, would not end entirely for a further four decades (in 1958 in Brussels), while the Jardin d'Agronomie Tropicale in the Vincennes woods had exhibited villagers from the remaining outposts of French colonial territory as recently as 1907. This last point will cast a slightly different inflection on *Shrouds* than it does on *Blue Ravens*, but in the latter context particularly, it gestures to the orientalist equation of modernism and primitivism—exemplified in modernity's construction of the primitive. That Vizenor not only utterly refuses his characters' subsumption by that grammar, but has them directly implicated as producers in the vanguard indicates a further refusal of the rhetorics of encounter and empire. In doing so, he renders his characters actors in a cultural exchange that has long interpreted their presence as that of the passive historical object.

It is tempting, in both books, to read the artist as a proxy for the writer—indeed, Vizenor's own emphasis on the analogical positively invites us to. And although he makes several pertinent distinctions that maintain separation between the two forms—that suggest, in fact, an admiring acknowledgement that the writer's craft is fundamentally more limited, more mundane, more rational, than the painter's, though nonetheless significant—there is a clear, complementary, intersection of forms. I will develop some of these distinctions in the ensuing discussion, but it is worth pausing at this stage on one of them. Toward the beginning of *Blue Ravens* in a relationship very explicitly framed as that between a rather liberated, "natural" artist—a "blue raven painter of liberty" (Vizenor 2014, 12)—and a writer driven by the need to create and interpret, and record and report (influenced, in other words, by both the newspaper they sell, the double duty of documenting both history and travel, and the chance creations of his brother), the narrator makes a small but significant comparative concession:

> My brother actually inspired me to become a writer, to create the stories anew that our relatives once told whenever they gathered in the summer for native celebrations, at native wakes, and funerals at the mission. . . .
>
> Aloysius inspired me to create visionary stories and scenes of presence, stories that were elusive and not merely descriptive. . . . He created abstract ravens in motion, the very scenes of his vision and memory, but words were too heavy, too burdened by grammar and decorated with documented history to break into blue abstract ravens and fly. (12)

Comparison made, he nevertheless confirms the influence of those qualities of the visual arts his brother exudes when he says: "My recollections of the words in stories were not the same as artistic or visionary scenes, *not at first*. Dreams are scenes not words, but one or two precise words could create a vision of the scene. That would be my course of literary art and liberty" (12; emphasis added). Such a statement echoes a comment by the artist-narrator Dogroy Beaulieu of the earlier *Shrouds of White Earth*, who declares, "Yes, the brush of a painter, and the pen of a literary artist create scenes of liberation, critical and chancy" (Vizenor 2011, 65). While maintaining and appreciating the difference, then, these last statements infer a gestural connection of intent and effect/affect between the visual and verbal that speaks very directly to those aspects of Vizenor's aesthetic discussed already.

There is one further influence that, given its prior treatment here and in chapter 6, is worth drawing attention to. "Frances Densmore visited the reservation that summer," we're told, "and provided me with the intuition and the initial tease of visionary songs and stories" (Vizenor 2014, 12–13). In chapter 6, I examine Marcie Rendon's critique of overreliance on source material such as Densmore's in her play *SongCatcher*. There, she suggests that the recordings Densmore made, and the work of recovery in which they are involved among Anishinaabeg who have moved, or been moved, some distance from community or roots, generate further alienation from the spiritual aspects of cultural heritage, in which seeking and finding one's own songs or interpretations give way to the attempts to replicate the songs of ancestors. While the tension between these positive and negative views of Densmore's legacy is somewhat suggestive of debate of acceptable and, dare I say, authentic cultural practice, this is not a suggestion I will indulge—not least because neither writer is didactic on these matters. More to the point, though, it reflects a range of responses to such materials within communities themselves, which is the kind of internal debate no outsider can enter. I want, then, to leave that tension sitting here between these two chapters, acknowledging only that while Basile celebrates the inspiration of Densmore's output here, Vizenor's stinging criticism of ethnographers' methods is no less vigorous than Rendon's.

More specifically still, however, it was "the stories of the songs" that inspired Basile, "and by intuition the actual creation of written scenes and stories became much easier" for him (Vizenor 2014, 13). He goes on to describe Densmore's recording of a song by Odjibwe, "*little plover, it is said, has walked by*," noting that "only eight words were translated. . . . The song scenes were active and memorable because the listeners understood the story. The song story is what inspired me to create the presence of listeners in the story" (13). The quality of visuality, then, is at least partly effected by the literary generation of audience—or the generation of communitas between reader, writer, and text. The presence of the listener is partly generated by the first-person narration and the sense it gives of both a community back home and a readership that is explicitly being written to—which may be one and the same. In this moment, too, the invocation of the visual act and potential, at least, of its reflection in language partially recalls Barnett Newman's infamous celebration of "The Ideographic Picture." Describing the work of "the" traditional

Kwakwaka'wakw artist he writes: "The abstract shape he used, his entire plastic language, was directed by a ritualistic will toward metaphysical understanding. . . . To him a shape was a living thing, a vehicle for an abstract thought-complex, a carrier of the awesome feelings he felt before the terror of the unknowable" (O'Neill 1992, 108). Strip back the hyperbolic tone, the evocation of the Romantic sublime, and what Newman invokes is a vision of art in which "the abstract shape was . . . real rather than a formal 'abstraction' of a visual fact, with its overtone of an already-known nature" (108). Addressing the "modern counterpart of the primitive art impulse" in 1947, then, there is an echo of Newman's sense in Basile's description of what and how his writing achieves the translation of the visionary on a par with painting. Newman expands:

> The basis of an aesthetic act is the pure idea. But the pure idea is, of necessity, an aesthetic act. Here then is the epistemological paradox that is the artist's problem. Not space cutting nor space building, not construction nor fauvist destruction; not the pure line, straight and narrow, nor the tortured line, distorted and humiliating; not the accurate eye, all fingers, nor the wild eye of dream, winking; but the idea-complex that makes contact with mystery—of life, of men, of nature, of the hard, black chaos that is death, or the grayer, softer chaos that is tragedy. For it is only the pure idea that has meaning. Everything else has everything else. (108)

While the implementation of the "primitive" must, of course, be further examined,[17] Newman's sense of the relationship between idea and aesthetic act has some resonance in Vizenor's haiku aesthetic—and, by turns, in the dreamsong and mythic story invoked but never actually told in *Blue Ravens*. There, by leaving the stories untold, invisible, an idea in themselves that contrasts with the reportage and description of the novel itself, he conjures a representation of that relation in the repeated rendition of Aloysius's painted ravens, as both drivers for the narrative, inspiration for the writer, and, ultimately, metonym for the inspired stories themselves.

Unlike Newman, it is not to American "new painting" that Vizenor turns in *Blue Ravens* to encounter the mainstream articulation of the primitive, but to the earlier moment of the modernist avant-garde in Paris in the post–World War I period, as it leaves les Fauves at the fin de siècle. Within the first eight pages of the novel, Vizenor (via Basile) makes three of what will be many direct references to European painters:

Aloysius Beaulieu, or *beau lieu*, means a beautiful place in French. That fur-trade surname became our union of ironic stories, necessary art, and our native liberty. Henri Matisse, we discovered later, painted the *Nu Bleu, Souvenir de Biskra*, or the *Blue Nude*, that same humid and gusty summer in France. (Vizenor 2014, 1)

Marc Chagall and my brother would be celebrated for their blue scenes and visionary portrayals. . . . Chagall declared his vision as an artist in Vitebsk on the Pale of Settlement in Imperial Russia. Aloysius created his glorious blue ravens about the same time on the Pale of White Earth in Minnesota. . . .

Chagall and my brother were the saints of blues. (1–2)

No one on the reservation would have associated the abstract blue ravens with the modern art movements of impressionism or expressionism, or the avant-garde, and certainly not compared the color and style of the inspired raven scenes on the reservation with the controversial painting *Les Demoiselles d'Avignon* by Pablo Picasso. Yet, my brother painted by inspiration the original abstract blue ravens at the same time that Picasso created *The Brothel of Avignon*, the translated title, in 1907. (7–8)

These early references locate us in time. The year 1907, when Matisse painted his Fauvist *Nu Bleu*—a reclining nude with a blue aura—was also the year of Picasso's famous cubist work. Vizenor thus temporally associates Aloysius's activities with two of the most influential French modernists of the moment. In 1907, Chagall, meanwhile, was a fugitive of sorts in St. Petersburg, where he had enrolled at the Imperial Society for the Protection of Fine Arts. Painting naturalistically at a time when Russian fashion still favored realism, Chagall would arrive in Paris in 1911 to find a very different art scene.

Vizenor's (or at the very least his characters') favored artists in this context are well known: "Picasso," he writes in *Shrouds of White Earth*, "chased his fame, an artistic comedy," whereas "Marc Chagall inspired me . . . to create an art of visionary liberty" (2011, 70). Along with Franz Marc, Wassily Kandinsky, and other members of Der Blaue Reiter, as well as war artist Otto Dix, Chagall features most prominently in the ranks of European artistic influences. Chagall's significance to this work aligns with another, more literary, influence—Albert Camus. In his paper "A Poetics of Recognition: Vizenor's *Shrouds of White Earth*," David J. Carlson examines Vizenor's frequent references to and invocations of Camus and Chagall in *Shrouds* as well as in *Native Liberty*, arguing that the figure of exile "is a vantage point [for Vizenor,] from which the modern artist engages in the creative, philosophical and narrative work that allows him to balance local and global consciousness in a politically engaged manner" (2015a). Carlson goes on to suggest that Vizenor reinscribes the negative—often tragic—logics of exile through his concept of transmotion, "the connotations of [which] are creation stories, totemic visions, reincarnation, and sovenance . . . that sense of native motion and an active presence, is *sui generis* sovereignty" (Vizenor 1998, 15). For Carlson, "paradoxically, one finds oneself 'at home' through the dialectical consciousness of exile, or, if you prefer, transmotion," going on to note that "Vizenor has embraced the notion that the creative artist, through the dialectics of transmotion, is particularly empowered to envision analogies between the local and global . . . without collapsing those terms into one another" (2015a).

In a similar focus on the impulse toward the expatriated/exilic artist, but with slightly different connotations, James Mackay writes, "By setting Morrison in [the] company [of Chagall and others, such as Edmond Jabès], and thus implying a commonality, Vizenor performs an act of what he has termed 'transmotion,' recognizing both the grounded nature of art and its ability to transcend borders and ethnic lines" (2015, 175). These exilic themes are clearly significant, and I will return to them, but in light of the excellent arguments forged by both Carlson and Mackay, they need not be my focus here. Both critics, in different ways, express fascination for, and some puzzlement at, Vizenor's intensive shift in this recent work to a European (modernist) aesthetic. The fascination is certainly warranted, since it renders Vizenor's work even more nuanced, an aesthetic kaleidoscope that complements his already varied theoretical landscape, lending it what Carlson identified in a paper delivered at the Western Literature Association conference in 2015 as a "curatorial sensibility." The puzzlement, meanwhile, is inevitable, given, for instance, some of the contradictions its emphasis on modernism provokes or, even more searchingly, given Mackay's provocative observation that Vizenor's "concern with reconceptualizing the primitive may end up simply reifying the category in a climactic act of museum masturbation" (2015, 171). All of these matters demand comment before the end of this chapter, but what I want to focus on first complicates what I have already discussed in terms of the straight relationship between image and text that the earlier literal and figurative juxtapositions of text and glyph imply. In fact, Vizenor's association with a painter like Morrison over and above those such as Norval Morrisseau, whose work more readily, or more immediately, appears to speak to the pictographic forms Vizenor celebrates earlier—an association that is both self-identified and noted by others such as the art critic Jackson Rushing III—embraces modernism as a means of both reconciling and resisting the ideological separation implicit in the term "primitivism" and refusing the epistemological grounds of its formation. In other words, it is a means of ushering the Native into the globalized discourses of modernity as a means of asserting the force and validity of Native aesthetics and politics, not only in contrast but resistance to the balkanization, under the rhetoric of literary or artistic or indeed tribal nationalism, of Native ontologies. It is a simple argument: that those elements of Native cultures he celebrates have always already flowed through the various currents of modernity and that the historic exclusion zones marked out by terms such as "primitive" are perpetuated in the exclusionary politics of contemporary settler-colonial societies as enacted by the politics of nationalism.

Dogroy's first aesthetic manifesto, as it were, and the moment that most clearly (to my mind, at least) connects these various issues, occurs in the "Casino Walkers" chapter of *Shrouds*. In this chapter, Dogroy lays claim to both Morrison and Chagall as his major inspirations. With regard to the latter, he declares an affinity that is almost spiritual in its intensity, where he explains, "Hiram Bingham and Varian Fry are as much a presence in my stories, the stories of a native artist, as the stories of Marc Chagall. My artistic practice would not be the same without the inspiration of the visionary artist who was rescued by two great humanitarians. Dogroy and Chagall, a union of chance, and we bear the stories of survivance with two saints" (Vizenor 2011, 62). Expanding his methods in relation to this "union of chance," then, Dogroy continues: "My artistic visions were never touched by the murky revisions of naturalism, modernism, cubism, and the discovery of primitive arts as a source of subject, composition, and style" (62). Rejecting the "murky revisions" of modernism and favoring instead the place-based "imagic perspectives" of Morrison and Chagall, Dogroy opposes the "realistic outlines" of the Santa Fe School under Dorothy Dunn. "My only art teacher," Dogroy begins, "started with the usual outlines, basic colors, and then she introduced a curious style of primitive impressionism—the sense of natural motion, light, and brush marks—a radical departure from the Flat Studio Style promoted by Dorothy Dunn" (63). Believing in her students' innate artistic ability—acknowledged by Dogroy's "the notion that natives were innate artists prevailed at the time. Yes, of course, only innate primitive native artists" (63)—Dunn favored illustrative and narrative forms, and specifically cultural topics.

Dogroy's unnamed teacher enables his avoidance of such forms, while "five of the seven students that summer continued with precise outlines of tree bark, drums, mongrels, and beaded dance vestments" (63). There is, undoubtedly, a nod here to the Woodland School painters—Norval Morrisseau et al.—who were dubbed the "Indian Group of Seven" by journalist Garry Sherbain, after the 1920s impressionistic "Group of Seven" in Canada. Expressing an ambivalence about his exclusive company (this was a selective summer school, after all), Basile continues: "The students only slightly pushed the lines with heavy paint, but not enough to escape the mundane contours of naturalism," while he "was the only student that summer who boldly distorted the outlines by motion, proportion, figuration, wild contrary colors, the suitable curvature, balance, and natural symmetry" (64). And there is one final statement about the influence of Chagall and Morrison that is significant to this particular thread: "Marc Chagall, and George Morrison, of course, are my only visionary teachers of abstract cosmoprimitive art" (64). Two things, arguably, occur here. Firstly, in light of the invocation of Native arts scenes such as the Santa Fe and Woodland Schools, it is significant that Dogroy nevertheless repeats his affiliation with a European outsider artist and an Anishinaabe artist who spent much of his career at some remove from the cultural and geographical heartlands of the Anishinaabeg. That Morrison's own trajectory is likely echoed in that description of the summer school is suggested in his self-assessment as "becoming more radical[,] more individual" (qtd. in Anthes 2006, 106). Secondly, the inference, however cloaked, of the collective style speaks directly to Vizenor's deconstruction in this novel and elsewhere of the *indian*, cultural expectations and misperceptions that equate the native with ideas of primitivism, ahistoricism, and other static signifiers, and, intrinsically, to the delimiting and above all dangerously reductive implications of cultural nationalisms on the one hand and imposed markers of cultural "authenticity" on the other.

The Group of Seven, renowned landscape artists such as Tom Thomson, A. Y. Jackson, and others, have only relatively recently been reevaluated in light of debates about what constitutes the nation, imagined à la Benedict Anderson or otherwise. In their moment (1920 was the year they formed), they, and the Canadian imagination more broadly, were in a process of self-discovery relative to two things: the United States—an ongoing project—and the wilderness. Then, the "wildercentric" project maintained the "practice of ascribing psychic value to the myth of an unpossessed wilderness [and] reflected the values of the dominant social classes of the time" (O'Brian 2007, 24). As John O'Brian claims in *Beyond*

Wilderness, the colonizing implications of a national art founded on landscape are clear in an icon of the movement, A. Y. Jackson's 1913 *Terre Sauvage*. That it was painted in a studio above a bank in Toronto implicates capitalism in both the production of wilderness and the artistic production of the nation. Meanwhile the title both evokes a rhetoric that in Canada as in the United States, legitimated the "civilizing" mission of colonialism and, ironically in light of Jackson's erasure of the presence of habitation in his choice of scene of Georgian Bay, invokes that other rhetorical spur of imperial expansion, terra nullius (see O'Brian 2007, 24, 26).[18] The manipulation of artistic form, then—both literally in terms of subject matter and ideologically—created a naturalism that in turn distorted the sociopolitical landscape it purported to represent. The partial and, above all, artificial "nation" thus produced can continue to ignore, oppress, and exploit those whom it does not represent, while self-legitimating as representative.

Such moves have resonance here despite being Canadian because of the landscape component, the imagery of wilderness and the *sauvage* so closely associated with broad notions of the primitive in the early twentieth century. Nevertheless, it represents a form of nation building deeply implicit in U.S. art, too, from the Hudson School wilderness painters even to the Ash Can School, whose leading proponent George Bellows painted the equally iconic *Cliff Dwellers* (1913, and exhibited in the Armory Show)—a painting of overcrowded Manhattan tenement life, whose title invokes the cliff dwellings of Mesa Verde, fairly recently rediscovered in the late 1880s and turned into a national park in 1906. Critics then and now were divided on whether to read Bellows's painting as a celebration of "the modern scene as one of energetic social interaction between people . . . caught in a moment of daily life" or, as a *New York Sun* reviewer saw it, possibly unrivalled by any of the debauchery in Bedlam or Hogarth's prints (Piott 2011, 115). Either way, the evocation of the ancient Puebloan ancestors whose disappearance from the cliff dwellings is still not wholly explained cannot help, from our own vantage point, but imply a host of possibilities with potentially negative racial, ethnic, economic, and even evolutionary connotations.[19]

The point I am making here is not that Vizenor is suddenly picking on Norval Morrisseau et al. in the "Indian Group of Seven." Rather, he is sending up the inherent small-c conservatism in the generation of cultural nationalism, which produces aesthetic schools that, on the one hand, as they become increasingly derivative also become increasingly self-parodic and, on the other, establish notional bounds of membership—both overt and implied—that increasingly restrict the freedom of imagination and originality of the individual artist. In evoking those groups mentioned above, he also uses artistic affiliation by way of refusal to participate in the co-option of artistic and literary movements into national narratives of (often false) cohesion and collective endeavor—whether those nations be Canada, the United States, or the Anishinaabeg of White Earth. The inherent transnationalism of Vizenor's points of reference, and the incipient transnationalism of Morrison's concerns, particularly after his sojourn in Paris and so on, are key to this element of engaged resistance to collectivizing—even totalizing—narratives. This unsettles at a microlevel the same kind of logic that invents and then imposes the *indian*, the primitive, and all those other manifest manners against which Vizenor and, as it happens, Dogroy rail. The correlation between the two—by no means a new vein for Vizenor—is perhaps most explicitly rendered in the penultimate chapter of *Shrouds*, titled "Tradition Fascists."

Here, again, he castigates technique—"Excessive technique undoubtedly reveals the flakery" (Vizenor 2011, 88)—as he recognizes the returned antiquity, the *Rose of Birch Bark*, as counterfeit. Like the hard lines of realism and naturalism, the fake document lacks the spontaneity and energy of the original—it lacks the presence of the mark maker. Father Beeg—the returner of the scroll, whether fence or counterfeiter himself—has, we discover, also been involved in trade of the eponymous shrouds: "You know, he practically stole my very first shrouds over drinks at Hello Dolly's. At the time, however, no one else wanted to buy my exotic, uncertain, arcane art. I learned many years later that he sold my shrouds as precious ancient native cerements to museums in France, Italy, and Germany" (89–90). At one level, this sequence raises an implicit critique of capitalism, as capital networks of exchange enable value in relation to forgery and the misappropriation of artifacts. It contrasts with Dogroy's own explicit manipulation of a form of meeting-ground between capitalism and patronage in his "Casino Walkers" series. "Casino Walkers," Dogroy's series of grotesque murals on the walls of the casino, takes advantage of the casino operators' desire for original (Native) art to proffer Hogarthian satirical insight on the nature, function, and impact of/on the casino and its users. In this sense, Dogroy takes the patron's coin while holding a mirror up to its flaws. As a muralist, the scene sits somewhere between the Renaissance model of architectural patronage and an early to mid-twentieth century (Latin American) tradition of radical political art.

In this instance, then, art performs a political function, offering a textual mirror to a clientele and a corporation that the literary text itself then reinscribes in its own satire of contemporary tribal politics. The eponymous shrouds of White Earth, though, replicate and significantly complicate this aspect, rendering both capitalism and (both alongside and in its intricate relationship with) imperialism objects of a satirical barb that continues to implicate certain (shall we say conservative) attitudes within the nation and toward its heritage, as well as broader abstract notions of tradition, heritage, culture, and so on. This results in discourse on ideas of nationhood, cultural policing including appropriation and theft versus artistic freedom, and, of course, discourse on ideas of the primitive and primitivism itself, each of which is worth briefly dwelling on.

James Mackay's reading of the shrouds themselves is uncompromising:

> Dogroy Beaulieu's shrouds, from which the book takes its title, are artistic creations in which white sheets are laid across the corpses of totemic animals, that are then left to rot. The resulting trace staining the sheet forms the artwork. This is obviously a gesture of survivance, in that new art emerges and continues from the deceased body in a new form. However, it also seems that for Vizenor the tribal tradition can be metaphorically seen as corpse-like. At one with Jacques Chirac and the designer of the Musée du Quai Branly, he rejects living and continuing traditions as fascistic, and celebrates exilic, diasporic, modernist identities that share an ability through art to transcend human difference. (2015, 181)

It is "obviously" a gesture of survivance. Vizenor's engagements with artistic practices by and large all gesture in such a fashion, either at the first-order level at which the act of creation itself signifies a form of resistance to the subjugated narrative of defeat and victimry, or in more complex ways. Here, the "trace staining the sheet" simultaneously indexes the presence of the animal and, allegorically speaking, the trace of presence in the "sheet[s]" of text that narrate American history. Thus, just as despite the vanishing of the animal through decomposition, "survivance" inheres in the literal stain on the shroud, the native presence endures in the traces that "stain" the manifest manners of Native American historiography.

It is a simple analogy, and one that I am not sure entirely explains the work of the shrouds. One could counter Mackay's corpse metaphor for tribal tradition by noting that the theme of destruction (decomposition) leading to new life (the artwork) is a common motif in Anishinaabe stories, although given Vizenor's propensity for setting false trails, one may be stepping into a snare. Reading them as representative of the "corpse-like" nature of "tribal tradition," then, perhaps avoids that snare, while also understanding the artwork from within a Vizenorian lexis wherein "totemic shrouds" carry echoes of those "dead voices" of the earlier novel. In both instances, the "death" is consequent to imposed definitions, orientalist expectations, and romantic cultural assumptions. If the dead voices effect the erasure of the Native in the presence of the *indian*, then, the totemic shrouds ironically symbolize the simulated absence of that which they purport to portray—the deathcloths of Anishinaabe culture or religion in the context of the cycle of exchange that would circulate them as exotica. That they are ultimately sold on as "precious ancient native cerements" by Father Beeg both confirms that subject of the satire and participates in it. In this respect, they have an antecedent in the form of the blank books made and distributed by Almost Brown in earlier stories (see, e.g. Vizenor 1991; 1997). In *Landfill Meditation*, Almost explains, "Our blank books said everything, whatever you could imagine in a picture. One pictomyth was worth a good story in those days" (1991, 9–10). Inferring a form of literacy that is at once inclusive and exclusive (if we recall the "illegibility" to which Daniel Heath Justice refers), the blank books—particularly in *Hotline Healers*—also feed on the myopic appetite for *indian* artifacts that renders the blank slate no less than a screen for the projection of readers' desires. What is generated is a dual text both pregnant with meaning and entirely meaningless. Complicit in the latter deceit—arguably—are the "tradition fascists" whose policing of "tradition" represents, to all intents and purposes, the death of culture. If his own banishment from White Earth despite the constitution's explicit prohibition of such an act forecasts the death of its political coherence, the shrouds themselves convey the death of its cultural vivacity under the same totalizing yoke.

As both Carlson and Mackay imply, then, the artist's banishment from White Earth Nation and his ostracization by the art world share an analogical relationship, each deriving from the artist's refusal to be confined by false standards and artificial boundaries. While, as Carlson clearly demonstrates, the intent behind Vizenor's contributions to and understanding of the Constitution of the White Earth Nation stands in the very starkest contrast to the type of nationalistic statecraft that underlies Dogroy's banishment, Mackay's commentary on tradition is, I think, apposite, albeit Vizenor's attitude to modernism is, as I have suggested, a little more ambivalent than he suggests. More to the point, though, the polarization implied in Mackay's comment between tradition and modernism, and avowedly implicit in the discussion of primitivism in both novels, is similarly relatively ambivalent. It would be banal to enunciate the false polarity of tradition and modernism in any greater detail—this polarity is neither Mackay's nor Vizenor's, and it assumes a kind of settled misunderstanding in popular accounts of the avant-garde. Rather, the break that modernism sought with Enlightenment thought and with the prevailing emphasis on more formal, less experimental, techniques turned away from particularly limited notions of tradition and culture in order to find anew that which generated and moved. Thus, Ezra Pound's dictum to make it new, driven as it was by major social, political, theological, and philosophical transformation, was not so much an abandonment of the past as its aesthetic reorientation.

The key deliberation here, then, is in the microdistinctions in the art world itself as they play out in the macroworld of art's economic cycles and power relations: art as imperial allegory. But there is a very clear distinction, as I have already mentioned, between the authenticity (philosophically speaking) of Chagall and the less ardently received incursions by the likes of Picasso. There is, on the one hand, a certain proximity of the artist to his chosen influence, in the sense that Chagall draws on the folk cultures of his childhood and Russian cultures more broadly, while Picasso's drawing on African masks commutes rather than celebrates or participates in the evolution of "traditional" forms to serve both political and commercial ends. In the latter instance, and on the other hand, there is a certain proximity to the market itself, which perhaps separates out Otto Dix's attempts to depict the horrors of his own experience from the many and varied ways in which Picasso, again and for want of a better example, actively sought to generate and sustain a market for his work—creating an art market network not dissimilar to that which forms around the brothers in *Blue Ravens* (see Fitzgerald 1996). Whether this constitutes a judgment call on Vizenor's part (it is not on mine) is neither here nor there. In fact, it resounds with arguments Vizenor himself has inferred in his habitual criticisms of overly commercialized Native American writing. Running parallel to these questions, meanwhile, is the theme developed in *Shrouds* itself of the difference between theft (cultural and literal) and authentic relation to influence that underpins mainstream ideas of artistic freedom and artistic license.

The question of appropriation is a continuous background noise in Vizenor's work—particularly in the treatment of primitivism and Native art in *Shrouds* and *Blue Ravens*. As with all narratives that encourage fugitive posture, Vizenor eschews the pose of tragic victimry by establishing ironic juxtapositions and allowing the playing out of false logic. Although it is not explicitly set in contrast, the damage done to Dogroy's standing in the art world by a critic's suggestion of plagiarism on the one hand and the accusation of harboring stolen property on the other establishes an ironic echo in respect of these questions. The plagiarism—purportedly of the style of British painter Francis Bacon—refers to the graphic and grotesque nature of Dogroy's depictions. The theft, meanwhile, is of Chagall's *The Pinch of Snuff,* one of many confiscated by the Nazis, which was given to him by Father Beeg. Incidentally, that this is the Chagall that instills Dogroy's lifelong love for the artist alludes to the recurrent trope of the "pinch" in Vizenor's work—from asemaa offerings (pinches of tobacco) to the "pinch" coffee of his early story *Reservation Café*. Much more could be made of the ironies of this choice, of course, since the snuff in the 1912 painting is a highly secular interruption in a painting replete with Jewish religious iconography. Suspicious of Beeg's motives, Dogroy had insisted on a certificate of authenticity; the irony deepens. It is not authenticity that is at stake—a profoundly fraught scenario in the post–American Indian Arts and Crafts Act era—but provenance. And yet, it would seem, Father Beeg (and, of course, many others) is at liberty to procure Native art, categorized as artifact, for resale and circulation. Similarly, in the context of the European art world from which many of his influences come, the irony of Dogroy being accused of plagiarism is palpable. As is more directly confronted in *Blue Ravens*, the turn by the avant-garde to non-Western societies such as China, various African societies, Breton, and Tahiti and, in the United States and Canada, to Indigenous societies, for both subject matter and formal inspiration, indicates a clear imbalance in understandings of appropriation (see Castro 1991; Rushing 1999; and Hutchinson 2001, among others).

The colonial logics underpinning that imbalance are very neatly summarized by the narrator, who complains that "when tutored or cultured artists create colored creatures in flight, the scenes are considered inspirations of primitivism . . . but when a native visionary artist creates creatures in bold colors on papers, canvas, birch bark, and on rocks, the images are pronounced primitive" (Vizenor 2011, 16). It is an asymmetry that both extends from and clearly sustains the balance of power in favor of the namer/appropriator. Mackay urges us to consider the likelihood that "Vizenor explicitly constructs *Shrouds of White Earth* as, among other things, a response to the primitivism represented by the Blaue Reiter group" (2015, 177). Another site of ambivalence, Der Blaue Reiter combined their primitivist aesthetic and ethos—drawn not only from tribal arts but also from children's art and the artworks of inmates of prisons and sanatoria—with particular emphasis on mark making and color, of ready significance and attraction to Vizenor and his artists. On the other hand, they sustain the asymmetry described above, both indirectly —"Early in the first chapter, Dogroy Beaulieu notes that the critical reactions to 'colored horses' by the ledger artists discuss such figures primarily in terms of 'native traditions,' while similar scenes of unusually coloured animals in flight painted by Chagall or other 'tutored or cultured artists' are seen as inspired by 'primitivism,' a certain value of artistic style" (Mackay 2015, 177, citing Vizenor)—and directly, as he has already pointed out: "Rather than understanding the artistic, social or religious contexts for the art that they elevated, primitivists such as the contributors to 1912's Der Blaue Reiter Almanach . . . 'recruited the primitive as a means of addressing the complexities of the modern world in terms that lay outside the post-Renaissance tradition'" (Mackay 2015, 177, citing Rhodes). More famously, but with no less directness, Lovejoy and Boas wrote that "cultural primitivism is the discontent of the civilized with civilization, or with some conspicuous and characteristic feature of it," explicitly placing the sources of primitivism outside "civilization"—almost the metonymic scapegoat to the postindustrial world (1935, 7).

Although neither Vizenor nor Mackay relates it in these terms, the Rhodes quotation speaks to the authentic relation of the painter to his material. Ledger artists, appearing toward the end of the nineteenth century, are nevertheless "seen as more representative of ancient . . . traditions" than so-called "primitive artists" such as Chagall, who, as Mackay points out, draws very directly from the folk traditions of his homeland. He, however, is celebrated as an "innovator and colourist" (Mackay 2015, 177). That question of authentic relation is in fact confronted head on in Dogroy's own deliberations over Chagall. "Jewish separation scenes are not entirely mine by imagination," he concedes, "but the creative figuration, ironic contours, dislocation and colors, blue and green faces, *we share by our chance union as artists*" (Vizenor 2011, 68; emphasis added). With this statement of affiliation and implicit analogy, Dogroy subtly refutes inferences of imitation or the claiming of direct influence in a way that distinctly separates his and Chagall's art from the "movement" that claims the latter. Thus, when he satirically refers to his own coterie as "the Red Rider Circle, or Cavalier Rouge" (14), he achieves two subversions of the art-historical narrative. The first sees further illumination—and therefore deconstruction—of the colonial logics that underpin primitivist practice and designation. Who, after all, can ignore the racialized connotations of the ironic name, which also connotes a readily discernible static signifier of the *indian* on horseback? At the same time, however, it also refuses the homogenizing rhetorics of historiography, which tend to lump all non-Western artists into a homogenized mass—for whom "primitive" is a pejorative noun rather than an adjective—by claiming "school" status in a way that simultaneously ironically deflates the pomposity of nomenclature.

This general imbalance is further hinted at to as Dogroy continues to assess the work of the tradition fascists following his exile. Dogroy's banishment from the art world in *Shrouds* is followed by the French exhibition of his *Homage Nu* series, "fleshy teases of familiar portraits by six distinguished painters" (114). Again, evocative of his haiku aesthetic, he explains, "Yes, the portrayals are aesthetic, figural traces, and visionary sensations, but not merely artistic representations. The painterly tease of familiar figures creates a sense of natural motion by color and contour" (114–15). Rather, exceeding the act of representation, "the portrayals are traces of nature, visionary memories, and . . . the afterimages of great works of art" (115). So, again, the description of visual art parallels the natural tease and reason of Vizenor's use of language. Yet he also reveals more about his committed railing against the monologic—or monoimagic—stasis of representation and about the institutional control imposed on the art world as further analogy for the totalizing functions of establishment authenticators: "The mighty truth games of national museums would never consider the traces and common associations of the baroque *Bacchus* by Rubens, and the hyperbaroque homage *Putto and Sumo Bacchus* by Dogroy Beaulieu in the same context of art" (118). In this latter instance, meanwhile, the popular audience Dogroy attracts for his iconoclastic grotesques is rapidly lost when they encounter his other work: "The irony of my hyperbaroque painterly style was appreciated, but the viewers were not as generous with their sense of irony over the romance of native cultures" (119). Indeed, he continues, "This, my friend, might be the actual reversal of the sentiments of native irony" (119).

There are three levels of cultural policing at work here—at an ideological, institutional, and popular level—all of which in some way delimit the artist's freedom to make art, to make meaning, and to assert or construct identity-through-representation that counters deeply entrenched prevailing expectations. The resulting restrictions allegorize the ways in which Indigenous identities more broadly—indeed, identity per se—are delimited by the impositions of standards, codes, and expectations from without and within. The analogical proximity of this scenario to the literary sphere itself thus cannot be ignored, wherein the category of Native American literature establishes a range of expectations that variously signal cultural authenticity and against which cultural performance can be gauged. Most immediate to the questions raised in *Shrouds*, the most forceful critiques of Vizenor's art in recent years have come from positions of self-declared nationalism—from strategic locations of cultural protectionism that, however well intentioned, seem ideologically contrary to Vizenor's notion of native liberty. In "A

Sovereignty of Transmotion," Sinclair delineates—without judgment—the various critiques through and about Vizenor's work that hold him at various removes from Indigenous-centered and/or tribal nationalist discourses, suggesting that he "most interests himself in how Anishinaabeg discourses resist, confirm, or coalesce with Western theories, colonial practices, and rhetorical imperialisms" (2009, 136). While other nationalist critics accuse Vizenor of a "grab-bag relationship with theory" (Craig Womack) or of working within "a distinctly Western and elite discourse" (Joanne DiNova), Sinclair insists that "Vizenor is [nevertheless] grounded in an Anishinaabeg intellectual tradition, and that [his concept of] transmotion is, in fact, a cultural, political, and historical Anishinaabeg method of continuance" (all citations Sinclair 2009, 136–37). Transmotion, in fact, enables the shift between Anishinaabe intellectual frameworks and European epistemologies, or between Anishinaabe aesthetic frameworks and the influence of European modernist artists. It underpins the gestural self-abnegation of the haiku and the temporal collapse inherent in his "fourth person perspective," which renders artist, inscription, and viewer present to the moment of perception.

In the context of the move in *Shrouds* toward an apparently ever-stronger declaration of affinity with modernism in counter to the fascistic motions of "tradition," Mackay expresses a legitimate concern. First noting that "Vizenor, who seemingly denies the attitude of primitivism, nonetheless celebrates notions of shamanism and native visionary art and has done so since his earliest work" (2015, 177), he goes on to celebrate and complicate the impact of *Shrouds*:

> he rejects the trappings of colonial dominance while simultaneously crafting a way to celebrate the random possibilities of artistic inspiration. Nonetheless, the difficulty remains that which Mattar has identified: by opposing the shaman to the modern Vizenor's cosmoprimitivism runs the risk of allowing the rejected fundamental concept of the primitive a way back in. (178)

Noting, more particularly, that "he rejects living and continuing traditions as fascistic, and celebrates exilic, diasporic, modernist identities that share an ability through art to transcend human difference" (181), Mackay identifies an essential paradox in Vizenor's approach, an irreconcilable contradiction between his career-long identification with the song-spirit of the Ojibwe to this aesthetic and apparently political identification with aspects of modernism. Earlier assessments of Vizenor have emphasized the hybridity of such a position, wherein hybridity represents a condition of possibility; to do so here, I think, might suggest the kind of bicultural entrapment refuted by the tribal literary nationalist critics and, indeed, resisted in Vizenor's dynamic use of the term "crossblood." More to the point, though, the concept of the crossblood has played a far less prominent role, particularly in *Blue Ravens*, where specific ties to place (White Earth and Paris) and kin (the Beaulieu forebears and the fur trade diaspora) transcend reductive implications of race and ethnicity. Conceptually speaking, too, "what Chagall inspires in Dogroy (and what he, Dogroy, and Vizenor share) is the notion that one can take a powerful personal sensibility, rooted in tradition and 'native' ground, and work with and through conventions and forms from other places, cultures, and even languages to 'modernize' oneself" (Carlson 2015a). This is an attitude far less redolent of hybridity discourse than of the transnational modernity Carlson himself elucidates.

Returning to Sinclair, then, while he acknowledges that Vizenor is "perhaps repulsed by certain attachments to 'tradition' as a formative claim for identity"—or, one could add, as a basis on which to build monolithic notions of nationhood and collective sovereignty—"Vizenor himself writes, 'Natives have been on the move since the creation of motion in stories; motion is the originary'" (2009, 137). At the heart of the cosmoprimitivism/cosmototemism that Vizenor celebrates is that sense of motion, its manifestation across different times, locations, media, and purposes—the foundation of native liberty in transmotion. In *Blue Ravens*, which is less politically orientated toward White Earth and its then newly drafted constitution, Vizenor's lead characters entirely voluntarily choose their exile in France, emphasizing a broader relationship between politics and aesthetics than *Shrouds*. It is no less politically vigorous for that, but its targets are arguably more diffuse. While the cousins' work selling copies of the *Tomahawk* directly illuminates the significance of the press, and of the newspaper, to Ojibwe involvement in national and even international modernity, it also foregrounds a technology that, in and of itself, comments on modernity's status, according to Walter Mignolo, as always already colonial. As such, participation alone—the active reprinting of syndicated news—could be classified (although it is not in the novel) as an assimilative act. As a corollary to the young men's participation in the war, and then in the art scene in Paris, the undertone of cultural distinctness at risk of consumption by the technological, political, commercial, and aesthetic march of modernity's machinery is palpable. It is not, of course, in any measure, the result of Vizenor's transnational forays.

Indeed, indigenizing activity frames the aesthetic actions of the novel such that they engender a politics of decolonization that seeks, quite literally, to re-place Native contributions to modernity. World War I is, inevitably, a somewhat fraught location for such work, but it serves as a clear reminder of the degree to which those displaced from mainstream histories have participated in and, in many instances, underpinned the so-called West. As one of modernism's key moments of fracture, then, the war and the immediate postwar environment ironically open an avenue in which the cousins—and Vizenor—can trace the wider permutations of Anishinaabe diasporic mobility. To too-readily understand this movement as a form of displacement or exile, however, is to miss one central element of the construction of Anishinaabe identity in this novel—and, indeed, elsewhere in Vizenor's work. "Many native fur trade families," Basile recounts, "came together with new and obscure traditions, the union of blood and treasure to honor and defend France" (Vizenor 2014, 9). He comes, as did many Indigenous residents of former colonies, to the imperial heartland with a sense of kinship rather than alienation. As such, his and Aloysius's presence in Paris is performed as a rite of belonging, rather than exile or exotic anomaly—the widening of the circumference of "homeland."[20]

Aloysius's re-presentation of the Anishinaabeg, then, begins in his articulation and evolution of that visionary tradition described earlier. It manifests in his totemic blue ravens, painted onto every available surface, from paper to signs to shop windows and bridges. In one respect, in doing so, Aloysius participates in an ancient tradition of visionary art: "Aloysius revealed his visions in the creative portrayals of blue ravens, and the abstract ravens became his singular totem of the natural world" (11). That participation, though, is very deliberately stripped of its connotations of fixity when Basile continues: "He was convinced that his totemic associations were original, and there were no other blue raven totems or cultures in the world" (11–12). At this point, while affirming ancient practice, Aloysius also demonstrates authentic relation (rather like Rendon's insistence that the singer find their own song rather than learn the songs of dead ancestors in *SongCatcher*; see chapter 6); in addition, he declares a certain modernistic affinity in his emphasis on originality with regard to a mechanism that reaches back to "primitive" forms. In toto, he presents as an individual in relation to a wider community, simultaneously refusing the homogenizing nature of the primitivist label and tying his art to its genealogical basis. Those forms, in turn, both mark (and thus map) a terrain that testifies to his presence and mark the way for those that follow, *and* transform the urban landscape from a space from which Native bodies are implicitly alienated to a space in which Indigenous presence is embodied and not just imagined through hyperreal simulations.

More than this, however, Vizenor offers an examination of the relationship between visionary art as a form of expressive communication and the quality of that subject matter as it is subsumed into a commercial, canvas-based discipline in Aloysius's evolution from graffitist to exhibiting painter. For instance, first he paints his ravens on the bridges of Paris. Later, exhibiting his work in Galerie Crémieux, he produces paintings of the bridges themselves, adorned with their visionary ravens. As such, they retain their visionary quality without reifying the "primitive" by blurring the distinction between what we might see as sacred and secular forms. In the same instance, the latter become a circulating form of the same process of marking and mapping implicit in the former, again, transforming the Paris landscape through art as a terrain that contains, rather than displacing, Indigenous presence. Combining—transforming—the urban with signifiers of indigeneity, which call up "the French romance of natives and nature" (Vizenor 2014, 161), the brothers embody a cosmopolitan modernity that at once precedes and is contemporaneous with their Parisian milieu. That same effect is generated by their regular mingling with the movers and shakers of Paris's Left Bank. There are few major writers, thinkers, artists, gallery owners, and collectors left out of their social scene, and their presence alongside these men and women offers a rejoinder to art historiography. In *The Indian Craze: Primitivism, Modernism, and Transculturation in American Art*, Elizabeth Hutchinson explains that the members of the Society of American Indians "turn[ed] primitivism to their own advantage" and that "the self-conscious appropriation of primitivism was a strategy Indian people adopted for political, as well as personal, ends" (2009, 172, 170). Here, that is decisively the case, in the sense that Aloysius's cachet relies at least in part on his background. But what he deals in is far from "primitivism" in the conventional sense, and far from "appropriating" form and style, he brings it with him, a unique and original signature that holds its own ground in the Paris scene. Where his contemporaries, such as Angel DeCora, were "compromised by her own vulnerability to the romanticizing nostalgia that made mainstream critics continually define Indian art as a thing of the past" (Hutchinson 2009, 173), Aloysius, like Basile, and of course like Vizenor, develops an aesthetic that is entirely contemporary, as at home in the urban sphere as it was back on the reservation, and yet deeply planted—like Chagall's own work—in a specific geographical and cultural context.

While always retaining that sense of themselves as outsiders, then, the Beaulieu brothers place themselves in the midst of the throng, as generators and agents of the modernist moment. Their cosmoprimitivism is far from antimodernist as they embrace the city, turning their art even to the technology of war as Aloysius determines to paint the masks of mutilated soldiers with raven designs, before transferring that desire into his series *Corbeaux Bleus: Les Mutilés de Guerre* (Vizenor 2014, 276). Here, again, the politics of Native presence in Paris, and in the art world, is demonstrably precarious, as the implacable masks of André and Henri, the two mutilated soldiers on whom the twenty raven paintings are based, are juxtaposed with the figurative "masks" of "native pretenders" Olivier Black Elk and Coyote Standing Bear: "The native feign of a romantic presence, and the disguise of a broken face. The cruel connections were ironic and obscure, but the agony of that moment was never forgotten, and became one of my best trickster stories of endurance" (277). That such stories of endurance are also stories of resistance is reinforced in an echo, when a collector comments that "the blue ravens were tourist scenes" and receives a lecture from Basile for his trouble. The precarity of slippage between the real and the artificial, countered by the necessity to create art and literature that does not shy away from confrontation, is underlined in this allegorical exchange, as the embarrassed collector "actually engaged André and Henri in conversation," nervously telling them tourist stories as they "appeared to listen ... but the pleasant artistic expressions of the metal masks remained the same" (277).

The sight of the collector spilling his stories as an outpouring of guilt while the impassive faces of his audience indicate neither exoneration nor forgiveness—nor even, for that matter, that they are actually listening—is not a minor comic interlude. It is followed immediately by another brief but significant conversation:

Daniel-Henry Kahnweiler returned several times to consider *Dreyfus in Natural Motion* and *Natchez Liberty*. He told me that the references to French colonialism, the commerce in slavery of natives, and the biased and wrongful prosecution of Alfred Dreyfus were subjects considered much too risky to present or even discuss at an art exhibition. (277–78)

Kahnweiler was a displaced German Jew and then doubly dispossessed Parisian gallery owner, whose "collection of incomparable cubist and avant-garde art" (278) was seized and sold during the Great War. Within France, the Dreyfus affair precipitated a struggle between republicans and monarchists over the significance of class and state power (see e.g. Cottington 1998). Imprisoned in 1896 under accusations of espionage, Alfred Dreyfus, a Jewish artillery office in the French Army, was the innocent but fomenting center of discord for the next ten years.

While the scandal reverberated for many years afterward, and its racial—anti-Semitic—overtones would have repercussions in France and clear resonance here for the status and vulnerability of the outsider artists, its placement alongside *Natchez Liberty* conjures further connotations. Dreyfus was, on the surface at least, an "internal" affair, which rocked French democracy through the battle between Bloc des gauches and Action Française. One cannot help but remember, however, that Dreyfus was imprisoned in French Guiana, a residual colonial outpost in South America and the location of the infamous Devil's Island penal colony. The colonial connection, then, is reiterated in *Natchez Liberty*'s title, which refers to what is colonially referred to as the Natchez Revolt in the early eighteenth century. Resisting continual incursion by the French in Louisiana—their nominal allies—tensions under the abusive watch of Commandant Chépart at Fort Rosalie reached a head when the commandant demanded lands used historically as a temple and gravesite for his own use (see e.g. Bond 2005). The ensuing "revolt," a Trojan-horse style affair under cover of an apparent peace envoy in November 1729, which resulted in the slaying of most of the Frenchmen in the fort's vicinity, ultimately also led to the total demise of the Natchez as a political entity after the French response decimated and scattered them.

The multiple connotations of the word "liberty" in reference to the Natchez uprising of course incorporate the ironic—the bid for liberty was anything but, although a kind of liberty from the colonial yoke ensued—and Vizenor's own "Native liberty," which codifies all of the various imaginative possibilities of his narratives of sovereignty and survivance. The reclaiming of the definition—liberty rather than revolt—is certainly one of those. Equally ironically, however, it also echoes French historiography itself, its own "revolt" being a bid for *liberté*. Although the colonial insurrection was bound by race rather than divisions of social rank, the shadow of an oppressed class trodden down by a bourgeoisie who controlled land and trade does not require much imagination to trace to both the French Revolution and, of course, the American Revolutionary War. In both cases, a reminder of the degree to which freedom in France and the United States was built on the oppression of others and of the degree to which the nation-state's narratives of liberty and equality depends on the suppression of counternarratives of colonization and dispossession is apposite. The complicity in the chattering classes—even those who have themselves, like Kahnweiler, been objects of similar violence—in silencing such dissent by declaring it off limits, addresses the deeper irony yet: that the very bourgeois structures that gave rise to the avant-garde as leftist opposers of the cultural mainstream enable a renewed colonial plunder, objectification, and silencing of the colonial subject.

––––––––––––

"Tradition," in Vizenorean vernacular, denotes a condition of stasis. Stasis, as his reiterative catchword "transmotion" connotes, is cultural death, anathema to what he sees as the vital dynamics of Anishinaabe currents. In a move that may seem perverse—indeed, Mackay makes just such a point above—Vizenor seeks to reabsorb static signifiers of Indigenousness in modernism, codified as "primitivism," in ways that reenliven them. Where we might expect a Native writer or artist to seek to displace or resist or debunk such motifs, Vizenor combats such cultural theft through a process of reabsorption that includes the retooling of the concept of primitivism itself. Bill Anthes has written:

> Primitivist artistic identification with Native American cultures initiated a cultural dialectic between the non-Native artists and critics of the American avant-garde and the Native American artists, who were never merely passive witnesses in this cultural exchange. In return, modernism bequeathed to Native artists an ambivalent legacy, the implications and ramification of which are still being addressed by contemporary Native American artists. (2006, xxii)

In *Blue Ravens*, the Native American artists are not only not "merely passive witnesses," they are generators of the cultural focus—at the heart of the artistic community in Aloysius's case, and narrative documenters of it in Basile's. The other artists and writers they encounter, although repeatedly described as creators themselves, do not explicitly add to the material of the novel, but rather act as its relatively passive backdrop.

In this respect, they echo Euro-modernity's witness to what Vizenor describes as cosmoprimitivism and cosmototemism, both of which terms reclaim an aesthetic genealogy from European cannibalization—an engaged resistance to that "ambivalent legacy" that Anthes describes. Calling it a "genealogy" is to invoke a Nietzschean sense of connection, rather than to claim lineage, since, in Vizenor's view, "there are no direct traditions or evolution of art, of course, but the scenes of natural motion and the elements of artistic perception and dimension were obvious connections between some ancient rock art and innovative painters" (2013, 46). In *Blue Ravens* he reorients the contingencies of such connections such that the Native artists take central agency and mock the pose of victimry.

The *cosmo*totemism he describes, then, while Indigenous in a very clear sense and while specific in the contexts of his novels to the ancient art of the Anishinaabeg, addresses that wider humanity present in the Parisian landscape. Underlining that commonality, Vizenor begins his discussion of "Native Cosmototemic Art" for the Global Indigenous exhibition *Sakahàn* (National Gallery of Canada, 2013) with a brief discussion of the Chauvet-Pont-d'Arc and Lascaux caves in the Ardèche and Dordogne regions of France. Relating these endeavors to caves and rocks elsewhere in the world, he continues: "These artists created the most memorable scenes of native presence and natural motion by sunlight on stone and by the shimmer of torchlight in thousands of caves on every continent in the world" (2013, 42). A number of the depictions at Lascaux and Chauvet, as elsewhere, appear to depict single animals in motion, while the fact that the caves would have originally been lit with flame adds further nuance (motion, quite literally) to Vizenor's claim that "the shadows in native stories and painted scenes give rise to the theory of *transmotion*, an inspired evolution of natural motion, survivance and memory over time, and a sense of visionary sovereignty" (42). The shadows are literal—thrown, like Plato's allegory, onto the walls of the caverns—as well as figurative, the signs and marks of presence in absence, and the signs and marks of futures revealed through vision. Here, as in all the visual media Vizenor evokes, presence is embodied, through touch, proximity, and the pictured presence of the body in photographs.

It is that presence, in the visual if elusive forms of Vizenor's literary play, that breaks down the binaries that have tended to structure the literary and oral, and that the work that I have elaborated on in this chapter unsettles either directly, through the displacement of the primacy and certainty of print, or through the more metaphorical deconstruction of those fixed categories that documentary textuality enables. Thus, the shifts he describes in *Dead Voices* and even in Aloysius's transition from sketcher and street artist to gallery/salon artist in *Blue Ravens* are not a trajectory toward assimilation but an evolution of forms pertinent to the function of art. And yet here, in the final scenes in the gallery, and clearly in the spirit of Otto Dix, Basile and Aloysius end on a note of common experience focused on the *mutilées de guerre*, captured not only in the paintings but in Basile's poem, "Prefects of the River Seine," which takes its inspiration directly from Aloysius's ravens:

Mighty blue ravens
prefects of wounded memories
seasons of war
in the *mutilés de guerre*
mustered on the ancient tributaries
down to the River Seine. (Vizenor 2014, 280)

The sense of affinity generated in these scenes presents cohesion between a group of cosmopolitans—refugees even—united by their outsiderness, their art, their experience of war, and their ability to tell "stories by visual memory" (283).

CHAPTER 6

Performance, Resistance

Countering the *indian* and Sovereign Aesthetics
in Contemporary Anishinaabe Drama

With the odd exception such as Lynne Riggs's *The Cherokee Night* (1932), formally produced theater productions depicting Native North American characters and themes were largely dominated by non-Native playwrights until well into the 1960s and 1970s. Such productions did not entirely exclude Native actors; for instance, George Ryga's *The Ecstasy of Rita Joe* (1967) included First Nations actors such as Chief Dan George. Indeed, Indigenous cast members were not unheard of much earlier in the century, as film scholarship has recently highlighted with the restoration of Edward Curtis's *In the Land of the Headhunters* (1914/2014) and Richard Banks and Norbert Myles's *The Daughter of Dawn* (1920/2012), two among a handful of early black-and-white movies with all-Indigenous casts. Furthermore, Indigenous cast members were often far more than passive vehicles for the views and interpretations of Euro-American writers. Perhaps the most striking example of Indigenous actors performing agency through a vehicle offered them by European dramaturgy occurred in the Sault Ste. Marie area of Ontario around the turn of the twentieth century. The considerable popularity of dramatic parlor-room readings of Longfellow's *The Song of Hiawatha* in the late nineteenth century saw it "issued in multiple editions, translated into many languages, anthologized widely and adapted for—among other things—songs, operas, musicals, symphonies, paintings, cartoons, and films" (Fruhauff 2007, 79). Gaagigegaabaw, or George Copway himself, an unacknowledged source for some of Longfellow's ethnographic detail, proudly offered performances of *Hiawatha* in his best regalia. At Garden River First Nation in 1900, a quite different version of the poem-play was performed for the first time, the result of a collaboration between Canada Pacific Railroad's colonization agent, Louis Oliver Armstrong, and the Anishinaabeg of Garden River, for whom Longfellow's/Schoolcraft's source material must have seemed intimately familiar.[1]

As Margot Francis describes it, those performances were, themselves, sites of decolonial resistance. A narrator stood on shore at the "theater" set up at Kensington Point on the shore of Lake Huron, while a troupe of Anishinaabe actors performed traditional songs and stories in Anishinaabemowin on a floating stage just offshore. For Francis, this amounts to a reappropriation of *Hiawatha*'s sources on the one hand, and a significant political exercise on the other: at a time when Native religious ceremony and traditional practices were largely prohibited, and when the nearby Shingwauk Residential School had banned the speaking of Anishinaabemowin, this troupe of actors publicly acted out aspects of traditional culture and spoke their language. As such, "the play both preserved a space for the public use of an Indigenous vernacular and legitimated its currency in the circuits of international performance" (Francis 2011, 133). That scene is at once picturesque and deeply ironic. Visually, the Anishinaabe performers will have played their part in a living montage of the exotic specimen of man-in-nature that Longfellow's Romantic fantasy drew on. Moreover, the scene of Hiawatha himself departing in his canoe across the bay explicitly brought to life the myth of the vanishing American, making the troupe effectively complicit in its embodiment. Yet their very presence, their apparently free "doctoring" of Longfellow's material to include actual Anishinaabe material unfiltered by Euro-American interpretation, and, quite simply, their presence there offshore as they performed those elements of living Anishinaabe culture that were, in that moment, under conditions of oppression bring an entirely new significance to the poem.

Perhaps most significantly, given the considerable power of public performance of culture, such secular "translations" of performative traditions were echoed elsewhere throughout the twentieth century, while a more formal theater movement saw its genesis in the United States in the creation of what Heath calls "the first Native American theatre company in the United States" by Arthur Janaluska and E. Claude Richards in 1956 (qtd. in Däwes 2013b, 4). In Canada, Indigenous theater came to prominence through the formation of Native Earth Performing Arts by Denis Lacroix and Bunny Sicard (1982) and Debajehmujig by Shirley Cheechoo and others at M'Cheeging First Nation on Manitoulin Island (1984). Although developments in Canada came later than in the United States, as W. H. New notes, where prose fiction shone the spotlight on Native writing in the United States, it was theater that effected the breakthrough to public attention in Canada (2002, 370).

Echoing both that sense of theater's importance as well as common sentiments around the culturally specific significance of the performing arts, Ojibwe playwright Drew Hayden Taylor claims:

> in terms of, I guess, per capita art form, it seems that theatre, for one reason or another, has become the predominant expressive vehicle for Canada's Native people. I believe the reason is that theatre is just a logical extension of storytelling. (1997, 144)

Certainly, if we extend the category to encompass the performing arts more generally—dance, performance art, video art, and so on—Taylor's first claim is incontestable. The second is possibly a logical fallacy, since storytelling of one kind or another is arguably at the root of all expressive art forms. Nevertheless, it emphasizes the significance of that relationship of continuity between writing—insofar as contemporary drama demands a script—and storytelling implicit in, for example, Louise Erdrich's *Books and Islands*. Within that relationship—somewhat "spinning the binary" in similar-but-different ways to the visual arts—Indigenous performance operates along a spectrum bookended by "two modalities, which are not always mutually exclusive" according to Helen Gilbert (2013, 174). Gilbert's bookends follow Judith Butler's understanding of performativity on the one hand, in which "self-fashioning acts . . . contingently constitute subjects through the embodied processes of enactment" (Gilbert 2013, 174). We might more simply think of this as "activism," not least because Gilbert directly references the deliberate "iterative performance" drawn on by figures such as Gerald Taiaiake Alfred and Jeff Corntassel as distinct from Butler's "repetition of normalized acts" (174). On the other hand—or at the other end—"highly aestheticized acts of performance, sensual but ephemeral, rehearsed and executed with an eye to effect, inclined towards ambiguity and forged with/in creative semblances rather than any putative reality" suggest something closer, I suppose, to what we tend to think of as "art" (174). The plays and performances I will examine in this chapter very much attend to both ends of this spectrum and points in between. This subject matter differs from the preceding chapters in several ways: at the first-order level, of course, they either are or imply performances rather than "texts" in a conventional sense, although much of what I will discuss pertains to the playscripts themselves, rather than productions of the plays, which are rare. Beyond that first-order level, I argue, they share much common ground with the texts I have discussed to this point. They approach and evoke common stereotypes, enacting resistance to the legacy of (mis)recognition that attends Indigenous identities, certainly, but they are also concerned with exploring decolonial aesthetic practices—illuminating ways in which aesthetic practice and performative indigeneity are intertwined. Further, they attend to questions of memory and history, engaging and producing, as they do so, forms of visual sovereignty. Although—through production—they explicitly invoke literal images, unlike many of the texts included here (*Summer in the Spring* and "Pre-Occupied" notwithstanding), those images perform functions in the plays that are not dissimilar to the ways their literary invocations operate.

In her introductory chapter to *Indigenous North American Drama*, Birgit Däwes claims that the creative engagement "with historical encounters between people of European American and Native American descent . . . marks a characteristic feature of the genre" (2013b, 3). To characterize contemporary Native drama in this way, however, is not to imply that a focus on the historical and the historiographic renders them detached from the contemporary—a lens on a distant past, as it were—nor that encounter itself marks the raison d'être of Indigenous theater. Indeed, although Däwes lists a number of plays with key historical events and personae at their core, in many if not even most cases the correction or adjustment of the historical record to reflect Indigenous experience is also mindful of a certain reorientation of the present. In other words—and as Däwes's own epigraph from Muriel Miguel's "Director's Notes on Persistence of Memory" makes explicit when she writes "it is important to connect . . . our stories of the past to our stories of the future" (qtd. in Däwes 2013b, 1)—drama has become a particularly effective means of critiquing and correcting colonial grand narratives, while also enlivening Indigenous memory, and offering renewed frameworks of interpretation for current and future generations. More abstractly, then, they also explore the relationship between the documentary record and embodied memory—not in the service of binary construction so much as in the delivery and maintenance of alternate histories that account for the interchange between both.

This is certainly true of the first of the plays I will examine here. Marcie Rendon's

SongCatcher (1998; the Great American History Theater) collapses the span of time between its present and the early twentieth century as Jack, a "modern, young, native man" (Rendon 2003, 3) turns to the work of ethnomusicologist Frances Densmore (presumably either *Chippewa Music* or its condensed highlights *Songs of the Chippewa*) in his endeavors to fill in the cultural knowledge he feels he lacks. Bringing Densmore into the present figuratively through Jack's attention to her work, the musicologist comes, quite literally, to haunt the apartment he shares with his girlfriend, Chris. What begins at first as dream sequences depicting Densmore's work and gradual estrangement from sister Maggie and friend Lizzie filter through to a ghostly reality, becoming thoroughly enmeshed in, if invisible to, the present. In this, they are joined by Spirit Woman, the song-giver, whose presence opens the play, and Old Man Spirit. In the course of seeking self-knowledge, Jack copies pictographs from Densmore's text onto the body of his drum, an instrument central to his sense of his Ojibwe identity. As Chris and the couple's "friend and spiritual consultant" Bill express their uncertainty about the appropriateness of this act—a corollary to their insistence that he will not find *his* song in a book—those pictographs become part of the stagecraft, as they are projected onto the backdrop and even onto the bodies of actors in the course of the play. The relationship between spoken (or sung) word, vision, and image, then, is absolutely central to the play's examination of Densmore's legacy. As Bill and Chris infer the manipulative strategies and problematic power dynamics of Densmore's fieldwork, they draw attention, too, to the potentially distortive power of Densmore's "salvage ethnography" on present-day tribal members like Jack who were raised physically and spiritually removed from the traditions he seeks to emulate.

The second play I want to consider here—a play that has, to date, had only limited performance—similarly turns to a historical relationship in order to appraise and recalibrate its particular legacy as it proceeds to the present. Heid Erdrich's *Curiosities: A Play in Two Centuries* is based around the travels of Ojibwe entrepreneur Maungwudaus (George Henry) circa 1840.[2] Again, as in *SongCatcher*, the span of time between the scenes depicted and the audience's present is elided—in this instance by a stage instruction that reads: "Performers become 1840-era Ojibwe performance troupe and return to present day" (H. Erdrich 2012). Interacting between the present (including conversation about summer camp) and the literal historical figure of Maungwudaus who, as their troupe leader, is rendered through the text of his own early nineteenth-century writings, the performance troupe generate a comic dialogue in which they exaggerate the strangeness of

Maungwudaus's encounters through their often ironic responses to what they witness. Since Maungwudaus's best-documented stint in Europe was when he joined George Catlin's traveling Indian Gallery in Paris, the artist himself features in the play, conjuring the curious interaction between artist-showman and his paradoxical object/agent status that saw "Maungwudaus ch[o]ose to perform in a colonial spectacle as an 'Indian curiosity' in order to preserve his sense of being Anishinabeg" (Nanibush 2010). Beyond that representation, however, the stage instructions outline a significant use of projection and even creation of artwork throughout:

> Slides in the background could suggest setting changes via historical or other images such as contemporary urban images, scenes of London, Paris, Glasgow and Boston of 1840's. Several images of Maungwudaus are available on-line including a noted portrait by the Canadian artist Paul Kane. The paintings and journal sketches of George Catlin illustrate some of the activities (including the actual persons) in Maungwudaus' narrative and could also be projected on walls. Sketches attributed to Say-say-gon, who travelled with Maungwudaus, are included in Catlin's journals and should be projected. (H. Erdrich 2012)

Catlin first reproduced Say-say-gon's often-humorous sketches in his *Eight Years' Travels and Residence in Europe*. The play also includes instruction for the playing or singing of Ojibwe hymns, entities commonly associated with assimilation before Michael McNally's (2004) fascinating analysis of the ways in which Christian hymns translated into Ojibwe performed a vital function in the maintenance of cohesion and identity among Minnesotan Ojibwe communities. More importantly, perhaps, Maungwudaus himself translated a number of hymns into Anishinaabemowin, publishing those translations along with his *Account of the Chippewa Indians*. The veritable mash-up of registers and media at work in the play, then, promise a rich—and quite improvisational—performance that unseats the static authority of written history in favor of a dialogue across time and between expressive forms and figures both present (in both ontic and poststructuralist terms) and absent.

Closing out the chapter, my discussion of *Curiosities* segues into brief consideration of another piece that is part performance, part artwork, and wholly mixed media. Robert Houle's *Paris/Ojibwa*, similarly premiered in 2010, also takes Maungwudaus into its purview. Centered on a gallery installation in which Houle re-creates the corner of a Parisian salon circa 1840, *Paris/Ojibwa* presents a commemorative site, complete with burning sage, that both marks the presence of the Ojibwe troupe in Paris and gestures toward healing of the social and psychological rupture implicit in their journey. Taking it further, the exhibit's debut itself included a performance outside the Louvre by an Odawa dancer, Barry Ace, re-presenting Anishinaabe presence in a colonial center. Houle's installation and Erdrich's play—and, indeed, Rendon's—thus engage in equally performative acts of re-presenting Anishinaabe creativity and agency in the face of consumption, whether it be of material produce, otherness, *indians*, or exotic spectacle. As such, they echo what Leanne Simpson sees as the "political, intellectual, spiritual and emotional innovation" in Rebecca Belmore's performance art, which is "strategically designed to infuse a colonial space with non-authoritarian power, presence and connection" (Simpson 2011a, 96),[3] and to participate in decolonizing projects on the stages, galleries, and salons of a greater Ojibwe mobility.

In each of these performances, the visual image, the made mark, the artist and the artifact, play pivotal roles. These elements of the plays differ in terms of dominance and specificity, but consistently between them the visual is both diegetic and dramaturgic, a vital element of the staging as well as the story. In all three—and to labor the cliché—the image speaks a thousand words, contributing to the play's message and playing a functional role in its analytical toolkit, in terms of both reassessing historical images of *indians* and their legacy and, far more significantly, communicating the relationship between word and image, speech and vision in the contemporary moment. These are just three among a significant number of Anishinaabe plays and performance pieces that I could have chosen—writers and artists include John McLeod, Nancy Paul Good, Ian Ross, Marc Anthony Rolo, Tina Mason, E. Donald Two-Rivers, Gerald Vizenor, Drew Hayden Taylor, Cecelia Martinez, Jim Northrup, and many, many others who contribute to a strong and lively scene. Unable to survey them all, I have instead been highly selective; the grounds for that selection, in the specific themes of temporal (historical) elision, mixture of media, and subject matter, will become clear as the chapter develops. I propose the readings here not as a canonical gesture, nor as a claim to what is most vital or important in Anishinaabe theater, but because they are intriguing examples of the interrelationship between performance and projection, collaboration and relationality, art and artistry in the form. The two plays, in particular, bring that strong visual element, the projected form, to what Gilbert calls "the phenomenological thickness of performance as a means of communication" in ways that add further layers to current understandings of Indigenous performance "not only as an aesthetic medium but also, and expressly, as 'a system of learning, storing and transmitting knowledge'" (2013, 175).

––––––––––––––––

Gilbert's further elaboration of the importance of Native theater has significant resonance for Rendon's *SongCatcher*, particularly where Gilbert writes: "Communal memory, a key concern in many indigenous societies, builds contingently from such knowledge systems, reiterating the embodied basis of cultural transmission" (2013, 175). Communal memory and indeed the knowledge system it pertains to is precisely what Jack is locked out from and what he therefore seeks to tap into through Densmore's work. In a playwright's note, Rendon makes explicit what this nexus of memory and knowledge comprises, writing that "for Native peoples of this continent, stories of social, familial, and historical consequence were passed generation to generation, either through the practice of oral storytelling; the creation of songs, sometimes with accompanying dance movement; or, as in the case of the Ojibwe Midé religious society, pictographs inscribed on birchbark scrolls" (2003, 4). A combination of forms, of course, is well evidenced by pictographic scrolls depicting songs, or functioning as mnemonic scripts for specific stories and histories. Jack equally explicitly clarifies his relationship to this archive when he tells Chris, "Here I am an old man . . . and don't know half the songs [other drummers] know. I have to catch up" (12–13). Chris, meanwhile, articulates Rendon's own anxiety about both the collecting and recovery by both Densmore and Jack, simply expressing, "I think those songs are sacred. I don't understand why they let some white woman record them" (13).[4] In saying this, she channels another of Rendon's prefatory notes, wherein "an individual's song was their sacred possession, not to be sung by others or recorded for posterity" (5). Thus, the groundwork is laid for an exploration of both the ethics of capture and reproduction.[5]

The figurative capture is clearly illustrated three ways in the play: firstly, in the actual voices on the tape-recording Jack has acquired from Charlie Stately "down at the Indian Center," hundred-year old voices about which Bill is uncertain and that positively unsettle Chris (8); secondly, in the pictographs Densmore records alongside the songs; and thirdly, in the anthropologist's photographs of her sources, which, though not as famous as Edward Curtis's images, are relatively iconic nevertheless. In the context of the anxiety expressed by Chris and, albeit to a lesser degree, Bill about the appropriateness of these "captures," one cannot help but be reminded of Christopher Vecsey's observation that "the Ojibwas considered a person's image, including the external shadow, as an integral part of the person" (1983, 61). Like Irene America, shadows tagged to an atemporal plane through the capturing of their images, the recording of their voices, exert—in this instance at least—an unsettling influence on the stability of present-day relationships and on the sanctity of the home. Hand in glove with these figurative captures, the play raises a series of questions about reproduction—beginning, of course, with Densmore's own reproduction of Native materials, including much considered sacred and secret, but honing in on their secondary reproduction by Jack. In both his quest to find "his" song on Charlie Stately's tape and in his decision to copy pictographs from Densmore's book onto his own drum, Jack's positive intentions belie the negative effects of basing his understanding of his culture on the white anthropologist's documentary interpretation at the expense of its living vitality in community.

Chris's response to Jack's use of the pictographs is commensurate with her general opposition to his actions: "You can't do that. Those are religious drawings. Our elders kept the religion alive through those pictures. They aren't supposed to be public. What if Bill comes over and sees that? You're going to have to paint over them" (Rendon 2003, 21). Meanwhile, Jack's response, "It's just a book, Chris. They're just drawings" (21), underlines his indifference—born of lack of knowledge—to their significance. They function, in other words, as cultural motifs, making his drum look "cool" and offering him a sense of connection to cultural material he does not understand or know how to access. Jack's attempts, as a result, resemble more the simulations of the tribal "poser" than the cultural insider he aspires to be. The contest over cultural appropriation looms large in Indian country at present; eschewing the common targets of mascots and headdresses, and of course placing its lens on a Native man rather than on non-Native appropriators, Rendon's illumination of the issues adds a layer of nuance, laying bare the entanglements and potentially harmful consequences for Native communities of cultural misrepresentation. While Densmore's activities are reflected in terms of what Orin Starn calls the "almost parasitic disciplinary dependence" of anthropology's development—an indictment tempered by appreciation for the archive she produced (2011; see notes 2 and 3)—Jack's recovery of song, though well intentioned, gestures to the ongoing impact of that initial "removal" and the distortive effect it can have on the idea of "recovery" itself. In this case, recovery is less about understanding cultural processes, or the means by which an individual comes by a song or story, not least because such details were rarely recorded by Densmore. Rather, it is more about the replication of a moment fixed in time—a performance, if you will, of an anthropologically legitimated, monolithic past. Culture, in this scenario, becomes what Scott Lyons calls a "political theology" (2010, 90), or Gerald Vizenor a "terminal creed" (see, e.g., 1990), rather than, as Lyons, Leanne Simpson, Winona LaDuke, and others describe it, the active production of new life in biimaadiziwin.

Illustrating almost exactly what it is Jack emulates, the stage directions that accompany his first explanation to Bill indicate a series of projections: "*Midé drum image is flashed on theater walls. Pictures of men who sang for [Densmore] are interspersed with drum image*" (Rendon 2003, 9). This early set of images functions as a metacommentary, making visible that which is being discussed in the play through a dramatic device that allows the audience to visualize (and that, effectively, embodies) that historical moment. They also suggest materiality, as if the images stand in for the people themselves as objects to be collected by the anthropologist. Furthermore, the juxtaposition of the singers with the drum reflects both the transience and ephemerality of the moment transfixed and, particularly for Anishinaabe audiences, the disruption of the sacred life of the mide that Densmore's interference (and even Jack's repetition of it) suggests. That interference itself recalls an oppressive history in which the authority and sovereignty of Native peoples was repeatedly undermined—although it must be acknowledged that for many Anishinaabeg, Densmore's recordings provide a vital (and revitalizing) resource. As Chris tells Jack, "They're sacred. Our people went to prison or mental institutions for practicing our religion. All this stuff had to go underground. People kept these teachings secret for a long time because it was dangerous to practice them" (21). The inference of (over)protectionism that counters arguments against appropriation, then, loses its charge in the face of colonially bound cultural genocide. In this way, too, Jack's actions are presented as disrespectful, regardless of his ethnic connections to that cultural material.

The taboo that Jack breaks here operates on several fundamental levels, then. Tied to spiritual traditions, his (after Densmore's) trampling over the privacy of songs not just as elements of the midewiwin but as manifestations of a recipient's vision, also constitutes a dangerous play with power. As Vecsey says, "Ojibwas kept their visions secret because telling a vision brought the manitos to the teller and that should be done only when the manitos were actually needed" (1983, 123). Whether or not Densmore's sources believed they were breaking such a taboo themselves, it is clear that both Chris and Bill—neither of them stereotyped "traditional Indians" but what Birgit Däwes (after Helmbrecht Breinig) identifies as "transdifferent" characters (2007), eschewing or perhaps embracing both hybridity's synthesis and deconstruction's deferrals—are deeply uncomfortable with the tape's invocation of the dead and the material's dubious provenance. That this material also invokes colonial suppression of Indigenous religious practices further underpins the political need to reclaim cultural authority that Chris and Bill's protective attitudes infer. Jack's pictographs, then, become symbolic of both the misappropriation of cultural motifs as emblematic of the asymmetrical power relations that render Native art and artifacts "available" to those who seek to profit from them and of the abuse of power and protocol that the taking of another's visions represents.

The double impact of Densmore's collecting, for the way it compromises her contemporary informants and contributes to the continued ironic distancing of men like Jack from his heritage, is palpable. Again, the play's depictions do not so much chastise those who, like Jack, seek to recoup painful losses, as illuminate the damaging and often unconsidered generational impact of misrepresentation.

Meanwhile, Jack is consistent in his requests from Chris and Bill to teach him; they, similarly, are consistent in their repeated admonitions that he needs to start "listening" for his own dreamsong. The tension this scenario creates steadily develops in the increasing presence of the spectral anthropologist, whose own relationships similarly break down as her work engrosses her more and more. In a twist in the logic of Vizenor's infamous "fourth person" court-room witness (see, e.g., 2009), wherein Charles Aubid recalls Old John Squirrel to testimony through oral story, destabilizing the authority of printed text in so doing, the tape in the play appears to recall not the singers-as-witnesses but Densmore herself, a silent scriptor, quite literally disrupting the dialogic circle. Meanwhile, the colonial structures that underpin and persist in Jack's attempts to learn his songs echo LeAnne Howe's observation that "in the western intellectual tradition, the act of writing stories has been given hegemony over the act of telling stories. This phenomenon led to a privileged view of text, so much so that written stories of the past became labelled as 'history,' and their authors 'historians'" (1999, 122). Self-evidently, the according of expertise to the writer/recorder and knowledge to the written/recorded text is precisely the trap that Chris and Bill hope to free him from, liberating Jack from the tyranny of the document. In one very fundamental respect, Jack's reliance on the document—and the "evidence" the tape furnishes of Densmore's judgments—is precisely what denies him the ability to emulate those ancestors. The text, in a sense, represents a false witness, the Euro-American spirits invoked by the hundred-year old Indigenous voices mischievously blocking Jack's ability to listen.

The turning point for Jack comes about when Chris, who ultimately treats Jack very gently when she sees his agony at not having inherited her store of knowledge, shows him the variety of objects she has been given over the years during ceremonies and other encounters. Handing him a stone given to her by an Aboriginal woman from Australia, Chris tells him, "See these markings, it looks like a woman. The woman who gave it to me said that with this rock she could hear the spirits of her ancestors. Here. Maybe it will help you hear your song" (Rendon 2003, 66). Jack is skeptical at Chris's (and perhaps the playwright's) apparent idealization of Indigenous interconnection, but a laughing Chris tells him "I think indigenous ancestors all reside in the same spirit world" (67). If at first this raises the question of appropriation again, we must remember both context and intent. The items Chris has been given emanate from her "choice to go to ceremony. To listen to elders. To put myself in places where I would learn and people would talk to me" (66). The implication, in other words, is that these items were given to her for a reason by people similarly spiritually motivated, and that her passing on of the stone is therefore appropriate rather than co-optive or disrespectful. That it is engraved with the markings of a woman—possibly readable here as Spirit Woman, who has joined Densmore's apparition in the apartment along with Old Man Spirit?—ties the stone in with the pictographic images Jack has transposed onto his drum. The marked difference between them, of course, is that between an image received and freely given and one that has been taken and, however inadvertently, misused.

Ultimately, then, while the play does "interrogate[] the privilege of anthropology to define the Ojibwe people," its real power lies in the reclamation of "cultural authority" (Darby 2002, 71), as well as reenactment of the very conditions absent from Jack's quest. Integral to this scenario—what Jaye T. Darby sees as the transformation of the stage into a sacred space—are the pictographs copied by Jack, projected this time onto the theater walls and the stage-setting itself. Act 3 opens with two sets of preparations. While Frances prepares packages to send up to White Earth in advance of her visit to record Ojibwe songs, Chris and Bill prepare the apartment for a ceremony. A change in Jack is registered as he sits on the couch *"slowly thumbing through FRANCES's book and periodically pull[ing] rock out of his pocket"* (Rendon 2003, 68). Looking a little less tired and worn, the implication is that the rock—whether its influence is symbolic (psychological) or material—is helping him prepare for the ceremony. Both Bill and Chris, sensitive to the spirits Jack has unwittingly called up, both remark on how "crowded, for sure" (68) the apartment is. With brilliantly satiric effect, Frances is drawn to their preparations, sensing more material through the temporal gauze.

The dream phase of the ensuing ceremony is signaled by the projected pictographs, as "*Spirit lights dance throughout theater, pictographs flash around walls and become stationary as blue light comes up on Ojibwe encampment*" in act 3, scene 2 (70). Here, Bill (as an ancestral elder) admonishes Main'gans (played by the same actor who plays Jack) for "sing[ing] for the chumakamon-iqway and . . . put[ting] us all in danger" (70). Cleverly mapping the present-day problematizing of Jack's appropriation back onto the original theft/giveaway, Rendon connects the coercive influences of the past and the tainted traces of their repetition in the present. Despite having promised only to sing his own songs, Main'gans is persuaded, largely by Frances's younger sister Margaret Densmore, to record some mide songs, material beyond his right to share. Visually, the damage of this act is emphasized in the lighting instructions: as Main'gans sings, "*pictograph symbols disappear one by one until only about half are left. Spirit lights falter*" (72). Underlining the damage, other elders then turn their backs on Main'gans and, shortly afterward, echoing rumors attached to Odjib'we's early demise, Main'gans's wife dies.

While Spirit Woman indicates that the diminishment signified by the disappearing pictographic symbols is not total ("Nothing sacred is ever lost / No matter what they take / Our spirits still live on" [73]), Old Man Spirit concentrates on making sure Frances knows how she damages herself through her actions, as well. Witnessing her burning her own writings and letters, he tells her: "I cry for your spirit. The songs you recorded were always The People's. The work you clung to was never yours. Once you've burned the stirrings of your heart, you will be no more" (73). Rather like Blaeser's examination of Mary Inez Hilger's fieldwork at White Earth in "Housing Conditions of One Hundred Fifty Chippewa Families" (2007, 79–83), Rendon proposes a more personal consequence to the act of cultural pillage. She implies, indeed, that the theft of souls imputed by several characters in the play, including Main'gans and Geronimo, involves a certain loss, or even submission, of the anthropologist's own soul. Although, as Wendy Geniusz informs us, "Densmore explains that she stopped accepting 'material that is surrounded by superstition'" once Main'gans was banned from the mide (2009, 25), her texts reveal a willingness to manipulate her subjects for specific information (see Geniusz 2009, 99).[6]

Scene 2 closes poignantly, first with Main'gans's accusation to Densmore: "My songs, my wife, my religion. You took them all" (Rendon 2003, 73). As he speaks, "*All spirit lights stop and Midé images disappear at once. Stage and theater go completely black."* From the darkness, Spirit Woman's voice sings the song Jack has been straining to hear from the beginning of the scene. I have already quoted the final three lines above, but its opening line probably carries most affect relative to Jack's endeavors: "I sing the songs of ages past," she sings, the song about singing those old songs both expressive of Jack's efforts and yet specifically up to date—a commentary and a reenlivening but explicitly not a reenactment of the voices on the tape. Spirit Woman's presence, Bill's smudging with sage, and the presence of the spirit lights and mide pictographs dramatically emphasize the way the stage has become a sacred space, as Darby suggests. Then, at the opening of scene 3, Spirit Woman's *"voice is heard—a strong song"* (74). Along with flickering spirit lights, mide images return with drumming, and Jack joins in with Spirit Woman. The dream sequence in which Main'gans first sings and then confronts Densmore is the first such sequence in the play in which consequences, rather than just Densmore's actions, are confronted, a cathartic release that means "things seem a lot lighter in [the apartment] now" to Chris. In addition to the "exorcism" of Densmore's specter, Jack finally has his song and, more pertinently perhaps, jokingly asks Chris for "32 bucks" so that he can pay the fine when he returns Densmore's book to the library (74).

In *Native American Drama*, Christy Stanlake describes *SongCatcher* as "a contemporary play with a haunted feeling, as [Rendon] contrasts those Native values [of orally transmitting Native cultural property] with Frances Densmore's method of capturing on wax cylinders disembodied voices singing Native songs" (2009, 108). While this is certainly true, it misses the nuances of the play's rumination on cultural appropriation and misuse, on the ignorance of Eurocentric ethnographic preservation founded on notions of vanishing, hierarchies of race, and misaligned perceptions of value, and on the continued legacy and cultural dislocation through which such texts perpetuate the ruptures of colonization. Nowhere is any of this more clearly illustrated than in the difference between the pictographs Jack paints on his drum and those projected onto the walls of the theater during the dream sequences, a highly immediate and visceral contrast of forms that demonstrates the important differences between cultural preservation as emphasis on the material artifact and cultural preservation as attending to spiritual concerns and intellectual heritage. The charge—which would be fairly understandable—that such a reading fails to understand the importance of many of these misbegotten cultural archives to the work of reclamation would miss what I think are the wider ramifications of Rendon's concerns about overreliance on documentary material. Such reliance, beyond its static rendering of a dynamic oral tradition, also diminishes the wider circles of relation involved in generational transference on the one hand and its interchange between physical and spiritual worlds on the other; while the play is not entirely unsympathetic to Jack's desperation to reclaim his heritage, it also makes clear that that community exists for him if he would only engage. Equally significantly, the play boldly embodies the interdependence of image, song or spoken word, and performance in the realization of both the material's significance and its recovery.

In "A Nexus of Connections," Kimberly Blaeser writes that "if, as Tom King suggests, Native writers are creating in words a Native universe, the assertion of our own author-ity especially in relationship with an other's authorship of our story, becomes not only an act of resistance, but also an important step towards reclamation and recovery" (2012a, 352). Although the medium is different, relying on embodied and not just imagined performance, Blaeser's assessment of resistance and recovery encapsulates the achievement of Rendon's play perfectly. Similarly, the play's structure and staging resounds in Blaeser's reading of the palimpsestic nature of much Native writing and in the multilayered relation between oral, graphic, and written spheres: "Language leads us to the non-verbal. Image is sign, trace. Words and picture finally dissolve into gesture. Words invoke motion rather than static reality. As readers, listeners, or viewers, we are invited into an experience that moves beyond the writing on the page, the image, or the spoken. We arrive at a dynamic nexus of connection" (Blaeser 2012a, 333). Rendon's authority, invested in the dynamism of those connections, which wrests cultural authority for Ojibwe song, is embodied in ceremony. The theater becomes a site of transformation in which projected pictographs play a vital, visual role in both the marking of that sacred space and in their very visual cue to audiences of both the visionary nature of song traditions and, at a diegetic level, the shifts in significance of the giving and receiving of song. In doing so, the lighting and projection palpably, and highly affectively, communicate the sense of spiritual imbalance and rebalancing generated not only by the original trespass, but by the paths the authoritative documentation of the anthropologist, like a map of misdirection across the cultural landscape, laid down.

The play not only reveals these absences in the document but works to amend them, both representing and becoming the resistance and recovery demanded by engagement with Densmore's text—in much the same way, if in different format, to Vizenor's "reexpressions" of the dreamsongs in *Summer in the Spring* (see chapter 5). As such, Stanlake could more explicitly, I think, describe the play as visiting a hauntology inferred in particular by the "disembodied voices" of Densmore's wax cylinders. The tape, the book, and the play itself directly engender the always already absent presence of these figures of knowledge. In doing so, it suggests a form of liberation both for those whose souls are "trapped" in the wax cylinders and those, like Jack, for whom that white noise prevents the listening required to access his own song. Thus, the dead do not "return" as revenants in the contemporary moment, but rather the temporal gap is collapsed at the site of the song/text, calling forth historical and spirit-world figures and tracing that genealogical array to the present moment in which the authority of knowledge must be untangled from the weave of colonial encounter and its asymmetries. In doing so, the play transforms the *power* of anthropological entrapment in an act of "performative recovery" (Blaeser 2012a, 333).

———————————

Temporal compression also characterizes Heid Erdrich's *Curiosities*, a play that, perhaps more satirically than Rendon's, also revisits the nineteenth century to recover the voices of ancestors. Whereas *SongCatcher* valorizes the oral over the written, and the spontaneous over the recorded, Erdrich turns specifically to the written text produced by Maungwudaus after his travels in Britain and France, invoking his presence through the textual absence in a powerfully comical exploration of his time in Europe. As with Rendon's play, Erdrich certainly enters the fray of the "reoccurring battle [to deconstruct] stereotypical representations and [reclaim] self-images" (Stanlake 2009, 180). But also like Rendon's play, its theme is survivance—not the recovery of voice but its re-presenting; not the contest with coloniality but its reorientation through Native agency. This is partially achieved through the palimpsestic technique Blaeser describes, gesturing toward a kind of postmodern pastiche, but with an absolute sincerity in the appropriation of voice: "Long before I began to think of Native literary works as similar in intent to the layered commentaries provided by ledger art, I sought to turn my poetry into a tool of recovery and resistance. I did this partly by incorporating in my works words of those beyond myself" (2012a, 348). For Erdrich, the primary incorporation is of course that of verbatim quotation from Maungwudaus himself, but the play's first interlude brings in a story of Gitche-ee-gaw-gonish about his father On-daig, which was illustrated by Say-say-gon.[7] In other words, in recounting that anecdote, Erdrich not only brings those three Ojibwe men into her narrative, but also calls forth, through direct but unattributed quotation, George Catlin in whose *Travels* the story (as reported speech) and its illustration were first published. Both a heteroglossic space and a palimpsestic scene, then, the combination of playscript, oral tale, image, and projection puts the contemporary and the historic, the stereotypical and the resistant into immediate dialogue.

Framed by a prologue and epilogue, and intercut with interludes, each of the play's five acts foregrounds Maungwudaus's (and, to a much lesser degree, Catlin's) account of his travels, incorporating some humorous anecdotes as well as brief accounts of the deaths of his wife and three of his children, and the death of Mrs. Catlin, in different parts of the UK. These segments of their text are set as dialogues and interact both directly and indirectly with dialogue from and between the troupe and the play's wider cast, including five Ojibwe actors plus Maungwudaus, a further two-four Ojibwe "ensemble," Catlin himself, and a small number of English, Scottish, and American characters and voices. The staging is divided—a table set for a feast on one side, an open space for ensemble on the other—with a hoop "representing the door to the next world" between them (H. Erdrich 2012, 3). The prologue effects a ceremonial opening, including lines from Gordon Henry Jr.'s "Ghost Supper Karaoke" spoken by Uh-Was-way-geezhig-gookway, who first introduces herself in Anishinaabemowin; meanwhile, 5-Troupe (who must be an artist according to the stage directions) *"sets up supplies as if to sketch or paint"* (4). All the while, 2-Troupe (also identified as Say-say-gon) plays a hand-drum and sings. Act 1 sees the immediate entrance of Maungwudaus, who declaims, formally and dramatically, introducing himself in much the same way as he introduces his *Account of the Chippewa Indians, Who Have Been Travelling Among the Whites, in the United States, England, France and Belgium.*

As Maungwudaus shuffles his papers, the modern-day troupe enters with accouterments and begins discussing their plans, while 5-Troupe takes up a position with the art materials. As Maungwudaus begins to direct his oration at this group, the distinction between his moment and theirs becomes both blurred and jarring, the latter eventually noticing the orator and responding to his words and actions. When Maungwudaus begins to tell his infamous story about being jeered at as they watch a street musician's monkey, Catlin comes forward—invisible to the Troupe—and takes over the account, noting as onlookers did at the time that between the monkey, the jeering young men, and the Native Americans, it is the young men who seem least civilized. The Troupe's banter, meanwhile, both participates in and effects commentary on the actions of the orator. As they take a bus ride together, Maungwudaus's speech becomes a commentary on London, ironically eliding the

1840s and the present day as 2-Troupe's gift of Prince Albert tobacco, for instance, segues into his observations on Victoria and Albert, whom he met at the palace. In act 2, the players all move to the table, where they are joined by an English man and woman for a meal. As Maungwudaus describes English mannerisms and vocal qualities, the players all mimic them, sending up English etiquette, while also establishing a comic aside as Mrs. Maungwudaus gets increasingly jealous of the attention her husband pays to the English women. Catlin joins them, sketching, and Maungwudaus recounts the death of his wife in Paris before beginning to speak of his troupe's time with Catlin. The Troupe, meanwhile, begins to concoct a plan to dress up like Maungwudaus's nineteenth-century entourage to perform. This conversation takes up the beginning of act 3, until they are rejoined by Maungwudaus who continues to tell of the French and Belgian tours. Again, Catlin joins him but is invisible to the troupe. Act 3 sees more plates laid at the "ghost supper" table, this time for Say-say-gon, Aunimuckwuh-um, and Mishimaung.

In act 4 the Troupe intersperses Maungwudaus's anecdotes with a "MOVEMENT W/HOOP," a visual passageway, perhaps, from the present to the "ghost world" of Maungwudaus's time. His anecdotes veer from Norwich in eastern England to Scotland, then back southeast to Earlham in Norfolk. At Earlham, a conversation with their host is highly revealing, as Maungwudaus "translates" his comments highly selectively, and incisively pinpoints the ironic superiority of J. J. Gurney who says: "I trust [the Bible] will be soon translated into your language, that you may be able to read it," which Maungwudaus translates as "Pane n'daa minjimendanan'mi mii gaa aankenootananmaan Chitwaa mazinigan miinwaa name nagamowin mazinigan. He says to remember the Bible and hymns that I myself have translated." That he further entreats the Troupe to end their uncivilized, warlike, roaming ways, and settle down peacefully in one place, exhibits a willful ignorance of those sat before him, who represent for him a singular stereotype of the *indian*; of course, the same will doubtless be true for many non-Native audience members to this play. As the meal ends, a number of the members of the Troupe exit to the ghost supper, as does Maungwudaus's wife who carries a cradleboard with her. As act 4 closes, the "curiosity" element takes a macabre twist, with Maungwudaus recounting to Catlin his having learned that relatives of Say-say-gon had been told that the old man's skeleton was offered up by Maungwudaus for public viewing—as three thousand people a night come to watch them perform, his own sense of the burden of spectacle is palpable. The interlude between acts 4 and 5 is given over to the artist. The written-in spontaneity of this moment makes it impossible to comment on the script, but its intent, as I will suggest shortly, is intriguing. Act 5, meanwhile, sees them heading back to the United States. Midway through the act, the Troupe reenters as their modern selves for the first time in a while as, toward the end of the play, Maungwudaus himself passes away and is wrapped in a Pendleton blanket. Act 5 closes with them all sat at the Ghost Supper table, before 5-Troupe reveals his artwork to the audience at exeunt. The epilogue then closes at a modern-day rehearsal as 1-Troupe enters excitedly with a sheaf of Catlin's papers.

The script's pathos and humor—present in Maungwudaus's writings—are considerably shored up through interactions with and between the five troupe members, who intermittently change between nineteenth-century and contemporary costume, performing both the roles of Maungwudaus's original troupe and a kind of comedy chorus in the present. To illustrate these transitions, at the beginning of act 3, dialogue revolves around the proposed trip to Europe, where the present-day troupe discusses signing up to a performance website, before alighting on "Indian sign language" picked up from summer church camp as a potential act. Like Jack, the sign language speaker is a city kid, taken "to the lakes one summer. We had music and swimming and camping skills, that's where we learned Indian Signs" (H. Erdrich 2012, 22). Reflecting common ironic stories of summer camp—where cultural appropriation is often de rigueur—troupe members 1 and 3 continue:

> 1: I bet you did crafts, too, beads and leather, real original.
> 3: Yeah, I sucked at it. The other kids were better than all us Indians. But I liked it. The last day, we had a big party with a magic show. The magician put Bear Jones to sleep and made him waddle like a duck, quacking and squatting and stuff.
> (22–23)

The conversation leads into the reentrance of Maungwudaus who, picking up where they left off begins: "The King's man amused us with tricks. . . . He gave us a needle to stick those he made sleep" (23). The king's man, Charles Lafontaine, was a Swiss mesmerist who pioneered what we know today as stage hypnotism (then known as the Mesmeric séance) in the early 1840s. Here, "the King's man" indicates their presence in France (then under Louis Philippe I), although Lafontaine became famous throughout western Europe. The interaction between Maungwudaus's nineteenth-century text and the contemporary dialogue is then added a further layer by the entrance of Catlin himself, visible and audible only to Maungwudaus. Again, a coincidence occurs between Catlin's description of a regatta and the female troupe members' mime dance in which they mimic canoe paddling. The comical effect of this incidental collision across times lies partly in its dramatic irony. More so, though, the disconnection between expectation and action. In this instance, for example, Catlin's effusive description of the race is tempered somewhat by his expression of a collective regret that "the Indians were beaten" (24), as he goes on to suggest they overloaded their canoe.

That Catlin's display of "Indians" depended on the spectacle of natural man means that such a scenario must have entirely subverted the assumptions of his contemporary audience. In the present moment of the play's performance, meanwhile, Catlin's insider knowledge that they ought to have "put two squaws into it instead of men, as they are in Indian country much superior to men in paddling canoes" both exposes the prejudices of early nineteenth-century etiquette and, no doubt, would surprise many contemporary audiences too (H. Erdrich 2012, 24). The extraordinary scene that Catlin describes at the Château de Saint-Cloud on the banks of the Seine is given a little more cursory treatment in Maungwudaus's brief travelogue, in which he remembers that they "also rowed [their] birch bark canoe in the artificial lake, amongst swans and geese" (2011, 6). Audience members familiar with Maungwudaus's text, meanwhile, may well remember this particular scene as one in which he describes French women as "handsome, very gay in their dresses," while "many of the gentlemen never shave their faces; this makes them look as if they had no mouths." Those with moustaches, on the other hand "look as if they had black squirrel's tailes sticking on each side of their mouths" (6). Painfully self-evident though it is, the considerable difference of emphasis in these two accounts is salutary. Maungwudaus's reverse "ethnography" places a focus on that which is different for the Ojibwe troupe, bringing into sharp relief the ways Catlin's real and textual display at best renders them curiosities and at worst strips them of their humanity. Characterized by Heidi Hoechst as a "struggle for freedom in the illogical venture of indigenous masquerade" (2008, 175), Erdrich's emphases display both Maungwudaus's familiarity with "the processes through which Native life was often contingent on manipulating white desires" and the more earnest reclamation of agency from those processes (175).

W. Richard West, the founding director of the National Museum of the American Indian, has written of the "profound resentment" some Native viewers feel about the invasive quality of Catlin's production. Noting Catlin's "genuine concern" and "sincere respect" for his subjects, West, a Southern Cheyenne, nevertheless indicts Catlin as a "cultural P.T. Barnum, a crass huckster trading on other people's lives and lifeways," and "an emblematic exploiter of native peoples" (qtd. by Flint 2009, 58). Catlin is, West concedes, an "easy and large target," but his assessment of the "salvage" project in which he was involved very much echoes—or prefigures—Rendon's conclusions about Densmore. As in the latter's case, however, overt focus on Catlin, at the expense of those Native peoples who supported his work through their performance and participation, has tended to perpetuate a historical silencing—what Linda Tuhiwai Smith describes as the relegation to obscurity of Native informants (1999, 82)—that, of course, is highly contrary to the vocal, charismatic, and dynamic presence of those Iowa and Ojibwe men and women in their moment. Erdrich, acknowledging the co-constructive presence of Catlin, who was after all a point to which Maungwudaus's self-organizing troupe gravitated for obvious commercial reasons, nevertheless places her emphasis on Maungwudaus himself, giving his voice through his text significantly more prominence than Catlin's.

The visual figures in this inversion in interesting ways, as well. On the one hand, the suggested slides in the background perform several functions. Erdrich writes that they "could suggest setting changes via historical or other images such as contemporary urban images, scenes of London, Paris, Glasgow and Boston of 1840's," serving a relatively simple contextual role. In addition, "several images of Maungwudaus are available on-line including a noted portrait by the Canadian artist Paul Kane" while "the paintings and journal sketches of George Catlin illustrate some of the activities (including the actual persons) in Maungwudaus's narrative" (2012, 2). These latter images embody the actors themselves and contribute visually to the elision of the historical gap. Perhaps most importantly, though, "Sketches of Say-say-gon, who travelled with Maungwudaus, are included in Catlin's journals and should be projected" (2). These include images that match anecdotes told in the play by 2-Troupe/Say-say-gon. Like Maungwudaus, then, Say-say-gon's own voice is given prominence, rather than the quoted voice embedded in Catlin's text; that it is given prominence both through the oral performance of his anecdotes and the projection of his sketches throws the spotlight on his artistic production at the expense of Catlin's own, meaning that the expressive witness of the two Ojibwe men, embodied and enlivened, is liberated from the textual capture of Catlin's work.

This liberation is not without irony. For instance, Erdrich quotes Catlin saying "I was much shocked and distressed to hear of the death of Say-say-gon who had been of an extraordinary nature, who had been illustrating by his own rude designs a series of stories which I wrote down from his own lips" (26). The layers of irony begin, in this instance, with Catlin's attempt to give himself prominence. It is his distress we hear about, for example, while we are given to understand very clearly that Say-say-gon's stories survive because "I wrote [them] down from his own lips." Catlin does not, for instance, question the relationship of the sketches themselves to the story—the possibility that they, in their own way, constitute a textual document to which his own is supplementary. The irony deepens, however, relative to the visual imagery itself. Inadvertent though it may be, Catlin's declaration of Say-say-gon's extraordinariness becomes somewhat self-congratulatory in that he connects it syntactically to Say-say-gon's drawing. Having done so, he then asserts a sense of superiority in describing Say-say-gon's sketches as "rude designs." The true irony of this judgment rests arguably in the range of contemporary assessments of his own work, which while frequently laudatory, also included the label of "American primitivism" by witnesses who dismissed his output as "deficient in drawing, perspective and finish" (Combe 1841, 70). Now commonly recognized—by many Native people as well as non-Natives—as a vital record, the humanity of his subjects cannot be doubted in his portrayals, and he was certainly a pioneer among portraitists attempting to capture specific detail in home locations, rather than repeat caricature and stereotype in romanticized landscapes. As West among others has noted, however, one cannot really ignore the levels of exploitation and commodification in which the Indian Gallery was bound. In London, for instance, its staging at Egyptian Hall in Piccadilly attests to its spectacular, rather than high artistic or pedagogic, positioning. At Egyptian Hall, the portraits and accompanying artifacts would come to be shown alongside the likes of Norfolk giant Robert Hales and the dwarf General Tom Thumb, who were under the management of the controversial entrepreneur Phineas T. Barnum. If Catlin's principal motivation had been to record a passing moment for the purposes of posterity and education, that anthropological remit did not align well with his financial expectations. The *Times* in 1840 described the Indian Gallery as a "curious exhibition," one that would likely attract antiquaries, naturalists, and philosophers, but not the public shilling. The difference in purpose and intent between Say-say-gon's sketches and Catlin's oeuvre is profound.

That these depictions were, in their own moment, also bound and therefore culpable in the discourse of vanishing with which manifest destiny beat its path is more than amply illustrated in Catlin's own writing. Its inheritance from Romanticism is similarly palpable. His will to educate and his salesmanship combine in his relationship with a group of fourteen Iowa sponsored by George H. C. Melody in particular, promoting them as "the finest specimens of the Indian tribe that have ever visited the continent" and organizing programs around demonstrations of dancing, wigwam erecting, lacrosse, scalping, and more (1841, 22). If claims of his trading on lives and lifeways belied a genuine respect for the "noble savage," his opportunism became unmissable in this aspect; while serious commentators highlighted the superiority of his paintings over the inferior caricatures of James Fenimore Cooper's hugely popular Frontier novels, Catlin himself advertised his Iowa encampment in Vauxhall Gardens with the promise that "the public will have an opportunity of witnessing for the first time in Europe illustrations of the stirring descriptions given by Cooper in his celebrated novels" (see Flint 2009, 55). Indeed, even in his own moment concerns were raised among the press as to the exploitative nature of Catlin's involvement with the Native performers, while his and other similar human exhibits—early versions of what would become, by the 1870s, the ethnological expositions known as human zoos—were actively protested against.

The multiple nature of Indigenous representation at this moment, even within Catlin's project, consolidates around this juxtaposition of documented nobility and human degradation. Like Cooper, he anticipates the passing of an esteemed, but ahistoric and doomed culture—indeed, he constructs a monument to that passing that, logically, enshrines the Indigenous American as an American inheritance. Yet clearly in Europe such exhibitions would depend not on pity, or on a stirring of settler desire, but on excitement for their success; Catlin knew that what his public wanted was what the *Times* called the "incongruous," wild men, savages; the opposite, in other words, of those men and women of dignity, nobility, and renown he celebrated in his paintings. The confusion of Catlin's Romantic idealizations and the Indian Gallery's tacit acquiescence to its audience's appetites is, of course, writ large in Charles Dickens's belated, notorious response to the 1843 show:

> With his party of Indians squatting and spitting on the table before him, or dancing their miserable jigs after their own dreary manner, he called, in all good faith, upon his civilised audience to take notice of their symmetry and grace, their perfect limbs, and the exquisite expression of their pantomime; and his civilised audience, in all good faith, complied and admired. Whereas, as mere animals, they were wretched creatures, very low in the scale and very poorly formed; and as men and women possessing any power of truthful dramatic expression by means of action, they were no better than the chorus at an Italian Opera in England—and would have been worse if such a thing were possible. (1853, 337)[8]

"It is not the miserable nature of the noble savage that is the new thing," Dickens continued, "it is the whimpering over him with maudlin admiration, and the affecting to regret him, and the drawing of any comparison of advantage between the blemishes of civilization and the tenor of his swinish life" (337). Dickens's primary target here is British society and the liberal establishment itself, but his caricatures suggest that for all Catlin's intended recalibrating of Native humanity, public perception—and certainly political exhortation—favored its beloved stereotypes.

In the face of all this representation and imposition, then, Erdrich, like Rendon, reclaims authority for the Ojibwe. Less concerned in this case with cultural authority, Erdrich instead asserts a political authority that lies buried beneath official histories—not least, Catlin's. The starting point is Maungwudaus's writing itself, his own brief travelogue, along with Say-say-gon's images, which displace the textual and visual document that Catlin produced. The contemporary performance, then, of Maungwudaus and troupe, both re-presents the Ojibwe, exploring the genealogical traces of name' (see chapter 1), both in specific sites and in performance itself, and exposing the politics of performance and portrayal in which they were enmeshed. Catlin's texts reveal a great sympathy for his subjects—both the performers and the sitters for his portraits—albeit couched in the leading assumptions of his moment. That it is, therefore, a condescending sympathy, which implicitly victimizes Native peoples as explicitly tragic and doomed, renders it all the more important that Maungwudaus's voice overshadows his. Maungwudaus's pamphlet represents just a few short pages compared to Catlin's hundreds, but it also represents a constructive effort to maintain and assert his agency within a context that, at face value, severely limited it. That agency is further foregrounded in the even more important decision not just to perform but to lead. Kate Flint notes that "Maungwudaus is a clear example of a First Nations member preferring to act—and being prepared to act—as an impresario for . . . his own people" and also that "Maungwudaus's pamphlet is indicative of one particular desire to regain some agency within this changing order of [modernity], producing, as well as being present within, print culture" (2009, 82, 84). Flint goes further, quoting Johannes Fabian when she explains that, in writing, Maungwudaus refuses "that 'persistent and systematic tendency to place the referent(s) of anthropology in a Time other than the present of the producer of the anthropological discourse'" (84).

This refusal is explored further by Erdrich in *Curiosities*. At one level, making those who are the title's subject, the "Indian curiosities" themselves, the only ones in the play who give voice to their curiosity, she reflects the gaze back at her putative audience and reasserts Maungwudaus's part "in mediation and dialogue" with modernity (Flint 2009, 84). Furthermore, having Maungwudaus act as both orator and guide to both audience and modern-day troupe, Erdrich places him rather than Catlin, who remains ever in the shadows, as the locus of authority, his reverse ethnography literally enacted as a form of decolonial gaze. And, perhaps most significantly, in having the troupe act out both modern and nineteenth-century roles, often with little distinction between the two, Erdrich reinforces that refusal of the "denial of coevalness" that Fabian describes (2002, 35). Her characters all implicitly participate in the performance of their Nativeness (as both Anishinaabeg and, on the odd inescapable occasion, *indians*) in a simultaneous past-present, which highlights both the modernity of the nineteenth-century ancestors and the degree to which the modern troupe are drawn into a capitalist nexus of performance; in other words, it reveals the extent to which the present was denied their forebears, while the troupe's own present continues to be dictated (in ways they seek to take advantage of in a form of engaged resistance) by the past. Maungwudaus's textual presence in the play, of course, is translated to oral performance. As such, he performs the role not only of "Indian" but also of impresario, lecturer, and so on, adding a further layer to the complexity of his own (self-)production.

Like his older half brother, Peter Jones (Kahkewaquonaby), George Henry became a respected Methodist teacher. Jones went on to become one of his people's—the Mississauga Ojibwe—most powerful advocates. At a time when the Canadian authorities were trying to remove them from their land in south-central Ontario, Jones wrote, lectured, and preached on their behalf, raised money for both his people and the Methodist church, and even traveled to Britain three times between 1830 and 1845 in service of that mission. Clearly far distantly removed from Catlin's images of Indians, Jones nevertheless succeeded in maintaining his people as an autonomous community, writing: "I cannot suppose for a moment that the Supreme Disposer has decreed that the doom of the red man is to fall and gradually disappear, like the mighty wilderness, before the axe of the European settler" (1860, 29). Jones, in fact, was one of a number of significant nineteenth-century Ojibwe who, either self-educated or educated by the church, were defying the assumptions of assimilationists about the fate of "Indians." Bilingual poet Jane Johnston Schoolcraft; minister and campaigner for an autonomous Indian state George Copway; and interpreter, historian, and advocate against the dispossession of the Minnesota Chippewa William Whipple Warren all made significant interventions between the 1820s and 1860s.

Wild West historian Brian Dippie has called Maungwudaus a "slick operator," arguing that his intention was to exploit "the wild side of the native nature" (1990, 108). In response, Heidi Hoechst asks what it might mean for him to be exploiting the "already exploited representation" of his people (2008, 174), an implicit subversion, if you like, of the power balance. Journalist Wanda Nanibush, meanwhile, argues that "Maungwudaus chose to perform . . . in order to preserve his sense of being Anishinabeg" (2010): how wonderfully ironic that the opportunity afforded by one American's nostalgic misrepresentations should sustain a troupe whose very performance of a "vanishing past" was testament to their survival. If Catlin's images fix an invented notion of "Indianness" into the historical imagination, Maungwudaus's choices unsettle it; if Catlin's work is exploitative and perfidious, Maungwudaus's story at least resists a tale of passive victimhood.

If the resistance to textual capture as a means of enacting cultural persistence encapsulates Maungwudaus's tale, however, it is Say-say-gon's that becomes even more intriguing in relation to the play's performance. There, in a complete counterstrategy to the constancy of the colonial gaze with which they worked, 2-Troupe/Say-say-gon takes up station with the art materials and draws/paints his (or her, depending on the actor) way through the play. So, while Catlin remains in the shadows, unseen by the present-day troupe, 2-Troupe becomes the de-facto artist-in-residence, touring Europe, sketching what he observes, and—quite literally—producing by the end of the play bona fide original Native American artwork. Again, this scenario switches the emphasis of curiosity on its head. Where Say-say-gon's sketches were absorbed by Catlin's oeuvre, presented (though not without praise) in Catlin's accounts rather than on their own terms, 2-Troupe's displace them as the contemporary recording of a passing moment. Where Catlin traveled west to document a transition, 2-Troupe travels east and mirrors his actions. There are one or two cues in the play as to the intended subject of that work—the odd focus on individual players—but the otherwise open aspect of the artist's remit means that anything could be sketched in the course of the drama. It is not so much the product, then, as the process, the reversed gaze, the Native rather than Euro-American painter that restores a kind of balance to the asymmetries of power inherent to Catlin's project.

That "balance," as well as the various doublings, returns, and inversions I have mentioned, is mirrored, also, in the PowerPoint projections that accompany the play. The opening slide, which carries title, writer and director, and theater credits, includes two sketches based on famous Catlin paintings, signed "Carolyn Lee

Anderson, Oct. 2010."[9] On the left side of the diptych, the painting "Catlin Painting the Portrait of Mah-to-toh-pa—Mandan" is reproduced (in reverse, I believe), but instead of the expected backdrop of a crowd of Mandan onlookers (gazing at the artist gazing at the chief, in a perfect ouroboros), an outline sketch of a London street with the unmistakable outline of the facade to the long-since destroyed Egyptian Hall takes their place. On the right, meanwhile, one half of the well-known diptych "Wi-jùn-jon Before and After his trip to Washington, DC" sees the "assimilated" afterimage of the Nakota (Assiniboine) chief—besuited, top-hatted, carrying a fancy fan, and seemingly unsteady on his feet—posed in front of a prairie earthlodge. These two images unsettle viewer expectations, reminding audiences of the way the European spectacle highlights an interruption of life on the plains and the jarring juxtaposition of the impacts of settler-colonial lifeways on Native peoples. Yet, while Catlin's project sought to arrest the moment in its "decline," these images also point to their ongoing life, placing the "object" as human subject on the streets of London, and evoking the chief beneath the veneer of assimilation. In both instances, the images resist the kind of totalizing narrative Catlin's agenda endorsed. Similar effects are created by other slides in the program. The next image, for instance, is a photograph of a car's hubcap painted in the colors of the four directions, to look like a medicine wheel. A humorous juxtaposition of the traditional and modern, it superimposes the spiritual onto the mass-manufactured, fusing the notional separateness of the sacred and the quotidian and (or!), perhaps more immediately, puncturing the assumptions that consistently render "Indians" and the modern world, spirituality and the day-to-day, and so on, separate in the public imagination.

Another urban stock photo, this time of a tipi in front of an apartment block, adds to much of the scene already set, while two further images continue to unsettle expectation. The first, a picture of contemporary Native passengers on a school bus, speaks to the relationship between Native peoples and modernity consistently and persistently denied by narratives of "civilization," picturing Natives in modern spaces that are anything but spaces of encounter. And, inverting this, a slide that depicts Canterbury Cathedral—marveled at for the sheer magnitude of its structure by Maungwudaus, who maximizes the dramatic comparison of church-as-civilization versus precivilized man by commenting on how their arrows would not reach the top of the tower—also includes two images of heavily tattooed and mustachioed figures wearing breech-cloths and tunics and carrying spears accompanied by the simple label "British costume." Likely pre-Roman, and certainly pre-Christian, the figures are startlingly contrasted against the cathedral, which was begun on a once-pagan site after the visit of Augustine in roughly 600 AD.[10] The juxtaposition—again discombobulating—nevertheless strips away assumptions. Disrupting the problematic inference suggested by the juxtaposition that there is some sort of teleological ley line on which ancient Britons and Canterbury Cathedral both sit—the kind of narrative that underpinned the myth of the vanishing American and the justification of manifest destiny—the orientation of the image, as the cathedral "floats" in the upper left-hand corner, offers a reminder perhaps that Christianity itself was a foreign import, supplanting and, in form and feature, literally imposed upon the Britons who preceded its arrival.

Perhaps the most viscerally comical image of inversion and temporal collapse immediately follows: Montana artist Gary Carter's now famous painting of Plains warriors dancing with C3PO—yes, the *Star Wars* droid—wandering in their midst is followed by several of Catlin's sketches of Native dancers. Carter's image is clearly tongue in cheek; it harks back to the apogee of Western art when men like Catlin and Paul Kane traveled west to record such scenes, but in the context of his more conventional depictions of "Indian" and "Western" themes, it does so in a way that nods to the fantastical qualities of the frontier myth, drawing attention to the ways in which such scenes are, themselves, often fictive interpretations, projections, that tend to overwrite the real in the public eye. Both *Star Wars* and the *indian* are facets of popular culture based in a long history of Euro-Western myth-making—indeed, both, according to David Treuer (see 2006), have their genesis in the Greek classics. Accompanying a number of other images of Native peoples, particularly by Catlin, we are reminded forcibly of the ways in which such images, intended as they are to record faithfully, have nevertheless contributed to the mythical narrative.

From all of this Say-say-gon's drawings, three of which are included in the slide show, stand as an expression of agency. They are drawings that seek to represent experience and express individual vision, rather than image a people or transmit a notional exotica. As such, the role of the artist as 2-Troupe, participant-observer to the action but recording his/her observations, and capturing the spirit of stories in the way Say-say-gon may have, reinscribes that agency as Indigenous artistic production in the moment of performance and encounter. This strong visual backdrop becomes a reminder, too, of the overwhelming degree to which Maungwudaus's own role in the play depends on vision (looking). Whether he is talking about his observations of character, the lesson in discernment delivered by the monkey, reading a sign on a London bus, or looking through a microscope, the writings that Erdrich chooses for him to speak almost all relate emphatically to the visual.

Like so many Native writers of his times, Maungwudaus's relationship to what Catlin saw as the corrupting institutions of Western civilization were so strong as to justify, for many early scholars, the accusation of compromise or inauthenticity. This is precisely the self-perpetuating validity of the vanishing Indian myth, disrupted by the play's embodied performance of the past-in-the-present. Maungwudaus appears to have remained committed to his community, to what Nichole Biber describes as an Ojibwe sensibility, and yet he clearly also made the most of those tools of modernity available to him (n.d.). If we believe it renders him any less real than a Catlin portrait, we have bought into the false logic of imperialism. For Flint, Maungwudaus, along with numerous other Native visitors to London in the nineteenth century, provided "living proof that, in their capacity to react and respond to modern life, they refused to be consigned to that role of the mythical and prehistorical that was so frequently assigned them" (2009, 24).

That sense of refusal—and the admittedly painful sacrifice that attended it—is also central to another performance/performative piece by Sandy Bay First Nation artist Robert Houle, whose *Paris/Ojibwa* debuted in Paris in 2010. In a brief review of the piece's exhibition at the Art Gallery of Peterborough in 2011, Leanne Simpson writes:

> When I first stood in front of Robert Houle's reconstruction of a 1840s Parisian salon, I had tears in my eyes thinking about my Mississauga relatives at the centre of the installation. I felt the horrific pain and despair of Uh wus sig gee zhig goo kway, a young Mississauga mother and artist who watched her children die of smallpox in Europe while completely isolated from her land, culture and family. (2011b)

That pain and despair is palpable on three levels: first, and most basic, in the implied distance from homelands and the colonial circumstances that forced that distance, represented by the installation's reproduction of the salon; secondly, in each of the four wall panels of the corner-salon, a member of the troupe is depicted facing away from the viewer toward a Lake Manitoban landscape, while beneath them Houle has painted a depiction of the smallpox virus, which killed both Maungwudaus's wife and children; and thirdly, in a gesture that "speaks directly to our community" (Simpson 2011b), behind them "unrepresented and unseen, is a graveyard from Houle's homeland of Sandy Bay First Nation, Manitoba. One would have to go there and stand in the landscape to know that they are walking out of the graveyard and returning home" (Nanibush 2010). Accompanied with burning sage, the overall effect indicates, like Erdrich's play "a symbolic return—which also serves to highlight the absence of the history of the Ojibwa in Paris from our collective imagination" (Nanibush 2010).

Just as Maungwudaus himself drew intelligently from what was available to him, Houle's artwork reflects a transcultural dynamic—the salon interior and the imagery of a grassy horizon capturing the tension implicit in the virgule between "Paris" and "Ojibwa." A similar transcultural doubleness occurs with a more ironic slant in Erdrich's play, the title of which signifies both the Ojibweg's status as "Indian curiosities" and the insightful and often wry observations that the inquisitive—curious—Maungwudaus makes in his writings. Speaking to a sense of co-construction, again echoing the dialogue in Erdrich's play between historical voice and its contemporary interpretation, or between Catlin's colonial mastery and the Mississaugas' resilient agency, the tension invoked in such doubling as well as in Houle's virgule marks a settler-colonial moment transported to and reexamined in the present. This is further emphasized, as Nanibush notes, in the Greco-Roman columnar interior of the salon, as well as in Houle's borrowing from "the ennobling romanticism of Eugène Delacroix, whose 1845 pen and ink drawings of Maungwudaus' troupe influenced Houle's work" (Nanibush 2010). That ennobling aesthetic is principally to be found in the dress of the four figures—a dancer, a shaman, a warrior, and a healer—who all wear Greco-Roman style robes, indicative of the idea that "Indigenous Peoples could be compared to Greco-Roman cultures was part of the nineteenth-century French imagination" (Nanibush 2010). In fact, that notion is not peculiar to the French, but infuses nineteenth-century depictions of the noble savage more broadly—perhaps best illustrated by Peter Stephenson's sculpture *The Wounded Indian* (1848–50), modeled after the Roman statue of Galata Morente, or the Dying Gaul, which was central to Romantic enunciations of a vanishing noble race. *The Wounded Indian*, a monument to settler colonialism that, exonerating its culpability by depicting the warrior felled by an arrow (and, therefore, by another Native, see Flint 2009), contributes to the indigenization of settler culture, was sent to Crystal Palace in Hyde Park, London, for the 1851 Great Exhibition to contribute to the representation of the United States.

Like Erdrich's play, though, *Paris/Ojibwa* steps beyond mere borrowing for its aesthetic and turns to collaboration. At the Paris opening, for instance, Houle invited Barry Ace, an Odawa artist, to perform outside the Louvre, where he danced men's traditional style to powwow music. His dancing moved on to the Tuileries Gardens, Cleopatra's Needle, down the Champs-Elysees, and into the exhibit itself, both tracing and figuratively indigenizing a route through Paris. "With grace and power," writes Nanibush (2010), "Ace honored the Ojibwa (Anishinaabeg) dancers." In an even more intriguing move, Houle commissioned Hervé Dagois, a Parisian animator, to create a video. The resulting film, *uhnemekéka*, featuring jingle dress dancers against an abstracted background performing a healing dance, is a far cry from Delacroix's sketches, even as it encounters a similar "spectacle du sauvage" in the context of French colonial history. Effectively, Houle's installation—even, indeed particularly, through its interaction with Dagois's performative medium—recovers the agency of those Ojibwe actors. It is an agency that they never relinquished in their moment, but that dominant representative history has all but erased.

Leanne Simpson makes a distinction between the exhibition in Paris and its later installation in Peterborough: "Originally shown in Paris as part of a series of performance re-enactments, *Paris/Ojibwa*, installed in Mississauga territory, now becomes about healing and reconciliation—but this time from within our own world view. Houle shifts our gaze from 'Indians as objects in a museum' to the politics of power that allow us to exoticize and objectify 'Indians' in the first place, while also illuminating the resistance and resilience of the Nishnaabeg" (2011b). There is, clearly, a greater ideological and epistemological connection to the objectification of Native peoples in its Paris staging—not forgetting that Paris's Vincennes woods was a celebrated site for the early twentieth-century "human zoo" that was the Exposition Coloniale. Nevertheless, in its Parisian setting, Houle brings Mississauga territory to bear in the colonial metropole, representing its space within the salon, which in turn stood within the Canadian Cultural Centre in Paris. The resilience of the standing figures, the healing resonances of the jingle dance in Dagois's video installation, and the literal presence outside of Barry Ace, all of which collapse the time span between 1845 and 2010, render the artwork more than a reenactment. Houle's visual and Ace's embodied performance thus reenliven Anishinaabe presence in Paris by literally bringing the land—represented, felt, embodied—with them, and reorienting those Parisian spaces themselves as sites of reconciliation with Mississauga land at their center.

———————

What I describe above represents a variety of examples of, among other things, Michelle Raheja's definition of visual sovereignty, which is described by Stephanie

Nohelani Teves as "the creative practice of self-representation that engages and deconstructs white-generated representations . . . [and] allows communities to negotiate what sovereignty and self-representation can mean through new media technologies in order to reimagine Native intellectual and cultural paradigms" (2014, 9). The combination of forms each of these performances and their stagings employs function in a variety of ways to both challenge the discursive structures that have dominated Native representation—from the salon itself to the conventions of dramaturgy, for instance—and reorient and repurpose those structures by taking possession of them. So, 2-Troupe's live art-production *both* parodies and diminishes the power of Catlin's original project and the discursive structures of the colonial gaze *and* reasserts Native agency and visual sovereignty through the production of new artwork born of the re-created encounter.

The pictographs in *SongCatcher*, meanwhile, assert a more literal form of visual sovereignty—reflecting, as do Vizenor's pictomyths in *Summer in the Spring*—an Anishinaabe form that precedes the writing that overwrites. As Louise Erdrich notes in *Books and Islands*, "Songs belong to these islands," recorded and remembered in part through the painted rocks. The pictographs projected onto the stage, then, elements of similar spiritual and mnemonic processes, evoke the precolonial existence of the very songs and imagic forms Jack is trying to recover, both illustrating their colonizing and marking a decolonial strategy—that is, a strategy not just of resistance but of true survivance. While Houle's art, on the other hand, reproduces the mechanisms of capture, however voluntarily entered into, it is the individual's engagement with that space that reproduces it ultimately—in Mississaugas territory if not in Paris—as a space of commemoration and healing.

Both Houle's interactive space—a site that literalizes Simon O'Sullivan's sense that "this is what art is: a bundle of affects or, as Deleuze and Guattari would say, a *bloc of sensations*, waiting to be reactivated by a spectator or participant" (2001, 126)—and Erdrich's *Curiosities* emphasize the contingent, processual, and relational qualities of art performatively through the acts of participating and making anew. Rendon's play, though it does so differently, similarly enacts the process of coming to song; within the contours of the play, after all, Jack needs to go through his journey of frustration in order, at the end, to be able to receive his song. It is not, then, a play about a man's failure, upended by an epiphanic moment followed by catharsis; it is a play about the learning to listen, and listening to learn, that underpins the very process he so desires to participate in.

At the same time, Birgit Däwes argues that the spectator's gaze carries traces of the "historicized practice of colonial surveillance"; these performances, as she says Native North American theater does in principle, seek to undermine that practice, "disturb[ing] the linear gaze" (2007, 387). Moreover, they "respond[] to a history of silencing by transcending rather than reverting binary semantics of power" (14). The spaces of those performances, too—both literally in terms of galleries, theaters, and metropolitan streets, and figuratively in the form of Houle's reconstructed salon—are a reminder that "space is never neutral, but always infused with political and historical discourses that claim and shape it" (Däwes 2014, 33). Marked by signifiers of visual sovereignty, these performances enact the recovery of or claim to what Goeman calls "spatial sovereignty" (2013, 13), indigenizing public and institutional spaces that have, historically, been the repositories of representations of rather than by Native people.

CONCLUSION

I n this book I have deliberately focused on the literary—and dramatic[1]—use and representation of visuality, visual arts, image-making, and other aspects of the optical. My interest, in other words, has primarily been in the inferred relationship between written and other forms of the graphic, not just in pictures but in image in the broadest terms. I have written elsewhere on narrative in contemporary Anishinaabe visual arts (see Stirrup 2013). In that essay, my concern was with the relationship between painting and storying processes—and, ultimately, with the primacy of process in narrative constructions of Anishinaabe art. Although I have mentioned many of those artists—Andrea Carlson, Frank Big Bear, Star Wallowing Bull, Norval Morrisseau, Daphne Odjig, Blake Debassige, David Bradley, George Morrison, Patrick DesJarlait, all of whose work is complex, demanding, and often beautiful—at various points in this book, and not forgetting the scores of talented Anishinaabe artists whose names go unmentioned here, I have deliberately chosen to favor the book and the writer over the canvas and the painter in this project. Another version of it could easily reorient discussion in multiple directions.

In his discussion of the exhibition *Before and After the Horizon: Anishinaabe Artists of the Great Lakes*, which has been shown in both the United States (National Museum of the American Indian, 2013–14) and Canada (Art Gallery of Ontario,

2014), artist, curator, and scholar Gerald McMaster addresses the double-textuality of a range of the work. Of Bonnie Devine's diptych *Letter to William* (2008), he writes: "The diptych begins with a large, abstract close-up of a rock, on which she writes: 'I have come to listen, believing the rock is filled with stories. I have come to read, believing the rock is a text'" (2013, 94). On the opposing panel, a dense, tiny alphabetic text is superimposed with her own imagined glyphs. "The point of these works," McMaster continues, "is for us to understand two different types of text. We might not, however, understand either of them, as differing epistemologies form the basis of each reading" (94). The notion of two different types of text in juxtaposition and/or dialogue has been a current in this book. At times it has flowed smoothly; at others multidirectional streams produce a foaming eddy that at once illuminates my outsider position and illustrates the complex historical shifts and fractures that characterize Native aesthetic lineages and ideological practices and reflects the various colonial inventions and interruptions that make lines between Native presence and invented *indian*ness often hard to discern. Nevertheless, and epistemological exclusions and breaks aside, there is a (literary) textuality, as well as a narrative process, implicit to much Anishinaabe art that reflects, and perhaps even endorses, the visuality implicit to much Anishinaabe writing. It suggests, I believe, a common aesthetic that repeatedly insists on the importance of reading when one believes one is simply looking, and seeing when one believes one is reading: in both cases, ultimately, as Devine's statement infers, hearing also becomes part of their central dynamic. Going on to discuss the incredible beaded commitment of Nadia Myre's *Indian Act*, McMaster writes: "Similarly, we read Nadia Myre's art through text. Her *Indian Act* (2002) asks us not to read or understand the basis of an archaic piece of legislation or an 'original' text, an ur-text, an *authentic* text" (94). Rather it asks us to see and to respond to the ways the apparent act of aesthetic erasure of alphabetic script by a form—beading—that has been both decorative and communicative in many contexts, also represents an unsilencing of the Native voices whose contributions to the settler-colonial document have themselves been drowned out by the dominance of script. These texts are significant and, as these few comments suggest, speak closely to the central theses of this book; that I have opted not to include the visual arts in the parameters of my discussion here is as much a condition of pragmatism—and publishers' tolerance on word limits!—as it is an intellectual choice.

I have also chosen, with a few exceptions, to avoid the sometimes too-obvious ground of the visual text—the book interspersed with pictures, for instance, or the painting that utilizes text. The unusual juxtapositions of Vizenor's use of pictomyths, the wonderfully dynamic meshing of word, image, and sound in Heid Erdrich's video poems, and the highly evocative visual-verbal collages of Kim Blaeser's photo-poems aside, I have tried deliberately to restrict my discussion to evocations rather than indexical or illustrative use of images. That the dramatic works in chapter 6 are a departure from this methodology represents a particular relationship between image and script where, as in the written texts here, the images in question directly complicate the relationship between forms of textuality, entering into Teuton's graphic-oral-critical triad. Again, there are many artworks that meet any definition of the imagetext, including Nadia Myre's *Indian Act*, or much of Robert Houle's or Carl Bream's work, all of whom make provocative, challenging use of different kinds of document. Such productions, again, cry out for further consideration in this jurisdiction and absolutely form part of what we might see as a wider graphic continuum in which literary and visual arts bear the marks of a common relationship to both the graphic traditions of Anishinaabe artists, thinkers, and visionaries and the traditions of survivance and resistance that undergird an aesthetic-intellectual sovereignty. More importantly, perhaps, such artists, like many of the writers explored here, intervene more incisively in art and literary historical discourses that relegate the Indigenous artist to fugitive status. Margaret Dubin, for instance, notes that, as far as the art-historical narrative has been concerned, "Indian people . . . are not seen as equal participants in a shared modernity, their interpretations of non-Native forms and styles . . . frequently viewed as mimicry rather than intelligent responses to larger human conditions" (1999, 158). The range and subject matter of material under scrutiny lends the lie to such assumptions, both in terms of Native contributions to modernity's aesthetics and more generally to modernity in the round. Equally significantly, Dubin continues: "Conversely, the revival of tribal forms is often seen as a direct continuation of ancient traditions, rather than an appropriation of symbols in promotion of sovereignty, or a personal aesthetic choice" (158). As I have tried to elucidate here, even apparent continuities represent aesthetic choices—and vice versa: thus, while even Vizenor lauds "George Morrison, the eminent painter" who "resisted the notion that there were essential, traditional connections between culture and creative art," while insisting that fellow Anishinaabe painter "Patrick DesJarlait . . . was more involved in the romantic images of the traditional past" (2000, ix), he occludes the crossover between the two, and the ways both artists, and both of their sources of inspiration, contribute to modernity in ways that mainstream discourse has failed to account for. It is a distinction, indeed, that his recent turn to the "cosmototemic" renders less sharply delineated.

If we return to my discussion of Mirzoeff in the introduction, we remember his confirmation that "in a sense, all visuality was and is imperial visuality, the shaping of modernity from the point of view of the imperial powers" (2011, 196). The writers included in this work strip back the veil to reveal the imperiality of the image of the *indian*. They go much further, though. Their engagement with the visual image, from the simple mark on a surface to the full span of contemporary fine art, along with the televisual and cinematic image, also unveils the degree to which the discourse about Indigenous expression and about writing itself fulfills a colonial taxonomic logic. In so engaging, these writers both foreground the significance of the visual to the literary traditions of the Anishinaabeg and recalibrate the gauges that define and confine epistemic breadth and depth. They perform what Joanna Hearne refers to in relation to Indigenous cinema as the "politics of seeing" (2012, 2), significant to a further elucidation of survivance and sovereignty: "Embedded in the politics of seeing *and being seen*," she writes, "are the possibilities of recognition and repatriation" (2; emphasis added). There is, then, an affinity between this literary appropriation of a wide range of images and image making and what Hearne outlines as a cinematic repatriation of archival images of Natives and *indians*. She further argues:

> These reflexive filmmaking strategies register the power of active Native vision at all points across the arc of image production, text, and reception, to assert a Native presence and politics of seeing. Vanishing becomes visibility, absence becomes presence, when an image once symbolic of Indian finality instead elicits tribal recognition and supports discourses of contemporary political sovereignty. (5)

Along analogous lines, these writers enact a form of visual sovereignty more commonly associated, for obvious reasons, with the visual and performing arts. With regard to the notion of "being seen" in the context of literary visuality, we witness not the literal, embodied presence of Native subjects, so much as the graphic (and graphic description) of forms of the visual that precisely "repatriates" myriad means of visual production to a vibrant, living present, recuperated from the discursive "finality" established by a variety of colonial narratives of loss, vanishing, primitivism, and their analogues. Such observations, though confined here to Anishinaabeg writing, are certainly applicable elsewhere. In "Painting 'Word-Pictures' in Place," for instance, Lisa Brooks writes, "In [Mohawk Poet Maurice] Kenny's work [the] craft of creating 'word pictures' in place is rooted both in modernist imagism and Indigenous pictographic writing. Kenny, like his heroine Alquippa, seeks neither 'honor nor loot' but 'only to write / on the rock, paint color for the grandchildren'" (2011, 112). Writing on the rock, writing on the page, forming what Brooks calls a "glyphic representation" in words that conjure images to displace and re-place: image and text, verbal and visual; an integrated whole rather than a category divide. Literally and figuratively this relationship between image and word unsettles the heavy burden of text in favor of a relational aesthetic that simultaneously evokes ways of seeing alongside ways of reading, and a relational ethic that foregrounds the power and the pressure of making marks on surfaces, whether they be letters, images, or both. Kenny is by no means alone.

Active articulations of the relationship between narrative (both spoken and written) and visual art-forms in contemporary Native literature go at least as far back as the moment Kenneth Lincoln designated the "Renaissance" in Native American literature. Writing of an exchange between Kiowa author N. Scott Momaday and Gus Blaisdell at the University of New Mexico Press prior to the publication of *The Way to Rainy Mountain*, Lincoln cites Momaday's terse response to the suggestion of a third-party reader. The suggestion concerns the syntax governing Momaday's description of the sight of a cricket, perched on a handrail, framed against the moon. The viewer's proximity to the cricket, and the trick of perspective, render the tiny creature proportionate to its lunar ground. In a letter to Blaisdell, Lincoln reports, "Momaday replied simply: 'Leave it alone. You don't seem to realize (as of course X doesn't) that this is one of the great images in our literature. If you lay a hand on it, I will cut your heart out.' Momaday explained further, 'I give some thought to what I write; I consider the alternatives. In every detail, this image is exactly what I want'" (1986, 104).

As many commentators have noted, that same image is then represented visually in Al Momaday's line drawing on the following page (see Teuton 2010 and Bernardin 2011 among others). Representative of "landmarks, icons, that indicate the right way...signs on a path" (Rader 2014, 302), Momaday's response to Blaisdell also gestures to a number of other aspects. On the one hand, it expresses a kind of literary visual sovereignty, in the author's resistance to alteration of "one of the great images in our literature." Evocative of the relational aspect of traditional storytelling, this makes an obvious claim for an understanding of the oral archive as literature. Yet that "our" is deliberately ambiguous in the context of Momaday's emergence on the literary scene as both a self-identifying Native American writer and an arch proponent of high modernist technique. He lays claim here, then, to both the image itself and to formal imagism and, in doing so, to both the living oral literary archive and its fundamental centrality to what Craig Womack will later insist on as the inverse understanding of the American canon: "tribal literatures are not some branch waiting to be grafted onto the main trunk. Tribal literatures are the *tree*" (1999, 6–7). In this formative exchange, then, we note several of the particular intellectual, ethical, and aesthetic histories to which the visual-verbal relationship attends.

To be sure, Momaday's second book is probably the most high-profile of a number of composite texts in which the visual and verbal interplay, but it is by no means an isolated phenomenon, nor was it the first. In this and such texts as Vizenor's *Summer in the Spring*, the interplay between text and images "emphasizes the values of the oral language rather than a total imposition of the philosophies of grammar and translation," lending a sense of material, performative vitality to the literary rendering of oral songs and stories (Spry 2012, 20). Such visual-verbal experimentation was also occurring north of the colonial border, in a slightly different way. In 1970, the year after Momaday was awarded his Pulitzer, Shoshone-Cree-Salish poet and painter Sock-a-jaw-wu, or Marion Sarain Stump, published *There Is My People Sleeping*, a product of his "overtly visual poetic depictions" (McKenzie 2007, 79). Stump moved to Alberta from the United States in the mid-1960s, working as a rancher, as an art instructor at the Saskatchewan Indian Cultural Centre, and as an actor, exhibiting his paintings and working on his first book (Armstrong and Grauer 2001, 80). Influenced by an earlier generation of artists of the U.S. southwest, as well as contemporaries from Native art schools such as Santa Fe alongside select European artists, and drawing a direct correlation between image and text, Stump described "a fully formed pictographic tradition and how this concrete system serves as the basis for his poetic artistry" (McKenzie 2007, 79). Stephanie McKenzie pairs Stump's text with Marty Dunn's *Red on White: The Biography of Duke Redbird*, but she notes "the disproportionate number of works from the [Native Canadian] Renaissance which include images" (79). Stump's endeavor stands out in its milieu precisely because it is a creative production, albeit the text is minimal and highly fragmented. Nevertheless, significant editions of traditional stories preceded it in Canada at this time and were also illustrated. These include works by artist-writers who were also deeply invested in pictographic traditions, such as George Clutesi's *Son of Raven, Son of Deer* (1967), illustrated by Clutesi himself, and

Norval Morriseau's self-illustrated *Legends of My People: The Great Ojibway* (1965), discussed briefly in chapter 2. In Morriseau's case, the relationship between word and image, and the spiritual nature of his material—the revelation of which was objected to by some of his Nation—offers perhaps the most explicit correlation between the twentieth-century image-text and its older precursors.

The interweaving of visual and verbal, then, describes an aesthetic that, by no means universal, might nevertheless be said to offer common ground in an ethics of seeing and storying experience that embraces polyvalency and resists the absolute primacy of any one form. It persists in fairly direct illustrative terms, such as in the collaborations between Anishinaabe poet Mark Turcotte and artist Kathleen Presnell (*Songs of Our Ancestors* [1995], *The Feathered Heart* [1995], and more), or in Peter Blue Cloud's (Aroniawenrate) comical accompaniments to his own *Elderberry Flute Song: Contemporary Coyote Tales* (1982), and in more complex, dialogic expression in, for example, Sherman Alexie's *Old Shirts and New Skins* (1996; illustrated by Elizabeth Woody), or the deft interplay both through word and photograph, of poetry and clay figure in Nora Noranjo-Morse's *Mud Woman: Poems from the Clay* (1997). That these texts are reemerging in discussions that attend precisely to the interpenetration of movement and meaning between picture and text is perhaps testament to several factors, but there are three that are relatively self-evident: the first speaks to the extraordinary range (and powerful political implications) of decolonial articulations of Indigenous sovereignty. Although critical challenges to the territorially bound (and therefore colonially implicated) nature of sovereignty as understood in relation to the nation-state arguably find their champion in Vine Deloria Jr., it was in the early 1990s, with Robert Warrior's examination of Deloria and Warrior's call to recognize the intellectual sovereignty of Native-centered historiography that those bounded notions began truly to unravel. In a similar move, art and film scholars such as Jolene Rickard and Michelle Raheja have turned to questions of visual sovereignty within their respective fields, questions that perhaps underlie much of the inquiry into the image-text, and certainly offer means of understanding that interaction as more than simply the semiotic encoding of the marketing of "Indianness." The second context is simply the burgeoning of Native owned-and-developed visual media, which would include the ever-increasing exposure of Indigenous film and television media, along with other vehicles such as digital and graphic media.

Thirdly, but by no means finally, the rise to prominence of increasing numbers of exciting visual artists working variously and to different ends with narrative, text, Indigenous sign systems and decorative motifs, popular cultural narratives and symbols, and decolonizing methodologies related to "colonial" documents such as maps, treaties, ID cards, street signs, and so on, along with the embrace by literary scholars of the intersections between visual and textual forms, promises to continue in its significance. Thus, artists such as Nadia Myre, Andrea Carlson, Christi Belcourtt, Jeffrey Veregge, America Meredith, Hulleah Tsinhnahjinnie, and Rickard herself join other internationally renowned artists such as Hock E Aye Vi Edgar Heap of Birds, Jaune Quick-to-See-Smith, George Longfish, and numerous others in the critical purview of literary scholars as well as scholars of the visual arts. In a similar vein, the heightened visibility of Indigenous texts that relate not only to cultural identification but, explicitly, to political and diplomatic understandings, texts such as those represented by wampum belts, provides a meeting point between text (in all its possibilities) and image in the work of many Haudenosaunee visual artists, including Alan Michelson, Shelley Niro, Greg Hill, G. Peter Jemison, Joey David, and, of course, most pertinently in this context, the "innovative mash-ups" of Eric Gansworth (Rader 2014, 308).

Onondaga artist-writer Gansworth's interplay of image and text—sometimes an organizing metaphor, such as in *Nickel Eclipse* (2001)—is often more theoretically searching, such that, as Bernardin argues, "Gansworth's aesthetic collaboration of text and image reaffirms foundational Haudenosaunee ways of knowing aimed at ensuring survival" (2011, 178). Gansworth's work is also worth pausing on briefly for its insight into visuality. In her introduction to *Visualities: Perspectives on Contemporary American Indian Film and Art*, Denise K. Cummings notes that "visuality concerns the field of vision as a site of power and social control" (2011, xiv). While, for Mirzoeff, the image, and control of the image, paradoxically, becomes the means by which people as objects are "blinded" in the hierarchy of imperial visuality, it also becomes a significant means of resistance and reappropriation of autonomy. Central to this dynamic, the question of who controls the images and what those images are, can be seen to be central to the dialogue between text and image. We need think only of such iconic images as the various portraits of Pocahontas/Matoake/Amunate/Rebecca Rolfe, Benjamin West's *The Death of General Wolfe*, or John Vanderlyn's *The Death of Jane McRea* to glimpse the legacy of the visual rhetorics of empire; it is precisely through such images, the highly visual literary portrayals of "*indians*" by authors such as James Fenimore Cooper, and, of course, the visuality of the Wild West show and the cinematic Western that popular perceptions of who (and what) Native peoples are illuminates the dominance of images over the realities of lived experience. Writers such as Gansworth, along with many other contemporary writers, artists, and filmmakers, though by no means bound in a one-dimensional tussle with the colonial legacy, construct a form of countervisuality that entirely disrupts and displaces the singular identities placed on Native people through popular (mis)representation. This functions in a figurative sense in Gansworth's work, through his "densely cross-pollinated iconography of Haudenosaunee stories and referents drawn from popular culture and music" (Bernardin 2011, 178), as well as European art conventions and artists. It also functions in a more literal sense, in a novel such as *Mending Skins* (2005), featuring the Seventh Annual Conference of the Society for Protection and Reclamation of Indian Images, kitsch-Indian obsessed art historian Annie Boans (daughter of the intimidating Tuscarora woman, Shirley Mounter), and a comical-yet-nuanced examination of the internalization of and internal conflict over popular cultural stereotypes of Indianness.

While Heid Erdrich's recent poetry, as discussed in chapter 2, captures the vitality of contemporary Indigenous protest through the adaptation of old forms to new technologies, it returns us to a very different, but no less "resistant" form at the end of the nineteenth century. Ledger art as it developed in the nineteenth century (particularly after the imprisonment of warriors at Fort Marion, Florida) has a well-charted connection back to Plains graphic traditions (see Keyser 2000), maintaining and in some ways developing the narrative forms of pictorial art associated with inscription on bark and painting on stone and hide. That latter pictographic tradition—frequently designated a "supplement" (whether "dangerous" or not remains unspecified!) to the oral tradition (Hail 2013, xv)—found its expression among incarcerated warriors using colored pencils and used ledger books. Denise Low-Weso ascribes the winter count—often spiraling pictographic accounts of historic events—to this same tradition, insisting that "as my students and I have encountered these sign-texts, European categories collapse. The images assert a legitimate alternative literacy" (2006, 85). The sense of resistance to imposition is multiple in that notion. The ledger drawings themselves potentially sustained individual agency and Indigenous sovereignty through that final period of containment; they defiantly combined traditional techniques with contemporary materials such that practitioners created the palimpsestic ground of a "space of foreign calculations, thereby transforming the nature of their own drawing and the ledger book itself, creating a middle place, an in-between place, in a place of writing" (Blume 1996, 40); and we might, then, reintroduce Kulchyski's question here, and ask what kind of literature—and therefore what kind of destabilizing power—such creations represent in direct relation to the structural (state) forms of literacy the ledger books and the fort-prisons invoke.

Ledger art, of course, persists in a variety of forms from the relatively straight contemporary iterations of the historic form represented by Dolores Purdy Corcoran, Terence Guardipee, or Linda Haukaas, to the often more playful work of Dwayne Wilcox and especially Dallin Maybee. Beyond those representative practices, though, Low-Weso points out that ledger art texts "inform contemporary writers' history and methods. They are vehicles of continuity, following historic and personal narratives into the present time" (2006, 84). In particular, she picks out James Welch's *Fool's Crow* for its recounting of "events that are in the Newberry ledger book" (84–85), but other examples spring to mind. Lance Henson's poetry collection *A Cheyenne Sketchbook* (1985) evokes the form in its title alone, while Diane Glancy's *Lone Dog's Winter Count* (1991) more explicitly claims continuity to "this idea of commemoration[, w]ith contemporary pictographs in the form of poems" (jacket blurb).

The literalness of that latter claim does a disservice to the rich complexity of Glancy's poetry here—not because pictography itself cannot be complex, but because the blurb infers a kind of ekphrastic representation of the visual form that the poems do not simply (or simplistically) serve up. Instead, they evoke the full re-lational and processual nature of the multiform tradition in which the winter count performs. "The tribe waits for the voice of Lone Dog to pierce the silence," one triplet in *Lone Dog's Winter Count* begins; "to father thought / like children running into their heads" (13). The relationship between the act of recording and the document as utterance, the generalized audience and the select voice reading-remembering, and the temporal flow forward and backward across generations that the poems invoke speak to survivance, even as individual poems contrast the desire to draw with the violence of writing as instructed in residential schools ("The First Reader: Santee Training School, 1873"), or navigate the psychic and even epistemological ground, shifting in the sudden changes of the late nineteenth-century Plains ("Portrait of Lone Dog"). The appropriative gesture of Glancy's subject—she is of Cherokee descent, while *Lone Dog's Winter Count* is a Yanktonais Nakota text—is not isolated with regard to the Plains tradition. Indeed, over many years, ledger art in particular has engrossed and at times aesthetically motivated writers and artists across First Nations' boundaries.

While for a writer like Leslie Marmon Silko, whose well-known evocations of sand painting in *Ceremony* entwine that nation- and geographically specific form into a polyphonic narrative of healing, all immediately available cultural material is potentially the stuff of ceremony, Vizenor, as briefly discussed in chapter 2, reaches to the vital motion of the Plains pictographic tradition to complement his already extensive engagement with the practices of the Anishinaabeg.

> The warriors and their horses are pictured in motion, the artistic transmotion of native sovereignty. The scenes and motion were of memories and consciousness. . . . The transmotion of ledger art is a creative connection to the motion of horses depicted in winter counts and heraldic hide paintings. . . . Native transmotion is seen in the raised hooves of horses, the voice lines, traces of arrows, the curve of feathers, footprints, and the trail of buffalo blood in a hunt. (1998, 179)

The active, dynamic, and visionary presence of the visual motif here—not only a picture but lines, traces, curves, prints, trails, marks of narrative and markers of sovereignty—echoes, Low-Weso suggests, the obviative (fourth person) presence Vizenor identifies in oral testimony. As such, she writes, "the 'presence' is the body of tradition that, in the ledger texts, interacts with image-texts" (2006, 85). The transcendent (and transient) qualities are implicit in much of the work I have discussed in this book.

The direct engagement of artists is by no means unique to Vizenor. Chagall makes an appearance among other Native and non-Native luminaries in Gansworth's *Nickel Eclipse*, while Louise Erdrich treats the murals of Mexican artist José Clemente Orozco in poetic form ("Orozco's Christ," for instance, appears in her second book of poetry, *Baptism of Desire*; his *The Epic of American Civilization* is situated in the Baker Memorial Library at her alma mater, Dartmouth). Cherokee author Thomas King also deploys an artist—Monroe Swimmer—in his 1999 novel, *Truth and Bright Water*. There, Swimmer engages in various strategies designed, quite literally, to paint out the impositions of the colonial world. Beginning by painting Natives back into museum-held landscapes, Swimmer takes his work to an even more literal level in his pursuit of reversing the colonial erasure of Indigenous peoples and spaces by painting out a church that sits like the heaving prow of a ship overlooking the Canada-U.S. border in the Canadian prairies. Along with a quilt assembled by the protagonist's mother from all the detritus of life, King's novel navigates art as analogue for the literary endeavor through motifs of erasure and accumulation: the former arguably limited by its inability to remove the traces of the "real" placed under erasure; the latter replete with the sharp pins (literally) of painful memories. If each in turn represents a protest-art of anticoloniality on the one hand and more intimate memory on the other, King does not make a judgment call on either. The former has a political exigency to it, while the latter of course combines the joyful with the miserable; the former, arguably, is bound to fail in its largest ambitions, while the latter, though arguably more consummate to healing, makes of the quilt a promising cover that cannot warm without also pricking. That he chooses visual media, and the visual arts, to explore such terrain is, however, indicative of the power and indeed efficacy of these forms in the literary sphere.

Amid all of this discussion there is of course one type of text that is both book and visual art, that falls squarely into neither my insistence on the evocation of the visual in written language nor the wholly visual art that utilizes text in an aesthetic or instrumental fashion. Margaret Noodin, for instance, writes that "today, the tradition of telling stories through pictures continues in comics as Chad Solomon and others work to provide a more complex understanding of native people's identity and experience" (Noori 2010, 56). Add to this the fact that the graphic novel is among the fastest growing areas of popular publishing, and that graphic novels by Anishinaabe artists and writers are very much on the rise. As I hope my reasoning above shows, this project is not intended to be exclusionary on any grounds other than space. I have thus sought to prioritize literary-led over visual art–led productions. That said, this book—or at least a different version of it—could readily have included a chapter on the wealth of graphic fiction being written and drawn by Native writers and artists, and collaborations between Native and non-Native artists of both stripes. Anishinaabe producers, as ever, are never far from the foreground, and the new series at Michigan State University Press, *Sovereign Traces*, has recently produced its first volume. *Not (Just) (An)Other*, coedited by Gordon Henry Jr. and Elizabeth LaPensée (2018) includes graphic reimaginings of stories by nine Native writers, four of whom are Anishinaabeg (Henry, Vizenor, Niigaanwewidam Sinclair, Louise Erdrich), and include two Anishinaabe artists (LaPensée and Neal Shannacappo) among eight. In Henry/Shannacappo's "The Prisoner of Haiku," in particular, the images strip the already visual text of all extraneous detail, rendering it closer to the haiku that the titular character writes and emphasizing the relationship in that character's story between nonverbal, verbal, and visual forms of resistance to colonialism.

Meanwhile, Camille Callison, Indigenous Services librarian at the University of Manitoba, is responsible for the Mazinbiige Indigenous Graphic Novel Collection, a gathering of over two hundred titles, good and bad, both by and about Indigenous people. The collection's title—Mazinbiige—is readily recognizable as an

Anishinaabe word, that word "mazin," dwelled on at length by Louise Erdrich in *Books and Islands in Ojibwe Country*, making an appearance again. The title means, Hugh Goldring informs, "beautiful images and writing" (2015). Niigaanwewidam Sinclair, also at the University of Manitoba, teaches a course on graphic fiction, a "vehicle for self-determination" (Goldring 2015), has given public lectures on the form, and has written for various graphic productions. Portage and Main Press, where Sinclair edits the Debwe Series, also has a growing Indigenous graphic novels portfolio that includes Swampy Cree author David Alexander Robertson's *7 Generations* tetralogy and *Tales from Big Spirit* series. Among Anishinaabe comic producers, artist and game designer Elizabeth LaPensée currently has many to her credit, as writer or as writer and artist/colorist. Their subject matter ranges from the steampunk *How the West Was Lost* (2008) to retellings of traditional stories such as *The Nature of Snakes* (2012) to, particularly pertinent in this context, the one-page *Our Words*, which recalls the destruction of birchbark scrolls and featured in the #0 issue of the Indigenous Narrative Collective's *Universe* (2012). Jay Odjick, meanwhile, is the creator (as writer) of *Kagaga: The Raven*, a comic that has also been adapted successfully into a thirteen-episode animated series screened on APTN in Canada, while Chad Solomon and Chris Meyer's multivolume *Adventures of Rabbit and Bear Paws* gains increasing visibility. Solomon talks of guidance from community elders; meanwhile, the comic *A Hero's Voice*, "commissioned by the Mille Lacs Band of Ojibwe," was itself "written by tribal elders, writers, and artists" and "designed to help local children, native and non-native, get to know important figures not mentioned in the public schools" (Noori 2010, 64). Noodin also reports on "other comics, including *The Mitgwaki Strips* by Lynn Johnston; numerous editorial cartoons, most notably *Baloney and Bannock* by Perry McLeod-Shabogesic; the health and healing comics produced by the Healthy Aboriginal Network; *The Illustrated History of the Chippewas of Nawash*; and many more," arguing, like those mentioned above, that they "serve as examples that the tradition of combining visual and verbal narrative continues" (Noori 2010, 69). Noodin's approach to the comic or graphic novel takes a similar line to her insights in *Bawaajimo*. She argues:

> if centuries of Anishinaabe were able to develop and deploy a complex agglutinative structure made mostly of verbs to communicate images, ideas, and relationships across time, there must then be a way of interpreting them based on more than printed and published texts. Furthermore, the layered construction of the sound and meaning is perfectly suited to the comic format, where text, line, and color combine to communicate action and relationships. (Noori 2010, 58)

Future work in this area will doubtless develop a more incisive line in this direction than I am able to at this juncture. Equally, critics well versed in the broader conventions of the comic novel are, and will be, developing the discourse around the Indigenous graphic novel in fresh directions.

If I finish with a partial list of materials I have not covered in this project, it is not so much an attempt to plug the gaps as recognition of the sheer extent of the Anishinaabe—and broader Native—literary sphere. I have not ventured any rigorous analysis in these closing pages, but rather a series of observations with a view to highlighting intersections with the prior analysis here, and points of departure to which the examples I use necessarily point in their more literal use of visual imagery and more explicit play off between text and image. I do so not by way of apology for oversight—it was never my intention to include overtly visual texts in this analysis—but by way of recognition of the increasing significance (and indeed, brilliance) of this new generation of graphic artists, as well as the wealth of talent already well known. All of the material included in this study, though, embodies the highly diverse but nevertheless coherent and consistent visuality in the highly "textual" narrative traditions of Anishinaabe aesthetic and intellectual production. To say so is not, by any means, to imply an equivalence between highly discrete forms of alternative literacy. Indeed, as I have reiterated throughout, forms of graphic production in Anishinaabe culture have always operated in tandem with, through intersection with, and as complementary to the oral tradition. While there can be no doubt that settler-colonial mechanisms endeavored with purpose to alienate the people from their spoken heritage—through the manifest theft of language, and the ignorant traduction of intellectual and spiritual practices—it is largely through the practice of "salvage" and its ideological underpinnings that we understand the oral tradition, like the "Indian," to have vanished. In fact, and not underestimating the considerable violence of its suppression, which still impacts on many thousands today, the oral tradition persists in a variety of forms and contexts. Looking to the interactions posited here between vision, image, and story is far from a nostalgic notion. Neither is it a conservative countertestimony to modern technologies. Rather, flatly, it rejects the binary in the contexts considered—beginning with oral/alphabetic literacy—that maintains expectations of Indigenous arts practices, and insists on perpetuating narratives of Indigenous cultures at odds with technological modernity.

NOTES

Introduction

1. I am certainly not alone in this view of the inherently politicized world of Anishinaabe literature; see, for instance, Adam Spry's new monograph *Our Warpaint Is Writers' Ink: Anishinaabe Literary Transnationalism*. Unfortunately, the monograph came out in the final throes of editing this book, so it does not feature here in a way it otherwise might have done. The coincidence, however, speaks to the particular currency of Anishinaabe literature at this moment in time.

2. In *Dancing on Our Turtle's Back*, Leanne Betasamosake Simpson writes, "The act of visioning for Nishnaabeg people is a powerful act of resurgence, because these visions create Shki-kiin, new worlds" (2011a, 146).

3. Among those whose absence is a felt presence in the chapters of this book, one deserves specific mention: Basil Johnston. Johnston's impressive catalogue of fifteen books in English and five in Ojibwemowin, as well as the script of a film (*The Man, the Snake, and the Fox*, dir. Tony Snowsill, 1978) and a joint writing credit for a second film, *Native Indian Folklore* (National Film Board of Canada, 1993), underlines his standing, in Sinclair's words, as "one of [the Anishinaabeg's] greatest ancestral intellectuals and elders" (2013b, 83). The visual image is ever present in his publications, a manifestation of the mark of human hand on rock, bark, hide, and paper; of the intricacy of quill,

bead, sinew, and thread, and of the patterning on birchbark baskets. While Johnston does not overpopulate his publications with images, the relationship between story and image, between the imagined and what Gerald Vizenor calls the "imagic," vision and the visionary tradition, is well established in and through his work. I am, however, concerned with the visionary only insofar as it is represented through engagement with art and artists. It is ultimately a combination of this factor and the simple fact that he writes neither poetry nor fiction that excludes Johnston from this study.

4. Perhaps most instructive here is Teuton's observation that "the oral impulse is the impulse communities and individuals feel as the need to create and maintain knowledge in relatively direct response to one another. . . . This definition is essentially the opposite of how orality is understood in oral-literate theory (as redundant, conservative, homeostatic, etc.)" (2010, 31).

5. Joddy Murray explains, "the reason he called it 'pictorial' [reflective speech] . . . reveals itself through the imagistic qualities of non-discursive language. The 'intonation' that accompanies speech is, in effect, a non-discursive image made up of everything other than the actual discursive language being conveyed" (2009, 43).

6. Although it is important to add a caveat. Comic books and graphic novels are an increasingly popular form with Anishinaabe writers within the past few years, including such productions as *A Hero's Voice* and *Dreams of Looking Up* devised by the Mille Lacs Band (see Goff 1996; 1999); Chad Solomon and Chris Meyer's *Adventures of Rabbit and Bear Paws* series (2006); Joe Odjick's *Kagaga: The Raven* (2011); Elizabeth LaPensée's selection of short comics; collaborative work in collections such as the *Moonshot* volumes edited by Hope Nicholson (2016), which include authors and artists such as Niigaanwewidam James Sinclair and Beth LaPensée, and more. I will briefly return to them in the conclusion. However, these art forms are usually more of a collaboration between artists and writer, rather than writer-led projects. As such, they bring in complicating factors that I felt would not be conducive to this study.

7. While affirming its often strategic significance, Martínez nevertheless notes that "intellectual is a foreign word imposed upon individuals who never described their roles as writers and speakers in such elitist terms. Consequently, one can argue that *intellectual* signals a colonized mind more than it evokes an Indigenous perspective" (2014, 30). Nevertheless, there are Indigenous intellectuals and Indigenous forms of intellectualism.

8. I invoke Ngũgĩ partly in the spirit of Elisabeth Cook-Lynn, rather than because I wish to prioritize the mechanisms of postcolonial studies. In her essay "The American Indian Fiction Writer: 'Cosmopolitanism, Nationalism, the Third World, and First Nation Sovereignty'" (1993), she outlines affinities between politically motivated First Nations

and Third World writers grounded in anticolonial resistance. While Ngũgĩ focuses on language, I must leave that conversation to true linguists and to speakers and theorists of Anishinaabemowin: Anishinaabe scholars such as Margaret Noodin, Howard Kimewon, Gordon Jourdain, Anton Treuer, Roger Roulette, Niigaanwewidam James Sinclair, and Basil Johnston, or non-Native scholars such as John Nichols and Roger Spielman to name just a small sample.

9. We must not forget the importance of the material, tactile object itself. As Cree artist, writer, director, and activist Cheryl L'Hirondelle states: "What these historical Indigenous practices . . . suggest is our ability to take account of vital information with the creation of a physical object and move beyond what has been oversimplified as solely orally centered transmission processes. The 'object' is charged and embodies the interplay of processes between the oral and the written (notched/drawn) used to aid in its own retelling" (2014, 157).

10. In fact, she was long thought the first Native literary poet until Parker's *Changing Is Not Vanishing* (2011) in which he provides an example of an earlier possibility.

11. This—inevitably—includes his brokerage of Ojibwe cession of vast tracts of land (thirteen million acres) in the 1836 Treaty of Washington, for instance.

12. Sinclair describes *The Mishomis Book: The Voice of the Ojibway* as "one of the most popular books ever on Anishinaabeg culture" and notes that it was "originally produced for a small cultural revitalization program in Minneapolis" during the American Indian Movement era (2013a, 39).

13. Heid Erdrich restricts her theorizing in *"Name': Literary Ancestry as Presence"* (2013b) to a small number of nineteenth-century literary forebears, including Maungwudaus, Bamewawagezhikaquay, and Kahgegagahbowh. Margaret Noodin, whose insightful *Bawaajimo* (2014a) offers the first real example of single-authored, book-length Anishinaabemowin-derived literary criticism, limits her deft readings to four of the best-known authors: Louise Erdrich, Jim Northrup, Basil Johnston, and Vizenor. Other scholars, such as Leanne Simpson, are explicitly embedded in nation-specific (nationalist) endeavors, while still others, such as Joseph Bauerkemper, combine tightly focused nation-defined readings with broader transnational theoretical moves that promise significant developments in the trans-Indigenous and beyond. Niigaanwewidam James Sinclair and Adam Spry offer the most comprehensive study of Anishinaabe literature to date, in Sinclair's doctoral dissertation "Nindoodemag Bagijiganan: A History of Anishinaabeg Narrative" (2013a), with a monograph forthcoming, and Spry's *Our Warpaint Is Writers' Ink*, deriving from his own doctoral dissertation. Some significant names are left out either in their entirety or in relation to their creative

work. The influential Ignatia Broker, only belatedly coming to be recognized outside Anishinaabe readerships, is one; George Copway's fellow commentators Peter Jones (Kahkewaquonaby) and George Henry (Maungwudaus) likewise. The wider array might include non-Ojibwe Anishinaabe writers such as Simon Pokagan (Bodéwadmi) and Andrew Blackbird (Odawa); writers of traditional stories such as Eliza Morrin Morrison and John Couchois Wright; autobiographers, advocates, sharers of Anishinaabe environmental knowledge such as John Rogers, Keewaydinoquay Peschel, and Wub-e-ki-niew; journalists and advocates like Gus and Theodore Beaulieu and Waubgeshig Rice; novelists such as Richard Wagamese and, of course, David Treuer, to whose books I turn intermittently; not to mention the myriad published poets, dramatists, short story writers, and scholars who do not feature in these pages.

14. The contest between art-historical and anthropological approaches to precontact art forms/artifacts, for instance, has produced much debate, not least over redundant questions of "authenticity." It was, perhaps ironically, the modernist artists of Europe in the early twentieth century who forced the reevaluation of so-called primitive arts.

15. One objection that some readers may have is that the Anishinaabe writers included in this project are responding to wider movements in English-language literature and arts, particularly since the advent of modernism. To look at them in isolation, therefore, is to omit influences and inspirations that may be crucial to their art practice. To a certain extent, I agree with this point. However, I would respond that while such art movements as imagism, concrete poetry, visual poetry, and so on, have been considered widely, this is one of the very few studies to treat Anishinaabe writing as an organic whole. As such, I am happy to leave that global contextualization to other scholars—or a different project.

16. Etymological dictionaries often ascribe the origin of the word "book" to the proto-Germanic noun for beech (as in tree), referring possibly to the practice of inscribing runic patterns on beech tablets. The *OED* explains that this etymology has been contested but ultimately defended: "recent accounts have defended the hypothesis that BOOK *n*. and BEECH *n*. are ultimately related, citing parallel cases where the name of a material and the derived name of an item made from it belong to different morphological classes (e.g. Sanskrit *bhūrjá-* (masculine) birch tree, (feminine) birch bark used for writing: see BIRCH *n*.)."

17. In the words of Socrates: "And when [speeches] have been once written down they are tumbled about anywhere among those who may or may not understand them, and know not to whom they should reply, to whom not; and, if they are maltreated or abused, they have no parent to protect them; and they cannot protect or defend themselves" (Derrida [1976], qtg Plato). The "orphaning" of writing from speech sets up for Derrida the false

dichotomy of logocentrism.

18. Foucault's basic point is that word and image are irreducible into one another. At its most fundamental level, it is in the interaction between text and image, the expansive, supplementary and complementary function of the visual, that I embrace Mitchell's thinking. I argue that it is that productive convergence that challenges the ideological apparatus that have tended to relegate Indigenous art and Indigenous literatures to the margins.

19. I use the variant *indian* to invoke Vizenor's coinage for the hyperreal, colonially constructed simulation of the Native, present throughout his work.

20. I use the word here in the sense Mitchell does in "What Do Pictures Want?" (Grønstad and Vågnes 2006), where he contrasts images themselves with "pictures, the specific, material supports or embodiments of images".

21. This is a deliciously ironic example, since *The Right to Look* appeared during Occupy, and Mirzoeff himself had an Occupy blog (he saw it as a potential countervisuality): http://www.nicholasmirzoeff.com/O2012/.

22. Keya Ganguly writes of the postcolonial as a "particular mode of historical emergence" (2004, 162) rather than as an age or an epoch. Enabling the open-ended treatment of the postcolonial, Ganguly's phrasing admits the possibility that the post- does not necessarily signify that the colonial is over.

23. For further examination of the relationship between Native American studies and postcolonial studies, see Cook-Lynn (1993), Weaver (1997, 2013), Cheyfitz (1991, 2002), and Byrd (2011), among others.

24. Language revitalization programs are going from strength to strength, but language learning cannot, yet, be universally expected.

25. The exceptions to this, clearly, are the early nineteenth-century work of Jane Johnston Schoolcraft and the early twentieth-century recordings of Frances Densmore. In the case of the former, I will be dealing largely with her English writings, but will also follow the guides laid out by Robert Dale Parker (who himself collaborated with Anishinaabemowin speakers such as Margaret Noodin). In the case of Densmore, I will principally be navigating the cultural context of production and documentation rather than the specific content of the dreamsongs.

Chapter 1. An Indian Well Versed: (Con)Textualizing Anishinaabeakiing— George Copway and Jane Johnston Schoolcraft

1. It is no great surprise that Copway, the ex-Methodist missionary, considerably dilutes the spiritual functions and significance of pictography.

2. Potential cross-fertilization between Native and African American rhetoric in this period is inevitable. Douglass's *Narrative*, printed and distributed in 1845, sold in very great numbers; it cannot be believed that men such as George Copway were ignorant of the growing abolitionist movement and its use of both oratory and text. Meanwhile, some of Douglass's speeches carry echoes of earlier Native rhetoric—compare, for instance, Douglass's "What to the Slave Is the Fourth of July?" (1852) with sections of William Apess's "Eulogy on King Phillip" (1836).

3. In *Red Dreams, White Nightmares* (2015), Robert M. Owens closes with an epilogue in which he describes efforts by Black Hawk to create a Pan-Indigenous/African American alliance using foreign aid. Owens describes the limited likelihood of success for such an alliance by the 1830s due to generalized fear of such affiliations, fostered by public rhetoric about the threat each group posed to wider society.

4. Henry Louis Gates's important discussion in *The Signifying Monkey* of the gap between the slave narrative's bearing witness to common humanity and the manifestation of "literary culture" allows us, I think, to understand the ways in which writing, so commonly read as assimilative, remains subversive in the context of subjugation.

5. I will refer to Jane generally as Bamewawagezhikaquay in order to keep her clearly distinct from Henry (Schoolcraft throughout) whose famous surname has often obscured his wife's brilliance.

6. Justice, who also draws on Warkentin, notes that alphabetic literacy is a "central pillar of the civilized/savage binary . . . in that civilized peoples write down their ideas and knowledge in lasting textual form . . . whereas savage peoples, whose knowledge is limited to something vaguely understood as 'the oral tradition,' do not" (2015, 296). Bizarrely, this notion still has traction in some quarters, as Justice illuminates in his brief discussion of *Disrobing the Aboriginal Industry: The Deception behind Indigenous Cultural Preservation* by Frances Widdowson and Albert Howard (2008).

7. See, among others, Bellin (2001), Walker (1997), Donald B. Smith (1997, 2013), Peyer (1997), and of course early reviews of his *Traditional History*, such as one in *Literary World*, which suggests "he does not appear to have made up his mind whether to be a white man or an Indian" (D. Smith 2013, 199).

8. I say apparently counterintuitive here because, as Dale Knobel (1984) relates, members of the Order of United Americans advocated against removals and generally reached out to Native groups in ways that make such alliances slightly easier to imagine in light of Copway's push for a self-governing Indian territory. Similarly, Peyer points out that in spite of Copway's earlier abolitionist sentiment, his switching allegiance to the "avowedly racist and antiabolitionist party" is in keeping with the reformists' having "well nigh

forsaken the 'Indian problem'" (1997, 258).

9. Said confusion is exemplified by biographical reports of Copway's death. The *Dictionary of Canadian Biography*, for instance, asserts that he died at Lac-des-deux-montagnes in January 1869. That entry was written by Donald B. Smith, who tells this version of the tale also in "Kahgegagahbowh: Canada's First Literary Celebrity in the United States" (1997). Yet, in his most recent study of Copway in *Mississauga Portraits*, he relates a different tale, in which the Copway who arrived at Oka was, in fact, George's younger brother David, who "had appeared at the Lake of Two Mountains (Oka) Reserve, just west of Montreal. There he had declared himself a 'pagan,' eager to join the Roman Catholic Church. David died at the Lake of Two Mountains, in January 1869, just after his baptism as a Roman Catholic and immediately before his first communion" (2013, 208). George's death, meanwhile, was reported in the *Ypsilanti Commercial* of July 3, 1869, as having occurred recently in that Michigan city at the residence of Rev. Mr. Spear (208).

10. In "Self-Reliance," Ralph Waldo Emerson writes: "Speak what you think now in hard words and to-morrow speak what to-morrow thinks in hard words again, though it contradict everything you said today" (1841, 7). Emerson's commitment to individualism, his rejection of "foolish consistency" and commitment to false ideals, of course underpins his contradictions. And yet Emerson, too, makes famous calls for forms of collectivity—in art, in politics. Copway's vulnerability to the charge not simply of inconsistency but self-contradiction is driven in part by his apparent nostalgia for a Herderian national community on the one hand and the fact, one feels, that he is an American Indian on the other. As such, his frequent departures from the understood Native ethos of communal and community living becomes harder for critics to forgive than were he a white American. He suffers, in other words, under the burden of challenge and expectation for Native Americans both of his moment and of time immemorial.

11. Jill Lepore's account of "Indians who could read and write" in the seventeenth century is a classic iteration of a familiar "caught between two worlds but fully accepted by neither" scenario—a scenario that dominates our understanding of this figure. I suspect, however, that this is less true for the Ojibwe, particularly the Mississauga and other more easterly bands, in the mid-nineteenth century. I therefore place the onus here on how the writing "Indian" is perceived by non-Native society.

12. The first edition of *The Ojibway Conquest* presented Copway's Anishinaabe name in large font on the title page, which read "*The Ojibway Conquest: A Tale of the Northwest* BY KAH-GE-GA-GAH-BOWH." In significantly smaller font beneath, was printed "G. Copway, Chief of the Ojibway Nation."

13. Rex, a defender of Copway, responds with understandable vitriol to readings like

Walker's, where she writes that they

> position Copway as a transculturated individual with a conflicted sense of self
> who is unable, in both his life and his texts, to incorporate his Ojibwe heritage
> into the white, antebellum American society that was thirsty for exotic Indian
> curiosities. These readings conflate the events of Copway's life with the material
> in his texts, add a dash of speculation about his mental processes, and finally
> provide an unsupportable reading of Copway's psychological state rather than
> his literary endeavors. (2006, 2)

14. In fact, Schoolcraft differentiated between "kekeewin," which "could be read and understood by everyone in the tribe," and "kekenowin," which were understood only by mide priests (Angel 2002, 102).

15. Alexander Pope's *Essay on Man* (1734) includes the immortal phrase "Lo, the poor Indian," which would come by the end of the nineteenth century to signify in the popular media as a proper noun—in numerous op-eds concerning "Lo" and his demise.

16. And of course Schoolcraft is often self-contradictory: indeed, his own analysis of the "Indian mind" turns on the notion that they are unable to reflect on the past. This ultimately reflects his tendency—intrinsic to his desire to universalize human development—to compare Ojibwe pictography with other writing systems and, thus, rank it in a kind of hierarchy in which ideographs, phonetic signs, and alphabetic symbols each take their place in "the onward train of letters" (1860, 342), in which they represent that most immoral of pre-Christian stages—idolatry.

17. At this point all of this terrain—what is now Michigan, Wisconsin, and part of Minnesota—was the contiguous Michigan Territory. Michigan statehood would be achieved six years later in 1837, with Wisconsin Territory, briefly incorporating what would become Iowa, Minnesota, and parts of North and South Dakota, thus defined in preparation in 1836.

18. Parker writes: "Woolsey's effusive letters to JJS suggest that he had something of a crush on her. His description in a letter of 5 July, while lengthy . . . together with HRS's letter suggests a source or at the least a closely contemporary analog for the description in JJS's poem" (2007, 96).

19. James Duane Doty's journal reveals that the Doric arch was so-named during the 1820 Cass expedition to survey the western part of Michigan, which Schoolcraft participated in. Schoolcraft refers to it thus in his journals.

Chapter 2. X-ing Boundaries: Transmotion, Transformation, and the Art of Engaged Resistance in Contemporary Anishinaabe Poetics

1. The poem makes specific reference to the Mississippi ("the river that made us") and the Hudson ("where all this started"). The Mississippi as it runs through Minneapolis-St. Paul is the predominant artery depicted in the poem.

2. In another of very many reiterations of the term—and a classically evasive definition—Vizenor writes:

   > The concept of transmotion is a visionary consciousness of continental liberty, and constitutes the unmistakable traces and cues of a new aesthetic resistance and natural motion in the literature of Native Americans. The perception and sentiments of transmotion are incomparable and reach over, across and beyond, through creative stories of resistance and transcendence, the burdens of institutional dominance and state sovereignty. Native stories of natural reason and transmotion are not contained by discovery, treaties or reservations. (2010, 51 [n.2]).

3. That neglect is curious in light of the early work of poet-artists like Sarain Stump (Shoshone-Cree) and of course the artist Norval Morrisseau (Ojibwe), whose work (in Stump's case in *There Is My People Sleeping*, 1969) in the 1960s, coterminous with the consolidation of academic and popular interest in Native cultural resurgence, was directly influenced by the relationship between oral tradition and the pictographic traditions of the Plains and Great Lakes respectively. As noted in the introduction, it is a neglect highlighted in general terms by Craig Womack in *Red on Red* and among others, and addressed directly by a range of writers in the last ten or so years.

4. Ford confirms that this self-effacement is understood in the American tradition: Robert Blyth's assertion that "'haiku are self-obliterating' established the notion of haiku as a form of writing so suspicious of language and personality that it aims to dissolve when read, leaving the reader with an emotional experience rather than a representation of nature or a record of the self" (Ford 2009, 334).

5. Serving in Japan as a GI from 1953, Vizenor "discovered the power of literature, gained access to his own poetic heritage, and found a literary voice in occupied Japan. 'How ironic,' he says 'that my service as a soldier would lead me to haiku, and haiku and overture to dream songs'" (Lynch 2000, 204–5).

6. I use the term "vanishing" deliberately, since Ford argues that the haiku is the form of choice for Anglo-American poets invoking, and eulogizing, the "vanishing Indian."

7. Steven Leuthold, for instance, suggests that the prevalence for narrative history among

Plains filmmakers and films made about Plains peoples is grounded in the narrative practices that informed ledger art. Leuthold cites twelve films made between the 1970s and early 1990s before asserting that "historical narrative is emerging as a consistent trait of Plains and Plateau documentaries" (1998, 81).

8. I should point out that he is by no means alone. Tom Hill and Richard W. Hill Sr., for example, suggest that "ledger art—and, later, painting and sculpture—is a way of honoring . . . warriors" (1994, 140). This is true, but of course also potentially reductive. Without refusing that quality of resistance, Melanie Benson Taylor, for instance, offers an important rejoinder as she notes that the materials and ultimately some of the content of ledger art also reveal a complicity in its social and economic structures—"not a writing *over* but a writing inextricably tangled *within* all that the ledger represents" (2012, 190). One might contend, given his recent engagements with the modernist art market in *Blue Ravens*, that Vizenor's sense of the imagic moment both acknowledges and mitigates against such implications. Vizenor is well known for barbed comments about commercialized art; he is equally well known, of course, for the rejection of assimilationist argumentation, having long embraced artist George Morrison, among others, as a modernist painter who was also Anishinaabe (and vice versa).

9. This version was kindly sent to me in personal correspondence by the author on November 11, 2015.

10. PDF version kindly sent to me in personal correspondence by the author on November 11, 2015.

11. Loons migrate during both day and night and, like this escapee, cover significant distances in single migrations.

12. I have retained Noodin's choice of presenting the Anishinaabemowin in italics, as set out in the *Papers of the Forty-First Algonquian Conference*.

13. Language learning, like poetry, is an ever-evolving process. Since first publication of this poem, Noodin has reworked and revised it. I am very grateful to her for allowing me to reproduce the latest version here for comparison:

WAANIMAZINBII'IGANIKE

Ningii-ozhibii'amawaa Daphne Odjigiban.

Gimaajaamin ina gemaa maajitaayang igo
apii dibaajimoyang anaami-madogaaning?
Gidizhinaagwi'aanaanig ina gimishomisinaanig miinawaa gookomisinaanig?
Giwaabamaanaanig ina naasaab aanzheniig gaye Gichidebenjiged?

Ginisidawaabandaamin ina wiigwaasenaandeg,

oziigiwaabigwaniin gaye amooshimowin?

Gibizindawaanaan ina baapaase baapaagaakwa'aad akikaandagibanan?

Gigikendaamin ina maamawigaabawiyang mooka'ang?

Ginisidawendaamin megwaaj aanjiseyang

bingwiwiyang, biisibiisaawiyang.

Anaami-madogaaning apii dibaajimoyang

maajitaayang miinawaa maajaayang igo.

WRITING IMAGES IN CIRCLES
Written for Daphne Odjig.

Are we taking leave or taking off

when we tell stories under the stars?

Do we look like our grandfathers and grandmothers?

Do we see the same angels and Creator?

Do we recognize the color of birch,

the wrinkle of leaves and dance of bees?

Do we hear the woodpecker pecking on the dead pine?

Do we know to stand together at sunrise?

Do we understand that as we change

we are the sand, we are the showers?

As we tell stories beneath the stars

we are beginning and we are moving on.

14. Occupy Wall Street began on September 17, 2011. Its global movement was in full flow by October of that year. Most major camps had been cleared by February 2012. Idle No More itself launched in December 2012.

15. Occupy is not the focus of my critique here, and in offering this analysis I echo the prevailing critique of the movement by many Indigenous activists, who according to Brady and Antoine "wished to reframe problematic power relations as mechanisms of a colonial apparatus working to disenfranchize Indigenous peoples" (2013, 2). As they note, "Some [Indigenous critics] . . . actually participated in and helped shape the movement" (2). Like Brady and Antoine, I do not wish to propose a binary relationship here between Indigenous and non-Indigenous activism, and it is important to acknowledge that Occupy came to serve many different agendas for different constituencies.

16. An entirely irrelevant but quirky piece of trivia: briefs were first sold in Chicago in 1935,

making them every bit as au courant as the rise in land claims. Superman as we know him first appeared in commercial print on the front cover of *Action Comics* in 1938, but he was developed in 1933 when his creators, Jerry Siegel and Joe Shuster, transformed their first version—himself a villain bent on world domination—to the superhero we know now. The question remains to be asked, then, were his briefs the inspiration for the later invention? Fortunately, wearing them on the outside has not caught on.

17. The zombie supervillain Solomon Grundy did not appear until 1944 and was initially a foe to the Green Lantern, although we might read the mad scientist here as a prototype. That said, the Dummies are wrong: Superman generally finds out about the crimes he solves via his alter ego's work as a journalist—so he does get paid, if indirectly.

Chapter 3. Reckoning Beyond the Crossing/X-ing: Formal Diversity and Visual Sovereignty in Gordon Henry Jr.'s *The Light People*

1. I use the phrase "narrative relay" here quite literally—the novel is composed largely of stories that interconnect and are "passed on" from one situation or one teller to the next.

2. In this respect, Henry engages with theory in the way Blaeser outlines in her study of Vizenor's writing. She writes: "Nancy Hartsock writes of 'those who have been marginalized by the transcendental voice of universalizing theory' and insists that we should neither 'ignore' the knowledge/power relations inherent in literary theory and canon formation nor merely 'resist' them; rather, we must 'transform' them" (1996, 195).

3. Since publishing this essay, Sinclair has amended the spelling of his Anishinaabe name from Niigonwedom (as it is in Henry, Soler, and Martínez-Falquina 2009). I have used the current spelling both here and in the bibliography.

4. Also known as pukwudjie. These little people are forest dwellers, and are known to be highly mischievous. They are a distinct people from the memegwesiwag, who are water spirits and more commonly associated with children.

5. There is no small irony in my criticism of the author here, in that she acknowledges the potentially "unethical project" of criticism of "so-called minority" literatures, urging that we "try our best not to impose our own presuppositions and make the text fit into them" (Martínez-Falquina 2009, 192). To be clear, I am not accusing Martínez-Falquina of breaking this injunction in relation to Henry's novel, an overgeneralized context in relation to Native literature (especially twenty-first-century literature) more generally.

6. Much is made of the difference between English and Indigenous languages in terms of their ability to capture variety and texture in nature in particular. English often comes out of the equation being seen as fundamentally deficient. Authors from Copway to Louise Erdrich, for instance, have made a point of declaring Anishinaabemowin more

nuanced, whether for its songlike spoken quality (Copway) or its apperception of the landscape of the Great Lakes (Erdrich). I like Margaret Noodin's measured insistence that the two languages have different strengths, and here I am more mindful of Vizenor's take on Karsten Harries's observation that "there are moments when the inadequacy of our language [per se] seizes us, when language seems to fall apart and falling apart opens us to what transcends it" (qtd. in Vizenor 1981, xvi).

7. Traditionally visions may be recounted to elders for interpretation and would not necessarily then become public.

8. There were, in fact, several treaties from 1837 onward, with the Ojibwe, Dakota, and Ho-Chunk; Wisconsin only became an "organized incorporated territory" in 1836, being made up of the present-day states of Wisconsin and Iowa (until 1838) and land westward as far as the Missouri River; Minnesota would wait until 1849 before being formalized as organized territory. I refer here to the Treaty of St. Peters, also known as the White Pine Treaty and the Pine Tree Treaty. (An earlier Treaty of St. Peters had already acquired land in what is now Minnesota. Ceded by the Dakota, this land was purchased principally for military purposes and led to the establishment of Fort Snelling.) In July 1837, Governor Henry Dodge would write of "nine to ten millions of acres of land, and abounding in pine timber" (qtd. in Satz 1991, 13), acknowledging the importance of the latter, the securing of which would avoid, to his mind, later war with the Ojibwe.

9. I am grateful to an anonymous reader for pointing out the direct correlation between expectation and the written terms of the treaty: article 5 reserves for the tribes "the privilege of hunting, fishing, and gathering the wild rice, upon the lands, the rivers and the lakes included in the territory ceded." As is a familiar story throughout the history of treaty making with Indigenous peoples, the promises and the reality have differed markedly.

10. This is, of course, more true of totemic markers than of the X mark itself, but the former attains in the latter.

11. I use the term "postimperial" here advisedly and specifically in a sense that intends to historically delimit European expansionism in the New World. Hardt and Negri would, of course, contest the notion (2000).

12. Numerous scholars of photography, from Roland Barthes to Susan Sontag, have debated the indexicality of photography, its relationship to the real.

13. Borrows is writing about the Royal Proclamation of 1763, and particularly the way that document ignores or elides its own wider contexts. He writes: "The portion of the treaty confirmed at Niagara has often been overlooked, with the result that the manuscript of the Proclamation has not been integrated with First Nation understandings of this

document. A reconstruction of the events and promises of 1763–4, which takes account of the treaty of Niagara, transforms conventional interpretations of colonialism which allow the Crown to ignore First Nations participation."

Chapter 4. Picturing Absence and Postcolonial Presence: Unsettling a Colonial Grammar in Selected Works by Louise Erdrich

1. All references are to the original National Geographic Directions edition (2003) rather than the 2014 HarperCollins reissue.

2. See, among many other studies, Robert Warrior's *Tribal Secrets* (1994) and *The People and the Word* (2005); Kimberly M. Blaeser's *Gerald Vizenor: Writing in the Oral Tradition* (1996); Craig Womack's *Red on Red* (1999) and *Art as Performance, Story as Criticism* (2009); Jace Weaver's *That the People Might Live* (1997); Daniel Heath Justice's *Our Fire Survives the Storm* (2006).

3. Today, at least, such dentally produced pictures are generally decorative—visual art rather than literary in nature—but the connotation is irresistible.

4. This discussion is far larger than I can summarize or contain here, but a brief look at the *OED* reveals early scholarship around the relationship between "book" and "beech" focused on the scratching of runes onto beech wood, while more recent scholarship favors explanations based more generally on the use of wooden writing tablets. It is useful even if it serves as no more than a reminder that our idea of the book has itself evolved from that original relationship between tool and technology to signify a variety of material objects on a spectrum, and from inscription on a single surface to the collated text.

5. Multiple accounts of the origins of variants of "Ojibwe" exist. Among them, Noodin insightfully suggests that "it is possibly more productive to connect the initial sound *jib* to such other words as *jibwa*, meaning 'before,' and *jiibay*, meaning ghost, which carry implications of the past. In fact *jibakwe* itself connects back to the concept of putting a plate out for the *jiibayag* (the ancestors who came before us), which makes sense because the role of remembering or retelling stories is the role most often associated with the Ojibwe" (2014a, 6).

6. It is admittedly impossible for book histories of the Americas to exclude Mayan codices, although it is worth noting that their status as written texts was still disputed well into the second half of the twentieth century when Yuri Knorosov's work on the phonetic possibilities of Mayan glyphs began to bear fruit in the 1950s. The real point here—as is well documented—is that colonists went to considerable effort, both rhetorically and materially (in the case of Spanish burnings of Quechuan texts, for example), to deny the

existence of textual and written traditions. Indeed, Lopenzina recounts a fine instance of circular logic: "When Ignace J. Gelb first published his magisterial monograph *A Study of Writing* in 1952, he cited the inability of Western scholars to decipher Mayan script as evidence of its failure to have developed into a full-fledged writing system" (2012, 24).

7. Erdrich emphasizes her daughter's connections to this place, and even describes how it feels to experience a place through her daughter; she also notes, however, that her own family ancestry came through this area, "roam[ing] from Madeline Island in Lake Superior, along what is now the Canadian border, through Lake of the Woods and down to Red Lake, and then out onto the Great Plains" (2003, 80).

8. This scenario is exacerbated both by the repeated, though false, assertion that the 9/11 terrorists entered the United States through the overly liberal and security-lax Canada and by the continuing problem of human trafficking in the Great Lakes.

9. Erdrich herself draws on the account of John Tanner in highlighting this different nomenclature. "Why it is called 'Lake of the Woods' by the whites, I cannot tell," Tanner wrote, "as there is not much wood about it" (1830, 48). Henry Gannett's *The Origin of Certain Place Names in the United States* explains the name comes from the French *lac des bois*, referring to the "heavily wooded islands" in the lake, rather than its setting (1905, 179). Upham, meanwhile, asserts that it "is entirely surrounded by woods, though the border of the great prairie region is not far westward" (2001, 8).

10. "As in all of my books, no sacred knowledge is revealed. I check carefully to make certain everything I use is written down already. Thomas Vennum's *The Ojibwe Dance Drum: Its History and Construction* was particularly helpful to me" (Erdrich 2005, 277).

11. See, for instance, Johnston and Lawson, who argue that the "typical settler narrative . . . has a doubled goal. It is concerned to act out the suppression or effacement of the indigene; it is also concerned to perform the concomitant indigenization of the settler" (2000, 369).

12. Given the controversy of this portrait, I have not included a reproduction here.

13. There is, indeed, an ironic analogue between Gil as an "American Indian artist" whose productions, however sincere, are automatically interpreted as representations of tragedy and nostalgia by the critics and a slice of Erdrich's own critical treatment.

14. In a 2008 radio interview, for instance, Erdrich said: "I'm very proud as an enrolled member of the Turtle Mountain Band to be able to say that I'm doing something and that I'm writing books. . . . But again, in other venues if I get to be 'quintessentially American' what's wrong with that? Woman, mother, writer . . . people just have to use labels": "Writers on a New England Stage: Louise Erdrich" (May 16, 2008; qtd. in Kirwan 2013, 195 [n.137]; the original interview is no longer available).

15. The self-justifying nature of these affiliations is emphasized by the fact that when Gil was called a "Native Edward Hopper" because of his early reservation landscape scenes, he had found the comparison "irritating" (L. Erdrich 2010, 8). For a particularly rich discussion of the implications of Hopper's relationship to Jo in the characterization of Gil and Irene's relationship, see Kirwan 2013. Although he doesn't mention the origins of the comparison to Hopper, Kirwan astutely notes its pertinence to the increasingly disturbing nature of the poses and content of both artists' work.

16. Decoloniality, as Mignolo explains in various locations, refers to the radical critique of modernity, which moves beyond the postcolonial or anticolonial (both of which describe Gil's project) to a political and epistemological space separate from, not merely in antagonism with, the conditions of coloniality.

17. I have to confess my ignorance of American pronunciation here, but Irene, in British English, can be rendered I-reen *and* I-reenee. As such, it conjures both phonetic and visual puns, since the formal pronunciation of the word "irony" is usually rendered "aɪrəni."

18. Most notably, perhaps, Japanese influence was strong in the Impressionist period (Japonisme), and then again among many of the major modernists, although it has exerted some influence (both aesthetically and philosophically) almost continuously since the late seventeenth century. Zen Buddhism was popular in the U.S. countercultural movement of the 1950s.

Chapter 5. So, How Can You Hear Stones and Pictures?
Gerald Vizenor's Imagic Returns

1. My use of the term "visuality" here explicitly echoes its multiple inferences, including, quite simply, the fact of being visual. Its colonial ambivalence, however, is particularly germane to this chapter, forming, in Dylan Miner's words, a "reciprocity between visuality, modernity, and imperialism [that] runs deep." I echo his usage, then, where he writes that "the concept of visuality is usually evoked within contemporary scholarship to demonstrate an ideological move away from the disciplinary constraints of 'art history' [and toward what he calls "uniquely aboriginal forms of visuality"]," but, "as Mirzoeff demonstrates, even the concept of visuality is one tied to European (particularly British) imperial expansion and European society's engagement with modernity" (2010, 176).

2. *Shrouds of White Earth*, as if to cement the dynamic between art and literature he describes, includes illustrations by French artist Pierre Cayol.

3. The acknowledgements data for *Touchwood* indicate that the scrolls are reprinted from the July 1963 issue of *The Minnesota Archaeologist* and that they come from the George

A. Flaskerd collection at the Minnesota Historical Society.

4. "When I of Fish Eat" can be seen on the *Te Ao Hou/The New World* website of the National Library of New Zealand: http://teaohou.natlib.govt.nz/journals/teaohou/image/ Mao40TeA/Mao40TeA004.html. The poem is preceded by a simple line drawing of a fish head with eviscerated spine, and followed by an equally simple (and equally evocative) drawing of a shoal of fish. The illustrations—chosen by *Te Ao Hou* editor Margaret Orbell and her husband Gordon Walters according to Allen's description—were created by Māori artist Ralph Hotere.

5. Due to the controversial nature of reproduction of such items—and also the prevalence among anthropologists for dissenting views over how to read them, all of which tends to obscure the knowledge of their keepers and cultural insiders who can read them still—I am not going to attempt to interpret the scrolls in *Touchwood* here. While this may seem like a feint, and certainly represents a missed opportunity for comparative analysis, I do not feel it is appropriate for me to attempt this kind of work, which is more ethically the domain of those with strong links to the communities in which these texts were produced, and who have the permission so to do. There are numerous mide lodges in existence today in the United States and Canada, and there is good reason that many of the most important such documents were buried or hidden away for years at a time to avoid the eyes of snooping academics and cultural plunderers. For just one readily digestible example of dissenting views, see Christopher Vecsey's (1976) review of Selwyn Dewdney's *The Sacred Scrolls of the Southern Ojibway*, which is the best-known and fullest treatment of the scrolls to date.

6. Maps, in this context, refer not to Western cartographic principles but to Indigenous mapping strategies, which, according to McGlennen, "render far more dimension." Quoting Mark Warhus, she continues "maps were not created as permanent documents. . . . Native American maps were pictures of experience" (2015, 15).

7. Although Vizenor is discussing the particular moments writers Greg Sarris and W. S. Penn saw themselves in photographs of family members and predecessors, this sense of imagic presence—the trace of the subject and the trace of the maker—is discernible in all of his literary work in relation to all forms of visual image except *indian* simulations.

8. Describing Vizenor's depiction in *The Everlasting Sky* of Ted Mahto, Blaeser notes that "Mahto places great emphasis on 'visual thinking' as a key quality in oral tradition, noting how it generates a sense of connection with the past" (1996, 65–66).

9. The dish game, depending on dialect, is variously called, for instance, bahgaysay or pagessewin (pronounced bû'gese"wĭn).

10. To avoid confusion—Kristeva is using the Neoplatonic sense of hieroglyph meaning the

artistic representation of an esoteric idea, here: the language is consonant, but it does not carry the more common understanding of hieroglyphics as a complete writing system.

11. Krupat suggests of Vizenor's *Heirs of Columbus* that "in its sensitivity to a pervasive human suffering and its desire to act, in the Sartrean manner, on behalf of that suffering, this is a postmodernism that takes a position far less ambiguous than anything possible in the more usual postmodernisms of Europe and America" (1996, 68). This of course relies on a truism that insists on the fundamental amorality of postmodernist culture.

12. "In his book *Downcast Eyes: The Denigration of Vision in Twentieth-Century French Thought*, Martin Jay argues that the de-privileging of vision and image in favor of language and text was a central thrust of the French critical theory that has contributed so fundamentally to new art history" (qtd. by Phillips 1999, 99).

13. The teleological underpinning of that tripartite understanding posits: "For Rousseau, pictographs or hieroglyphs, ideographs and alphabet 'correspond almost exactly to three different stages according to which one can consider men gathered into a nation. The depicting of objects is appropriate to a savage people; signs of words and of propositions, to a barbaric people, and the alphabet to civilized peoples'" (Tomlinson 1995, 347).

14. Tomlinson joins both Brotherston and Mignolo, whose differences he notes in his second footnote, in turning to *Of Grammatology* for a starting point in understanding American nonalphabetic writing and for critique of "our Europe-inflected notions of the relationship between writing and speech" (1995, 344 [n.2]).

15. Having invoked Arendt, it is tempting to also cite Agamben's (1998) discussion of homo sacer—the banished figure whose ostracism extends as far as his permitted (and unpunishable) death. I do not think Vizenor strips Dogroy further than the scapegoated exile, but there is a potential reading here.

16. In fact, the figure who comes most immediately to mind in the early twentieth century is Frank "Toronto" Prewett, a Canadian poet who was taken under the wing of English poet Siegfried Sassoon. Prewett claimed Iroquois ancestry, although that claim is widely refuted now.

17. Indeed, Newman would later insist that he intended to connote man in his generality, rather than any specific group or peoples in this essay.

18. The deeper irony, of course, is that summer cottages themselves speak to a kind of capitalist advance guard—those wealthy enough to maintain houses that are empty for over half the year, which includes Jackson himself. O'Brian notes that the echo of terra nullius in Jackson's title is probably unintentional.

19. The name of the painting cannot help but invoke the title of Gustaf Nordenskiöld's 1893 study, *The Cliff Dwellers of Mesa Verde*.

20. This self-construction is interesting, not least since, as James Mackay points out, Vizenor's European heritage is largely Swedish.

Chapter 6. Performance, Resistance: Countering the *indian* and Sovereign Aesthetics in Contemporary Anishinaabe Drama

1. Michael McNally notes that "it would ultimately contribute to the spectacular nature of the Ontario Hiawatha pageants that the poem was performed just downriver from the Sault, where Schoolcraft garnered the material in the first place. It was even reported that a number of players in the 1901 pageant were grandchildren of his informants" (2006, 109).

2. *Curiosities* was first performed November 18–21, 2010, for Pangea World Theater at Intermedia Arts, directed by Dipankar Mukherjee.

3. Simpson is discussing Belmore's performance of "X" as part of the *Mapping Resistance* exhibition during Peterborough, Ontario's Ode'min Giizis festival, in 2010.

4. The problematic nature of Densmore's methodologies are well recorded (see, e.g., McNally 2000, Angel 2002). Jensen notes that harsh critiques of Densmore's and other pioneer anthropologists' methods written in the 1960s and 1970s, "responding to criticism of international imperialism and domestic colonialism," led anthropologists to "work more closely with their Native collaborators in re-creating the musical lives of Native singers and musicians" (2015). In the interests of balance, Michael Angel does note that "so accurate are [Hoffman's] transcriptions . . . that present-day Ojibwa have turned to his work in their attempts to preserve the Midewiwin" (2002, 133).

5. My analysis of Rendon's play is not intended to either endorse or judge the actions and views of her characters. Attitudes to, and uses for, Densmore's work differ widely among the Anishinaabeg. In *Just Too Much of an Indian: Bill Baker, Stalwart in a Fading Culture* (2009), Thomas Vennum portrays the Ojibwe singer with whom he worked for forty years as approving of the conservation and cultural continuance implicit in Densmore's practice. Other Anishinaabe scholars and singers today continue to use the recordings. Jensen reports similar feelings by Makah singer Helma Swan in the 1970s. Michael Angel similarly reports that the efforts of Densmore and, later, Hoffman "to preserve the vanishing cultural records . . . coincided with a similar desire on the part of some traditional Ojibwe Mide leaders. As a result, these practitioners were willing to pass on unusually detailed descriptions, songs, and pictographs that, in the past, had been considered highly secret" (2002, 179). Densmore's work was also central to the Federal Cylinder Project, which saw the repatriation of much music through copies of early recordings to originary communities in the late 1970s. This is to say, Densmore's work is

fraught with tension around the manner and appropriateness of its methodologies and practices, and the question of its legacy is highly complex!

6. Any apparent sensitivity to belief is also somewhat undercut by the manner in which Densmore discusses the midewiwin and its practices largely in the past tense—despite having seen it in action in the present. Geniusz remarks on this as a colonizing rhetoric (2009, 96–97).

7. I retain the spellings used in the play, which are in turn those used by Catlin and other contemporary documenters.

8. In his PhD thesis, Theo Van Alst footnotes this reference, noting with some feeling his desire to read it as sarcasm on Dickens's part (2008, 202 [n.24]). While the article does indeed carry a healthy dose of sarcasm, I fear Dr. Van Alst's distaste is well founded.

9. Anderson is a Minneapolis-based artist of Navajo descent.

10. Christianity arrived on the British Isles a long time before Augustine, but it was his mission (from 597 AD) that concerted efforts to convert Britons.

Conclusion

1. Chapter 6 departs from this principle in some ways, in that the dramatic productions I examine do, of course, contain actual images. This is not out of keeping with my discussion of the pictographs in *Summer in the Spring* and the video forms of Heid Erdrich's poems. At the same time, the thrust of my discussion is largely directed to the playscripts, which do not contain these images, since this is how the majority of readers of this book will encounter them.

BIBLIOGRAPHY

Agamben, Giorgio. 1998. *Homo Sacer: Sovereign Power and Bare Life*. Stanford: Stanford University Press.

Alexander, M. Jacqui, and Chandra Talpade Mohanty, eds. 1997. *Feminist Genealogies, Colonial Legacies, Democratic Futures*. New York: Routledge.

Allen, Chadwick. 2000. "Postcolonial Theory and the Discourse of Treaties." *American Quarterly* 52 (1): 59–89.

———. 2002. *Blood Narrative: Indigenous Identity in American Indian and Maori Literary and Activist Texts*. Durham, NC: Duke University Press.

———. 2012. *Trans-Indigenous: Methodologies for Global Native Literary Studies*. Minneapolis: University of Minnesota Press.

Anderson, Eric Gary. 1999. *American Indian Literature & the Southwest: Contexts and Dispositions*. Austin: University of Texas Press.

Angel, Michael. 2002. *Preserving the Sacred: Historical Perspectives on the Ojibwa Midewiwin*. Winnipeg: University of Manitoba Press.

Anthes, Bill. 2006. *Native Moderns: American Indian Painting, 1940–1960*. Durham, NC: Duke University Press.

Apess, William. 1833. "An Indian's Looking-Glass for the White Man." http://webpages.uidaho.edu/engl504trauma/WmApess.pdf.

———. 1836. "Eulogy on King Phillip." https://voicesofdemocracy.umd.edu/apess-eulogy-speech-text/.

Arendt, Hannah. 1994. "We Refugees." In *Altogether Elsewhere: Writers on Exile*, edited by Marc Robinson, 110–19. London: Faber & Faber.

Armstrong, Jeanette C., and Lally Grauer, eds. 2001. *Native Poetry in Canada: A Contemporary Anthology*. Peterborough, ON: Broadview Press.

Baraga, Frederic. 1992. *A Dictionary of the Ojibwe Language*. 3rd ed. St. Paul: Minnesota Historical Society Press.

Baudrillard, Jean. 1994. *Simulacra and Simulation*. Translated by Sheila Faria Glaser. Ann Arbor: University of Michigan Press.

Bauerkemper, Joseph. 2015. "The White Earth Constitution, Cosmopolitan Nationhood, and the Fruitful Ironies of Relational Sovereignty." *Transmotion* 1 (1): 1–22.

Bellin, Joshua David. 2001. *The Demon of the Continent: Indians and the Shaping of American Literature*. Philadelphia: University of Pennsylvania Press.

———. 2008. *Medicine Bundle: Indian Sacred Performance and American Literature, 1824–1932*. Philadelphia: University of Pennsylvania Press.

Bender, Margaret. 2010. "Reflections on What Writing Means, Beyond What It 'Says': The Political Economy and Semiotics of Graphic Pluralism in the Americas." *Ethnohistory* 57 (1): 175–82.

Benson, Melanie R. 2010. "Review Essay of *The Common Pot: The Recovery of Native Space in the Northeast*." *Wicazo Sa Review* 25 (2): 144–46.

Benton-Banai, Edward. 1988. *The Mishomis Book: The Voice of the Ojibway*. Hayward, WI: Indian Country Communications.

Berger, John. 1972. *Ways of Seeing*. New York: Penguin.

Berlo, Janet C., and Ruth B. Phillips. 1998. *Native North American Art*. Oxford: Oxford University Press.

Bernardin, Susan. 2011. "Seeing Memory, Storying Memory: Printup Hope, Rickard, Gansworth." In *Visualities: Perspectives on Contemporary American Indian Film and Art*, edited by Denise K. Cummings, 161–88. East Lansing: Michigan State University Press.

Biber, Nichole. n.d. "The Old World Display and the New World Displaced." In "Enduring Critical Poses: Beyond Nation and History," edited by Gordon Henry Jr., Margaret Noodin, and David Stirrup. Unpublished manuscript.

Bieder, Robert E. 1986. *Science Encounters the Indian, 1820–1880: The Early Years of American Ethnology*. Norman: University of Oklahoma Press.

Blaeser, Kimberly M. 1993. "Native Literature: Seeking a Critical Center." In *Looking at the Words of Our People: First Nations Analysis of Literature*, edited by Jeanette Armstrong,

53–61. Penticton, BC: Theytus Books.

———. 1996. *Gerald Vizenor: Writing in the Oral Tradition*. Norman: University of Oklahoma Press.

———. 1997a. "Like 'Reeds through the Ribs of a Basket': Native Women Weaving Stories." *American Indian Quarterly* 21 (4): 555–65.

———. 1997b. "'Interior Dancers': Transformations of Vizenor's Poetic Vision." *Studies in American Indian Literatures* 9 (1): 3–15.

———. 1999. "Writing Voices Speaking: Native Authors and an Oral Aesthetic." In *Talking on the Page: Editing Aboriginal Oral Texts*, edited by Keren Rice and Laura J. Murray, 53–68. Toronto: University of Toronto Press.

———. 2006. *Traces in Blood, Bone and Stone: Contemporary Ojibwe Poetry*. Bemidji, MN: Loonfeather Press.

———. 2007. *Apprenticed to Justice*. Cambridge, UK: Salt Publishing.

———. 2012a. "A Nexus of Connections: Acts of Recovery, Acts of Resistance in Native Palimpsest." In *Listening Up, Writing Down, and Writing Beyond: Interfaces of the Oral, Written, and Visual*, edited by Susan Gingell and Wendy Roy, 331–56. Waterloo, ON: Wilfrid Laurier University Press.

———. 2012b. "The Language of Borders, the Borders of Language in Gerald Vizenor's Poetry." In *The Poetry and Poetics of Gerald Vizenor*, edited by Deborah L. Madsen, 1–22. Albuquerque: University of New Mexico Press.

———. 2015. "Refraction and Helio-tropes: Native Photography and Visions of Light." In *Mediating Indianness*, edited by Cathy Covell Waegner, 163–95. East Lansing: Michigan State University Press.

Blume, Anna. 1996. "In Place of Writing." In *Plains Indian Drawings, 1865–1935: Pages from a Visual History*, edited by Janet Berlo, 40–44. New York: Abrams.

Bohaker, Heidi. 2010. "Reading Anishinaabe Identities: Meaning and Metaphor in *Nindoodem* Pictographs." *Ethnohistory* 57 (1): 11–33.

Bond, Bradley G., ed. 2005. *French Colonial Louisiana and the Atlantic World*. Baton Rouge: Louisiana State University Press.

Borrows, John. 1997. "Wampum at Niagara: The Royal Proclamation, Canadian Legal History, and Self-Government." In *Aboriginal Treaty Rights in Canada: Essays on Law, Equity, and Respect for Difference*, edited by Michael Asch, 155–72. Vancouver: University of British Columbia Press.

Bostwick, Todd W. 2005. "Rock Art Research in the American Southwest." In *Discovering North American Rock Art*, edited by Lawrence L. Loendorf, Christopher Chippindale, and David S. Whitley, 51–92. Tucson: University of Arizona Press.

Brady, Miranda J., and Derek Antoine. 2013. "Decolonize Wall Street: Situating Indigenous Critiques of the Occupy Wall Street Movement." *American Journal of Communication* 14 (3): 1–10.

Brehm, Victoria. 1996. "The Metamorphosis of an Ojibwa Manido." *American Literature* 68 (4): 677–706.

Breinig, Helmbrecht. 2010. "Transdifference in the Work of Gerald Vizenor." In *Native Authenticity: Transnational Perspectives on Native American Literary Studies*, edited by Deborah L. Madsen, 123–32. Albany: SUNY Press.

Brennan, Jonathan, ed. 2003. *When Brer Rabbit Meets Coyote: Africa-Native American Literature*. Chicago: University of Illinois Press.

Brooks, Lisa. 2008. *The Common Pot: The Recovery of Native Space in the Northeast*. Minneapolis: University of Minnesota Press.

———. 2011. "Painting 'Word-Pictures' in Place: Maurice Kenny's Empathetic Imagination of *Tekonwatonti / Molly Brant*." In *Maurice Kenny: Celebrations of a Mohawk Writer*, edited by Penelope Myrtle Kelsey, 97–118. Albany: SUNY Press.

———. 2014. "Writing and Lasting: Native Northeastern Literary History." In *The Oxford Handbook of Indigenous American Literature*, edited by James H. Cox and Daniel Heath Justice, 536–58. Oxford: Oxford University Press.

Brotherston, Gordon. 1992. *Book of the Fourth World: Reading the Native Americas through Their Literature*. Cambridge: Cambridge University Press.

Brownlie, Robin Jarvis. 2009. "First Nations Perspectives and Historical Thinking in Canada." In *First Nations, First Thoughts: The Impact of Indigenous Thought in Canada*, edited by Annis May Timpson, 21–50. Vancouver: University of British Columbia Press.

Buchanan, Brett. 2011. "Painting the Prehuman: Bataille, Merleau-Ponty, and the Aesthetic Origins of Humanity." *Journal for Critical Animal Studies* 9 (1/2): 14–31.

Byrd, Jodi A. 2011. *The Transit of Empire: Indigenous Critiques of Colonialism*. Minneapolis: University of Minnesota Press.

Callahan, David. 2005. "Narrative and Moral Intelligence in Gordon Henry Jr.'s *The Light People*." In *Towards a Transcultural Future: Literature and Society in a "Post"-Colonial World*, edited by Geoffrey V. Davis, Peter H. Marsden, Bénédicte Ledent, and Marc Delrez, 187–200. Amsterdam: Rodopi.

Cariou, Warren, and Niigaanwewidam James Sinclair. 2011. *Manitowapow: Aboriginal Writings from the Land of Water*. Winnipeg: Highwater Press.

Carlson, David J. 2015a. "A Poetics of Recognition: Vizenor's *Shrouds of White Earth*." Unpublished paper.

———. 2015b. "The Columbian Moment: Overcoming Globalization in Vizenor's *The Heirs of*

Columbus." *Transmotion* 1 (2): 26–45.

———. 2016. *Imagining Sovereignties: Self-Determination in American Indian Law and Literature*. Norman: University of Oklahoma Press.

Castro, Michael J. 1991. *Interpreting the Indian: Twentieth-Century Poets and the Native American*. Norman: University of Oklahoma Press.

Catlin, George. 1848. *Catlin's Notes of Eight Years' Travels and Residence in Europe with His North American Indian Collection*. Vol 2. Cambridge: Cambridge University Press.

Cheyfitz, Eric. 1991. *The Poetics of Imperialism: Translation and Colonization from The Tempest to Tarzan*. New York: Oxford University Press.

———. 2002. "The (Post)Colonial Predicament of Native American Studies." *Interventions: International Journal of Postcolonial Studies* 4 (3): 405–27.

Cohen, Matt. 2015. "A History of Books in Native North America." In *The World of Indigenous North America*, edited by Robert Warrior, 308–29. New York: Routledge.

Coleman, Daniel. 2013. "Grappling with Respect: Copway and Traill in a Conversation that Never Took Place." *English Studies in Canada* 39 (2/3): 63–88.

Comaroff, John L., and Jean Comaroff. 1992. *Ethnography and the Historical Imagination: Studies in the Ethnographic Imagination*. Boulder: Westview Press.

Combe, George. 1841. *Notes on the United States of North America during a Phrenological Visit in 1838–9–40*. Philadelphia: Carey & Hart.

Cook-Lynn, Elizabeth. 1993. "The American Indian Fiction Writer: 'Cosmopolitanism, Nationalism, the Third World, and First Nation Sovereignty.'" *Wicazo Sa Review* 9 (2): 26–36.

Copway, George. 1847. *The Life, History, and Travels of Kah-ge-ga-gah-bowh (George Copway), a Young Indian Chief of the Ojebwa Nation, a Convert to the Christian Faith, and a Missionary to His People for Twelve Years, with a Sketch of the Present State of the Ojebwa Nation in Regard to Christianity and Their Future Prospects*. Albany, NY: Weed and Parsons.

———. 1850a. *The Traditional History and Characteristic Sketches of the Ojibway Nation*. Boston: Benjamin B. Mussey & Co.

———. 1850b. *The Ojibway Conquest: A Tale of the Northwest*. New York: George P. Putnam.

———. 1997. *Life, Letters, and Speeches*. Edited by A. Lavonne Brown Ruoff and Donald B. Smith. Lincoln: University of Nebraska Press. First published in 1850.

Corachán, Anna Brígido. N.d. "Performing Identity: Zapatista Narratives of Resistance." http://hemi.nyu.edu/eng/seminar/peru/call/workgroups/indigabcorachan.shtml.

Cottington, David. 1998. *Cubism in the Shadow of War: The Avant-Garde and Politics in Paris 1905–1914*. New Haven: Yale University Press.

Coulthard, Glen. 2014. "From Wards of the State to Subjects of Recognition? Marx, Indigenous

Peoples, and the Politics of Dispossession in Denendeh." In *Theorizing Native Studies*, edited by Audra Simpson and Andrea Smith, 56–98. Durham, NC: Duke University Press.

Cox, James H. 2006. *Muting White Noise: Native American and European American Novel Traditions*. Norman: University of Oklahoma Press.

Cox, James H., and Daniel Heath Justice, eds. 2014. *The Oxford Handbook of Indigenous American Literature*. Oxford: Oxford University Press.

Cummings, Denise K., ed. 2011. *Visualities: Perspectives on Contemporary American Indian Film and Art*. East Lansing: Michigan State University Press.

Curtis, Edward S., dir. 1914. *In the Land of the Headhunters* (film). World Film Company.

Darby, Jaye T. 2002. "Re-imagining the Stage: Tradition and Transformation in Native Theater." In *The Color of Theater: Race, Culture and Contemporary Performance*, edited by Roberta Uno and Lucy Mae San Pablo Burns, 61–82. New York: Continuum.

Däwes, Birgit. 2007. *Native North American Theater in a Global Age: Sites of Identity Construction and Transdifference*. Heidelberg: Universitätsverlag Winter.

———, ed. 2013a. *Indigenous North American Drama: A Multivocal History*. Albany: SUNY Press.

———. 2013b. "Performing Memory, Transforming Time: History and Indigenous North American Drama." In *Indigenous North American Drama: A Multivocal History*, edited by Birgit Däwes, 1–15. Albany: SUNY Press.

———. 2014. "Native American Landscapes on Canvas and Stage." In *Aspects of Transnational and Indigenous Cultures*, edited by Hsinya Huang and Clara Shu-Chun Chang, 31–46. Newcastle: Cambridge Scholars Publishing.

Debord, Guy. 1994. *The Society of the Spectacle*. New York: Zone Books.

DeFrancis, John. 1989. *Visible Speech: The Diverse Oneness of Writing Systems*. Honolulu: University of Hawaii Press.

Deloria, Philip J. 1998. *Playing Indian*. New Haven: Yale University Press.

Densmore, Frances. 1979. *Chippewa Customs*. St. Paul: Minnesota Historical Society Press.

Denzin, Norman K. 2013. *Indians on Display: Global Commodification of Native America in Performance, Art, and Museums*. Walnut Creek, CA: Left Coast Press.

DePasquale, Paul, Renate Eigenbrod, and Emma LaRocque, eds. 2010. *Across Cultures / Across Borders: Canadian Aboriginal and Native American Literatures*. Peterborough, ON: Broadview Press.

Derrida, Jacques. 1976. *Of Grammatology*. Translated by Gayatri Chakravorty Spivak. Baltimore: Johns Hopkins University Press.

———. 1986. *Glas*. Translated by John P. Leavey Jr. and Richard Rand. Lincoln: University of Nebraska Press.

Dickens, Charles. 1853. "The Noble Savage." *Household Words* 168: 337–39.

Dippie, Brian. 1990. *Catlin and His Contemporaries: The Politics of Patronage*. Lincoln: University of Nebraska Press.

Dix, Douglas, Wolfgang Hochbruck, Kirstie McAlpine, Dallas Miller, and Mary Tyne. 2000. "Textual Interstices: Mirrored Shadows in Gerald Vizenor's *Dead Voices*." In *Loosening the Seams: Interpretations of Gerald Vizenor*, edited by A. Robert Lee, 178–91. Bowling Green: Bowling Green State University Popular Press.

Doerfler, Jill. 2014. "Making It Work: A Model of Tribalography as Methodology." *Studies in American Indian Literatures* 26 (2): 65–74.

Doerfler, Jill, Niigaanwewidam James Sinclair, and Heidi Kiiwetinepinesiik Stark, eds. 2013. *Centering Anishinaabeg Studies: Understanding the World through Stories*. East Lansing: Michigan State University Press.

Douglass, Frederick. 1845. *Narrative of the Life of Frederick Douglass, an American Slave*. Electronic Text Center, University of Virginia Library. https://babel.hathitrust.org/cgi/pt?id=loc.ark:/13960/t07w6h58h&view=1up&seq=7.

———. 1852. "What to the Slave Is the Fourth of July?" Teaching American History. http://teachingamericanhistory.org/library/document/what-to-the-slave-is-the-fourth-of-july/.

Dubin, Margaret. 1999. "Sanctioned Scribes: How Critics and Historians Write the Native American Art World." In *Native American Art in the Twentieth Century: Makers, Meanings, Histories*, edited by W. Jackson Rushing III, 149–68. New York: Routledge.

Emerson, Ralph Waldo. 1841. "Self-Reliance." https://math.dartmouth.edu/~doyle/docs/self/self.pdf.

Erdrich, Heid. 2005. *The Mother's Tongue*. Cambridge, UK: Salt Publishing.

———. 2008. *National Monuments*. East Lansing: Michigan State University Press.

———. 2012. *Curiosities*. Minneapolis.

———. 2013a. "Pre-Occupied." Heid E. Erdrich. http://www.heiderdrich.com.

———. 2013b. "'Name': Literary Ancestry as Presence." In *Centering Anishinaabeg Studies: Understanding the World through Stories*, edited by Jill Doerfler, Niigaanwewidam James Sinclair, and Heidi Kiiwetinepinesiik Stark, 13–34. East Lansing: Michigan State University Press.

———. 2017. *Curator of Ephemera at the New Museum for Archaic Media*. East Lansing: Michigan State University Press.

Erdrich, Louise. 1984. *Jacklight: Poems*. London: Flamingo.

———. 1995. *The Blue Jay's Dance: A Birth Year*. New York: HarperCollins.

———. 1998. *The Antelope Wife*. London: Flamingo.

———. 2000. *The Birchbark House*. London: Dolphin.

————. 2003. *Books and Islands in Ojibwe Country*. Washington, DC: National Geographic Society.

————. 2004. *Four Souls*. New York: HarperCollins.

————. 2005. *The Painted Drum*. New York: HarperCollins.

————. 2010. *Shadow Tag*. New York: HarperCollins.

Fabian, Johannes. 2002. *Time and the Other: How Anthropology Makes Its Object*. New York: Columbia University Press.

Fisher, Jean. 1987. "Frank Bigbear, Jr at Bockley Gallery, New York" *Artforum*, 25, no. 9 (May), 148–49.

Fitzgerald, Michael C. 1996. *Making Modernism: Picasso and the Creation of the Market for Twentieth-Century Art*. Berkeley: University of California Press.

Fleischer, Dave, dir. 1942. *Superman*. "Electric Earthquake. Released May 15. https://www.youtube.com.

Flint, Kate. 2009. *The Transatlantic Indian, 1776–1930*. Princeton: Princeton University Press.

Flys, Carmen. 1996. "Interview with Gordon Henry." *North Dakota Quarterly* 64 (4): 167–79.

Ford, Karen Jackson. 2009. "Marking Time in Native America: Haiku, Elegy, Survival." *American Literature* 81 (2): 333–59.

Foster, Tol. 2008. "Against Separatism: Jace Weaver and the Call for Community." *American Literary History* 20 (3): 566–78.

Foucault, Michel. 1980. *Power/Knowledge: Selected Interviews and Other Writing, 1972–1977*. Edited by Colin Gordon. New York: Pantheon Books.

————. 1994. *The Order of Things*. New York: Vintage Books.

Francis, Margot. 2011. *Creative Subversions: Whiteness, Indigeneity, and the National Imaginary*. Vancouver: University of British Columbia Press.

Fruhauff, Brad. 2007. "The Lost Work of Longfellow's *Hiawatha*." *Journal of the Midwest Modern Language Association* 40 (2): 79–96.

Ganguly, Keya. 2004. "Temporality and Postcolonial Critique." In *The Cambridge Companion to Postcolonial Literary Studies*, edited by Neil Lazarus, 162–80. Cambridge: Cambridge University Press.

Gannett, Henry. 1905. *The Origin of Certain Place Names in the United States*. Washington, DC: Government Printing Office.

Gansworth, Eric. 2001. *Nickel Eclipse: Iroquois Moon*. East Lansing: Michigan State University Press.

————. 2005. *Mending Skins*. Lincoln: University of Nebraska Press.

Geniusz, Wendy Makoons. 2009. *Our Knowledge Is Not Primitive: Decolonizing Botanical Anishinaabe Teachings*. New York: Syracuse University Press.

Gilbert, Helen. 2013. "Indigeneity and Performance." *Interventions: International Journal of Postcolonial Studies* 15 (2): 173–80.

Gilmore, Paul. 2001. *The Genuine Article: Race, Mass Culture, and American Literary Manhood.* Durham, NC: Duke University Press.

Gingell, Susan, and Wendy Roy, eds. 2012. *Listening Up, Writing Down, and Writing Beyond: Interfaces of the Oral, Written, and Visual.* Waterloo, ON: Wilfrid Laurier University Press.

Glancy, Diane. 1991. *Lone Dog's Winter Count.* Albuquerque: West End Press.

Goeman, Mishuana. 2013. *Mark My Words: Native Women Mapping Our Nation.* Minneapolis: University of Minnesota Press.

———. 2014. "Disrupting a Settler-Colonial Grammar of Place: The Visual Memoir of Hulleah Tsinhnahjinnie." In *Theorizing Native Studies*, edited by Audra Simpson and Andrea Smith, 235–65. Durham, NC: Duke University Press.

Goff, Cindy. 1996. *A Hero's Voice.* Illustrated by Steve Premo and Paul Fricke. Mille Lacs Band of Ojibwe.

———. 1999. *Dreams of Looking Up.* Illustrated by Steve Premo and Paul Fricke. Mille Lacs Band of Ojibwe.

Goldring, Hugh. 2015. "The Mazinbiige Indigenous Graphic Novel Collection & the Politics of Public Knowledge." *ad astra comix*, May 1. https://adastracomix.com.

Greenblatt, Stephen. 1991. *Marvellous Possessions: The Wonder of the New World.* Oxford: Oxford University Press.

Grønstad, Asbjørn, and Øyvind Vågnes. 2006. "What Do Pictures Want? Interview with W. J. T. Mitchell." Center for Visual Studies. http://www.visual-studies.com/interviews/mitchell.html. Reprinted from *Image & Narrative.*

Gross, Lawrence W. 2005. "The Trickster and World Maintenance: An Anishinaabe Reading of Louise Erdrich's Tracks." *Studies in American Indian Literatures* 17 (3): 48–66.

———. 2014. *Anishinaabe Ways of Knowing and Being.* Burlington: Ashgate.

Grover, Linda LeGarde, Jim Northrup, Marcie R. Rendon, and Denise Sweet. 2002. *Nitaawichige: Selected Poetry and Prose by Four Anishinaabe Writers.* Duluth: Poetry Harbor Publications.

Hail, Barbara. 2013. "Foreword." In *Women and Ledger Art: Four Contemporary Native American Artists*, edited by Richard Pearce, xiii–xviii. Tucson: University of Arizona Press.

Hardt, Michael, and Antonio Negri. 2000. *Empire.* Cambridge, MA: Harvard University Press.

Hearne, Joanna. 2012. *Native Recognition: Indigenous Cinema and the Western.* Albany: SUNY Press.

Heidegger, Martin. 1971. *Poetry, Language, Thought*, translated by Albert Hofstadter. New York: Harper Colophon Books.

Hein, Christina. 2012. "Enriching Prose with Haiku Poetics." In *The Poetry and Poetics of Gerald Vizenor*, edited by Deborah L. Madsen, 113–34. Albuquerque: University of New Mexico Press.

Hele, Karl S., and J. Randolph Valentine, eds. 2013. *Papers of the Forty-First Algonquian Conference, 2009*. Albany: SUNY Press.

Henry, Gordon, Jr. 1994. *The Light People*. East Lansing: Michigan State University Press.

———. 2017. "Anishinaabeskinuk: Writing Over Skins, Writing Over Imagi(natives)." *Wasafiri* 32 (2): 32–40.

Henry, Gordon, Jr., and Elizabeth LaPensée, eds. 2018. *Sovereign Traces*. Vol. 1, *Not (Just) (An) Other*. East Lansing: Michigan State University Press.

Henry, Gordon D., Jr., Nieves Pascual Soler, and Silvia Martínez-Falquina, eds. 2009. *Stories through Theories/Theories through Stories: North American Indian Writing, Storytelling, and Critique*. East Lansing: Michigan State University Press.

Herman, Matthew D. 2008. "'The Making of Relatives': Sovereignty and Cosmopolitan Democracies." In *Foundations of First Peoples' Sovereignty: History, Education & Culture*, edited by Ulrike Wiethaus, 21–42. New York: Peter Lang.

Hill, Tom, and Richard W. Hill Sr. 1994. *Creation's Journey: Native American Identity and Belief*. Washington, DC: Smithsonian Institution Press.

Hill Boone, Elizabeth, and Walter D. Mignolo. 1994. *Writing without Words: Alternative Literacies in Mesoamerica and the Andes*. Durham, NC: Duke University Press.

Hill Boone, Elizabeth, and Gary Urton, eds. 2011. *Their Way of Writing: Scripts, Signs, and Pictographies in Pre-Columbian America*. Cambridge, MA: Harvard University Press.

Hoechst, Heidi. 2008. "Refusable Pasts: Speculative Democracy, Spectator Citizens, and the Dislocation of Freedom in the United States." PhD thesis, University of California, San Diego.

Hoffman, W. J. 1891. *The Midē′Wiwin or "Grand Medicine Society" of the Ojibwa*. Seventh Annual Report of the Bureau of Ethnology to the Secretary of the Smithsonian Institution, 1885–1886, 143–300. Washington, DC: Government Printing Office.

Horse Capture, George, Duane Champagne, and Chandler C. Jackson. 2007. *American Indian Nations: Yesterday, Today, and Tomorrow*. New York: Alta Mira Press.

Houle, Robert. 2007. "Copper Thunder." Aboriginal Curatorial Collective/Collectif des commissaires autochtones. December 5. http://www.aboriginalcuratorialcollective.org/features/morrisseau.html. (site discontinued).

Howe, LeAnne. 1999. "Tribalography: The Power of Native Stories." *Journal of Dramatic Theory and Criticism* 24 (1): 117–25.

Huang, Hsinya, and Clara Shu-Chun Chang, eds. 2014. *Aspects of Transnational and Indigenous*

Cultures. Newcastle: Cambridge Scholars Publishing.

Huggan, Graham. 1989. "Decolonizing the Map: Post-Colonialism, Post-Structuralism and the Cartographic Connection." *Ariel* 20 (4): 115–31.

Hutchinson, Elizabeth. 2001. "Modern Native American Art: Angel DeCora's Transcultural Aesthetics." *Art Bulletin* 83 (4): 740–56.

———. 2009. *The Indian Craze: Primitivism, Modernism, and Transculturation in American Art, 1890–1915*. Durham, NC: Duke University Press.

Ingold, Tim. 2000. *The Perception of the Environment: Essays on Livelihood, Dwelling and Skill*. New York: Routledge.

Ireland, Corydon. 2012. "Artist Touts 'Primacy' of Images." *Harvard Gazette*, March 26. http://news.harvard.edu/gazette.

Jackson, Virginia. 1998. "Longfellow's Tradition; or, Picture-Writing a Nation." *Modern Language Quarterly* 59 (4): 471–96.

Jacobs, Connie. 2001. *The Novels of Louise Erdrich: Stories of Her People*. New York: Peter Lang.

Jensen, Joan M. 2015. "Gone but Not Quite Forgotten." In *Travels with Frances Densmore: Her Life, Work, and Legacy in Native American Studies*, edited by Joan M. Jensen and Michelle Wick Patterson, 242–86. Lincoln: University of Nebraska Press.

Jensen, Joan M., and Michelle Wick Patterson, eds. 2015. *Travels with Frances Densmore: Her Life, Work, and Legacy in Native American Studies*. Lincoln: University of Nebraska Press.

Johnston, Anna, and Alan Lawson. 2000. "Settler Colonies." In *A Companion to Postcolonial Studies*, edited by Henry Schwarz and Sangeeta Ray, 360–76. London: Blackwell.

Johnston, Basil H. 1990a. *Ojibway Heritage*. Lincoln: University of Nebraska Press.

———. 1990b. *Ojibway Ceremonies*. Lincoln: University of Nebraska Press.

Jones, Peter. 1860. *History of the Ojebway Indians, with Especial Reference to Their Conversion to Christianity*. London: A. W. Bennett.

Justice, Daniel Heath. 2005. *Our Fire Survives the Storm: A Cherokee Literary History*. Minneapolis: University of Minnesota Press.

———. 2015. "Indigenous Writing." In *The World of Indigenous North America*, edited by Robert Warrior, 291–307. New York: Routledge.

Kelsey, Penelope Myrtle. 2010. *Tribal Theory in Native American Literature: Dakota and Haudenosaunee Writing and Indigenous Worldviews*. Lincoln: University of Nebraska Press.

———, ed. 2011. *Maurice Kenny: Celebrations of a Mohawk Writer*. Albany: SUNY Press.

———. 2014. *Reading the Wampum: Essays on Hodinöhsö:ni' Visual Code and Epistemological Recovery*. Syracuse: Syracuse University Press.

Keyser, James D. 2000. *The Five Crows Ledger: Biographic Warrior Art of the Flathead*. Salt Lake

City: University of Utah Press.

King, Thomas. 1990. "Godzilla vs. Post-Colonial." *World Literature Written in English* 30 (2): 10–16.

Kirwan, Padraig. 2013. *Sovereign Stories: Aesthetics, Autonomy, and Contemporary Native American Writing*. London: Peter Lang.

Knobel, Dale T. 1984. "Know-Nothings and Indians: Strange Bedfellows?" *Western Historical Quarterly* 15 (2): 175–98.

Konkle, Maureen. 2004. *Writing Indian Nations: Native Intellectuals and the Politics of Historiography, 1827–1863*. Chapel Hill: University of North Carolina Press.

———. 2014. "Recovering Jane Johnston Schoolcraft's Cultural Activism in the Nineteenth Century." In *The Oxford Handbook of Indigenous American Literature*, edited by James H. Cox and Daniel Heath Justice, 81–101. Oxford: Oxford University Press.

Kristeva, Julia. 1986. "Word, Dialogue and Novel." In *The Kristeva Reader*, edited by Toril Moi, 34–61. New York: Columbia University Press.

Krupat, Arnold. 1996. *The Turn to the Native: Studies in Criticism and Culture*. Lincoln: University of Nebraska Press.

———. 2002. *Red Matters: Native American Studies*. Philadelphia: University of Pennsylvania Press.

Kulchyski, Peter. 2005. *Like the Sound of a Drum: Aboriginal Politics in Denendeh and Nunavut*. Winnipeg: University of Manitoba Press.

———. 2012. "Bush/Writing: Embodied Deconstruction, Traces of Community, and Writing against the State in Indigenous Acts of Inscription." In *Shifting the Ground of Canadian Literary Studies*, edited by Smaro Kamboureli and Robert Zachariasm, 249–67. Waterloo, ON: Wilfrid Laurier University Press.

LaLonde, Chris. 1997. "Stories, Humor, and Survival in Jim Northrup's *Walking the Rez Road*." *Studies in American Indian Literatures* 9 (2): 23–40.

———. n.d. "Louise Erdrich's *Books and Islands in Ojibwe Country*: Writing, Being, Healing, Place." In "Enduring Critical Poses: Beyond Nation and History," edited by Gordon Henry Jr., Margaret Noodin, and David Stirrup. Unpublished manuscript.

Lepore, Jill. 1999. *The Name of War: King Philip's War and the Origins of American Identity*. New York: Vintage.

Leuthold, Steven. 1998. *Indigenous Aesthetics: Native Art, Media, and Identity*. Austin: University of Texas Press.

Lewis, Michael. 2008. *Derrida and Lacan: Another Writing*. Edinburgh: Edinburgh University Press.

L'Hirondelle, Cheryl. 2014. "Codetalkers Recounting Signals of Survival." In *Coded Territories*,

147–68. Calgary: University of Calgary Press.

Liang, Iping. 2016. "Crossing the Bering Strait: Transpacific Turns and Native Literatures." In *The Routledge Handbook to Native American Literatures*, edited by Deborah Madsen, 379–89. Abingdon: Routledge.

Lincoln, Kenneth. 1986. "Tai-Me to Rainy Mountain: The Makings of American Indian Literature." *American Indian Quarterly* 10 (2): 101–17.

———. 2007. "Red Stick Lit Crit." *Indian Country Today*. https://indiancountrymedianetwork. com/news/lincoln-red-stick-lit-crit/ (site discontinued).

Longfellow, Henry Wadsworth. 1898. *The Song of Hiawatha: an Epic Poem*. Chicago: M.A. Donohue & Co.

———. 1891. *Life of Henry Wadsworth Longfellow, with Extracts from His Journals and Correspondence*. Ed. Samuel Longfellow. Boston: Houghton Mifflin. https://archive.org/ stream/lifehenrywadswo04longgoog#page/n10/mode/2up.

Lopenzina, Drew. 2012. *Red Ink: Native Americans Picking Up the Pen in the Colonial Period*. Albany: SUNY Press.

Lorde, Audre. 2018. *The Master's Tools Will Never Dismantle the Master's House*. London: Penguin.

Lounsbury, Floyd G. 1989. "The Ancient Writing of Middle America." In *The Origins of Writing*, edited by Wayne M. Senner, 203–38. Lincoln: University of Nebraska Press.

Lovejoy, Arthur Oncken, and George Boas. 1935. *Primitivism and Related Ideas in Antiquity*. London: Octagon Books.

Low-Weso, Denise. 2006. "Composite Indigeneity: Cheyenne Ledger Art as Literature." *Studies in American Indian Literatures* 18 (2): 83–104.

Lynch, Tom. 2000. "To Honor Impermanence: The Haiku and Other Poems of Gerald Vizenor." In *Loosening the Seams: Interpretations of Gerald Vizenor*, edited by A. Robert Lee, 203–24. Bowling Green: Bowling Green State University Popular Press.

Lyons, Scott Richard. 2010. *X-Marks: Native Signatures of Assent*. Minneapolis: University of Minnesota Press.

Mackay, James. 2008. "Ghosts in the Gaps: Diane Glancy's Paradoxes of Survivance." In *Survivance: Narratives of Native Presence*, edited by Gerald Vizenor, 247–69. Lincoln: Nebraska University Press.

———. 2015. "'Wanton and Sensuous' in the Musée du Quai Branly: Gerald Vizenor's Cosmoprimitivist Visions of France." *Journal of Postcolonial Writing* 51 (2): 170–83.

Madsen, Deborah L. 2011. "Out of the Melting Pot into the Nationalist Fires: Native American Literary Studies in Europe." *American Indian Quarterly* 35 (3): 353–71.

———, ed. 2012. *The Poetry and Poetics of Gerald Vizenor*. Albuquerque: University of New

Mexico Press.

———. 2015. "The Sovereignty of Transmotion in a State of Exception: Lessons from the Internment of 'Praying Indians' on Deer Island, Massachusetts Bay Colony, 1675–1676." *Transmotion* 1 (1): 23–47.

———, ed. 2016. *The Routledge Companion to Native American Literature.* Abingdon: Routledge.

Manuel, Carme. 2012. "Flying Gerald Vizenor Home in Words and Myths: Or, How to Translate His Poetry into Catalan." In *The Poetry and Poetics of Gerald Vizenor*, edited by Deborah L. Madsen, 43–62. Albuquerque: University of New Mexico Press.

Markovits, Benjamin. 2005. "*The Painted Drum*: Off the Rez." *New York Times*, September 11. http://www.nytimes.com.

Martínez, David. 2014. "Neither Chief nor Medicine Man: The Historical Role of the 'Intellectual' in the American Indian Community." *Studies in American Indian Literatures* 26 (1): 29–53.

Martínez-Falquina, Silvia. 2009. "The(st)ories of Ceremonial Relation: Native Narratives and the Ethics of Reading." In *Stories through Theories/Theories through Stories: North American Indian Writing, Storytelling, and Critique*, edited by Gordon D. Henry Jr., Nieves Pascal, and Silvia Martínez-Falquina, 191–208. East Lansing: Michigan State University Press.

Maungwudaus (George Henry). 2011. *An Account of the Chippewa Indians, Who Have Been Travelling Among the Whites, in the United States, England, France and Belgium. Written by, the Self-Taught Indian, Etc.* London: British Library, Historical Print Editions. First published in 1848.

McGlennen, Molly. 2013. "Horizon Lines, Medicine Painting, and Moose Calling: The Visual/ Performative Storytelling of Three Anishinaabeg Artists." In *Centering Anishinaabeg Studies: Understanding the World through Stories*, edited by Jill Doerfler, Niigaanwewidam James Sinclair, and Heidi Kiiwetinepinesiik Stark, 341–62. East Lansing: Michigan State University Press.

———. 2015. "'By My Heart': Gerald Vizenor's *Almost Ashore* and *Bear Island: The War at Sugar Point*." *Transmotion* 1 (2): 1–25.

McKegney, Sam. 2007. *Magic Weapons: Aboriginal Writers Remaking Community after Residential School.* Winnipeg: University of Manitoba Press.

McKenzie, Stephanie. 2007. *Before the Country: Native Renaissance, Canadian Mythology.* Toronto: University of Toronto Press.

McMaster, Gerald. 2005. "Contributions to Canadian Art by Aboriginal Contemporary Artists." In *Hidden in Plain Sight: Contributions of Aboriginal Peoples to Canadian Identity and*

Culture, edited by David Newhouse, Cora Voyageur, and Dan Beavon, 140–62. Toronto: University of Toronto Press.

———. 2013. "The Anishinaabe Artistic Consciousness." In *Before and After the Horizon: Anishinaabe Artists of the Great Lakes*, edited by David W. Penney and Gerald McMaster, 71–105. Washington, DC: National Museum of the American Indian.

McNally, Michael D. 2000. *Ojibwe Singers: Hymns, Grief, and a Native Culture in Motion*. Minneapolis: Minnesota Historical Society Press.

———. 2006. "The Indian Passion Play: Contesting the Real Indian in *Song of Hiawatha* Pageants, 1901–1965." *American Quarterly* 58 (1): 105–36.

Melville, Herman. 1851. *Moby-Dick; or the Whale*. http://www.gutenberg.org/files/2701/2701.txt.

Merleau-Ponty, Maurice. 1968. *The Visible and the Invisible*. Evanston: Northwestern University Press.

———. 2002. *Phenomenology of Perception*. New York: Routledge.

Meshake, Rene. 2006. "The Grand Entry." In *Traces in Blood, Bone, and Stone: Contemporary Ojibwe Poetry*, edited by Kimberly Blaeser, 137. Bemidji, MN: Loonfeather Press.

Meyer, Melissa L. 1994. *The White Earth Tragedy: Ethnicity and Dispossession at a Minnesota Anishinaabe Reservation, 1889–1920*. Lincoln: University of Nebraska Press.

Michaelson, Scott. 1999. *The Limits of Multiculturalism: Interrogating the Limits of American Anthropology*. Minneapolis: University of Minneapolis Press.

Mignolo, Walter D. 2011. "Crossing Gazes and the Silence of the 'Indians': Theodor De Bry and Guaman Poma de Ayala." *Journal of Medieval and Early Modern Studies* 41 (1): 173–223.

Mihesuah, Devon Abbott, and Angela Cavendar Wilson. 2004. *Indigenizing the Academy: Transforming Scholarship and Empowering Communities*. Lincoln: Nebraska University Press.

Miller, Cary. 2010. *Ogimaag: Anishinaabeg Leadership, 1760–1845*. Lincoln: University of Nebraska Press.

Miner, Dylan A. T. 2010. "'When They Awaken': Indigeneity, Miscegenation, and Anticolonial Visuality." In *Rhetorics of the Americas: 3114 BCE to 2012 CE*, edited by Damián Baca and Victor Villanueva, 169–96. New York: Palgrave MacMillan.

Mirzoeff, Nicholas. 2006. "On Visuality." *Journal of Visual Culture* 5 (1): 53–79.

———. 2011. *The Right to Look: A Counterhistory of Visuality*. Durham, NC: Duke University Press.

Mitchell, W. J. T. 1994. *Picture Theory*. Chicago: University of Chicago Press.

Mithun, Marianne. 1999. *The Languages of Native North America*. Cambridge: Cambridge University Press.

Momaday, N. Scott. 2015. "There Are 120 Years of Lakota History on This Calendar."

Smithsonian Magazine, January. http://www.smithsonianmag.com.

Monaghan, E. Jennifer. 2005. *Learning to Read and Write in Colonial America*. Amherst: University of Massachusetts Press.

Moore, David L. 2012. "Reinventing the Nature of Language: The Poetics of Gerald Vizenor's Prose." In *The Poetry and Poetics of Gerald Vizenor*, edited by Deborah L. Madsen, 135–63. Albuquerque: University of New Mexico Press.

Moreira, Goretti Das Neves. 2007. "O Novo Guerreiro em *The Light People* (Gordon Henry Jr) / The New Warrior in Gordon Henry's *The Light People*." Master's dissertation, Universite de Aveiro.

Morrisseau, Norval. 1965. *Legends of My People, the Great Ojibway*. Toronto: Ryerson Press.

Murray, Joddy. 2009. *Non-discursive Rhetoric: Image and Affect in Multimodal Composition*. Albany: SUNY Press.

Myles, Norbert A., dir. 1920. *The Daughter of Dawn*. Texas Film Co., Milestone Films.

Nanibush, Wanda. 2010. "Contamination and Reclamation: Robert Houle's 'Paris/Ojibwa.'" *Fuse*. http://fusemagazine.org/2010/12/961 (site discontinued).

Neihardt, John G. 2014. *Black Elk Speaks*. Lincoln: University of Nebraska Press. First published in 1932.

New, W. H. 2002. *Encyclopedia of Literature in Canada*. Toronto: University of Toronto Press.

Nicholson, Hope, ed. 2016. *Moonshot: The Indigenous Comics Collection*. Toronto: Alternate History Comics.

Noodin, Margaret. 2014a. *Bawaajimo: A Dialect of Dreams in Anishinaabe Language and Literature*. East Lansing: Michigan State University Press.

———. 2014b. "Megwa Baabaamiiaayaayaang Dibaajomoyaang: Anishinaabe Literature as Memory in Motion." In *The Oxford Handbook of Indigenous American Literature*, edited by James H. Cox and Daniel Heath Justice, 175–84. Oxford: Oxford University Press.

———. n.d. "Miikindizi Baapaawinad Jim Northrupan / Jim Northrup's Art of Teasing Shakery." In "Enduring Critical Poses: Beyond Nation and History," edited by Gordon Henry Jr., Margaret Noodin, and David Stirrup. Unpublished manuscript.

Noori, Margaret. 2010. "Native American Narratives from Early Art to Graphic Novels: How We See Stories / Ezhi-g'waabamaanaanig Aadizookaanag." In *Multicultural Comics: from "Zap" to "Blue Beetle*,*"* edited by Frederick Luis Aldama, 55–72. Austin: University of Texas Press.

———. 2013. "*Ezhi-waanimazinbiiganankewag*: The Way They Write Circular Images." In *Papers of the Forty-First Algonquian Conference, 2009*, edited by Karl S. Hele and Randolph J. Valentine, 195–207. Albany: SUNY Press.

O'Brian, John. 2007. *Beyond Wilderness: The Group of Seven, Canadian Identity, and*

Contemporary Art. Montreal: McGill-Queen's University Press.

O'Brien, Jean. 1997. *Dispossession by Degrees: Indian Land and Identity in Natick, Massachusetts, 1650–1790*. Lincoln: University of Nebraska Press.

Odjick, Jay. 2011. *Kagaga: The Raven*. Burnaby, BC: Arcana Studio.

Olmanson, Eric D. 2007. *The Future City on the Inland Sea: A History of Imaginative Geographies of Lake Superior*. Athens: Ohio University Press.

O'Neill, John P., ed. 1992. *Barnett Newman: Selected Writings and Interviews*. Berkeley: University of California Press.

Ortiz, Simon. 1981. "Towards a National Indian Literature: Cultural Authenticity in Nationalism." *MELUS* 8 (2): 7–12.

O'Sullivan, Simon. 2001. "The Aesthetics of Affect: Thinking Art beyond Representation." *Angelaki* 6 (3): 125–35.

Owens, Robert M. 2015. *Red Dreams, White Nightmares: Pan-Indian Alliances in the Anglo-American Mind, 1763–1815*. Norman: University of Oklahoma Press.

Parker, Robert Dale. 2007. *The Sound the Stars Make Rushing through the Sky: The Writings of Jane Johnston Schoolcraft*. Philadelphia: University of Pennsylvania Press.

———. 2011. *Changing Is Not Vanishing: A Collection of American Indian Poetry to 1930*. Philadelphia: University of Pennsylvania Press.

Pasquaretta, Paul. 1996. "Sacred Chance: Gambling and the Contemporary Native American Indian Novel." *MELUS* 21 (2): 21–33.

Penney, David W. 2004. *North American Indian Art*. London: Thames & Hudson.

———. 2013. "Introduction: Water, Earth, Sky." In *Before and After the Horizon: Anishinaabe Artists of the Great Lakes*, edited by David W. Penney and Gerald McMaster, 9–35. Washington, DC: National Museum of the American Indian.

Penney, David W., and Gerald McMaster, eds. 2013. *Before and After the Horizon: Anishinaabe Artists of the Great Lakes*. Washington, DC: National Museum of the American Indian.

Peters, Jesse. 2008. "'Remember the Last Voice': Motion and Narrative Flux in Gordon Henry's *The Light People*." Paper presented at the annual convention of Southwest Texas Popular Culture and American Culture Associations, Albuquerque, February 13–16.

Peterson, Nancy. 1994. "History, Postmodernism, and Louise Erdrich's *Tracks*." *PMLA* 109 (5): 982–94.

Peyer, Bernd C. 1997. *The Tutor'd Mind: Indian Missionary Writers in Antebellum America*. Amherst: University of Massachusetts Press.

Phillips, Ruth B. 1999. "Art History and the Native-Made Object: New Discourses, Old Differences?" In *Native American Art in the Twentieth Century: Makers, Meanings, Histories*, edited by W. Jackson Rushing III, 97–112. New York: Routledge.

Piott, Steven L. 2011. *Daily Life in the Progressive Era*. Santa Barbara: Greenwood.

Pitawanakwat, Lillian. 2006. "Ojibwe/ Potawatomi (Anishinabe) Teaching." Four Directions Teachings. http://www.fourdirectionsteachings.com/transcripts/ojibwe.pdf.

Pittman, Barbara. 1995. "Cross-Cultural Reading and Generic Transformations: The Chronotope of the Road in Louise Erdrich's *Love Medicine*." *American Literature* 67 (4): 777–92.

Pomedli, Michael. 2014. *Living with Animals: Ojibwe Spirit Powers*. Toronto: University of Toronto Press.

Pope, Alexander. 1891. *An Essay on Man: Moral Essays and Satires*. London: Cassell & Company.

Poulantzas, Nicos. 2000. *State, Power, Socialism*. New York: Verso.

Rader, Dean. 2002. "Word as Weapon: Visual Culture and Contemporary American Indian Poetry." *MELUS* 27 (3): 147–67.

———. 2003. "Engaged Resistance in American Indian Art, Literature and Film." *Peace Review* 15 (2): 179–86.

———. 2011. *Engaged Resistance: American Indian Art, Literature, and Film from Alcatraz to the NMAI*. Austin: University of Texas Press.

———. 2014. "Reading the Visual, Seeing the Verbal: Text and Image in Recent American Indian Literature and Art." In *The Oxford Handbook of Indigenous American Literature*, edited by James H. Cox and Daniel Heath Justice, 299–317. Oxford: Oxford University Press.

Rainwater, Catherine. 1990. "Reading between Worlds: Narrativity in the Fiction of Louise Erdrich." *American Literature* 62 (3): 405–22.

Rajnovich, Grace. 1994. *Reading Rock Art: Interpreting the Indian Rock Paintings of the Canadian Shield*. Toronto: Dundurn Press.

Raljevic, Selma. 2016. "'Words Are Crossbloods': An Interview with Gerald Vizenor." *Post45*, May 26. http://post45.research.yale.edu.

de Ramirez, Susan Berry Brill. n.d. "The Anishinaabe Ecopoetics of Language, Life, and Place in the Poetry of Schoolcraft, Noodin, Blaeser, and Henry." In "Enduring Critical Poses: Beyond Nation and History," edited by Gordon Henry Jr., Margaret Noodin, and David Stirrup. Unpublished manuscript.

Rasmussen, Birgit Brander. 2012. *Queequeg's Coffin: Indigenous Literacies and Early American Literature*. Durham, NC: Duke University Press.

Reder, Deanna. 2010. "Writing Autobiographically: A Neglected Indigenous Intellectual Tradition." In *Across Cultures / Across Borders: Canadian Aboriginal and Native American Literatures*, edited by Paul DePasquale, Renate Eigenbrod, and Emma LaRocque, 153–70. Peterborough, ON: Broadview Press.

Reder, Deanna, and Linda Morra. 2010. *Troubling Tricksters: Revisioning Critical Conversations.* Waterloo, ON: Wilfrid Laurier University Press.

Rendon, Marcie. 2003. "SongCatcher." In *Keepers of the Morning Star: An Anthology of Native Women's Theater,* edited by Jaye T. Darby and Stephanie Fitzgerald, 1–75. Los Angeles: American Indian Studies Center, UCLA.

Rex, Cathy. 2006. "Survivance and Fluidity: George Copway's *The Life, History, and Travels of Kah-ge-ga-gah-bowh.*" *Studies in American Indian Literatures* 18 (2): 1–33.

Rexroth, Kenneth. 1961. "American Indian Songs: The United States Bureau of Ethnology Collection." In *Literature of the American Indians—Views and Interpretations: A Gathering of Indian Memories, Symbolic Contexts, and Literary Criticism,* edited by Abraham Chapman, 278–91. New York: New American Library.

Riggs, Lynne. 2003. *The Cherokee Night and Other Plays.* Norman: University of Oklahoma Press.

Robinson, Laura. 2002. "Review: The Boy in the Treehouse / Girl Who Loved Her Horses." *Canadian Ethnic Studies* 34 (2): 152–53.

Rose, Anne C. 1995. *Voices of the Marketplace: American Thought and Culture, 1830–1860.* Lanham, MD: Rowman & Littlefield.

Ruffo, Armand Garnet. 1997. *Grey Owl: The Mystery of Archie Belaney.* Regina: Coteau Books.

———. 2001. *At Geronimo's Grave.* Regina: Coteau Books.

———. 2014. *Norval Morrisseau: Man Changing into Thunderbird.* Madeira Park, BC: Douglas & McIntyre.

———. 2015. *The Thunderbird Poems.* Madeira Park, BC: Harbour Publishing.

Rushing, W. Jackson, III, ed. 1999. *Native American Art in the Twentieth Century: Makers, Meanings, Histories.* New York: Routledge.

Russell, Steve. 2010. *Sequoyah Rising: Problems in Post-Colonial Tribal Governance.* Durham, NC: Carolina Academic Press.

Ryga, George. 1967. *The Ecstasy of Rita Joe.* Directed by George Bloomfield, Vancouver Playhouse, November 23.

Said, Edward. 1975. "The Text, the World, the Critic." *Bulletin of the Midwestern Modern Languages Association* 8 (2): 1–23.

———. 1983. *The World, the Text, and the Critic.* Cambridge, MA: Harvard University Press.

Sarkowsky, Katja. 2012. "Gaps, Immediacy, and the Deconstruction of Epistemological Categories: The Impact of Gerald Vizenor's Poetry on His Prose." In *The Poetry and Poetics of Gerald Vizenor,* edited by Deborah L. Madsen, 98–112. Albuquerque: University of New Mexico Press.

Sarvé-Gorham, Kristan. 1995. "Power Lines: The Motif of Twins and the Medicine Women of

Tracks and *Love Medicine*." In *Having Our Way: Women Rewriting Tradition in Twentieth-Century America*, edited by Harriet Pollack, 167–90. Lewisburg: Bucknell University Press.

Satz, Ronald. 1991. *Chippewa Treaty Rights: The Reserved Rights of Wisconsin's Chippewa Indians in Historical Perspective*. Madison: Wisconsin Academy of Sciences, Arts and Letters.

Schlereth, Thomas J., ed. 1999. *Material Culture Studies in America*. Lanham, MD: Alta Mira Press.

Schneider, Bethany. 2008. "Not for Citation: Jane Johnston Schoolcraft's Synchronic Strategies." *Journal of the American Renaissance* 54 (1–4): 111–44.

Schoolcraft, Henry Rowe. 1851. *Personal Memoirs of a Residence of Thirty Years with the Indian Tribes on the American Frontiers: With Brief Notices of Passing Events, Facts, and Opinions, AD 1812 to AD 1842*. http://www.gutenberg.org/ebooks/11119.

———. 1855. *Summary Narrative of an Exploratory Expedition to the Sources of the Mississippi River, in 1820: Resumed and Completed, by the Discovery of Its Origin in Itasca Lake, in 1832*. Philadelphia: Lippincott, Grambo, & Co. https://archive.org/details/summarynarrativ00schogoog.

———. 1860. *Aboriginal Knowledge: Containing All the Original Papers Laid before Congress Respecting the History, Antiquities, Language, Ethnology, Pictography, Rites, Superstitions, and Mythology, of the Indian Tribes of the United States*. https://archive.org/details/archivesaborknow01schorich.

———. 1991. *Schoolcraft's Indian Legends*. Edited by Mentor L. Williams. East Lansing: Michigan State University Press.

Schultz, Lydia. 1991. "Fragments and Ojibwe Stories: Narrative Strategies in Louise Erdrich's *Love Medicine*." *College Literature* 18 (3): 80–95.

Schwarz, Herbert T. 1969. *The Windigo and Other Tales of the Ojibways*. Illustrated by Norval Morrisseau. Toronto: McClelland & Stewart.

Sergi, Jennifer. 1992. "Storytelling: Tradition and Preservation in Louise Erdrich's *Tracks*." *World Literature Today* 66 (2): 279–82.

Simpson, Audra, and Andrea Smith, eds. 2014. *Theorizing Native Studies*. Durham, NC: Duke University Press.

Simpson, Leanne Betasamosake. 2011a. *Dancing on Our Turtle's Back: Stories of Nishnaabeg Re-Creation, Resurgence and a New Emergence*. Winnipeg: Arbeiter Ring Publishing.

———. 2011b. "Robert Houle: Honouring Ojibwa History." *Canadian Art*, July 28. https://canadianart.ca/reviews/robert_houle/ (no longer available).

Sinclair, Niigaanwewidam James. 2009. "A Sovereignty of Transmotion: Imagination and the 'Real,' Gerald Vizenor, and Native Literary Nationalism." In *Stories through Theories/Theories through Stories: North American Indian Writing, Storytelling, and Critique*, edited by Gordon D. Henry Jr., Nieves Pascal, and Silvia Martínez-Falquina, 123–58. East Lansing: Michigan State University Press.

———. 2013a. "Nindoodemag Bagijiganan: A History of Anishinaabeg Narrative." PhD dissertation, University of British Columbia.

———. 2013b. "*K'zaugin*: Storying Ourselves into Life." In *Centering Anishinaabeg Studies: Understanding the World through Stories*, edited by Jill Doerfler, Niigaanwewidam James Sinclair, and Heidi Kiiwetinepinesiik Stark, 81–102. East Lansing: Michigan State University Press.

Smith, Donald B. 1997. "Kahgegagahbowh: Canada's First Literary Celebrity in the United States." In George Copway, *Life, Letters, and Speeches*, edited by A. Lavonne Brown Ruoff and Donald B. Smith, 23–60. Lincoln: University of Nebraska Press.

———. 2013. *Mississauga Portraits: Ojibwe Voices from Nineteenth-Century Canada*. Toronto: University of Toronto Press.

Smith, Gregory Bruce. 1996. *Nietzsche, Heidegger, and the Transition to Postmodernity*. Chicago: University of Chicago Press.

Smith, Linda Tuhiwai. 1999. *Decolonizing Methodologies: Research among Indigenous Peoples*. London: Zed Books.

Smith, Theresa S., Blake Debassige, Shirley Cheechoo, James Simeon Mishibinijima, and Leland Bell. 1994. "Beyond the Woodlands: Four Manitoulin Painters Speak their Minds." *American Indian Quarterly* 18 (1): 1–24.

Solomon, Chad, and Chris Meyer. 2006. *Adventures of Rabbit and Bear Paws*. Little Spirit Bear Productions.

Spry, Adam. 2018. *Our Warpaint Is Writers' Ink: Anishinaabe Literary Transnationalism*. Albany: SUNY Press.

———. 2012. "'It May Be Revolutionary in Character': The *Progress*, a New Tribal Hermeneutics, and the Literary Re-expression of the Anishinaabe Oral Tradition in *Summer in the Spring*." In *The Poetry and Poetics of Gerald Vizenor*, edited by Deborah L. Madsen, 23–42. Albuquerque: University of New Mexico Press.

Stafford, Barbara Maria. 2001. *Visual Analogy: Consciousness as the Art of Connecting*. Cambridge, MA: MIT Press.

Stanlake, Christy. 2009. *Native American Drama: A Critical Perspective*. New York: Cambridge University Press.

Stark, Heidi Kiiwetinepinesiik. 2010. "Respect, Responsibility, and Renewal: The Foundations of Anishinaabe Treaty Making with the United States and Canada." *American Indian Culture and Research Journal* 34 (2): 145–64.

———. 2012. "Marked by Fire: Anishinaabe Articulations of Nationhood in Treaty Making with the United States and Canada." *American Indian Quarterly* 36 (2): 119–49.

Starn, Orin. 2011. "Here Come the Anthros (Again): The Strange Marriage of Anthropology and Native America." *Cultural Anthropology* 26 (2): 179–204.

Stirrup, David. 2010a. *Louise Erdrich*. Manchester: Manchester University Press.

———. 2010b. "'To the Indian Names Are Subjoined a Mark and Seal': Tracing the Terrain of Ojibwe Writing." *Literature Compass* 7: 370–86.

———. 2013. "*Aadizookewininiwag* and the Visual Arts: Story as Process and Principle in 21st Century Anishinaabeg Painting." In *Centering Anishinaabeg Studies: Understanding the World through Stories*, edited by Jill Doerfler, Niigaanwewidam James Sinclair, and Heidi Kiiwetinepinesiik Stark, 297–316. East Lansing: Michigan State University Press.

———. 2015. "Spinning the Binary: Visual Cultures and Literary Aesthetics." In *Routledge Companion to Native American Literature*, edited by Deborah Madsen, 340–52. New York: Routledge.

Stokes, Karah. 1999. "What about the Sweetheart?: The 'Different Shape' of Anishinabe Two Sisters Stories in Louise Erdrich's *Love Medicine* and *Tales of Burning Love*." *MELUS* 24 (2): 89–105.

Stratton, Billy J. 2015. "'Carried in the Arms of Standing Waves': The Transmotional Aesthetics of Nora Marks Dauenhauer." *Transmotion* 1 (2): 47–71.

Stump, Sarain. 1969. *There Is My People Sleeping*. Sidney, BC: Gray's Publishing.

Suleri, Sara. 1992. *The Rhetoric of English India*. Chicago: University of Chicago Press.

Swann, Brian, ed. 1996. *Coming to Light: Contemporary Translations of the Native Literatures of North America*. New York: Vintage.

Tanner, John. 1830. *A Narrative of the Captivity and Adventures of John Tanner during Thirty Years Residence among the Indians in the Interior of North America*. Edited by Edwin James. London: Baldwin & Craddock.

Taylor, Drew Hayden. 1997. "Storytelling to Stage: The Growth of Native Theatre in Canada." *Drama Review* 41 (3): 140–41 and 144–52.

———. 2000. "Girl Who Loved Her Horses." In *The Boy in the Treehouse / Girl Who Loved Her Horses*, 83–159. Vancouver: Talon.

Taylor, Melanie Benson. 2012. "Unsettling Accounts: The Violent Economies of the Ledger." In *Ledger Narratives: The Plains Indian Drawings of the Lansburgh Collection at Dartmouth College*, edited by Colin G. Calloway, 189–200. Norman: University of Oklahoma Press.

Teuton, Christopher B. 2010. *Deep Waters: The Textual Continuum in American Indian Literature*. Lincoln: University of Nebraska Press.

Teves, Stephanie Nohelani. 2014. "A Critical Reading of Aloha and Visual Sovereignty in *Ke Kulana He Māhū*." *International Journal of Critical Indigenous Studies* 7 (1): 1–17.

Thiong'o, Ngũgĩ wa. 1986. *Decolonizing the Mind: The Politics of Language in African Literature.* Nairobi: East African Educational Publishers.

Thomas, Nicholas. 2004. *Cook: The Extraordinary Voyages of Captain James Cook.* New York: Walker.

Timpson, Annis May. 2009. *First Nations, First Thoughts: The Impact of Indigenous Thought in Canada.* Vancouver: UBC Press.

Tomlinson, Gary. 1995. "Ideologies of Aztec Song." *Journal of the American Musicological Society* 48 (3): 343–79.

———. 2007. *The Singing of the New World: Indigenous Voice in the Era of European Contact.* Cambridge: Cambridge University Press.

Treuer, David. 2006. *Native American Fiction: A User's Manual.* St. Paul, MN: Graywolf Press.

Trevelyan, Amelia. 1989. "Continuity of Form and Function in the Art of the Eastern Woodlands." *Canadian Journal of Native Studies* 9 (2): 187–203.

Turcotte, Gerry. 2003. "Re-Marking on History, or, Playing Basketball with Godzilla: Thomas King's Monstrous Post-Colonial Gesture." In *Connections: Non-Native Responses to Native Canadian Literature*, edited by H. Lutz and C. Vevaina, 205–35. New Delhi: Creative Books. Reprinted (late draft) University of Wollongong: Research Online, http://ro.uow.edu.au/cgi/viewcontent.cgi?article=1063&context=artspapers.

United States v. Creek Nation. 1935. No. 2561. http://caselaw.findlaw.com/us-supreme-court/295/103.html.

Upham, Warren. 2001. *Minnesota Place Names: A Geographic Encyclopedia.* St. Paul: Minnesota Historical Society.

Van Alst, Theodore C. 2008. "'How Quickly They Forget': American Indians in European Film, 1962–1976." PhD thesis, University of Connecticut.

Van Dyke, Annette. 1992. "Questions of the Spirit: Bloodlines in Louise Erdrich's Chippewa Landscape." *Studies in American Indian Literatures* 4 (1): 15–27.

Vastoukas, Joan M., and Romas K. Vastoukas. 1973. *Sacred Art of the Algonkians: A Study of the Peterborough Petroglyphs.* Peterborough: Mansard Press.

Vecsey, Christopher. 1976. "*The Sacred Scrolls of the Southern Ojibway.* Selwyn Dewdney." *American Anthropologist* 78 (2): 162.

———. 1983. *Traditional Ojibwa Religion and Its Historical Changes.* Washington, DC: American Philosophical Society.

Vennum, Thomas. 2009. *Just Too Much of an Indian: Bill Baker, Stalwart in a Fading Culture.* Madison: University of Wisconsin Press.

Vizenor, Gerald Robert. 1963. *South of the Painted Stones.* Minneapolis: Callimachus Publishing.

———. 1964a. *Seventeen Chirps: Haiku*. Minneapolis: Nodin Press.

———. 1964b. *Raising the Moon Vines: Haiku*. Minneapolis: Nodin Press.

———. 1981. *Earthdivers: Tribal Narratives on Mixed Descent*. Minneapolis: University of Minnesota Press.

———. 1984a. *Matsushima: Haiku*. Minneapolis: Nodin Press.

———. 1984b. *The People Named the Chippewa: Narrative Histories*. Minneapolis: University of Minnesota Press.

———, ed. 1987. *Touchwood: A Collection of Ojibway Prose*. Minneapolis: New Rivers Press.

———. 1990. *Bearheart: The Heirship Chronicles*. Minneapolis: University of Minnesota Press.

———. 1991. *Landfill Meditation: Crossblood Stories*. Middletown: Wesleyan University Press.

———. 1992. *Dead Voices: Natural Agonies in the New World*. Norman: University of Oklahoma Press.

———. 1993a. "Trickster Discourse." In *Narrative Chance: Postmodern Discourse on Native American Indian Literature*, edited by Gerald Robert Vizenor, 187–212. Norman: University of Oklahoma Press.

———, ed. 1993b. *Summer in the Spring: Anishinaabe Lyric Poems and Stories*. New edition. Norman: University of Oklahoma Press. First published in 1981.

———, ed. 1993c. *Narrative Chance: Postmodern Discourse on Native American Indian Literature*. Norman: University of Oklahoma Press.

———. 1994a. "Envoy to Haiku." In *Shadow Distance: A Gerald Vizenor Reader*, edited by A. Robert Lee, 25–32. Hanover, NH: Wesleyan University Press.

———. 1994b. *Manifest Manners: Postindian Warriors of Survivance*. Hanover, NH: Wesleyan University Press.

———. 1997. *Hotline Healers: An Almost Browne Novel*. Middletown: Wesleyan University Press.

———. 1998. *Fugitive Poses: Native American Indian Scenes of Absence and Presence*. Lincoln: University of Nebraska Press.

———. 2000. *The Everlasting Sky: Voices of the Anishinabe People*. St. Paul: Minnesota Historical Society Press.

———. 2003. *Wordarrows: Native States of Literary Sovereignty*. Lincoln: University of Nebraska Press. First published in 1978.

———. 2006. *Almost Ashore*. Cambridge, UK: Salt Publishing.

———. 2009. *Native Liberty: Natural Reason and Cultural Survivance*. Lincoln: University of Nebraska Press.

———. 2010. "American Indian Art and Literature Today: Survivance and Tragic Wisdom." *Museum International* 62 (3): 41–51.

———. 2011. *Shrouds of White Earth*. Buffalo: SUNY Press.

———. 2013. "Native Cosmototemic Art." In *Sakahàn: International Indigenous Art*, edited by Candice Hopkins, Christine Lalonde, and Greg Hill, 41–52. Ottawa: National Gallery of Canada.

———. 2014. *Blue Ravens*. Middletown, CT: Wesleyan University Press.

———. 2016. *Treaty Shirts: October 2034—A Familiar Treatise on the White Earth Nation*. Middletown, CT: Wesleyan University Press.

———. 2015. "The Unmissable: Transmotion in Native Stories and Literature." *Transmotion* 1 (1): 63–75.

Vizenor, Gerald, and Jill Doerfler. 2012. *The White Earth Nation: Ratification of a Native Democratic Constitution*. Lincoln: University of Nebraska Press.

Waegner, Cathy Covell, ed. 2015. *Mediating Indianness*. East Lansing: Michigan State University Press.

Walker, Cheryl. 1997. *Indian Nation: Native American Literature and Nineteenth-Century Nationalism*. Durham, NC: Duke University Press.

Warhus, Mark. 1997. *Another America: Native American Maps and the History of Our Land*. New York: St. Martin's Press.

Warkentin, Germaine. 1999. "In Search of 'The Word of the Other': Aboriginal Sign Systems and the History of the Book in Canada." *Book History* 2 (1): 1–27.

Warren, William. 1987. "History of the Ojibway Nation" [1885]. In *Touchwood: A Collection of Ojibway Prose*, edited by Gerald Vizenor, 10–43. Minneapolis: New Rivers Press.

Warrior, Robert. 1994. *Tribal Secrets: Recovering American Indian Intellectual Traditions*. Minneapolis: University of Minnesota Press.

———. 2005. *The People and the Word: Reading Native Nonfiction*. Minneapolis: University of Minnesota Press.

———. 2009. "Native American Scholarship and the Transnational Turn." *Cultural Studies Review* 15 (2): 119–30.

———, ed. 2015. *The World of Indigenous North America*. New York: Routledge.

Washburn, Frances. 2013. *Tracks on a Page: Louise Erdrich, Her Life and Works*. Santa Barbara: Praeger.

Weaver, Jace. 1997. *That the People Might Live: Native American Literatures and Native American Community*. Oxford: Oxford University Press.

———. 2007. "More Light Than Heat: The Current State of Native American Studies." *American Indian Quarterly* 31 (2): 235–55.

———. 2013. "Turning West: Cosmopolitanism and American Indian Literary Nationalism." In *The Native American Renaissance: Literary Imagination and Achievement*, edited by

Alan R. Velie and A. Robert Lee, 16–38. Norman: University of Oklahoma Press.

Weeks, Rex. 2004. "Oral Traditions and Native North American Literacy: Rock Art, Writing and the Cadmus Myth." *New England Antiquities Research Association (NEARA) Journal* 38 (2): 3–17.

Weidman, Bette S. 2006. "Native American Languages in Print." *American Indian Quarterly* 30 (1/2): 166–260.

Widdowson, Frances, and Albert Howard. 2008. *Disrobing the Aboriginal Industry: The Deception behind Indigenous Cultural Preservation*. Montreal: McGill-Queen's University Press.

Wieser, Kimberly G. 2017. *Back to the Blanket: Recovered Rhetorics and Literacies in American Indian Studies*. Norman: University of Oklahoma Press.

Wilson, Waziyaṭawiŋ Angela Cavender. 2005. *Remember This! Dakota Decolonization and the Eli Taylor Narratives*. Lincoln: University of Nebraska Press.

Wilson, Michael D. 2007. *Writing Home: Indigenous Narratives of Resistance*. East Lansing: Michigan State University Press.

Wolfe, Patrick. 2006. "Settler Colonialism and the Elimination of the Native." *Journal of Genocide Research* 8 (4): 387–409.

Womack, Craig S. 1999. *Red on Red: Native American Literary Separatism*. Minneapolis: University of Minnesota Press.

———. 2009. *Art as Performance, Story as Criticism: Reflections on Native Literary Aesthetics*. Norman: University of Oklahoma Press.

Wong, Hertha D. Sweet. 1999. "Louise Erdrich's *Love Medicine*: Narrative Communities and the Short Story Cycle." In *Louise Erdrich's Love Medicine: A Casebook*, edited by Hertha D. Sweet Wong, 85–106. Oxford: Oxford University Press.

———. 2005. "Native American Life Writing." In *The Cambridge Companion to Native American Literature*, edited by Joy Porter and Kenneth M. Roemer, 125–44. Cambridge: Cambridge University Press.

Wyatt, Jean. 2011. "Storytelling, Melancholia, and Narrative Structure in Louise Erdrich's *The Painted Drum*." *MELUS* 36 (1): 13–36.

Yaeger, Patricia. 1996. *The Geography of Identity*. Ann Arbor: University of Michigan Press.

INDEX

A

acculturation and assimilation, 44, 47;
  alphabetic literacy as evidence of, 9,
  10, 20, 40–41, 48, 53, 161–62, 194, 200,
  296 (n.6) artistic practice as, 104, 162,
  182, 196, 241; literacy as resistance to,
  40, 51–55, 70, 163, 153, 194–95, 211, 229;
  refusal of narratives of, 248, 267, 269,
  300 (n. 8)

Ace, Barry, 272, 273

activism, 1; in *The Light People*, 130,
  146–51; literary, 5; performance as, 245;
  tribalography as, 9–10

African Americans: exploitation of, 185; and
  Native Americans, 38–40, 74, 217, 296
  (n.2), 296 (n.4); and writing, 38

Agawa Bay, 56–57, 138

Algic Researches, 13, 49

alternative literacies, 4, 6, 7, 19, 149, 153,
  194–95, 290; and alternative cartography,
  126, 170–72; blindness to, 8; landscape
  as, 74; legibility of, 29–30; in *The Light
  People*, 154–56; in nineteenth-century
  Indigenous writing, 41–43; 45–46, 48–49,
  51–56, 70; in Ojibwe poetry, 112; recovery
  of, 9; rock paintings as, 162–67; and
  treaties, 122; in Vizenor, 103, 193, 203,
  211–12, 229; winter counts as, 285–86; X
  mark as signifier of, 78, 82

Anishinaabeakiing, 11–16, 56–57, 126, 205; as
  Ojibwe Country, 20, 52, 56, 86, 160–71

Anishinaabemowin, 33–35, 61, 92, 148, 293
  (n.8), 293 (n.13), 302 (n.6); banning of,
  244; and Ojibwemowin, 91, 165, 170, 291;

speaking or writing in, 92, 259; teaching of, 164, 171; translation of, 26, 95, 248, 295 (n.25)

awikhigan, 7, 20, 165

B

bagwajiwinini (little person), 142, 145, 302 (n.4)

Barthes, Roland, 157, 206, 303 (n.12)

Beaulieu, Theodore Hudon, 55, 199, 293 (n.13)

Big Bear, Frank, 119–22, 139, 204, 277

birchbark: baskets, 292 (n.3); bitten incisions on, 156, 162, 172, 304 (n.3); canoes, 186; haiku written on, 79, 83, 100, 131, 156; inscribing on, 156, 161; messages, 18, 20; scrolls, 14, 76, 131, 138, 250, 289

Bradley, David, 4, 104, 196, 216

C

Canada-U.S. border: Anishinaabeakiing bisected by, 16; in *Books and Islands in Ojibwe Country*, 160, 168–69, 305 (n.7); in Thomas King's *Truth and Bright Water*, 287

Catlin, George: in *Curiosities*, 248, 258–70, 272, 274; in *Shadow Tag*, 176–79, 181, 182–83, 271; Vizenor on, 206

Chagall, Marc: in Gansworth's *Nickel Eclipse*, 287; in Vizenor's fiction, 222–25, 230–32, 235, 237; in Vizenor's poetry, 105–7

circulatory poetics, 4–5, 84, 89, 125

coloniality, 65, 74, 258; anticoloniality, 288; decoloniality, 65, 306 (n.16); postcoloniality, 28; writing as gauge of, 40

critical impulse, 3, 28–29, 43; in Blaeser's poetry, 111; in *Books and Islands in Ojibwe Country*, 166; and engaged resistance, 5; as ethical-aesthetic engagement, 79; in Heid Erdrich's poetry, 122; in *The Light People*, 83, 135, 152–53, 156; in Native narrative, 127; and pictorial turn, 151

cultural loss: depictions of, 49; rejection of, 5, 190; resistance to, 55, 79, 94, 101; writing as a response to, 161, 165, 190, 280

Curtis, Edward, 4, 176, 196, 243, 250

D

Debassige, Blake, 139, 277

Debord, Guy, 74

decolonizing: and activism, 1; aesthetics, 29, 112, 172, 236; the gaze, 26, 179, 267; methodologies, 31, 284; the mind, 9; through performance, 244, 246, 249, 274; power of story and, 2; of space, 5, 108, 114; Wall Street, 123; of writing, 32, 163, 210–11, 216, 283

Densmore, Frances: *Chippewa Music*, 99; with Margaret Densmore, 255; and modernist poetics, 198–99; and *SongCatcher*, 247, 250–58, 263, 309 (nn.4–5), 310 (n.6); Vizenor's treatment of, 55, 194, 197, 201, 204, 218, 220

Der Blaue Reiter, 106, 222, 231–32

Derrida, Jacques: context dependency, 67–68; *Glas*, 80; on history, 52; on Lévi-Strauss, 19; on speech and writing, 20–21, 152, 211–12, 294 (n.17); on trace, 94

Dix, Otto, 106, 222, 230, 241

double consciousness, 24

Douglass, Frederick, 38–39, 296 (n.2)

visual-verbal relationship: in Anishinaabe literary heritage, 18; art forms, 6; in Blaeser's photo-poems, 279; Brotherston on, 21–23; discourse around, 3–4, 282; in "Pre-Occupied," 74

W

Waabojiig, 57, 59

Wallowing Bull, Star, 120–22, 139

Warren, William Whipple, 131

White Earth: banishment from, 229; Constitution, 229; Nationhood, 15, 112; Reservation, 15, 95, 235, 254, 255

Woolsey, Melancthon L., 58, 60–61, 62–69, 298 (n.19)

writing: systems, 4–5, 7–8, 18–19, 52, 298 (n.16); as resistance and survivance, 9, 38, 40, 43, 45–46, 210–11; of the state, 28, 39–40, 42, 52, 55, 77–78, 167; as a tool of oppression, 40–41, 49, 53–55, 162

X

X marks: as critical impulse, 79; as engaged resistance, 77–79, 92, 107, 122, 157; in haiku, 102, 112; in *The Light People*, 81; as linguistic figure, 94; as mark of presence, 90; and nindoodemag, 82–83, 125, 148–49; as spatial marker, 86–87, 89, 154–55; as treaty signatures, 74, 100

Z

Zotom, 104. *See also* ledger art